Readings in
Psychological Tests
and Measurements

THE DORSEY SERIES IN PSYCHOLOGY

EDITORIAL COMMITTEE

READINGS IN PSYCHOLOGICAL TESTS AND MEASUREMENTS

Edited by

W. Leslie Barnette, Jr., Ph.D.

Professor of Psychology and

Director, Vocational Counseling Center

State University of New York at Buffalo

1964

THE DORSEY PRESS, INC.

HOMEWOOD, ILLINOIS

First Printing, January, 1964

Library of Congress Catalog Card No. 64–11716

PRINTED IN THE UNITED STATES OF AMERICA

To the Reader

The present volume is based on the experience of the editor in teaching undergraduate classes, largely populated by majors in the Department of Psychology, in Tests and Measurements. Experience has shown that it is desirable to use supplementary readings of recent origin in addition to the basic text used in the course. It is usually impractical to ask fairly large groups of students to read journal articles directly from journals in the periodical room of the campus library; it is also costly to have all such material reproduced for local use. For these reasons, the present selection of recent articles has been assembled.

The selection of the particular articles to be included here was also governed by another consideration: that the material so ably presented in the *Test Service Bulletins,* published by the Psychological Corporation in New York City, would not overlap. It is assumed that this collection of readings would be utilized in conjunction with this excellent series.

The editing job has been considerable. Only a very few articles are here presented as they originally appeared; most have been considered or abbreviated in one way or another. The focus here has consistently been the undergraduate psychology major whose knowledge of statistics is modest. Articles presenting extensive tables and elaborate statistical analysis have been drastically edited solely from this point of view. The editor has been frequently irritated, when using other books of readings in other courses, when such editing has not been done and, as a result, the beginning student meets up with an analysis of variance or some complex Rorschach nomenclature. The student reader here, however, is expected to understand elementary statistical concepts: correlation, various measures of central tendency and dispersion, and the simpler ways of expressing confidence limits. In a word, it is assumed that the student in a Tests and Measurements course which utilizes this collection of readings will have completed at least a one semester course in Elementary Statistics.

The bibliography at the end lists all publications mentioned in the main body of the readings. Articles which have been abstracted and used as actual selections in this collection are not included in this bibliography; for a survey of this material, the reader should refer to the Table of Contents. Unlike most collections of readings, this volume has been composed to conform with regular textbook format: tables and charts are numbered in sequential order rather than as they would appear in the original reference. Similarly, all references to other research have been collected in one final bibliography at the end of the volume.

WLB

Acknowledgements

The common attribution of credit to other persons for any merit a book may have is especially appropriate in a book of readings such as this. It is to these authors, herein reprinted and with their permission, that the editor owes the first debt of gratitude and, in the name of these contributors, a portion of the royalties from this volume has been assigned to the American Psychological Foundation.

In addition, the following journals and publishers are to be thanked for their permission to use materials: *American Journal of Mental Deficiency, American Psychologist, College Board Review, Educational & Psychological Measurement,* Educational Testing Service, *Harper's Magazine, The Humanist, Journal of Abnormal & Social Psychology, Journal of Applied Psychology, Journal of Consulting Psychology, Journal of Counseling Psychology, Michigan Journal of Secondary Education, Newsletter of Elementary School Principals' Association of Connecticut,* New York State Psychological Association, *Personnel Psychology, Physics Today,* Prentice-Hall, Inc., *Psychological Bulletin, Review of Educational Research, Scientific American,* and the U.S. Department of Labor.

The editor would also like to express sincere appreciation to Mrs. Katherine Wejnarth for her devoted work in connection with the initial typing of this manuscript and to Mr. N. C. Rao for assistance in the preparation of the indexes.

WLB

Table of Contents

PART ONE. GENERAL MEASUREMENT PROBLEMS

PAGE

Mental Testing and the Logic of Measurement, *Andrew L. Comrey*.................. 2

Basic Problems of Measurement, *Herbert Dingle*.. 11

Testing Programs—Misconception, Misuse, Overuse, *Frank B. Womer*.......... 17

Ethical and Professional Considerations in Reporting of Test Information,
  Dorothea McCarthy 26

PART TWO. TEST ADMINISTRATION PROBLEMS

An Adventure in Psychological Testing Abroad, *Frederic R. Wickert*........... 34

After the Samoans Come of Age, *Abraham S. Levine*................................... 39

The Effects of Warm and Cold Interaction on the Administration and
  Scoring of an Intelligence Test, *Joseph Masling*..................................... 45

Playing Games, *Catherine Landreth*.. 51

PART THREE. NORMS

Norms Are Not Goals, *Robert Dion*... 58

Are Sex Norms Necessary? *Robert H. Bauernfeind*.................................... 68

PART FOUR. RESPONSE SET

Systematic Biases in the Keying of Correct Responses on Certain
  Standardized Tests, *Newton S. Metfessel and Gilbert Sax*..................... 74

Deviant Responses and Deviant People: the Formulation of the Deviation
  Hypothesis, *Irwin A. Berg*.. 76

Negative Response Bias and Personality Adjustment, *Morton J. Asch*........... 87

PART FIVE. RELIABILITY

Some Effects of Speed in Test Use, *Alexander G. Wesman*............................ 95

The Reliability of a Response Measure: Differential Recognition-Threshold
  Scores, *Donn Byrne and Joan Holcomb*.. 102

PAGE

PART SIX. FACTOR ANALYSIS

What Is Factor Analysis? *John W. French* 108

Primary Mental Abilities and Psychological Implications, *L. L. Thurstone*.... 113

The Structure of Intellect, *J. P. Guilford* 124

PART SEVEN. VALIDITY

Development of Occupational Norms, *Beatrice J. Dvorak* 132

Validity, Reliability, and Baloney, *Edward E. Cureton* 145

Cross-Validation of a Forced-Choice Personality Inventory,
James J. Kirkpatrick 148

Validity for What? *John G. Jenkins* 155

The Experimental Evaluation of a Selection Procedure, *John C. Flanagan* 163

Relative Pilot Aptitude and Success in Primary Pilot Training,
John D. Krumboltz and Raymond E. Christal 171

Research on the Selection of Aircrew Personnel, *American Institute
of Research* 178

Gain in Proficiency as a Criterion in Test Validation, *Winton H. Manning
and Philip H. DuBois* 183

Predicting Long-Range Performance of Substation Operators,
G. M. Worbois 189

Advantages of the Multiple Cut-Off Method, *Beatrice J. Dvorak* 195

Dimensional Problems of Criteria, *E. E. Ghiselli* 197

The Twisted Pear and the Prediction of Behavior, *Jerome Fisher* 203

Output Rates among Coil Winders, *Harold F. Rothe and Charles T. Nye* 212

Differentiation of Individuals in Terms of Their Predictability,
Edwin E. Ghiselli 218

A Study in Synthetic Validity: Exploratory Investigation of Clerical Jobs,
C. H. Lawshe and M. D. Steinberg 225

Reducing Training Costs by Employment Testing, *J. T. Rushmore and
G. J. Toorenaar* 229

Must All Tests Be Valid? *Robert L. Ebel* 233

PART EIGHT. INTELLIGENCE

The Motivation Factor in Testing Supervisors, *Eugene E. Jennings* 245

A Study of Individuals Committed to a State Home for the Retarded Who
Were Later Released as Not Mentally Defective, *S. L. Garfield and
D. C. Affleck* 249

PAGE

PART NINE.   PERSONALITY

What Is "Objective" in "Objective Personality Tests"? *Raymond B. Cattell* 260

F—K in a Motivated Group, *James Drasgow and W. Leslie Barnette, Jr.* 267

A Validation Study of Naval Neuropsychiatric Screening, *William A. Hunt,
Cecil L. Wittson and Henrietta W. Burton*.. 271

Use of the Sugar Pill by Industrial Psychologists, *Marvin D. Dunnette*.......... 276

The Fallacy of Personal Validations: A Classroom Demonstration of
Gullibility, *B. R. Forer*.. 281

PART TEN.   INTERESTS

Permanence of Interest Scores over 22 Years, *Edward K. Strong, Jr*................. 289

Long-Term Validity of the Strong Interest Test in Two Subcultures,
Charles McArthur 294

Expected Developments in Interest and Personality Inventories,
G. Frederic Kuder.. 303

PART ELEVEN.   CRITIQUES OF TESTING

The Fallacies of "Personality" Testing, *William H. Whyte, Jr*...................... 310

The Tyranny of Multiple-Choice Tests, *Banesh Hoffmann*............................ 321

Mental Testing and Modern Society, *John M. Shlien*.................................. 337

BIBLIOGRAPHY 345

SUBJECT INDEX 349

AUTHOR INDEX 353

PART ONE

GENERAL MEASUREMENT PROBLEMS

Measurement which purports to be scientific in any sense of the word has a logic of its own. This logic has largely been developed, because of historical priority, in the area of the physical scientists. The claims of social scientists, and especially workers in the field of psychometrics, must be evaluated against these same standards. It is well that the beginning student of psychological measurement know something of these principles. Writers such as Bridgman, Campbell and Carnap have published treatises in this area from the vantage point of physics and mathematics. In the following article, Dr. Comrey, psychologist at the University of California in Los Angeles, who is well known for his research in psychometrics, spells out some of the fundamental facts of measurement as these relate to the mental testing movement. The reader is urged, however, not to confine his thinking when he reads this article merely to "mental" tests but, rather, to generalize these arguments to the wider field of aptitude testing. The article originally appeared in Educational & Psychological Measurement, *1951, Vol. 11, pp. 323–34.*

Before attempting to understand all of Dr. Comrey's article, it would be wise for the student to be acquainted with the differences between and among nominal, ordinal, interval and ratio scales.

Mental Testing and the Logic

of Measurement

Andrew L. Comrey

By comparison with measurement in the physical sciences, psychological measurement has always enjoyed a somewhat unsavory reputation and has even been called by some the "queen of the inexact sciences." Many writers have pointed out deficiencies in the techniques employed in psychology; some have based their criticisms upon alleged violations of the traditional "laws of measurement." In a previous article (Comrey, 1950) certain implications of the logic behind measurement were given some attention. The traditional requirements were stated, criticisms of psychological measurement were discussed, and an interpretation of the position of psychological measurement with respect to these requirements was offered.

In the present paper, some of the general problems of psychological measurement will be discussed as they apply to the mental-test field. A brief review of the requirements of fundamental measurement will be given, together with a discussion of some difficulties in applying this model to mental testing. Some of the consequences of these difficulties for measurement practice will be mentioned and, finally, some suggestions regarding criteria for evaluating mental-test methods will be made which depart from the customary criteria of conformity to the pattern of fundamental measurement. The point of view will be expressed that the excellence of measurement methods in mental testing may be judged by the practical validity of those methods for the purposes at hand, in addition to comparing them with the model of measurement in the physical sciences. Reasons for giving greater emphasis to the former criterion will be offered.

CRITICISMS OF MENTAL TESTING

Perhaps the most comprehensive treatment of the requirements for fundamental measurement has been given by Campbell. Some of the more important requirements will be summarized with respect to ordinal characteristics, the relation of equality, and the operation of addition. The requirements for order specify that a class of elements must be defined unambiguously so that the elements vary with respect to some particular property. To be measurable with respect to that property, the elements must vary only in degree, not in kind. Furthermore, a relation "greater," which is transitive and asymmetrical, must be physically defined. That is, if Stimulus A is greater than Stimulus B, and B is greater than C, then A should be greater than C; also, if A is greater than B, B cannot be greater than A.

To satisfy the requirements for equality, a physical definition of the relation "equals" is needed. This definition must be such that physical equality is transitive and symmetrical, i.e., if $A = B$, and $B = C$, then $A = C$; also, if $A = B$, then $B = A$. And, finally, the requirements for addition state, among other things, that some experimental operation must be found whereby two elements possessing the measurable property can be added together to get an element containing an amount of this property greater than that of either element added. For properties which satisfy these requirements, a complete, or *fundamental* measurement is possible. Numbers assigned to elements of such classes of measurables can be manipulated in accordance with the rule of arithmetic. Furthermore, such measurements are made on scales with equal-unit and ratio properties. A few properties so measurable are weight, length, period of time, and electrical resistance.

It is fairly well known that certain difficulties are involved in trying to apply the model of fundamental measurement to the mental-test area. One of the first criticisms laid at the doorstep of mental testing is that classes of measurables are not even defined, i.e., the class of degrees of some property supposedly indicated by different scores on some test do not represent merely differences in degree but differences in kind as well. A Gestalt interpretation of mental organization would tend to contradict the notion that merely a quantitative difference is reflected by different test scores. Furthermore, the relation of equality does not meet the necessary conditions. It is stated that equal test scores do not mean identity with respect to some ability. Individuals may get the same test scores by solving correctly different combinations of items. Furthermore, by this line of reasoning, if $A = B$ (i.e., equal test scores), and $B = C$, there is no reason to suppose that the underlying ability organizations of A and C are the same, even though their numerical test scores are identical.

Interesting as these objections may be, the psychologist can minimize their importance on operational grounds. He can state that by the only measuring instrument available to him, i.e., the test, $A = B$ if they have the same test score. Aside from the question of differences in kind represented by different test scores, no contradiction in the actual numbers assigned can occur with respect to the relations "greater" and "equals." The fact that different combinations of items add up to the same score does not bother him too much because he feels that if the items themselves are of the same sort, the total score should be fairly indicative of the person's level of achievement.

That mental testing has no suitable operation of addition is quite apparent, and critics have not failed to mention this point. There seems to be no way to add physically one psychological magnitude to another to get a third even greater in amount. With fundamentally measurable variables, such as weight, length, resistance, and so on, this can be accomplished easily and, from such an operation, numbers can be assigned such that differences and ratios are endowed with the desired experimental meaning. The fact that the operation of addition is not defined in mental testing leads to considerable difficulty, since this operation is employed in fundamental measurement to endow measurement scales with equal-unit and ratio properties. Thus, it would appear that mental-test workers may not be able to develop test scales with equal units and ratio properties.

Let us consider, for a moment, two opposed points of view which might be adopted with respect to the nature of measurement involved in a mental test. First, it might be assumed that the human mind is composed of an undetermined number of abilities. A test may tap, so to speak, a few of these abilities which inhere basically in the physiological structure of the organism, but the test can be only an indirect measurement in terms of certain behavioral manifestations. A direct measurement is out of the question, at the present state of our knowledge of physiology, for there is no way that variations in these abilities can be directly observed. Behavioral products represent the only available indicators of such underlying variables at the present time.

Taking a simple case, suppose there were such an underlying ability and a test which measured this variable alone, plus some error variance. What is the functional relationship between the performance variable and the underlying ability? If a performance variable is to be used to yield a measure of ability in this sense, it is obvious that such functional relationships must either be determined experimentally, or assumed to follow a certain form. This functional relationship must be known before the task of securing equal-unit scales, with respect to the underlying variable, can be accomplished, for the equality of units must be in terms of the underlying ability, not the performance.

Unfortunately, it is not now possible to determine the nature of such functional relationships. An independent measure of the underlying ability would be necessary before the relationship of such measures to scores on the performance test could be found. Since no independent measurements (e.g., physiological determinations) for the underlying variable can be taken, this method of proceeding is impractical. It should be mentioned at this point that an approach to this problem can be made through the use of certain types of judgments. For example, one might employ fractionation and equal-appearing-interval methods for the scaling of the subjective difficulty of digit series and words in a vocabulary test. These methods do not comprise an experimental verification of unit equality on an underlying mental-ability variable, however. They do allow an operational meaning to be attached to unit differences on the subjective scale, but such units do not represent those of a fundamental type for the underlying variable.

From this analysis, it appears evident that one cannot prove that a performance or behavior test yields equal units along the scale of some basic underlying ability which in itself is not directly observable. It should be emphasized that the task of disproving an assumption of equal units in such cases is equally difficult, for this, too, would require experimental checks of the relationship between the performance variable and independent measurements of the underlying ability.

An opposite position which might be assumed by some persons with respect to the nature of measurement involved in a mental test is the point of view that a test measures a variable of some kind, or variables, and these behavioral products themselves are what concern us. It amounts to behavioristic approach, so to speak, which denies the necessity of dealing in terms of concepts which have no basis in observation. The extreme behaviorist might ask, "What is the point of assuming an underlying ability which cannot be measured, observed, or proved to exist?"

If the second approach is taken, what are the consequences? First, the matter of a functional relationship between the behavior variable and a hypothetical underlying variable is no longer of importance. The behavior itself is the variable, as determined by the performance on some test. The emphasis with this approach is switched from a consideration of whether the test measures the underlying variable properly to that of whether the variable measured is a useful one. It is assumed that the measures obtained from a test represent some variable in a one-to-one fashion. Since the variable is defined by the test scores, there can be no question as to whether the units on such a test are equal, because that is implicit in the assumptions. It follows from the general approach involved that the units of such tests are equal by definition. It is not the intention of the writer to advance either of these positions as his own. These points of view are considered as represented opposed positions which may flank most observers rather than represent them. The point of importance in this discussion is merely that, regardless of what systematic position one adopts, we do not have equal units of the fundamental type with any mental test and we will not have them until means are devised for direct observation of underlying physiological phenomena.

SOME POSSIBLE CONSEQUENCES OF THE DIFFICULTIES

It has already been suggested that the objections raised against mental-test methods with respect to the requirements for order and equality are crucial. The issues raised by the failure to achieve an operational definition of addition in mental testing are more serious, however. Since equal-unit and ratio properties of measurement scales are based upon addition, mental testing faces the task of evaluating the effects of this deficiency.

The most obvious conclusion which might be drawn is that measurement in this area is confined to the ordinal level. That is, numbers assigned by means of mental tests can indicate only the rank-order positions of performances to which those numbers have been given. This is the sort of conclusion which is often made by critics of psychological measurement.

Now, it is quite clear that many of the statistical procedures which are applied to mental-test results demand something in the way of a unit of measurement. (1) Means, standard deviations, product-moment correlations, and all the statistical procedures based upon these must necessarily depend upon interval sizes along the scale of measurement. This is no less true of the rank-difference correlation method, which is derived from the product-moment formula, and hence involves the same concepts. (Ratio characteristics of measurement scales do not constitute as much of a loss to mental testing as the lack of equal units, for most purposes, since the typical statistical treatments need not involve such relations between test scores.)

These considerations suggest that one of two courses of action must be taken by those attempting to use mental tests for measurement purposes. First, they may show that using methods involving unit assumptions does not introduce serious errors or that certain procedures can be employed to minimize such error in spite of the absence of fundamentally equal units. Secondly, they may avoid the use of methods of analysis which depend upon interval interpretations. The multiple cutting-score methods, for example, do not demand such assumptions. Further, non-parametric methods may be used for statistical tests of hypotheses.

It is likely that further development of measurement techniques in mental testing will proceed along both these lines. Certainly, there is a vast unexplored territory in the area of the second procedure suggested above. With respect to the first program, it can be stated that insufficient attention has been given to the problem of determining the degree and kind of error introduced into the results of measurement by virtue of the fact that such measurements lack certain characteristics they are presumed to have. In the next section, criteria for judging the work of measurement methods will be treated in the light of the discussion to this point.

CRITERIA FOR EVALUATING MENTAL TEST METHODS

The fundamental-measurement model has typically been used as a criterion by which measurement procedures should be evaluated. Those procedures which fit this scheme are termed "good" methods, and procedures which fail to do so are held to be primitive and unsatisfactory as scientific instruments. Mental tests fall in this latter category, for they certainly fail to fit the fundamental-measurement model in at least one important respect, namely, in their defection with respect to the operation of addition. Are there other criteria by which mental tests can be evaluated which may be more useful? Under the first criterion mentioned above, all mental tests are unsatisfactory, and no discrimination among them is provided. Certainly, some tests are better and more useful than others.

The obvious answer to this question is that other criteria are available for judging the value of procedures in mental testing. These criteria are to be found in the validity of such instruments for the practical purposes of assessing and predicting status under a variety of conditions. Lest some misunderstanding on this point arise, it should be hastily added that the logic of fundamental measurement should not be forgotten or ignored. It is a good thing to know where one's methods fail to meet this more exacting pattern in order to avoid the errors which are likely to occur in the absence of this knowledge. The fact that mental-test methods do not satisfy such criteria need not blind us to the possibility and usefulness of evaluation in terms of these other more practical criteria.

Whereas many difficulties are involved in the use of mental tests for the purpose of establishing scientific laws, there seems to be little doubt as to their value for certain practical purposes. It seems reasonable to assert that mental testing is and will be for some time essentially an empirical science with certain rather well-defined practical objectives, rather than primarily a theoretical scientific enterprise. At least, in terms of relative proportion of activity in this area, such a position could scarcely be questioned. Some individuals may object to this point of view, since personal preferences in matters of emphasis are involved. Be that as it may, this position will be adopted with respect to the objectives of mental testing.

These considerations lead to certain conclusions regarding the attitude which practical mental-test workers should adopt toward the logic of measurement. In the first place, they should abandon attempts to manipulate their test scores for the purpose of making their measurements approximate fundamental measurement. It is quite clear that such objectives can never be attained in this manner; they can be attained only through experimental operations upon the underlying physiological determiners of behavior. The practical test worker is not in a position to engage in the type of research activity which might conceivably succeed in reaching such ends. This fact would be evident to anyone familiar with the logic of fundamental measurement, so mental-test workers should by all means be acquainted with measurement theory.

It should be pointed out in this connection that scaling procedures which are apparently designed for obtaining measurement properties beyond rank order are not necessarily bad. What is not defensible is to assume that such procedures can stand on their own because they appear to resemble, in the end result, measurement in the physical sciences. Whether such methods are good or bad can be assessed in terms of their capacity to help achieve the practical objectives of mental tests. Ultimately, methods may become available for checking the claims of such procedures with respect to measurement properties beyond rank-order but, for the present, such claims must rest upon assumptions for which there is insufficient experimental evidence.

Attempts to improve quantification techniques in mental testing should not be confined to the pattern of fundamental measurement but should be spread over a much wider area. Any and all techniques should be explored which might conceivably lead to better predictions or assessments of status, even though such techniques do not appear to have any possibility of making mental-test measurement more like fundamental measurement.

As a matter of fact, some such successful techniques may appear to be in contradiction to a goal in terms of the fundamental-measurement pattern. An article by Richardson (1936), for example, emphasizes the importance of considering the effects of test difficulty on validity. Richardson states that the validity of a test depends in large measure upon whether the test is properly tailored to the job with respect to difficulty. He states:

> Suppose, for example, that a test of clerical aptitude is meant to sort out the best 15 per cent of all applicants. This is on the assumption that the labor market is such that one hundred persons will apply for 15 positions. It is then clear that the optimal difficulty of test elements should be in the neighborhood of plus 1 sigma and that easier tasks would give us discriminations between individuals in whom we are not interested. . . . Under any circumstances involving educational or psychological measurement, the distribution of difficulty of the elements to tasks can be arranged to fulfill more accurately the purposes of measurement.

If, by some procedure, it were possible to develop a test of clerical aptitude which would represent truly a fundamental-measurement scale with a given number of items, the scale would be the same whether 15 per cent or 85 per cent of the applicants were being selected. Under conditions where error variance is not present in the test, success would probably be equal for any cutting score. However, under the conditions of testing existing, this fixed scale could not do the measuring job at a given level as well as a test tailored for that level, although this fixed scale might conceivably be the best general-purpose scale. Thus, the approach to better measurement through meeting the requirements for fundamental measurement, were it possible, would not necessarily give the best practical methods, since it ignores at least one of the important factors affecting test validity.

The methods to be employed in mental testing, then, have a definite purpose and they can be evaluated in terms of that purpose. From the standpoint of the ideas presented here, the primary value of item analysis and factor analysis, for example, lies in the possibility of using such techniques to increase predictive efficiency. Developing batteries of pure tests to predict some criterion through factor analysis of tests and criteria, constitutes a method the value of which can definitely be assessed in terms of higher validity coefficients. The same criteria can be applied to other methods introduced into the mental-test field.

Where such good means are available for evaluating measurement methods it seems inappropriate to rely principally on comparisons with abstract logical criteria that were designed for a different context.

SUMMARY

1. Many difficulties lie in the path of securing for mental-test measurement the type of rigor found in the fundamental type of measurement. Among these, one of the most serious is the impossibility of obtaining equal units without independent physiological assessment of the variables under consideration.

2. This failure brings up many important problems with respect to the treatment of mental-test data by statistical methods, since many of these methods presume that a unit of measurement has been established. Some justification for the use of such methods should be offered.

3. It would be desirable to attain a fundamental type of measurement for mental testing but, at present, such a goal seems out of reach. If fundamental measurement is made the sole yardstick by which the excellence of measurement procedures are to be judged, mental-test methods are automatically classed as primitive and virtually without prospect of substantial improvement.

4. The objectives of mental testing are held to be primarily empirical in nature. Testing techniques are designed mainly for the prediction and assessment of status. These objectives provide additional criteria by which mental-test methods can be judged, namely, the practical validity determinations for the purposes at hand.

5. Mental-test workers should certainly be aware of what is involved in fundamental measurement, but they should devote their major efforts toward developing measurement techniques which give some hope for better satisfying the practical validity criteria rather than the fundamental-measurement criteria. This position is taken because (a) the fundamental-measurement criteria cannot be attained by the methods available to the mental-test worker, if at all, and (b) the practical-validity criteria and the fundamental-measurement criteria may sometimes be contradictory objectives in the practical situation.

The comments which follow represent a condensation of a book review published in the Scientific American *(June, 1960, Vol. 202, No. 6) by Dr. Dingle. The author was writing about a volume which contained the contributions to a symposium on measurement held at the 1956 meetings of the American Association for the Advancement of Science. Dr. Dingle uses this occasion—which is the reason sections of the review are reproduced here—to write about the general operational approach to valid measurement, something which is applicable to physics as well as to psychology. The author takes issue with the first sentence of this book: "Measurement presupposes something to be measured, and, unless we know what that something is, no measurement can have any significance."*

Dr. Dingle is an English astronomer and physicist. He is Professor Emeritus of History and Philosophy of Science at University College, London.

Basic Problems of Measurement

Herbert Dingle

To understand what measurement means we must turn to the physical sciences as the field affording the potentialities of measurement their widest scope; there alone are all the known processes of measurement exemplified. Consequently a true conception of measurement must cover physical measurements in their widest generality. Such a conception shows that measurement is a self-contained process, a process that implies nothing beyond that of which it gives a numerical estimation.

It is perfectly legitimate to ask an astronomer to measure the area in the sky of the constellation Orion as defined by the International Astronomical Union. But what is the "something" that he measures? We no longer think in terms of a "sky," and from another viewpoint the constellation ceases to exist. There is no "something," but beyond question there is a measurement.

Pursuing the matter, we see not only that all physical measurements are of this kind, but also that, far from starting with a something and then measuring it, we start with a measure and then try to find something to which we can attach it. We measure the weight, W, of a body, and its height, h, above the ground, and form the product Wh. This we regard as significant because it is equal to the kinetic energy with which the body, having been released, reaches the ground. We therefore invent something that Wh measures and call it the potential energy of the body. When the body falls, and h becomes 0, it loses its potential energy. We are delighted, and think we have "discovered" potential energy. But we are now forced to say that when a body moves toward or away from the sun, it similarly loses or gains potential energy. Suppose, then, that our body falls to the earth when the sun is directly overhead. Has it gained or lost potential energy? We can take our choice, which means that potential energy is not "something to be measured," but a quantity devised after the measurement has shown its importance. In its devising we are free to exercise our choice among various possibilities; and, if we do not devise it at all, the measurement has exactly the same status it had before.

Take another example. We make a measurement with a diffraction grating and call the result the "wave length" of light. But we do not first perceive the waves and then measure their length; we make a measurement and then invent "wave length" to attach to it. The invention is just as arbitrary as that of potential energy, and at present it is even less satisfactory. Another observer, moving away from us in the direction of the light, gets a different value. It is the same light. Which observer determines the "right" wave length? Clearly, at least one of our measurements does not imply a "wave length to be measured." But if the something is not wave length, what is it? We do not know, though there can be no doubt that this measurement is important.

So we could continue. For this reason I some years ago proposed the rudiments of a theory in which measurement was defined as "any precisely specified operation that yields a number; that is, measurement is related to the operation performed and not to the hypothetical "something" on which it is supposed to be performed. This theory appeared in *The British Journal for the Philosophy of Science* (Vol. 1, page 5), and as it seems not to have been noticed by any of the contributors to the present volume, I shall take the liberty of outlining its basic idea. But first of all I think it will be useful to take a step still further back and see how measurement came to be practiced at all. This point is not touched upon in the volume, yet it is of some relevance and is indeed essential if we are to understand fully what measurement signifies. The contributors to the volume take measurement for granted and then discuss—often admirably—what it is, but they do not ask why it must be taken for granted. They tacitly assume the strategy of the campaign, and concentrate on the tactics. Let us see why the strategy commits us to measurement.

The fundamental problem of philosophy is that of making sense of our experience. We are originally aware of a haphazard succession of experiences. After a while some regularities force themselves on our attention—night and day alternate, falling is followed by a pain, and so on. The first philosopher is the man who first conceives the possibility that other—perhaps all—experiences are related; that is, experiences form a rational system. Given a knowledge of some experiences, therefore, other experiences that seem quite independent can be predicted.

The earliest philosophers accepted the obvious relations and tried to supplement them—the alternation of night and day was associated with alternations of heat and cold, falling on grass hurt less than falling on stone—until in such a system as that of Aristotle, with its generalizations in terms of matter and form, a considerable area of experience became organized into a rational system. Two things characterized this approach: first, it was concerned entirely with involuntary experience; and second, progress in it was painfully slow.

By the 17th century the patience of philosophers was exhausted (I am of course describing not what consciously went on in their minds, but what we, knowing the outcome of their actions, can see to be the truest rationalization of them), and they said: "Look here; we aren't getting anywhere with ordinary experience; it is too difficult. Let us make some artificial experiences and find relations between them. Then perhaps ordinary experience will fit in later." So instead of studying the natural motions of birds and smoke and rivers, they made artificial motions—balls rolling down carefully prepared grooves. Thus was born scientific experiment: the deliberate production of artificial experiences more simply related to one another than those that come naturally.

The aspect of the artificial experiences that was examined was the metrical aspect. The rolling ball did not pass from potentiality to actuality; it merely gave readings on a measuring scale and a form of clock, readings represented by numbers. What was the advantage of this? Simply that, since rational relations were required, it brought into operation the most highly developed form of reasoning known: pure mathematics. The artificial experiences were reduced to experiences of numbers, and then metrical science was born. Thus the original aim of relating all natural experience was transformed to that of relating the numbers yielded by contrived operations.

But this was not at all understood. It was thought that each measurement represented a property of something in the "external world." The object of philosophy was conceived to be the study of this external world. Our experience—which is ultimately all that is of any importance to anybody—was simply a trivial effect of the casual impinging of the "world" on our bodies; the "world" would be exactly the same if this had never occurred. This idea could persist because there happened to be a pretty close correspondence between the other "things" that were thought to be measured and the "things" that we actually experience, but in fact this correspondence is illusory. Take mass, for instance. This is the name given to something conceived to be responsible for the recordings of certain measuring instruments. But mass was imagined to be "the quantity of matter in a body," and this was plausible, because when the instrument recorded a big number, a large body was usually seen. Hence it was believed that Newton's law of gravitation described the path of a planet around the sun. In reality it describes the path of a mass-point in a gravitational field, and both mass-point and gravitational field belong to an invented world that only in part corresponds to the common-sense world of material objects. If the earth should explode to smithereens through internal stresses, the mass-point (the "center of gravity") would continue on its orbit undisturbed, but there would be no matter where it was situated.

Every symbol in every physical equation stands for the result of a measurement or a combination of such results, and fundamentally for nothing else. In a simple case like that of mass, the correspondence between symbol and some element of ordinary experience is fairly close; usually matters are more complex. Take, for example, Avogadro's number, N—the number of molecules in a cubic centimeter of gas in a certain state. N actually stands for a combination of measurements with thermometers, pressure gauges, balances and so on. (There are various combinations that give the same result; that is why the "number" is important). But we describe N as "a number of molecules"— the name given to the result of the operation of counting. And we think of it as such. But in fact the operation of counting molecules is impossible. We can delude ourselves into believing that the operation of weighing is a discovery of the mass of a body, but no honest man can claim that when he is finding N he is counting anything. Yet such is our faith that each measurement is a measurement of "something" that we are ready to make such a claim in order to maintain that faith. Nor is that the worst. We even analyze the intricate concept that we call "the momentum of an electron" as though we had a particle of matter before us and were applying the process for measuring momentum to it; and then we imagine that we are learning something about the world of experience. God help us!

The whole world of physics is a set of relations between concepts that represent combinations of the results of measurements, i.e., of artificially created experiences. Nothing that this world contains would ever have happened if we had not made it happen. To verify any of the relations you must adjust the conditions with the greatest care; let experience come naturally, and their supposed requirements are always violated. Go on dropping an object to the ground, and it will come to rest at a different place every time. Go out one day, and you feel warm; do the same the next day, and you feel cold. The laws of falling bodies and of heat are obeyed only in laboratories. Physics tells us a tremendous amount about the world, but it is not the natural world; it is a world of our own making.

How is it, then, that we have turned the results of physical research to such significant account in ordinary life? Simply because of a purely empirical relation between the natural and the artificial worlds. Over a large part of experience they maintain a close parallelism. When a balance gives a big number, we usually do see a big object (but we have seen that a large value of M does not always mean that). When the thermometer has a high reading, we usually feel hot (but in outer space we should probably die instantly of cold, although astronomers tell us that the temperature there can be over 1,000 degrees centigrade). Why the sight of a big object is usually attended by a large M, and feeling of heat by a large O, we understand no more than Thales could have if he had known the facts. With all our science we have learned nothing about the relations existing in the world of natural experience. We have discovered how to create a world between the elements of which rational relations do exist, and we exploit the empirical fact of its close parallelism with the natural world.

This is of the greatest importance in regard to the function of measurement in other sciences such as psychology and sociology. Here exactly the same considerations hold good, but whereas in physics the parallelism between the metrical concepts and ordinary experiences is the rule and its breakdown the exception, in the other sciences the reverse is more nearly true; at least any supposed measurement of a psychological attribute is much less uniformly related to actual experience than is normally the case in physics. To take but a single example, the primary importance of Intelligence Quotient is not that it measures "intelligence," whatever that may be, but that it stands in simple relations to other measurements (in particular, a relation approaching identity with further determinations of the same quantity with the same person). We may expect that in time a considerable system of relations between psychological measurements will be built up, but woe betide us if we imagine that its relation to the world of experience is other than purely empirical. A large IQ may go with a good performance in other specified operations, but its possessor may well be a gambling addict, and so one of the most "unintelligent" of persons.

It is in view of such facts as these that measurement must be defined in terms of its origin in the operations we perform, without reference to anything external. Having so defined it, we can begin its analysis. Each measurement includes a manual and a mental part; for example, in measuring length we lay an object along a specified scale (the manual part) and subtract the smaller from the larger of the end-readings (the mental part). We deliberately relax the precision of the specification in two respects. In the manual part we allow one element of the operation to be changed ad lib.; in the example of length we can make "the object" anything we like, and we call the result (merely as a name) the length of that object. In the mental part we allow ourselves to multiply the result of any fundamental measurement (that is, a measurement that does not include another measurement as a part of its prescription) by any number; we call this (again merely as a name) "changing the unit of measurement." The whole process is thus described without wandering outside into a hypothetical "something to be measured."

There is currently some vociferous objection to testing programs, especially since these programs have so proliferated. Possibly if testing programs were not so misused or overused, these critics would be less disturbed. Dr. Womer, who is Assistant Professor of Education and consultant on testing and guidance in the Bureau of School Services, University of Michigan, spells out several of these misconceptions and misuses. The article originally appeared in the Michigan Journal of Secondary Education, *Spring 1961, and was subsequently widely distributed by the Cooperative Test Division of the Educational Testing Service.*

Testing Programs—Misconception, Misuse, Overuse

Frank B. Womer

We are in a boom period of standardized testing in elementary and secondary schools. To pupils at all grade levels, millions of tests are administered each year—achievement tests, mental ability tests, aptitude tests, and interest inventories, as well as several types of tests and inventories. Some of these tests are given for college scholarship purposes and some for college admissions purposes. Title V of the National Defense Education Act has stimulated, and in some instances, required, additions to testing programs at the secondary level. In general, however, these external influences account for a relatively small percentage of the total standardized testing undertaken by a school system.

There are at least two factors which have had a greater impact upon the amount of testing done in the schools than NDEA or college requirements. First, there has been and continues to be a natural growth of standardized testing at all grade levels. Second, the rapid growth of the guidance movement has meant a corresponding rapid growth in testing. This latter influence may well be the most influential one operating, for in many schools the testing program is developed by and operated by guidance personnel.

Inauguration or expansion of a testing program is relatively easy. Decisions made one day can be implemented within a week or two. The only time lag is that of the United States mail in delivering orders for tests and getting test materials from the publisher to the school. Machine methods for test scoring have reduced, and in many cases eliminated, objections that a testing program is a burden upon individual teachers. The school budget and allocation of time for testing are the only real problems to face if an administrator or faculty decides to enlarge the testing program. Thus it is relatively easy to test.

The values of standardized testing, however, cannot be dismissed so quickly. Such values are dependent upon two processes: (1) establishment of proper goals of testing and the development of a testing program to meet those goals, and (2) proper use of test results. Both of these processes are essential to the operation of a successful testing program. Most educators feel, and rightfully so, that the major weakness of testing today is in the area of test use.

Many writers have made this point, and most school administrators are acutely aware of the fact that the ultimate criterion for judging the effectiveness of their testing programs is the correct use of test results. Accumulating test scores in cumulative files is not evidence of test use. Correct use depends upon getting test results into the hands of counselors, teachers, administrators, pupils, and parents and of being sure that each consumer of these results is made knowledgeable enough to interpret them. In this latter statement—"made knowledgeable enough to interpret them"—lies the key to proper test use.

There are a number of ways that test scores are misused or overused, and a number of misconceptions about tests and test scores that are common enough to warrant special attention. While one could think of innumerable examples of specific errors in test interpretation, the purpose of this article is to point up some of the more common mistakes, in order to help increase the knowledgeable use of test results. Ten points have been selected for discussion; others could have been added.

CATEGORIZING A PUPIL AT A SPECIFIC LEVEL OF ACHIEVEMENT OR ABILITY

One of the most common mistakes made by persons unskilled in interpreting test results is the assumption of perfect reliability of a test score. Too often it is assumed that an IQ of 105 represents performance definitely superior to that represented by an IQ of 104 and definitely inferior to that represented by 106. Too often we fail to realize that a test score is best interpreted as a good estimate of the general level of performance, and that it will vary from test to test and from time to time. Test users must accept the concept of variability of test scores over time and over tests. The assessment of human traits and abilities is not at the same level of accuracy as that found in a physics laboratory. It probably is closer to the level of accuracy found in the predictions of weather, in which temperature predictions are generally within a few degrees of actual temperatures, but in which differences of ten or more degrees are common enough to be remembered vividly by critics.

Another aspect of this assumption of greater accuracy than actually prevails is the use of a single estimate (test score) to predict human performance. It is generally wise to insist on having two or three reading scores, or two or three aptitude scores, before putting much confidence in them. This is a direct result of the unreliability present in all test scores. If a pupil receives percentiles of 35 and 40 on arithmetic tests given in two different years, one can have greater confidence that his level of achievement in arithmetic is in the average range than if only one of these scores is available.

CONFUSION OF NORMS AND STANDARDS

Norms are test scores which tell us the level of performance attained by an average or typical group of pupils. Standards represent human judgments of the level of performance that "should be" attained by a group of pupils. A test user should not assume that "typical" pupil performance is automatically the "proper" level of performance for pupils in a particular school system. It is reasonable, of course, to assume that pupils in many school systems will tend to perform at a level close to the level of test norms. In others, however, it is reasonable to assume that pupils will perform at a higher level or at a lower level.

One occasionally finds a test user who completely fails to grasp the conception of what a test norm is. Since a test norm represents "typical" performance, then, of necessity, half of the pupils in a typical or average group will have scores at or below the average score. If a teacher of a typical group of pupils finds that 40 per cent of his pupils are below grade level in reading, he is to be congratulated. In the norm group for whatever test is being used, 50 per cent of all the pupils were at or below grade level. The assumption that all pupils in a class should be at grade level is patently impossible, unless one knows that the poorest achieving pupil in one's class is in the top 50 per cent of all pupils his own age or grade.

ASSUMPTION THAT TEST SCORES PREDICT SUCCESS OR FAILURE FOR INDIVIDUAL PUPILS

One way that test results often are overused is the assumption that a particular score or series of scores does in fact predict success or failure with unfailing accuracy. It is well established that students who succeed in colleges of engineering generally make high scores on numerical ability tests. Yet it is not correct to conclude from such data that Johnny, with a 50th percentile rank on a test of numerical ability, will not succeed in an engineering course. It is correct to conclude that of every 100 students with numerical ability scores the same as Johnny's, only a small percentage will succeed in an engineering curriculum. The test score does provide information of a probability type; it enables a student or parent or counselor to know the odds for success or failure. It is a well-known fact that long shots occasionally win the Kentucky Derby, but year in, year out, the favorites generally win.

It is not unusual for two counselors to look at the same test scores for an individual pupil and to come to somewhat different conclusions. For this reason, it is well to face the fact that while test scores do provide information that can be helpful in decision making, the decisions for courses of action are made by human beings, not by the scores.

Added to this overuse of test scores is the failure of some people to utilize all pertinent data available about a student when test scores are known. To allow test scores to outweigh all other judgmental data is a misuse of these scores; to ignore test scores in favor of other judgmental data also is a misuse of these scores.

DETERMINATION OF VOCATIONAL GOALS

"Mary's scores from a clerical speed and accuracy test and from a spelling test are only average. Therefore, Mary should not consider secretarial work as a career possibility." Or, "Since Jim's interest profile shows high scores in 'Scientific' and 'Social Service' he should elect a premed course in college." How often can vocational counseling be summed up in just such simple statements? It is so easy to make the jump from test score to occupation, and it seems so logical that this type of interpretation should be accurate. Unfortunately, the predictive validity of test scores in high school for success in specific occupations is not good enough to permit such interpretations. Most evidence of the predictive efficiency of test scores relates those scores to academic curricula. We can say with a fair degree of accuracy that certain patterns of test scores predict fairly well in different curricula. That is the type of validity data that is generally available.

The use of test scores in vocational counseling should tend to open doors of possible occupations rather than close them. Again, presenting the relationship between test scores and occupational areas on a probability basis can be helpful, and is certainly more accurate than making the assumption that certain test scores assure success in one field and failure in another.

ASSUMPTION THAT INTELLIGENCE AND ACHIEVEMENT ARE SEPARATE AND DISTINCT

Here are two sample questions from standardized tests:

1. Extraneous
   a. extra b. foreign c. transparent d. noisy
2. Make indelible means
   a. indistinct b. permanent c. purple d. identical

Both are vocabulary items. One of them is taken from a widely-used intelligence test (California Test of Mental Maturity) and the other from a widely used achievement battery (Iowa Tests of Educational Development). Vocabulary items measure the learned meanings of words; vocabulary items are our best single measure of general intelligence or scholastic aptitude. Arithmetic items and general information items are also found in both achievement tests and intelligence tests. It is true, of course, that some items suitable for an intelligence test (number series, verbal analogies) are not good measures of achievement. It also is true that many direct measures of achievement (capitalization, punctuation, spelling) are not good measures of intellectual potential.

There is considerable overlap between standardized tests of achievement and standardized intelligence tests. One of the important differences between the two is the way the results are used. When analyzing achievement test scores, one is generally considering past performance, what has been accomplished. When analyzing intelligence test scores, one is generally looking forward to the future; predicting performance.

It is well to keep in mind the fact that intelligence is inferred from achievement. We have no direct measures of intelligence completely divorced from achievement.

ASSUMPTION THAT INTERESTS AND APTITUDES ARE SYNONYMOUS

Probably few users of standardized tests would acknowledge a belief that interests and aptitudes are the same thing. Webster defines the terms in different domains. Yet how many users of standardized interest inventories can truthfully say that they have never made the jump from a high percentile score in "Persuasive" to the suggestion that Bill probably could succeed in sales activities? To say that Bill seems to be interested in many of the same things that are of interest to people who work in occupations that require influencing other people may be accurate. But to say that Bill will likely succeed in one of these occupations is to make the unwarranted jump from interest to aptitude.

There is evidence that interests and aptitudes are correlated, but not at a level that allows us to predict one from the other with a high degree of accuracy. This is not to say that interest inventories are useless, but their use might well center on their motivational attributes, on their power to stimulate pupil concern over long range planning.

MISCONCEPTION OF THE MEANINGS OF CERTAIN TYPES OF DERIVED SCORES

Students of education have been and are continuing to be taught that an intelligence quotient is obtained by dividing mental age by chronological age, and that mental age is determined by the test performance of students at different levels. Yet, as a matter of fact, very few of the IQ's to be found in the cumulative folders of elementary and secondary schools today are quotient scores at all. IQ's are standard scores, just as are z scores, T scores, stanines, College Board scores, and others for almost every widely-used intelligence test.

It is true that IQ's originally were quotient scores. But, primarily for statistical reasons, the deviation IQ was developed some years ago and has since met with almost universal adoption. Even the Stanford-Binet test switched to a deviation IQ in 1959. The change from a quotient score to a standard score has not necessitated any drastic change in interpretation. Yet it seems to the writer that test users would be well advised to stop paying lip service to a type of score that no longer exists, and to become familiar with standard scores, the type of scores actually being used with our intelligence tests.

The grade placement or grade equivalent score is another type of derived score that is frequently misinterpreted or overused. All too often it is assumed that a grade placement score is an indication of the grade to which a pupil should be assigned. It does not provide that type of information; it simply tells a user whether a pupil is doing high, average, or low quality work. A percentile rank also provides the same assessment of level of work, yet avoids the danger of over-interpretation. If one wishes to compare a pupil's achievement on two different tests in an achievement battery (e.g., reading level versus arithmetic level), a grade equivalent score may lead one to an important misinterpretation. Because of the variability (standard deviation) of grade placement scores from test to test it is possible for a sixth grade pupil to be at the 90th percentile in both reading and arithmetic, yet receive grade placement scores of 8.8 in reading and 8.0 in arithmetic.* If a teacher sees only the grade placement scores of 8.8 and 8.0 he may assume superiority in reading, whereas the two scores represent equivalent performance. For test-by-test comparisons in elementary level achievement batteries, percentile scores should be used.

GRADING OR PROMOTING PUPILS

Standardized achievement tests are designed with certain purposes in mind. In general, test authors attempt to identify those skills and understandings that are common to most educational programs. They look for the common denominators; they make no attempt to cover those unique aspects of content that a particular school system may incorporate in its curricular offering. They cannot attempt to reflect a particular teacher's goals for his own pupils. Thus, while achievement test results represent very useful assessment of certain skills and understandings that are common to many classrooms, they should not be used to replace a teacher's own assessment devices.

In many schools standardized achievement tests are given toward the beginning of the school year. They are used to look ahead rather than to look back, to diagnose rather than to evaluate or grade. In those schools that use standardized achievement tests at the end of the year, it may be interesting for a teacher to compare the results with his own judgments. It is not wise for the test results to be used to replace his judgments, in either grading or promotion.

JUDGING EFFECTIVENESS OF INSTRUCTION

Just as standardized tests are not designed to be used for grading pupils, they are not designed to be used for grading teachers. Many of the outcomes of classroom instruction cannot be programmed in standardized tests. Those that can be programmed in tests may not be meaningful because of different emphases, different content, and different grade placement in a particular school.

Of special concern is the attitude engendered in teachers in a school attempting to assess instruction through achievement tests. When test results are used to judge teachers, teachers soon learn to teach for the tests.

It is interesting to note that in some instances teachers even feel compelled to "teach for" ability tests. They somehow feel that it isn't respectable to turn in a set of IQ scores for filing in a cumulative record

---

*Iowa Tests of Basic Skills, end-of-year percentile norms for sixth grade pupils.

unless all or almost all of them are at least 100. Such a feeling, of course, is based on a misconception of the meaning of intelligence. A teacher may be cutting his own throat with such high scores, for if his pupils are all above average in ability they may be expected to show equally high achievement levels.

COMPARING RESULTS FROM DIFFERENT TESTS

There is a very natural tendency for test users to assume that a language usage score from one test is directly comparable to a language usage score from another test, that an IQ from one test means the same thing as an IQ from another. When making such assumptions one tends to forget two very important characteristics of standardized tests:

1. Test authors do not build their tests on the same specifications, following the same blueprints. Each one develops his own specifications for test construction. There usually is considerable overlap between the plans for a language usage test developed by one author and the plans developed by another. However, there is never a complete overlap. Scores from two tests measuring the same attribute vary to a certain extent because the test designs vary.

2. The norms for different tests are based upon different groups of pupils. Each test author aims at securing a truly random population of pupils for use in standardizing his test. Each author falls somewhat short of his goal. While it is correct to assume that test norms for two different arithmetic tests are based on groups with considerable overlap in achievement, it is not correct to assume 100-per cent overlap.

Thus, two IQ's derived from two different intelligence tests are not exactly equivalent. It has been demonstrated that IQ's can vary as much as 5 or 10 points between different tests for no other reason than that they are different tests.

Sometimes one hears this objection: "But how can IQ's be different from different tests? I thought that all good intelligence tests correlated well with each other." It is true that the correlation between different intelligence tests are generally sizable, and many times are almost as high as the reliability of the separate tests. Such correlations do not guarantee comparability of norms. Such correlations simply say that pupils taking the different tests will tend to get scores putting them in the same relative rank order but not with the same scores. For example, suppose one were to take a set of IQ's (or any other test score) and add 50 points to each score. The correlation between the original IQ's and the new scores would be perfect, yet the two sets of scores would be 50 points apart.

As was mentioned earlier, we are in the middle of a boom period of testing. If the users of tests do a good job of interpreting the results for the improvement of our understanding of boys and girls and for the improvement of instruction, the boom will level off on a satisfactory plateau of test use. If the users of test results fall into the various misuses, overuses, and misconceptions that are possible, the boom will most certainly be followed by a "bust."

It is the thesis of this article that the consumers of test scores must be thoroughly conversant with proper methods of test use and must studiously avoid misuses, overuses, and misconceptions.

"A little knowledge is a dangerous thing."

At the 23rd annual meeting of the New York State Psychological Association in 1961, the Division of Personnel Psychology sponsored a symposium on the reporting of test information. Dr. Dorothea Mc-Carthy, Professor of Psychology at Fordham University, presented the main paper in which she summarized the significant questions any test user should ask about tests and then continued with the communication aspect of such results. The student should also read, in conjunction with this, Test Service Bulletin #54, *by Dr. James R. Ricks, "On Telling Parents About Test Results."*

Ethical and Professional Considerations in Reporting of Test Information

Dorothea McCarthy

Mental test data of all sorts are coming into increasing use in schools, in mental health and community clinics, in employment agencies and in business and industry, as well as in the military services. For a long time tests were administered in schools, and the practice was considered generally desirable, but the information often remained in files on cumulative record cards and was not used or interpreted to the testee himself or to his parents, teachers, or counselors. Such testing programs are utterly useless and a waste of time and money unless the test results are to be made known and unless they are to be used in decision making about the individuals who have been tested. On the other hand, school administrators who are convinced of the potential value of testing programs sometimes make specific test results known in numerical terms without adequate interpretation to members of their staff who have very limited understanding of their meaning. In a school situation where every teacher can immediately associate each child's IQ with his name in her roll book one cannot help but feel that an overemphasis on test results has occurred somewhere along the line, without due recognition to the limitations of the instruments, the conditions of taking the tests, or of the importance of motivation and other personality characteristics in the makeup of the individual.

This discussion is limited to the communication of test results as distinct from all forms of confidential information which comes to the knowledge of the clinical psychologist. Yet as tests have spread more widely in the coverage they give, there are several areas of test information which must be recognized. The first is the area of general intelligence usually in the form of a verbal test of intelligence. Secondly, there is the measure of non-verbal intelligence or performance ability, which in most cases gives a comparison score. A third major area of test information concerns a person's level of academic achievement and his relative strengths and weaknesses in the various skills and subject matter areas. The fourth area in which fairly specific test information may become available is in the category of special aptitudes and interests. There is also the area of personality and adjustment in which there are two types of test results: the objective, quantitatively-scored inventory type of test, and the more subtle and less objectively-scored projective techniques. Finally, we have the important but nebulous area of test of impairment of mental functioning.

These seven types of test results from a series of criteria or gradients along which they should be evaluated prior to interpretation. The first gradient is that of *reliability*. How certain are we that the results in each of these areas really characterizes the client and is likely to characterize him in the near or distant future? What is the margin of error we are dealing with in each of the obtained scores? How much is the particular secured score on this occasion likely to change on retest due to chance alone? How much is the particular score likely to change and in which direction, due to anticipated growth or environmental changes in the life of the individual?

The second gradient is that of *validity*. How sure are we that the test in each of these areas really measures what we think it measures, or what the test designer intended it to measure? Is the test properly named, or is it a misnomer? It seems to me we are most certain of validity in the area of achievement and least certain in tests of mental impairment, or perhaps in the more subtle aspects of personality assessment.

The third gradient to be considered in evaluating the degree of confidence to be placed in the test results we are interpreting to others is that of the adequacy of the *norms* and the suitability or applicability of the norms in the particular case to which we wish to apply the instrument. Is it fair, right and proper to apply this instrument to the case at hand? Are there norms available for the group to which this client belongs or in which he will find himself competing?

The fourth and perhaps the most important gradient when it comes to matters of interpreting test results is the degree of *intimacy* of the information yielded by the test. How *sensitive* would most clients be about having these aspects of his total makeup known to others? How *personal* is this information usually conceded to be? In general, the more personal or intimate the information, the more conservative one must be about communicating it to others.

These remarks go back to some of the fundamentals of testing, but I think it is a healthy thing to remind ourselves, as practitioners and appliers of tests, of the limitations of our instruments. When we report experimental results of research we report the level of confidence with which the results or conclusions are presented. Often, we get in the habit of applying tests on a routine basis and forget to look at newer and perhaps better instruments, or sometimes we forget things we once learned about instruments we use habitually. Such matters as the fact that a certain test has a much smaller variability than another with which we constantly make mental comparisons, the fact that its standard deviation varies markedly from one age to another, or that it is based on very few cases at the upper and lower ends of the scale, even though it may be adequately standardized in the middle range, are points often forgotten by the psychometrician. If a test is designed to get at a pathological condition, how normal were the control cases from which the pathological cases were supposed to have been differentiated? Can we honestly answer all such questions about our instruments and answer them favorably? It seems to me that if we review these fundamental principles, we become rather humble with regard to our fallible instruments, and this humility can be our best guide in matters of test interpretation.

It is my observation and experience that the person who knows the *most* about the tests is likely to be most conservative and cautious in interpretation. When we hear of some horrible example of misuse of test results, it usually arises from ignorance, or from that little knowledge which can be such a dangerous thing.

When the knowledgeable and conscientious psychologist has applied the best tools at his command which are appropriate for the evaluation of the particular subject, and has given due consideration to the fallibility of the instruments employed in the light of the above-mentioned criteria, he must then ask himself a number of additional questions in deciding how much information to divulge, and *to whom* and *how* the information can best be communicated, so as to do the most good for the client and for society, and lead to the least possibility of harm or misinterpretation.

First should be considered the right of the person to the information. The client himself has a right to know the results of the tests he has taken if he is an adolescent or an adult who is not feebleminded or severely disturbed. Some limited interpretation can often be given to children, especially for reassurance. This is particularly true in cases where there is a severe feeling of inferiority or doubt as to one's competence and when the test results are normal or superior. Parents of normal or superior intelligence who are reasonably normally adjusted certainly have a right to information about the test results of their minor children, but here care must be exercised as to *how much* information is given and in *what terms* it is to be given. Opportunity must be afforded to confer about test results which may be unfavorable and difficult for the parents to accept emotionally, even though he or she may be fully capable of intellectual understanding of the material. Those who may have had a role in referring the case are entitled to a courteous note of acknowledgement. If they are in continuing contact with the client in school or in a medical or other professional capacity, they may be entitled to a general statement about the results of test findings. If such persons are professional people familiar with handling and interpreting test results, it may be appropriate to divulge actual test findings, but in such instances it is best to clear with the client or his deputy regarding the sending of a report to the school, the doctor or whoever the party may be. In addition, it is best not to assume too much psychological sophistication, even on the part of other professional people. A pediatrician may be amazingly ignorant when it comes to interpreting an IQ! When in doubt, it is best to make such reports conservative. A meager and conservative report can always be elaborated upon later should the need arise, if one later learns more about the competence of the person to whom the information is being given.

It is best to avoid giving information over the telephone to anyone who may ask for it. First of all, clients may have relatives who are busybodies who are fishing for information they have no right to know, and the client should be protected from such inquiries. Also there is great likelihood of being misunderstood and misquoted concerning information given over the telephone. If there is some degree of urgency it is always best to call the person back, so as to check on the identity of the inquirer, if he or she is not personally known.

Another important consideration in divulging test information is whether the person will be able to *understand* the information. Information given in conference is usually the best method, for one can usually tell from facial expression, accepting remarks, etc. whether the factual information is understood. The good psychologist can judge the intellectual level of the parent, teacher or principal, and couch his information in language which can be understood by the person to whom the information is being given. One would use very different words in explaining a test IQ of 75 to a bilingual parent with a fourth grade education and to a parent holding an MA degree in social work. A disturbed mother undergoing psychoanalysis can tolerate relatively little information concerning the pseudo-mental retardation of her unloved child.

Mere intellectual understanding of test results is not, however, the only matter to be taken into consideration in deciding what and how to communicate test results. One must consider whether the test *results* are *favorable* or *unfavorable* or *likely to be regarded as such* by the person receiving the information. The relationship of the person to the client is important, for if the mother is pushing and overly ambitious for a child who is only average, her acceptance of his mediocrity may be very difficult. On the other hand a parent who has been told by a pediatrician that his child is "brain damaged," and who has been living with fear and panic, imagining imbecility and institutonalization ahead for the child, may be greatly reassured to learn that his child has mentality in the dull-normal range. It can readily be seen then that there is no ready rule of thumb to be followed in giving test results. We must ask ourselves what tests were used, how good are they, what level of rapport and effort were achieved, who should get the results, in how much detail and under what circumstances.

I shall conclude with a few thumbnail sketches of actual experiences which will illustrate the tremendous variety of discriminations the psychologist must make in his professional judgments concerning the communication of test results.

Two delinquent boys in a reformatory had similarly high IQ's of 136 and 138. Quite different interpretations were given to them, however, because of their very different personalities and attitudes. To one who was extremely cocky and overconfident, the discrepancy between his high verbal and poorer performance score of 115 was stressed, and it was pointed out to him that he was not equally good in all kinds of skills and that perhaps there were areas in which he needed to improve. The other boy who suffered from a severe inferiority complex and feeling of utter worthlessness was given a very enthusiastic interpretation of his verbal IQ which raised his morale appreciably.

In another instance the Army Signal Corps inquired about our earlier clinical study of a recruit who was now in the service. We felt obligated to point out the finding that the boy was color-blind and should not be assigned to duty involving color discrimination.

A school principal was having difficulty trying to decide whether or not a child belonged in a class for gifted children. He was using a cut-off point of 130 IQ. The child in question had an Otis Group Test score of only 124 but his Stanford-Binet IQ was 138. When the differences in Standard deviation of the two tests were interpreted to the principal he realized that 124 on the Otis (SD:12 pts.) would be equivalent to 132 on the Stanford-Binet (SD:16 pts.) so that the two scores were really not so far apart, and the child really would meet the criterion for the special class when the scores were properly interpreted.

A mother of a retarded reader in fifth grade received a report that her child's reading level was 3.2. She was so impressed with the seriousness of the child's reading retardation that she thought he read at 3.2 years instead of a 3.2 grade level.

A clergyman learned that a young man who was about to be married had been known to a child guidance clinic because of non-reading. The clergyman thought only mental deficiency could account for such a difficulty. He merely wanted reassurance that the young man had sufficient intelligence to understand the nature of the marriage contract.

The mother of a nine-year-old in fourth grade referred the child to the clinic because she though he was retarded in reading. The child was found, however, to be reading normally at the middle of the 4th grade and the mother was told his score of 4.5 grade level. She replied, "Oh, but is that good enough? He'll soon be going into fifth!"

My final example concerns a young intern who, while a medical student, chanced to see his score of 84 on a mental test. Since he thought all mental test scores were IQ's, he found a book on mental testing and looked up to see what an IQ of 84 meant. He found it was in the "dull-normal" range. He decided that he had only been able to get through medical school because he had "a good memory," but he really wasn't very bright. When it was interpreted to him that results on college level mental tests were usually in percentiles, and a percentile score of 84 was interpreted to him, a great weight was lifted from his mind.

These are but a few illustrations of the confusions and difficulties which can arise when there is lack of proper communication concerning test results.

PART TWO

TEST
ADMINISTRATION
PROBLEMS

Test-wise Americans often expect little difficulty with aptitude testing programs in other cultures, despite extensive anthropological and sociological evidence that culture and individual values are intertwined. In our easy adaptation to aptitude and achievement tests of all sorts, particularly in school situations, we are apt to forget that psychological testing is a very different sort of experience to foreigners, especially non-Westerners. Presumably "culture-free" tests (a clear misnomer, since no psychological tests can be constructed outside of any cultural value system) hope to minimize some of these difficulties; evidence that they can do this, however, is sadly lacking. The following four articles all deal with various aspects of test administration, both in "foreign" cultures as well as in USA sub-cultures.

The first of this group relates some of the difficulties, as well as some very amusing sidelights, that one psychologist met in his attempt to devise a selection battery for police officers in Viet Nam. The author, Dr. Wickert, is Professor of Psychology at Michigan State University. During 1955–57 he was in Viet Nam on a technical assistance mission to this government. The article amusingly relates some of the difficulties met on this assignment. It is reproduced in its entirety from American Psychologist, 1957, Vol. 5, pp. 86–88.

An Adventure in Psychological

Testing Abroad

Frederic R. Wickert

In the room at the north end of the first floor of President Diem's Freedom Palace in Saigon, one day in September, 1955, several members of the "police team" and I were in a conference. We all belonged to the Michigan State University group sent to Viet Nam to give technical aid to the government of that new country.

The police team members, one of several teams in the MSU group, had the mission of helping the Viet Nam government improve the internal security of the country as rapidly as possible. In the States the police team members had all been engaged in professional police work. Normally, I am one of the regular teaching members of the MSU psychology department. Temporarily I had agreed to go to Viet Nam as coordinator and deputy adviser for in-service training.

We MSU technical aides were conferring with Mr. Ro, something like a chief of staff to the Minister of the Interior, whose offices were in the palace. Mr. Ro, in addition to his many other duties, had been named to head the new police academy which our police team had been instrumental in establishing.

During the conference the subject of student selection arose. Mr. Ro asked whether we could give a test in order to make sure that only students who could benefit from the instruction would be included in the class. This request had a familiar ring to a psychologist. Further discussion indicated that the students should have completed the equivalent of sixth grade. From this it was concluded that an "intelligence" (educational achievement type) test, pitched at the level of students at the end of sixth grade, would be in order. We told Mr. Ro that we could, with help from him, prepare a suitable test in the short time remaining before the opening of the academy. Mr. Ro then arranged a visit to the Ministry of Education, where discussion with officials indicated that a test consisting partly of Vietnamese language items and partly of arithmetic items would be appropriate. Two "professors" who taught Vietnamese language and two who taught arithmetic, all at the sixth-grade level, were borrowed from the Ministry of Education. I spent some hours trying to explain to them how to construct objective items in language and arithmetic. The Far East edition of *Reader's Digest* fortunately contains a page of multiple-choice vocabulary items. These items provided a pattern for the language professors to follow. The idea of objective-type items came more readily to the arithmetic professors. It was most difficult to get both the language and the arithmetic professors to prepare items of a wide enough range of difficulty. Specifically, they wanted to make difficult items only. Finally, some of the interpreter–translators around the office helped to construct items too. It got to be a game.

Vietnamese language is a tricky thing to work with. Basically it is monosyllabic. Complex, abstract concepts are sometimes expressed by combining two or three monosyllables. Since, however, Vietnamese is basically a peasant's language (with, for example, about twelve different ways of expressing the idea "to carry," a different word depending on what part of the body is doing the carrying), it is poor in abstractions, even when one tries putting Vietnamese monosyllables together to express more complex ideas. It borrows heavily from Chinese monosyllables, and combinations of monosyllables, for abstractions. Vietnamese who would do well on Chinese-type language items were said to be overly pedantic and would not necessarily make too good policemen.

In addition, the Tonkinese or North Viet Nam dialect is quite different from the South Viet Nam dialect. Almost the only persons available to construct vocabulary items were North Vietnamese intellectuals who had fled from the North as the Communists took over following the Geneva conference. But most of the persons who would take the test would know only the South Vietnamese dialect. Eventually these problems were largely overcome. A 60-item Vietnamese language and 60-item arithmetic test, including a test booklet and a separate answer sheet, was finally prepared.

The Ministry of Education was asked to provide a large number of average boys, just beginning seventh grade, as a tryout group. After much negotiating, only one class of about 50 boys was made available. Instead of average boys, they turned out to be probably the best seventh-grade class in all Viet Nam. The Vietnamese were out to show how well they could do. Naturally the items were too easy for this group. The item difficulty analyses did not show as much as would ordinarily have been expected.

Administering the test was an eye-opener for us Americans. It turned out to be necessary to give much supplemental instruction on the use of the separate answer sheet, on how to mark answers, etc. Boys would turn to each other for help, notwithstanding frequent instructions that they were not to talk to each other. Maintaining order was all the more difficult because of the Vietnamese habit of thinking out loud as they work problems or even study. How much neighbors listened to each other and benefited from this listening could not be determined. The test administrators and proctors could not be sure whether the students were communicating to each other or were merely doing the usual thinking out loud. The boys all seemed to try hard on the tests and remained in good spirits but looked very puzzled when we tried to keep them from talking. How to maintain "standardized" testing conditions under these circumstances?

Results showed that the arithmetic test took unnecessarily long, while the language test was too easy and too short. Odd-even reliabilities of the two-part scores were reasonably satisfactory, judging by the scatter diagrams of odd-versus-even scores.

In view of the above experiences, the test was reconstructed. The language test was expanded from 60 items to 100; the arithmetic was cut from 60 items to 40. The items were arranged in the order of their difficulty, as well as could be done from the data. Types of items thought to be difficult turned out to be relatively easy, and other types, thought to be easy, turned out to be difficult. Instructions were reworked in the light of specific difficulties encountered in the tryout testing.

The big day finally arrived when approximately 130 candidates, all policemen on the active force, appeared for testing. The two classrooms available for testing held but about 70 students each, so the group was split in two. Group 1 was started without much apparent difficulty. Its members were especially cautioned not to talk, and they stayed surprisingly quiet. We then went next door to Group 2. They had scarcely started when the slight rumble from the direction of Group 1 increased to a roar. We rushed back only to find that they had gone back to thinking out loud, each one trying to outshout his neighbor. In two hours practically all had finished and the papers were collected.

Results showed that we had guessed well on many things. Scatter diagrams showed odd-even reliabilities on both parts of the test to be about in the eighties or low nineties. The correlation between the two tests was probably in the low thirties. This time the items were fairly well arranged in the order of their difficulty. The test was rather easy, so that those subjects toward the lower end of the distribution were well spread out and discrimination among these persons was reasonably dependable. Incidentally, I had no time to work out any statistics. It was easy to teach Vietnamese assistants to score the tests, to make frequency distributions and scatter diagrams and to do simple item-difficulty analysis. In the rush of far more pressing matters, there was no time to teach them how to calculate correlation coefficients, and I had no time to do them myself.

Administratively the decision was made to send back to duty the 26 men with the lowest scores. A number of persons, both Vietnamese and American, objected to sending these men back on the grounds that they were the ones who most needed training. It was finally worked out that the low men from four or five classes would be accumulated and put through as a class for which the instruction would be especially adapted.

It developed that about three-fifths of the group tested was made up of municipal police and the remaining two-fifths were from the "Sureté," the plain-clothes, undercover men. Much to the surprise of the Americans, the Sureté men did no better on the test than the ordinary municipal police. To the Vietnamese this was no surprise. They did say that at least the test results would provide them with ammunition to try to convince the higher-ups that the Sureté should be given better men. The idea of using tests in selecting new men for the Sureté they have not yet been able or willing to grasp.

The staff of the Police Academy were most impressed by the speed with which test results were made available. They said that never before had they seriously considered using selection testing in a crash program like the present one. In the past, tests had always taken weeks and even months to score.

The speed-of-scoring feature of the tests had another by-product. The academy staff decided to give their classes weekly objective tests. Their first attempts to make true-false items were very crude, but they did better on multiple-choice items. In view of their obvious interest, I then gave the instructors some help on how to construct objective items. The students were much interested in the weekly achievement tests and demanded to have their scored papers returned to them quickly. Other parts of the government have begun to hear about the testing and have expressed an interest in learning more about how it is done. However, I have had no time to develop this field further.

Upon the graduation of the first class at the academy in late December, 1955, the candidates for the second class took the test. This time there was far less talking. According to some Vietnamese the word had gotten around with respect to how to behave during Western-style testing. This "word" was apparently far more potent than any test instructions. The volume of talking out loud during testing was down markedly.

A strongly worded request had gone out to all administrators sending candidates to the academy to refrain from sending any but good men in the future. A comparison of the first and second testings showed that in the first class 16 per cent of 130 men made scores below 67, a kind of minimum passing score. In the second class, however, a little under 10 per cent of the 165 candidates scored below 67. Although these results look as though either the statement to the administrators or other factors were operating to make the performance of the second group better, the difference is not significant.

Some other testing had been done in Viet Nam. There is still a large sign over a courtyard leading to a government-type building which indicates that a psychotechnical center once existed there under the French occupation. The Vietnamese military have developed two tests which were used in selecting men to technical military specialties. This little bit of testing, done in the past, had apparently made no imprint on the culture, judging from our experiences.

Testing in another culture, then, can have its surprises. It also can be useful in that culture. With more time and effort, testing in Viet Nam could play an increasingly important role in an awakening movement to adopt improved personnel practices and to modernize educational procedures.

Also from Asia comes a second report of efforts by the local testees to "beat the test." Here, in Samoa, these Navy tests were in English rather than in the native language, so a "mental" translation problem presented itself to the candidates. Not only was the local populace most enthusiastic about the arrival of this U.S. Navy Recruiting Team, since it opened up the possibility of lucrative jobs, but also their response to the USA testing situation was otherwise from what many Americans would expect. Here, again, knowledge of cultural anthropology would have been most helpful to the team and the troublesome problem of "culture-free" tests again arises.

The author, Dr. Levine, is Psychological Research Advisor in the Navy Department. The following article is a condensation of the original report which appeared in American Psychologist, *1957, Vol. 5, pp. 259–263. Additional comments concerning the reported superiority of the Samoans on the Radio Code Aptitude Test have taken from a rejoinder to the Levine article by Ford which appeared in the "Comment" columns of this same journal.*

After the Samoans Come of Age

Abraham S. Levine

After the Samoans come of age—then what? They want to join the U.S. Navy!

The first Samoan recruiting mission arrived in 1954 and was enthusiastically greeted by all hands. The total stay on the islands of this popular team amounted to little more than a month. They were given a quota of 100 by the Chief of Naval Personnel in Washington. The first week was spent publicizing their mission and administering the Applicant Qualification Test which is the official Navy prescreening test made up of verbal, arithmetic, and mechanical items. This test was administered ostensibly to 1,410 applicants. However, it turned out that 1,410 did not represent the actual number. During this first week it did not occur to the Officer in Charge that a candidate would: (a) use any name but his true one, (b) take the examination more than once, (c) have someone else take the examination for him.

A bit of anthropology soon came to light. To "save face" is a trait of these people. Fictitious names were used so that in the event that names were published no one would know who had failed. This backfired: a successful candidate was unable to identify the examination as his paper. Also, many noneligibles took the examination hoping that either the fact that they were married, had dependents, or were underage would be overlooked or perhaps waived. Worse yet, some candidates took the examination more than once under different names or had friends take the examination for them. Taking an examination for someone else does not represent the kind of breach of ethics it would be in the United States. For the Samoans, it merely represents a bit of transfer of training from the well-established courtship custom reported on by Mead when a friend (if he doesn't speak for himself) serves as proxy.

When all the smoke had cleared away and the interviewers had completed their work, a total of 131 Samoans were considered eligible for the final screen—the medical examination. Of these, 84 were found physically acceptable and enlisted.

The 84 Samoans who successfully met all the requirements and became enlisted men in the U.S. Navy were subsequently administered a number of Navy aptitude and achievement tests for assignment purposes. The results of these psychometrics provide some interesting material for cross-cultural comparisons and represent the raison d'être of this article despite the rather discursive introduction. In view of the many limitations of these data, it would be presumptuous to regard them as being any more than suggestive, i.e., springboards for hypotheses and speculations which are perhaps better grounded than the well-meaning romanticizing which oft occurs in the absence of cold psychometric evidence.

It should be emphasized that these test data were obtained in connection with an operational mission rather than as part of a research project designed by psychologists or other competent social scientists. Also, it should be pointed out that the 84 Samoan males, selected out of an original pool of several hundred legitimate applicants, constitute those who achieved a passing score on a written test printed in English and devised for continental U. S. Navy applicants. The passing score for the Samoans was fixed at the same point as for applicants in the United States, i.e., the 10th percentile of a World War II Navy enlisted population. This selection standard was probably a good deal more rigorous for Samoans than for Americans. In other words, the Applicant Qualification Test was not a "culture-fair" test for the Samoans. This theme will be elaborated on when the test data are examined. Since the Recruiting Team was assigned a quota of 100 Samoans, it would not have been practicable to attempt to devise a specially tailored instrument for them. Besides it may be argued that, since the Samoans will have to adjust to the same complex subculture as will the recruits from the States, they should be selected and assigned on the basis of similar functional abilities as reflected in test scores. Even if this meant that in many instances a particular test score actually represented for the Samoans a greater potential to learn certain skills than would be the case for American recruits, this would be all to the good since it might serve to compensate for certain subtle cultural handicaps.

The battery of tests administered to the Samoans included:

1. General Classification Test: 100 completion and analogy items to measure verbal ability.

2. Arithmetic Test: 40 purely computational items and 60 problem-solving items.

3. Mechanical Test: pictorial items with a minimum of verbal descriptive material to measure basic mechanical and electrical knowledge and understanding of mechanical principles.

4. Clerical Aptitude Test: two sets of numbers to be rapidly and accurately checked as same or different.

5. Sonar Pitch Memory Test: items to measure ability to make fine pitch discriminations presented on phonograph records.

6. Radio Code Aptitude Test: a speed test to measure the ability to identify a few code characters at rapid rates of transmission. There is, first, a learning unit where examinees are taught three code characters; then a testing unit where examinees are tested at four different speeds on these learned characters.

7. Non-Verbal Classification Test: a general ability test, with items in pictorial or geometric form, designed for testing persons who can understand English but cannot read it.

Table 1 lists the mean scores obtained by the Samoans on this series of Navy aptitude and achievement tests. The screening test (Applicant Qualification Test) is also included. Several considerations should be kept in mind while examining these data:

TABLE 1
MEAN SCORES OBTAINED BY SAMOANS ON
U.S. NAVY APTITUDE TESTS

Test	N	Mean
Applicant Qualification Test	84	40.8
General Classification Test	84	33.6
Arithmetic Test	84	48.1
Mechanical Test	84	36.6
Clerical Aptitude Test	84	46.6
Sonar Pitch Memory Test	69	48.8
Radio Code Aptitude Test	80	63.2
Non-Verbal Classification Test	56	53.3

1. All of the test scores, with the exception of the Non-Verbal Classification Test, are expressed in standard score units. Mean standard score for Navy enlisted men is 50 and the standard deviation is 10. These statistics are based on a 1944, Navy enlisted, normative population. Actual means and standard deviations have fluctuated somewhat on both sides of these values, depending on a number of conditions, mostly of a supply-quota nature.

2. The Samoans in this sample represent a highly restricted segment of their population in education and ability variables. Moreover, they are rather difficult to characterize accurately in terms of psychometric referents generated in our culture. Consequently, it would not be too meaningful an enterprise to make comparisons on the basis of standard deviations and intercorrelations, since these statistics are particularly sensitive to the various kinds of influences which make for range restrictions in the specific test variables under consideration. In view of all of these limitations, perhaps the most meaningful comparisons may be made between mean scores of the Samoans on the different tests. While making this intra-Samoan comparison, it should be remembered that Navy recruits in general tend to get about the same mean score on all the tests (except Non-Verbal Classification), i.e., 50.

On the General Classification Test, which may best be characterized as a verbal reasoning test, the Samoan sample mean is more than 1.5 standard deviations below the mean of American recruits; but on the Arithmetic Test, the Samoans fall just slightly short of this general mean (.2 of a standard deviation). Apparently, the Arithmetic Test represents more of a culture-fair test than the General Classification Test for reasons which are not hard to guess—most important of which is probably the higher vocabulary level of the General Classification Test.

Interestingly enough, the Mechanical Test is almost 1.5 standard deviations below the general mean. This, of course, may be attributed primarily to the relatively nonmechanical nature of the Samoan culture despite the impact on it of the gear-laden American Navy.

On the Clerical Aptitude Test, the Samoans score almost .5 of a standard deviation below the mean. There are no obvious cultural handicaps, except perhaps less opportunity for practice in related activities which may account for the slight, apparent depression in performance on the number-checking test. Any further speculation about such a thin disparity would be indefensible.

Results on the Sonar Pitch Memory Test provide nothing of special interest, since it corresponds closely to the general mean. However, as a group the Samoans perform exceptionally well on the Radio Code

Aptitude Test (63.2—almost 1.5 standard deviations above the general mean). The reason for this is far from apparent; but, if it could be successfully tested out, it is probable that it would be a significant nugget of information. However, one could hypothesize that these islanders living so close to nature have developed more acute sensoria and hence can more rapidly integrate auditory stimuli, which would account for superior performance on a test of ability to rapidly receive and decipher radio code. A corollary of this would be that our urban culture tends to restrict the development of certain of our perceptual skills, even as it stimulates the development of other types of cognitive abilities, e.g., verbal. Another kind of hypothesis with some plausibility is that, since the Radio Code Aptitude Test correlates about .50 with tests of either verbal or arithmetic reasoning (for American recruits), the superior performance of the Samoans on the code test derives from the fact that they represent a highly select group with respect to the kinds of potentialities measured by standard intelligence tests in our culture. However, this was not reflected in their scores on Navy tests which did not give them a fair shake.

The mean score on the Non-Verbal Classification Test is at about the same relative level for the Samoans as their Applicant Qualification Test score (about one standard deviation below the mean for a general Navy recruit population). The Non-Verbal Classification Test scores are expressed in raw score units. They were never converted into standard score units, as were most other Navy tests, since the test was devised for American illiterates, has a relatively low ceiling, and consequently was never administered to a general Navy population for standardization purposes. However, in a sample similar to those for the other tests, the mean raw score was determined to be 61 and the standard deviation about 9. The mean raw score of the Samoan sample under consideration is 53.3, which is almost a standard deviation below the general mean. This raises an interesting question regarding the difficulty of devising culture-free or culture-fair tests for use in other cultures. The Non-Verbal Classification test comprises a total of 75 items, 25 of which are made up of pictures of objects familiar to Americans and 50 of which are composed of abstract geometric designs that ostensibly give no advantage to individuals from any particular cultural background. In each item, the examinee is required to select the alternative which either does not belong with the other components or is in a similar analogical relationship to the third term as are the first two terms, i.e., the test is made up of classification and analogy type items. In view of the low scores obtained by the Samoans (substantially lower than on the Arithmetic Test, for example), it would seem that modes of thought as well as specific content are culturally conditioned. This would tend to make a test which is quite adequate for rank-ordering American illiterates in relation to some accepted ability criterion, one that is quite inappropriate for members of another culture, even those who have been exposed to more than a smattering of our cultural heritage. All of this points up some of the excruciating problems inherent in devising a satisfactory culture-free test.

(Note: The Navy, to cope with American illiterates, has established Recruit Preparatory Training Units which furnish a maximum of 13 weeks of special literacy and Naval orientation instruction, and has thus been able to enhance the usefulness of many of its marginal recruits. Groups of Samoan, Guamanian, and Filipino recruits, many with definite English language handicaps, were found to be unusually successful in this training—more so than with the typical American recruit. It would appear that such groups as the Samoans evidence greater adaptability to the Navy situation than do Americans with similarly low test scores.)

*   *   *   *   *

Comments by Ford on the superior test performance of the Samoans on the Radio Code Aptitude Test (American Psychologist, 1957, Vol. 5, p. 751) *who sets down the reactions of a former Governor of American Samoa to the Levine article.*

No one who spent any time in Samoa should find this surprising. The basic elements of Samoan music are percussive rhythm instruments, principally sticks, hollowed logs, rolled-up bundles of matting, and empty biscuit tins. Any group of Samoans engaged in group dancing will employ several of these rhythm instruments producing a total effect of very complex rhythmic patterns, against the background of which dancing and singing are performed. Consequently, from childhood the Samoan is accustomed to highly varied and rapid systems of rhythmic beats similar to that found in radio transmission. So proficient do the Samoans become as radio operators that on the naval circuits between Samoa and Hawaii, which are in use to this day, it was customary to employ Samoans at the Hawaiian end because of the difficulty in obtaining any other kind of personnel who could receive messages sent from Samoa, so great was the rapidity of the Samoan operators in Pago. Since nearly everything in Samoa is done rhythmically, it is not at all surprising that the Samoan radio operators are among the finest transmitters of CW messages in the world.

Especially with psychological tests that require individual administration, such as the Stanford-Binet or the Wechsler scales, to say nothing of projective tests, all test manuals exhort the test administrator to be neutral and objective and to establish good rapport with the testee. Beyond general statements, such as the admonition to the examiner to remain interested and attentive and, in the instance of incomplete answers, to ask for further information, little more is done with this general topic of rapport. A little reflection on the business of interaction between tester and testee, especially in an individual test situation where something as critical to the testee as an intelligence rating, would lead one to pay close attention to this aspect of test administration. Partly because the entire situation is supposed to be "objective" and because scoring instructions are so detailed, it is often assumed that this personal interaction phase of test administration can be minimized. The following report, one of the few in the research literature, shows that significant differences in test scores can result with testees (accomplices) who put on a "warm" or "cold" facade to the examiner, and that even in an objective situation of this type, relatively experienced examiners can be adversely influenced.

Dr. Masling, the author of this report, is Director of the Clinical Psychology Ph.D. Training Program at Syracuse University. A previous report by him, employing a projective test situation (1957), showed significant effects of such "warm" and "cold" facades. In the present report, condensed from the Journal of Consulting Psychology, *1959, Vol. 23, pp. 336–341, the same effects are to be seen in a more objective and standardized test situation.*

The Effects of Warm and Cold Interaction

on the Administration and Scoring

of an Intelligence Test

Joseph Masling

Several studies have examined the psychologist-subject relationship in projective test situations. The ambiguity which faces both examiner and subject here makes it probable that each will be influenced by the other in attempting to complete their respective tasks. In intelligence testing, however, the instructions are specific, the stimuli are clearly defined, and there are right and wrong answers. Here the examiner is required to read the questions as stated in the test and to evaluate the answers with the aid of a scoring manual.

The examiner-subject relationship in intelligence testing has not received a great deal of attention. During the course of their training most examiners are exhorted to establish "rapport" and admonished to be "objective." The "objective" examiner is charged with the responsibility of deriving as valid an estimate of the intelligence of the subject as can be obtained, without regard for his personal attitudes about the subject. He is thus expected to be standardized and depersonalized. The purpose of the present study was to investigate the extent to which an examiner could divest himself of personal bias in administering and scoring an intelligence test—in this case, three verbal subtests of the Wechsler-Bellevue I* (hereafter called the "W-B I")—when the subject acted in either a highly approving, interested (warm) manner or in a persistently rejecting, disinterested (cold) manner. The specific hypotheses which were tested were as follows:

I. When an examiner tests two subjects, one of whom acts warm to him and the other cold, he will be more generous in scoring the responses of the warm subject.

II. During the course of administration of an intelligence test to two subjects, one of whom is warm and the other cold, an examiner will: (a) make more reinforcing statements to the warm subject than the cold; (b) ask more questions of the warm subject, giving him the opportunity of clarifying or reformulating an answer.

METHOD

The Interaction. Manipulation of the interaction was effected through the use of attractive female accomplices, posing as test subjects (S's), who acted either warm or cold to the examiner. In the warm condition, the accomplice acted interested in the examiner and in the test; she responded freely to his questions and tried to communicate respect and liking for him. In the cold condition, the accomplice acted disinterested and bored with the test and the examiner; her attitude was that of fulfilling an unpleasant class assignment which she wanted to complete as soon as possible. She tended to answer pre-test interview questions in monosyllables and throughout avoided eye contact with

---

*Listed incorrectly in the original report as "W-B II."

the examiner. In the middle of each cold session the accomplice in a deliberate, calculated fashion put on sunglasses, thereby increasing the psychological distance between herself and the examiner.

Examiners and Procedure. These were 11 graduate students at Syracuse University, all of whom had completed at least one course in the administration of individual tests of intelligence. Six of these also had had further work with individual tests. The most experienced of the examiners who had previously given over 200 W-B's. The median W-B administrations for the entire group was 21.

Each examiner was told that the author was interested in the comparability of various short forms of the W-B and that he would be asked to administer two or three subtests to subjects chosen at random. The subjects would be two undergraduates participating in the experiment as part of their Introductory Psychology course requirement.

Each examiner administered three subtests (Information, Comprehension, Similarities) to both subjects, one of whom acted warm to him and the other cold. Each accomplice had five cold and five warm roles. To insure uniformity in scoring, each examiner was directed to use the instructions in Wechsler's manual (third edition). The experimenter prepared a script for each accomplice to memorize and to repeat to each examiner, regardless of whether this was a warm or cold interaction. Fourteen of these responses were written to maximize difficulty in scoring. All test situations were tape-recorded.

RESULTS

There was no mistaking the impact of the warm and cold conditions on the examiners. All reported that one S seemed particularly disinterested in the test, with some emphasizing the notion that this represented "sick" behavior. One examiner correctly guessed that the S's were really accomplices, and he was therefore replaced and his data were not used.

Hypothesis I was tested by comparing the way in which each examiner scored the responses given him under the two conditions. Since the experimenter had intentionally written responses that gave a higher "true" IQ for one of the accomplices than for the other, the bias of the examiner scoring was determined from the mean of the 10 scores given each accomplice, rather than from the raw scores. Once a mean score for each accomplice had been obtained, the extent and direction of differences from each mean were derived for such examiner. A statistical test showed that the probability of obtaining such a distribution of differences by chance was remote ($p = .056$).

Hypothesis I can also be evaluated by looking at scores assigned above and below the subject's mean. Of the five examiners who tested Accomplice A under the warm condition, four gave her scores greater than the mean, while of the five examiners who tested her in the cold condition, four gave her scores smaller than the mean. The identical results were obtained for Accomplice B: four of the five examiners who interacted with her in a warm manner gave her scores greater than the mean, while four of the five examiners who interacted with her in the cold condition gave her scores smaller than the mean.

Hypothesis II was tested by having independent judges go through the tape recordings (all identifying data being removed) and rating examiner statements as reinforcing ("OK," "swell," etc.) or questioning ("Can you be more specific?"). There were 285 examiner remarks culled from the testing sections of the interviews. The judges independently agreed on the ratings of 89 per cent of the remarks; the remainder were eventually agreed upon in conference. Once the number of reinforcing and questioning statements had been obtained, a comparison was made of each examiner's verbal behavior during the warm interaction and with his verbal behavior during the cold interaction. All examiners made more reinforcing statements to the warm subjects and they asked more questions of them. The sum of reinforcing and questioning statements was also greater for the warm condition than for the cold.

While the experimental hypotheses were substantiated, the differences between conditions seemed much smaller than the differences among examiners. For example, Examiner 1 made a total of only 14 remarks to his S's, while Examiner 7 made 64. Examiner 8's scoring favored the warm condition by 4.8 points, while Examiner 5's scoring was biased in favor of the cold condition by 1.8 points. Since it was possible that the more experienced examiners were least biased by the interaction, rank-order correlations were computed between the number of W-B's previously given and the dependent variables. None of the $rho's$ were significantly greater than zero.

DISCUSSION

The results of this study indicate that the examiner-subject interaction influenced the psychologist's behavior in the administration and scoring of the three subtests of the W-B I. When the instructions to the cold accomplice are considered, i.e., to answer in monosyllables, to appear disinterested, and the typescripts of the sessions studied, it becomes clear that the examiners tried to make contact with the Cold S and, in failing to do this, became silent. While the examiners were undoubtedly trained to encourage the S, this was difficult to do when friendly overtures elicited disinterest and rejection. The feelings which the interaction aroused in these examiners obviously influenced the manner in which they administered the tests. With warm, responsive S's they tended to encourage and question; with cold S's they tended to remain silent.

It is difficult to predict the extent to which this particular finding can be generalized to nonlaboratory situations. Probably few individuals taking intelligence tests act as hostile and nonparticipating as the cold accomplice. However, some S's, notably children, may become threatened by the testing situation, responding with belligerence or silence or other variations of avoidance.

The interaction also affected the examiners' "objective" judgment of the scoring of relatively "objective" material. Even though they had the Wechsler manual available, a response given in the warm condition tended to be given greater credit than the identical response given in the cold condition. This bias is even more striking when it is considered that the scoring occurred some time after the testing, allowing the examiners some perspective regarding the events of the session. Again, this study exaggerated the situation found in most clinic settings, since the examiners were given responses that were selected because they were difficult to evaluate. However, an examination of the scoring records indicated that there were systematic differences in scoring even for those responses which were cited as examples in the scoring manual.

The artificial nature of this study—the use of accomplices and relatively unsophisticated examiners, the exaggerated nature of the interjection, the use of ambiguous responses—together with the inadequate sampling of both the examiner and accomplice populations limits severely the generalization of these findings to nonlaboratory settings of psychologists and S's. What has been demonstrated is that in giving an intelligence test under these conditions, an advanced graduate student examiner will respond to the way S's interact with him and will act out his feelings about the interpersonal situation in administration and scoring.

SUMMARY

1. Eleven graduate students, each of whom had completed at least one course in the administration of individual intelligence tests, administered the Information, Comprehension, and Similarities subtests of the Wechsler-Bellevue I to two subjects. The test subjects were accomplices who acted in either a warm or cold role to the examiners, giving

as their responses memorized answers, 14 of which were specifically devised to be difficult to score. One examiner became aware of the purposes of the experiment, and his data were not used. Each accomplice had five cold and five warm roles, and each examiner saw one subject who acted warm and one who acted cold.

2. From the typescripts prepared from these tapes, every examiner remark during the course of the testing part of the interview was rated. Of the 285 examiner statements, two judges independently agreed on the rating of 254 of them, for an agreement of 89 per cent.

3. The results indicated that in scoring the responses, the examiners tended to be more lenient to the warm subject than the cold. The examiners also tended to use more reinforcing comments and to give more opportunity to clarify or correct responses to the warm subject. The magnitude of the differences in behavior to the two subjects was generally small, with individual differences more marked than differences due to the effect of the interaction.

*   *   *   *   *

Not only may client behavior influence test results and the interpretative comments derived from test protocols, client "stimulus input" may also clearly influence an interviewer's or therapist's behavior. The behavior of the therapist, for example, may be very specifically determined by the stimulus characteristics of his client. Heller et al. (1963) decided to study these effects by using trained student actors who acted out hostile-friendly and dominant-dependent roles during a half-hour intake interview conducted by 34 graduate student trainees in clinical and counseling psychology. Clear results were obtained (with the exception of the "client" who portrayed the dependent-hostile role— who, in actuality, was not very hostile) to show that clients could evoke reciprocal behaviors from therapists even though these influences were not perceived. The interviewers or therapists used in this study, incidentally, varied in experience from that of one semester's clinical practicum to those with several years of field experience.

All test manuals stress the importance of the examiner rapport with the testee, especially where individual tests of mental ability are involved. In many cases this is easier said than done. Especially is the problem acute when preschool children are the subjects. People with little experience in this area simply have no idea of the difficulties and "emergencies" that arise. Too frequently the entire problem is apt to be disposed of with a bland or cavalier sentence or two.

This is exactly what the writer Dr. Landreth, Professor of Psychology and Director of the University of California's Nursery School (at Berkeley), is complaining about. The original appeared in a "Letters to the Editor" column in the American Psychologist, *1961, Vol. 16, pp. 604–607. Besides the entertaining quality of this writing, the reader will also acquire some useful child psychology.*

Playing Games

Catherine Landreth

In a recent *Handbook of Research Methods in Child Development* (Mussen, 1960) a subsection "Ethical Problems of Research" disposes of the problem of eliciting preschool children's cooperation in research projects with the following statement: "With preschool children the request to play some games with the experimenter is probably as good as can be done."

Is it?

Since this handbook is "addressed to present and potential investigators—as a basic reference and a guide," let us consider what happens when one of them approaches a preschool child with only this games cliché to guide him. Immediately the experimenter will be struck by the fact that the preschool child is not waiting around for an invitation to "play games" with a psychologist. To the contrary, he is likely to be deeply absorbed in a project of his own devising. With a fireman's hat on his head, a wagon tied to his tricycle, and a length of hose tucked in his belt, he is speeding to a four-alarm blaze with accompanying firemen and accompanying sound effects. If the experimenter does not move out of the way he may be a casualty.

Clearly the outcome of an invitation to "play games" depends on what the invited child is doing at the moment.

Looking around him at vigorous projects, cooking operations, and ambulance activities in full swing, the experimenter may begin to wonder what chance an invitation to play unspecified games has against vivid child-to-child and teacher-to-child invitations to engage in interesting activties developing before the invited children's eyes. Though, recalling his basic reference "in the case of younger children it may be quite impossible to make the child understand the purpose of the experimenter" our experimenter decides to take a chance. He can see as well as any three-year-old that the success of an invitation to play games depends on how attractive the proposed game sounds to the invited.

Polishing his sales pitch to include some account of what activities his game involves, the experimenter hopefully approaches an unoccupied girl. She is four years of age, an urban child whose mother has warned her never to go off with people she does not know. Even without this advice she shares with most children her age a conservative suspicion of the unfamiliar. It is soon clear to the experimenter that he is going to get nowhere with this girl without an introduction. His basic reference with the statements "children are half human, half animal" and "in terms of traditional research operations, somewhere between animals and adults" serves no warning that a child's willingness to play games with an adult depends in part on how well the child knows the adult, and how favorably.

Not all girls say no, despite their mother's advice, so it is possible that the experimenter will eventually get a little girl's hand in his—but not for long. When it becomes clear to the child that the games are to be played in some place unknown to her, it is a fairly safe bet that she will balk before leaving the familiar nursery school surroundings. Invitations to play games are, as the experimenter can now see, more likely to be accepted when the games are played in a familiar place with some of the same inviting quality as the preschool.

This, however, is not all the experimenter has to learn. He must still approach 4-year-old games veterans who meet his invitation with a calculating: "What do we get?" Having previously endured a tedious learning game merely to get a handful of trinkets, they are not to be had for the asking but may consider bargaining on their own terms. Clearly children's past experiences with playing games affects their response to a gamesy experimenter.

At this point, when the experimenter may well feel he has his own games in progress, he meets a child who feels the same way. The child refuses his invitation politely and firmly, explains that he has played games today, yesterday, or whenever, and that he intends to play right where he is. After all, it is a poor preschool in which experimenter's games are, in general, more interesting than the activities of the preschool.

With this final rebuff our experimenter might sum up his conclusions much as follows: a preschool child's response to an experimenter's request to play some games depends on what the child is doing when the request is made, on how well and favorably he knows the experimenter, on how attractive the games appear to him, on his familiarity with and feeling about the games room, on his past experience with games, and on the number of times he has recently been asked to forego his own activities to cooperate in those of the experimenter.

But is this what a rebuffed experimenter concludes? If it were, some hint of his conclusions would surely appear in the basic reference.

What is more likely is that during his unsuccessful encounters with preschool children, the experimenter notes the relative ease with which the nursery school teacher interacts with the children and decides to bypass his difficulties by having her withdraw the children for him. What happens then?

Does he cajole or coerce the teacher into supplying him, against her better judgment, with a steady stream of children, regardless of what activities have to be interrupted? If so, what does he learn and what does he lose in the way of experience and understanding, and what is the effect on the children, the teacher, and the function of the nursery school?

Since these inquiries are more likely to embarrass than enlighten, let us consider instead what could be done to make games players more perceptive and games playing more productive. The need for such consideration is implicit in the preface of the handbook. There, the editor notes wistfully: "Research in this field since the mid-twenties has not generally improved in quality or increased in quantity as much as research in many other scientific disciplines." In another section of the handbook, a contributing author enjoins: "We must understand (children) . . . somewhat, even to conduct research with them." No clue is given, though, as to how this is to be accomplished.

Though there is indeed no sure formula for understanding children —even somewhat—there is something that can be done to increase the probabilities that a potential experimenter will develop some understanding of preschool children's behavior before he conducts research with them.

Preparatory Course in Participant Observation: Experimenting with preschool children calls for skill in interacting with them as well as some understanding of them. Since an experimenter's future observations of children's behavior will generally take place under circumstances in which he is a participator, systematic training in observing while participating can help him become more sensitive to the various elements in a behavior episode—the behavior setting and the participant observer's actions as well as those of the child.

What makes a preschool admirably suited to this purpose is that the children, to a great extent, create the behavior settings which have meaning for them—something quite different from an experimenter creating behavior settings that have meaning for him. It is the children who decide that a wagon load of dirt is a poison consignment for putting on flies, or that a packing box and pole are a fire or service station, calling for actions and accessories appropriate to such a setting.

As the experimenter moves unobtrusively and helpfully among them, being accepted as a collaborator and "teacher," he cannot help learning something about children's behavior. If he compares his perception and recall of an episode with that of a companion observer behind a screen or with a televised film of the episode's action, he can sharpen his perception and recall. The value of such participant observation shines through in the writings of Susan Isaacs and Jean Piaget. Though participant observation will not of itself produce an Isaacs or a Piaget, without participant observation, nothing else will.

A fringe benefit of this experience is the ideas the experimenter will get for his own games. As a simple illustration from my own experience: Incidental observation of the ways three- and four-year-olds used the cylindrical and rectangular building blocks of different sizes, suggested their possibilities in family representation. This led to a game that furnished a record of the order in which family members were built (by each child), their relative heights and block complexity, their cylindrical or rectangular character, and their positions relative to each other. The children enjoyed this game, and as publication will reveal, it helped to throw some light on their concepts of family status.

Preparatory Period in Any Preschool from Which Children Are to Be Withdrawn. Given experience in participant observation, a potential experimenter can appreciate the need for spending a preparatory day or two in any preschool group from which he hopes to withdraw children. Time spent in getting acquainted not only saves time in the withdrawal process, it favors a freer response from the children in the games situation itself. Since it gives the teacher an informal opportunity to introduce the experimenter, he is able to tell the children about his game and show them some of the games materials and the place where the game will be played. Again illustrating from my own experience: last year on a research project in New Zealand, I spent part of a get-acquainted period sitting on the fringes of a four-year-old music group. After a song and some drum beating about Indians, the teacher looked and smiled in my direction. "We have a visitor from Indian country," she said. "Maybe she can tell us about the Indians she knows." Thanks, in part, to a summer in Taos, New Mexico, from then on I was "in." I arrived each morning to a greeting of "me first" or "my turn next." As each child finished his turn, he passed the word to the next in line. It helps to do something for children before asking them to do something for you.

Consideration for the Characteristics of the Games Room.   Other factors that affect the outcome of games playing are perhaps not as much under the individual experimenter's control. One of these is the character of the games room and the children's association with it. Again illustrating from my own experience: In a children's play center, from which I decided not to withdraw children, the only room available for games was one used for giving inoculations. Since many centers, where preschool children gather, have no adequate games room facilities, a trailer or mobile unit, attractively equipped for such a purpose, is worth considering.

Freedom from unpleasant association is, however, not the only prerequisite for a games room. Many now in use and designed for this purpose have the stark compelling character of a line-up room at police headquarters. A games room should be at least as attractive to children as the preschool from which they are withdrawn.

Pretesting and Scheduling Games in Consultation with the Preschool Staff.   Since one poorly conceived experiment conducted by a graduate student or faculty member who is inept in interacting with children can produce protesting resistance to games for weeks, the length of time a game requires, its appeal or lack of appeal for the children, and the materials and directions it involves, all deserve careful consideration. Talking these over with a preschool teacher who has years of experience in working with young children can conserve the time, effort, and good will of all concerned.

Since parents pay preschool fees for their children's education, not for their cooperation in experiments, careful scheduling of games playing is necessary in consultation with the preschool staff in advance of each semester. Experimenters' desire to use the children should be balanced against the children's desire to use the preschool facilities.

Only in this way can withdrawal demands be kept within the children's tolerance.

Preparation for playing games thus involves a little more than acquiring a stereotyped request. A potential experimenter can be helped by preparatory training in participant observation, by a preparatory get-acquainted period in any preschool from which children are to be withdrawn, by having available an inviting games room, and by pre-testing and scheduling games in cooperation with preschool staff members.

As for the injunction to understand children—somewhat—before conducting research with them, Rogers and Hammerstein are more helpful. As Anna in *The King and I* makes lyrically clear, understanding children is largely a matter of: getting to know them, getting to like them, getting to know what to say, seeing it their way, as well as putting it your way, but nicely.

PART THREE

NORMS

With the troublesome concept of test norms, it cannot be stressed sufficiently that norm represents normal: if the average eight-year-old child completes 15 arithmetic problems correctly on Test X, then 15 is the norm. In actual fact, norms not only give the average; they also provide the relative frequency of the varying degrees of deviation from this norm—i.e., norm tables. There are, furthermore, many kinds of norms: local, class, grade, geographic area, and national norms, to mention only a few. Adequate normative data does not have to be based on millions of cases to insure accuracy and stability. The crux of this problem lies in the standardization procedures that were employed and, most importantly, sampling procedures themselves.

In the history of psychological testing, the best sampling procedures have typically been with standardized mental ability scales for which national norm data are to be computed. In the USA the prime example of this was the work of Terman and Merrill (1937) when they standardized Forms L and M of the Stanford-Binet and where they used a stratified sampling technique.

Random sampling, let alone 100 per cent sampling, is rarely employed but, when it is carefully done, very accurate results occur. Probably the best example of this sampling technique is the famous Scottish survey in 1939 (Macmeeken, 1940), very likely the most nearly complete testing of an entire population yet managed. All children born in Scotland on four days (1 February, 1 May, 1 August, 1 November) were to be tested. As one might imagine, this meant a diligent, painstaking search to the remotest corners of Scotland in order to secure a final and complete sample. (There was a loss of only one case!) This search resulted in a total of 443 boys and 430 girls between the ages of 8 years, 11 months and 11 years, 9 months. All testees were administered the 1916 Stanford-Binet and eight of the performance measures devised by Pintner and Paterson. To illustrate one of the norm results: for the Stanford-Binet the researchers secured a generally normal, but not perfect, curve. Here it should be remembered that all of these tests were standardized on USA children.

With achievement tests, the sampling problems in regard to school and grade populations are no less difficult. Normative data from these types of tests are typically expressed in terms of grade placement indices. Among the most widely used of such tests are the California Achievement Tests. Mr. Robert Dion, Area Director for the California Test Bureau, has written about the sampling procedures employed in standardizing the 1957 edition of these tests. His article, reproduced from the October, 1958 Newsletter of the Elementary School Principals Association of Connecticut, *is here presented because he spells out so clearly what is involved in a stratified sampling technique.*

Norms Are Not Goals

Robert Dion

After users have compared obtained results with the norms supplied with a test, the following reactions are not too uncommon: "The norms are too high."—"The norms are too low."—"The test must be off because our group is below the norm."—"The test is too easy because our group is above the norm."—"Our group is below the norm, but we'll work to bring it up to the norm."—"More cases should have been used in establishing norms." Searching for reasons for such reactions and other comparable reactions reveals that there is confusion and misunderstanding about norms; misuse of norms; and invariably no consideration is being given to a variety of factors that may account for deviations from test norms. Replies to the foregoing reactions embrace several concepts and procedures.

A test is merely a sampling from a broad area of knowledge, information and skill, and the preparation of a test involves two major aspects—(1) content (items, reliability, validity), and (2) assigning norms which will serve as reference points indicating the typical performance for described groups. This discussion concerns the latter aspect.

Although there are many ways of describing or recording performance on a test, numbers are the least cumbersome and complicated for practical use because they simplify communication, comparison and manipulation. Thus the raw score is an essential or fundamental piece of information. However, the raw score by itself is meaningless. Determining the total number of items in the test and expressing the score in terms of the per cent of the total number of items in the test may have more meaning; however, the per cent score may indicate a good or a poor score depending upon the difficulty of the items. To interpret raw scores it is necessary to know how others perform on the test. Raw scores have to be related to other types of information that may affect performance, so raw scores are converted into derived scores.

Derived scores can be expressed as grades, ages, percentiles, standard scores, etc., and the use of one type does not exclude the use of others. One of the most commonly used derived scores is the grade placement or grade equivalent, so let us examine what it means. If a pupil makes a raw score of 55 and 55 is the median score made by pupils tested at the sixth month of the fifth grade, he is said to have a grade placement of 5.6. This 5.6 grade placement is the norm and merely reflects or describes the typical performance of all tested in a described group who are at the sixth month of the fifth grade. Consequently, all examinees shouldn't be expected to reach or exceed a norm which has been established by a score achieved or exceeded by only 50 per cent of the examinees in a group. Norms should not be considered standards of work, because standards are levels of performance or attainment fixed for an individual school or a pupil and expressed in terms of outcomes of instruction. It cannot be presumed that a given group is doing satisfactory work if the group is up to the norm without considering the objectives of the school and the background and ability of the pupils. For example, the standard of accuracy in arithmetic is 100 per cent; however, the norms of sixth graders may indicate that only 85 per cent of the computation has been done correctly.

The user of a test must understand the nature of the group upon which the test has been standardized, and he must determine that the norms yield meaning in terms of the particular purpose for which the testing is done. Large numbers of cases are no guarantee of an adequate sampling, and naming the localities (without additional information) where norms were obtained does not indicate the nature of the population. These two elements were established quite forcefully following the huge mail canvasses of ten million or more post-card ballots sent out by the *Literary Digest* back in 1936. Actually the number of cases required for an adequate sampling is a statistical problem, and in view of a number of criteria the amount required is relatively small. If the standardization group is not comparable to the group upon which the test is to be used then comparable results cannot be expected. If the norms are not based on groups with whom it is sensible to compare individuals we are testing, they are meaningless and misleading. Therefore, the main consideration is a definition of the standardization or normative group and the relevancy of the norms. Find the evidence in the manual.

Although standardization is complex and very often one procedure is preferred to some other procedure because of the philosophy of the test maker and the objectives underlying the test, it may be helpful to give an example of the procedures followed in the standardization of a series of achievement tests (Clark and Tiegs, 1958).

SAMPLING

1. Nation-wide Representation—Students from 48 states and the District of Columbia were included in the over-all standardization population. For selection and statistical purposes, eighteen geographical homogeneous areas were established. Data used in assigning states to an area were from the Biennial Survey of Education in the United States, 1952–54, published by the United States Office of Education and from other sources. Primary consideration was given to the following factors: average expenditures per student for instructional purposes; comparability of average scores on draft deferment examinations; length of school term; urban-rural characteristics; and type of school organization, attitudes and cultural characteristics. The areas were as follows:

Area 1.   Maine, New Hampshire, Vermont, Massachusetts, Connecticut and Rhode Island (5.04% of school population)
Area 2.   New York (7.40%)
Area 3.   New Jersey (2.53%)
Area 4.   Pennsylvania, Delaware and Maryland (7.63%)
Area 5.   West Virginia, Virginia and District of Columbia (4.61%)
Area 6.   Ohio (4.87%)
Area 7.   South Carolina, Alabama, Georgia and Mississippi (9.78%)
Area 8.   North Carolina and Florida (5.73%)
Area 9.   Tennessee, Arkansas and Kentucky (6.55%)
Area 10. Illinois and Indiana (7.38%)
Area 11. Michigan (4.00%)
Area 12. Minnesota and Wisconsin (3.77%)
Area 13. Iowa, North Dakota, South Dakota, Kansas, Nebraska and Colorado (5.92%)
Area 14. Missouri, Oklahoma and Louisiana (6.53%)
Area 15. Texas (5.75%)

Area 16.   New Mexico, Idaho, Montana, Utah, Wyoming, Arizona and
Nevada (3.20%)
Area 17.   Oregon and Washington (2.78%)
Area 18.   California (6.53%)

2. Population Density Categories—Within each area the schools
were divided into the four population density categories from which
the schools draw their pupils.

(a) More than 100,000.
(b) 10,000 to 99,999.
(c) 2,500 to 9,999.
(d) Less than 2,500.

3. Basic Sampling Pattern—For each grade level (Grades 1 through
12), representative classes were selected for each of the four population density categories in each of the eighteen geographical areas. Thus,
the sampling procedure of the nationwide sample at each grade from
1 through 12 was identical. In computing the norms for the W-X-Y-Z
series, the test statistics for each population density category and each
geographical area were weighted in direct proportion to the per cent
the school children in these specific categories are to the school children
in the United States as a whole.

4. Data from about 65,000 selected cases were utilized in the dual,
two-stage standardization program. The first stage of sampling provided
a large pool of subjects from which the second stage sampling drew
stratified groups having statistically and educationally controlled characteristics. In addition to the sampling design, a number of other quality
restrictions and controls are imposed on the standardization testing.
Some of these were:

a. Only one grade per level was utilized in any one participating
school. The rationale for this requirement was to avoid undue influence
by any school system.

b. Special efforts were made to have the participating schools include
only the designated normal or typical classes for the community. Neither
accelerated nor retarded classes were included. Even mixed classes,
i.e., those consisting of more than one grade level, were avoided. The
purpose of this restriction was to maintain the normal homogeneity of
classroom units in the standardization program.

c. No classes were included if they had recently been administered
either a California Achievement Test Battery or the California Test of
Mental Maturity. This restriction was imposed to avoid the possibility
of spurious practice effects.

d. Most testing was done on Tuesdays, Wednesdays and Thursdays which did not immediately follow or precede holidays or athletic events. Any detrimental influences of fatigue after a holiday or the disturbance of anticipation of a special event or holiday were thus minimized.

e. Because the total testing required for both batteries was over two hours, testing was distributed over two or three days. The purpose of this was to avoid having examinees become test-weary and fatigued.

In their final form the norms for the California Achievement Tests have been based on a controlled (stratified), two-stage sampling which constituted a normal distribution of mental ability, typical age-grade relationships and other characteristics as follows: the median IQ for pupils in Grades 1 through 8 was 100 with a standard deviation of 16 points; for grades above the eighth, the median IQ for each grade was as follows: ninth—101.5, tenth—103, eleventh—104, twelfth—105; 70 per cent were making normal progress through the grades; about 20 per cent were retarded one-half year or more; 10 per cent were accelerated one-half year or more; the norming sample contained various ethnic and cultural groups and pupils with bilingual problems. The two-stage national sampling design assumes a random sampling of examinees within the required cell design rather than the cluster sampling of total classes traditionally used which can give undue weight to some communities or regions. Weights were applied to obtain the number of sample cases proportional to the total of pupils enrolled in schools over the nation when classified with respect to population, geographic area and school grade.

Note that the above example defines the population, reflects a well-planned sample rather than data collected on the basis of availability, and reports the number of cases and details methods.

Differences in courses of study, materials of instruction, time allotments, emphasis on certain skill areas, differences in the quality of teaching, and age and intelligence of pupils are factors which may account for deviations from test norms. Among the foregoing let us consider three principal factors that influence test scores of pupils from a particular elementary school—

a. Curriculum—If, in a particular school, instructional materials tend to be taught earlier in the school program, then the test performance of that school at this grade will tend to be higher with respect to norms. Conversely, if materials are not taught until later than usual, the test performance of that school at this grade will tend to be lower with respect to norms. However, when all materials have been taught, it is expected (other things being equal) that the performance of the two groups will be about equal. Variations in curriculum primarily influence rate of growth and are detected by analyzing the test results in a longitudinal manner from Grades 1 to 8. The school introducing materials earlier and stressing the basic skills will have results that start out high at Grades 1, 2, and 3, but tend to drop somewhat at Grades 7 and 8. Those schools using a delayed approach start out lower, show more rapid growth, but end up at about the same level at Grades 7 and 8.

b. Age-grade relationship—Acceleration-retardation policies of a school influence test results. Consider a school system with a "no failure" policy. This policy will tend to lower the test results for a school in relation to the norms which are based upon 70 per cent of the pupils making normal progress through the grades with 20 per cent being retarded and 10 per cent being accelerated by one-half year or more. Take a pupil in Grade 5 whose test score is 4.0 grade placement units. Here his performance is 1.0 grade placement units below norms and he tends to pull the class average down. Now assume that this same pupil has been in a school system that followed the policy of retarding pupils low in achievement. In this school the pupil would have been retarded and so would be in Grade 4 rather than Grade 5. At a Grade 4 classification his performance would be at the norm and he would not tend to pull the class average down. Thus the more pupils are retarded in a school system the higher will be the average performances of the various grades. An analysis of the age-grade relationships is important in interpreting test results.

c. Mental ability—It is estimated that curriculum and age-grade factors account on the average for about 30 per cent of the variations from the norms in test results of a particular school, and about 70 per cent of the variations may be attributed to variations in mental ability. Schools whose pupils have an average IQ above 100 (median mental ability of the norm group for Grades 1–8) would be expected to have achievement results above the norm. There are several ways that the median IQ of a school may be raised. In some schools all pupils with IQ's below 80 or 70 are withdrawn from regular classes and classified in opportunity rooms. This procedure will raise the median IQ of the general classes. In independent schools entrance requirements establish certain selective criteria. As a result it is found that pupils in these schools usually have median IQ's in excess of 100. Consequently, we would expect the median performance for such schools to exceed the norms. Conversely, schools whose pupils have an average IQ below 100 would be expected to have achievement results below the norm.

Test norms should serve as the point of departure both in investigating the reasons for obtained results and in determining the desirability of possible modifications of the factors which account for the obtained results. The elements which constitute a norm provide somewhat of an average of all the combined successes and failures of teachers and pupils ranging from the poorest to the best. To use norms as goals, objectives or standards is to encourage mediocrity.

Sex norms for psychological tests of many types are so frequently met that it may be a surprise to the reader to discover a test specialist who seriously questions their worth. The basic argument in the following paper is that, since the USA is primarily a competitive, heterosexual society, sex norms for tests are frequently not needed. The author believes that this is one of the population variables no longer very useful in norms development. On the other hand, he would emphasize another population variable, if one were out to make a case for sub-group norms, and this would be socio-economic status. Much data from social psychology indicate most Americans tend largely to interact with individuals within their own social class. If, then, we want sub-group norms, a more culturally realistic proposal would be for socio-economic level norms.

The author, Dr. Bauernfeind, is now Associate Professor of Education at Northern Illinois University. The paper, of which this is a condensed version, originally appeared in the Journal of Counseling Psychology, *1956, Vol. 3, pp. 57–62.*

Are Sex Norms Necessary?

Robert H. Bauernfeind

When a journal article is titled in the form of a question, it often follows that the writer has no answer and that the phrasing of the title is as meaningful at the end of the article as it was at the beginning. Such a generalization might be applied by the reader to the present article as well, although there is an attempt by the writer to go beyond this journalistic "norm" and to offer a qualified "no" to the question posed.

It is readily acknowledged that counseling is a highly personal skill, and that to a considerable extent each counselor's choice of tests and test norms is a matter of interest and of personal preference as well as a matter of systematic analysis. The importance of this consideration is attested by the fact that some widely used tests provide norms by sex only, yet have for many years been used effectively in counseling situations. Moreover, we are mindful of the fact that many research workers, counselors, and reviewers for the Buros' Yearbooks on tests critically call attention to the absence of sex norms on a test, while few if any critically call attention to their presence.

On the other hand, a search of the literature reveals that work with these kinds of data has been accompanied by a dearth of systematic argument justifying the development, publication, and use of sex norms. Rather, there is a tendency to rely heavily on t-tests of statistical significance between sexes—a procedure that permits a high degree of mathematical precision but short-circuits the question.

THE PURPOSES OF TESTS

To facilitate our discussion, four major purposes of psychological and educational tests are proposed in the following paragraphs. These purposes, drawn from many sources, are illustrated using the frequently encountered analogy of a ruler.

Purpose 1. To enlarge our universe of knowledge regarding the nature of man; to provide behavioral data for the enrichment of psychological, sociological, and educational theories and systems.

Example: Use of a ruler to survey the general relationship of height to other biosocial variables such as verbal intelligence, introversion–extroversion, or perhaps birth order.

Purpose 2. To enlarge our capacity for quantitative research; to furnish investigators in schools, industries, clinics, and psychological laboratories with reliable tools for measuring modifications of behavior.

Example: Use of a ruler to study experimentally the effects on height of a particular diet.

Purpose 3. To enlarge our universe of predictive validities; to provide data for improved personnel selection and for more informed educational, vocational, and avocational planning on the part of guidance counselees.

Example: Use of a ruler in counseling an individual on his plans to enter a field for which success-group cutoff points on the height variable have been established.

Purpose 4. To enlarge our pool of "yardsticks" with which an individual personality may be appraised; to provide tools for improved educational or clinical diagnosis; to provide tools for improved self-understanding on the part of counselees.

Example: Use of a ruler to enhance a counselee's self-concept, e.g., reporting to him, "You are average in height for your age."

TEST PURPOSES AND SEX NORMS

Having defined these major purposes of testing, it is now possible to examine the sex norms issue in a value context. In the ensuing paragraphs the contribution of these data to Purposes 1, 2, and 3 will be examined briefly. Their contribution to Purpose 4—the purpose to which they seem most strongly to relate—will then be examined in greater detail.

Explicitly, the following question will be considered: "If it is demonstrated statistically that there are significant differences between the sexes on a given test, does it follow that detailed tables of norms by sex will prove useful?"

Purpose 1. A study of sex differences on a particular test is highly consistent with our first purpose—expanded systematic knowledge. In this context, statistically significant differences are important. Findings from such studies will be of value to instructors in psychology courses and to authors of textbooks in general, social, personality, and developmental psychology.

Purpose 1 is achieved, however, by reports of means, standard deviations, and the results of significance tests; publication of detailed norms by sex is not essential to its accomplishment.

Purpose 2. To realize this purpose, investigators seek answers to the question, "What complex of variables accounts for the variance in a particular measure of behavior, e.g., test score?" In this test purpose, the test score is treated as a dependent variable—a function of many independent variables of which sex is at best only one.

As a dependent variable, test performance data may be recorded and analyzed as either raw scores or standard scores. In the case of the former procedure, we need no norms of any sort. In the case of the latter procedure, we need only one point of reference for communication among investigators and for drawing generalizations (including generalizations regarding sex differences) from specific studies. While standard scores based on both sexes combined meet the "only one point of reference" criterion nicely, separate tables of standard scores by sex can actually confuse communication of research on test scores functioning as dependent-variable data.

Purpose 3. To realize this purpose, investigators study the question, "How can this test score be used for improved educational, vocational, and avocational planning?" In this aspect of research, the test score is treated as a predictor variable—a datum hypothesized to be related to successful performance in a particular situation.

With reference to Purpose 3, the question of sex norms may be divided into two considerations:

First, it is clear that norms by sex should be provided within a defined success-group if there are significant differences between the sexes in the group. For example, it will certainly be helpful to a counselor to know that a standard score of, say, 60 on a particular test represents the 50th percentile among men successful in the occupation but only the 20th percentile among women successful in the occupation. In such an instance he would treat a score of 60 quite differently in counseling a man than he would in counseling a woman.

Second, it seems equally clear that general population norms by sex would be diversionary—unrelated to Purpose 3. Indeed, such data might promote confusion by providing a counselor two different points of reference from which to enter tables of success-group norms. The "one point of reference" criterion for general population norms mentioned in our discussion of Purpose 2 seems also to be desirable as a starting point in the area of Purpose 3.

Purpose 4. To achieve this purpose, investigators ask the question, "What does the test score tell us about the individual?" Note that this purpose is not concerned with specific predictions of success; it is concerned only with personality appraisal. The investigator seeks to supply more intelligent answers to such questions as "Am I more an introvert or extrovert?" "How much musical interest do I have?" or "Is my intelligence above average?"

These questions can be answered either in terms of relatives within the individual (e.g., the six-score profile derived from the Allport-Vernon Study of Values), or in terms of a comparison with the test scores of some standard group.

No norms of any sort are necessary to the former approach. It is in the latter case that we encounter the issue of sub-group norms. Thus the problem of test norms for Purpose 4 turns on the question, "With whom does (will) this person associate?"

Judgments concerning an individual's current and projected associations do not come easily in a society such as ours; rather, they require as high a degree of sensitivity to population structure and trends as we can command. When flexibly conceived, we should expect such judgments to vary both in terms of cultural space and historical time.

In answer to the question, "With whom does (will) this person associate?" it has been argued that state norms, sex norms, private school norms, big city norms, and the like are desirable. Yet, the present writer believes that in the United States today, a stronger case can be made for total-population national norms, developed through rigorous stratified sampling, as the *sine qua non* for personality appraisal and self-understanding.

There are important exceptions to this generalization. Scores that separate testees into explicitly defined groups, as with masculinityfeminity scales, would be one illustration. Other scores that logically have meaning only for a specific sub-group would be another (example: "interest in remaining in Salt Lake City" would demand Salt Lake City norms).

Our case for total-population national norms derives from four general qualities of the population in twentieth-century America— increasing interdependence, competition, communication, and equality of the sexes.

Increasing competition with men on the part of women is a current social reality; increasing communication, interdependence, and competition within the nation are current social realities. In the past generation, we have witnessed the gradual passing of urban–rural differences on psychological tests. Similarly, we may project the lessening of regional and racial differences within the next generation. And we may project further increases in interaction and competition between the sexes, with resulting decreases in sex differences on many psychological tests. The facts of increasing numbers of women in the national labor force and increasing numbers of women in various educational programs are illustrative of this trend.

The point to be made here is that, in twentieth-century America, each member of the society associates with, competes with, and is dependent upon every other member of the society in an ultimate sociological and economic sense. Further, while this generalization is not true in the sense of direct interactive experience, considerations of mass communication, "going away to college," universal military training, and migration for job opportunities indicate that it will often be seriously unrealistic to evaluate and counsel in terms of constricted sub-group populations.

To return to the immediate issue of "sex norms": Granted that statistically significant differences between the sexes on certain types of tests now occur and may continue to occur; the crucial question for personality appraisal and counseling remains: "With whom does (will) the person associate?" The nature of American families, schools and colleges, popular recreational and social activities, and trends in the national labor force all attest that, in the vast majority of their interactive experiences, most Americans today function in a heterosexual environment. It follows then that heterosexual norms should often provide a desirable point of reference for counseling in the area of Purpose 4.

The validity of the above conclusion is certainly not absolute; rather, each counselor will want to judge its applicability in view of (a) the test used and (b) the individual counselee's needs, current environment, and plans. Obviously, one who is not involved in an individual counseling situation cannot attempt to comment effectively on this second consideration. With reference to the former consideration, however, the present writer believes that the conclusion does apply rather strongly in the case of cognitive tests—measures of general educational achievement, intelligence, and vocational aptitudes; and, further, that the conclusion might more often be applied in the case of various inventories—measures of interests, values, temperament, and attitudes.

TEST PURPOSES AND PURPOSEFUL NORMS

It is important that counselors distinguish carefully between norms developed for Purpose 3 and norms developed for Purpose 4 in planning their interpretations of test scores.

Purpose 3, for which criterion-group norms are developed, is concerned with specific predictions of a criterion. Representative examples of normative data devoted to this purpose are found in the Strong Vocational Interest Blank, the Law School Admission Test, the AGCT Scores for Civilian Occupations, and the Kuder Scores for Occupations.

Purpose 4, for which general population norms are developed, is concerned only with general appraisal of personality. Representative examples of normative data devoted to Purpose 4 are found in the Stanford-Binet, the Primary Mental Abilities profiles, the Bernreuter Personality Inventory, and the Kuder profiles.

No one set of normative data can meet both Purpose 3 and Purpose 4; attempts to use one set of data for both purposes can eventually lead to serious misinterpretations. In defense of sex norms, one might cite the general population norms by sex on the Mechanical Reasoning Test of the Differential Aptitude Test battery. These data indicate that a score of 40 corresponds to the 75th percentile for both sexes, but only the 50th percentile for boys. The use of the heterosexual norms in counseling a boy about plans to enter a mechanics class (in which the competition is primarily male) would provide misleading information. Some writers then conclude that a boy should be counseled from the boys' norms.

This suggestion violates our principle that general population norms are developed for general appraisal only (Purpose 4), not for predictions of specific criteria (Purpose 3). For adequate prediction performance in a specific situation, the counselor needs evidence of validity and success-group norms. On this same test, it might be found that a score of 40 in fact corresponds to the 25th percentile among those who actually enroll for a particular mechanics class, and an even lower percentile among those who pass the course. In this event, the 50th percentile interpretation recommended would also provide seriously misleading information.

As an investigator acquires proper criterion-group data it is a matter of complete indifference, from the standpoint of prediction, whether his general population norms are based on the total group or on the sexes separately. The suggestion that the general population boys' norms be used when counseling a girl about plans to enroll for a mechanics class also appears misleading, in that it attempts to make one set of normative data serve these two distinct purposes.

An investigator who wishes to work simultaneously toward both Purpose 3 and Purpose 4 must plan to develop both general population norms (Purpose 4) and criterion-group norms (Purpose 3). An example of this approach would be normative data for a particular test which supplied "general population percentiles" (for both sexes, males only, females only) as well as norms for some particular educational or occupational group (as student nurses at hospital X or Y or both). Data reported under "general population percentiles" are related to Purpose 4 and may be used to improve understanding of the individual by showing how he compares with the total population. Data given for student nurses are related to Purpose 3 and may be used in vocational counseling for this one specific occupation.

It is important to note that the former (including "females only") would be inappropriate for use in counseling about a nursing career and, in turn, the latter would be inappropriate for use in the general appraisal of a person.

SEX DIFFERENCES AND PUBLICATION PROCEDURES

Categorical pronouncements that there is an obligation to develop and publish general population norms by sex seem inappropriate. Apropos of this conclusion, the publication "Technical Recommendations for Psychological Tests and Diagnostic Techniques" (APA, 1954) includes no explicit recommendation that separate sex norms be published. Statement F–7.3, "The manual should report whether scores differ for groups differing on ... sex ..." appears consistent with our Purpose 1 and special cases of Purpose 4.

In developing normative data for Purpose 4, each test author must elect one of the three alternative courses of action: (a) to develop and publish norms for each sex alone, but not for the sexes combined; (b) to develop and publish norms for each sex alone and for the sexes combined; (c) to develop and publish norms for the sexes combined, but not for each sex alone.

The second procedure—that of presenting heterosexual norms only, along with a discussion of any sex differences—reflects the considerations cited earlier in this article, while at the same time providing necessary information for counselors who may wish to refer to the consideration of sex differences on the test in question.

SUMMARY

Four major purposes of psychological tests have been summarized, and the question of "sex norms" has been examined as it relates to each of the four purposes. These types of data were found to be unrelated to Purposes 1, 2, and 3, and to be of debatable value to Purpose 4.

While this article has not been specifically concerned with the development and use of other types of sub-group norms, it is hoped that the considerations presented will be helpful to counselors and other individuals who are planning norms studies for various psychological tests.

PART FOUR

RESPONSE
SET

A relatively recent development in test construction is the concern over response sets of one type or another. These are usually regarded as undesirable in the sense that they lower the validity of a particular test. In two significant articles (in 1946 and 1950), Cronbach has extensively discussed these so that now most test constructors, especially with personality measures, take pains to minimize or delete these adverse influences. Cronbach's two papers summarize extensive evidence that response sets (such as bias in marking one particular alternative to a test item, tendency to guess, working for speed as against accuracy) also operate in the more conventional objective measuring devices. Such response sets can also be altered fairly easily by direct coaching or by suitable changes in directions to the testee. In these two papers, Cronbach has recommended the following: (a) response sets should be avoided, with the occasional exception of personality tests where traits such as carefulness are being measured, since such traits are psychologically similar to response sets; (b) the multiple-choice type of tests in forced choice format, or utilizing paired comparisons or "do-guess" items, is to be preferred over other forms of test items. If, however, an item form is used where response sets do occur, the test constructor should take certain precautions to minimize these: (a) phrase the directions so as to reduce ambiguity and require every testee to respond with the same set; (b) avoid administering the particular test to a group for whom the test is quite difficult; (c) provide for a response-set score to be obtained, and use this to identify testees whose scores are probably invalid. Cronbach further believes that, if test constructors adhere to these general guide lines, future tests will *increase their saturation with the particular factors these tests are attempting to measure.*

Even standardized scoring keys for well-known psychological tests can be shown to be contaminated (unwittingly, it is assumed) by response bias. This has resulted from inattention on the part of test makers to the general rule that correct answers to true-false or multiple-choice items should be randomized as to position. Metfessel and Sax in a brief report in Educational & Psychological Measurement, *1958, Vol. 18, pp. 787–790, have shown that this is fairly common, especially in "older" personality inventories where the true-false item form has been employed. Here follows a brief abstract of this report.*

Systematic Biases in the Keying of Correct

Responses on Certain Standardized Tests

Newton S. Metfessel and Gilbert Sax

Inaccurate measurement results also because of the keying of the correct responses, by a test constructor, in certain alternative positions on multiple-choice and true-false tests according to a pattern not in harmony with randomization. For example, in a multiple-choice test consisting of 100 items and four alternative response positions, one would expect by chance randomization that approximately one-fourth of the correct responses would be "keyed" by the test constructor to each of the four choice positions. If a statistically significant difference in the number of correct response placements at each of the alternative positions was in evidence, a bias on the part of the test constructor would be indicated.

There is evidence of the presence of response-set patterns on the part of subjects in responding to multiple-choice tests, and there is further evidence showing that subjects presented with true-false items tend to negate the false scores in favor of the affirmative ones. However, it should be explained that response sets for both multiple-choice and true-false tests operate only when the subject is in doubt or does not know the answer to a question. Cronbach reports in the case of true-false tests that this tendency (to mark items true rather than false) makes false items more valid and reliable than true items, reduces the range of test scores when the number of true and false items are equal, raises the mean score when a majority of the items are true, or lowers it when the majority are false, and causes the R–W formula to be inappropriate in many cases.

The purpose of our investigation is to determine which of a number of standardized tests have biases in their keying patterns. Instances where these biases were known to "test-wise" students or were in harmony with tendencies of compulsive subjects, results which are incongruous with "true" scores would be obtained. In this study, chi-squares were obtained for the distribution of correct responses on approximately twenty currently popular tests, all of them in wide use. Examples of the frequencies of keyed correct responses for each alternative position, some of which frequencies are clearly randomized and others not, are as follows:

	Response Alternative					X^2 Significant at
	1	2	3	4	5	.01 Level
Army General Classification Test	36	37	36	38	—	No
California Test Mental Maturity	13	42	37	26	—	Yes
Otis Quick-Scoring Test Mental Ability	5	14	24	13	10	Yes
Co-op Test Reading Comprehension	30	31	31	29	29	No
Bell Adjustment Inventory	133	27	—	—	—	Yes
California Test Personality	71	109	—	—	—	Yes
Thurstone Temperament Scale	109	31	—	—	—	Yes

Considering all the tests covered in this report, approximately 42 per cent yielded chi-square values significant at the .01 level. There is a tendency for the authors of multiple-choice tests to place the correct response at the center of the response distribution. Also, test constructors tend to place the correct response at the "true" position on true-false tests. Thus, subjects who are test-wise or who have a compulsive tendency to avoid the "false" response have a greater-than-average chance of doing well on the test. It is suggested that test constructors become more aware of the bias which is involved in the tests themselves as well as the response-set of the subject.

There are other test situations, however, where the presence of response sets is welcome and where a researcher, especially in the field of personality measurement, might actively hope to capitalize on these. Here, rather than try to remove such response sets, one would actively encourage and promote them but, again, always with their measurement in mind. Professor Berg, among others, has written a series of reports from just this point of view where his emphasis is not on item content but on the deviant responses that are obtained. The ubiquitous principal of individual differences again can be used here. Professor Berg would then make into an asset what, from another point of view, is often seen as a liability in psychological test construction.

The report of his Deviation Hypothesis is taken from an informal and what the author terms "a highly personal account" which appeared in the Journal of Counseling Psychology, 1957, Vol. 4, pp. 154–160. *What appears here is a condensation of the original article. It is hoped that the student reader will also enjoy the highly informal writing style. Professor Berg is Chairman of the Department of Psychology at Louisiana State University in Baton Rouge.*

Deviant Responses and Deviant People:

the Formulation of the Deviation Hypothesis

Irwin A. Berg

This is a highly personal account of a research area and a concept which grew out of this research which has, during the past dozen years, held my interest with varying degrees of intensity. Conventionally, one does not write highly personal discourses dealing with research; at least, it isn't done more than once in a blue moon. Yet the haunch and the hoof, the bone and the gristle of the problem are for me intimately bound to the personal involvement.

This preamble sounds as if I am about to unveil something of heroic size and import, complete with final results. While the Deviation Hypothesis is perhaps ample in scope, I certainly have no final results to offer. What I have to offer is only a road that does have a few signposts, but makes its way like the River Meander and may end in a bog instead of leading to Rome. At times, I have been temporarily convinced that I was chasing a wild goose or the chimera of the ancients. When this conviction became strong, I turned to other studies, uttering sighs of relief between Anglo-Saxon expletives. But like a half-welcome suitor, I sooner or later returned to the object of my affections and received some encouragement in the form of small favors, only to be roundly spurned anew and left to repeat the cycle once again.

The problem I have been concerned with is an aspect of the old, old problem of "set" or einstellung, specifically, the problem of biased responses and what they mean. It has been known for a long time that when subjects respond to a stimulus pattern, the distribution of their responses often does not follow a normal probability pattern. A flipped coin, for example, is not a 50–50 "heads-tails" proposition insofar as human responses are concerned. On the first toss, 80 per cent of the subjects will call out, "heads." When ascending to the balcony of some movie theaters, to consider another example, patrons may take either a stairway to the right or to the left and reach about the same point upstairs. Yet theater managers have noted with some exasperation that three times as many persons will use the right-hand stairway and the carpet wears out three times as fast.

RESPONSE BIAS IN TESTS

In psychological tests, similar biases often appear, and they are something of a headache to those who are aware of the problem. When subjects do not know the answer to certain items or when the test is otherwise unstructured for them, there is a demonstrable tendency for them to favor certain options which indicate aquiescence such as "true," "agree," or "like," as opposed to negative options as "false" or "disagree." Other biases may appear as preferences for "uncertain," "?," "cannot say," indicating evasiveness, when the test provides for such answers. Cronbach (in 1946) called such biases in tests "response sets," and he described a large number of them in detail. Incidentally, response sets are quite stable; and they affect test validity and reliability, often spuriously raising the latter. Curiously, although it is more than ten years since Cronbach published his excellent review of the significant role played by response sets in tests, a surprising number of psychologists appear to be unaware of what these response tendencies mean.

A number of writers have provided evidence that biased responses are related to personality characteristics. But while the evidence is clearly positive, it is not strong and, at best, indicates that only a moderate relationship exists. To take but one example: a reported correlation of −.43 between Bernreuter self-sufficiency scores and the number of noncommittal responses on a social attitudes test. That is what one usually finds: correlations in the .30's and .40's or, among groups, differences that just reach the 1 to 5 per cent levels of statistical significance. Yet, to my mind, it seemed clear that anything highly stable and related to personality ought to be capable of being refined into a usefully valid instrument for measuring personality characteristics. Furthermore, there is something intriguing in the cloak-and-dagger sense of taking materials totally unrelated to personality, such as an algebra test, and from it deriving a valid scale for paranoid tendencies. Unfortunately, it didn't work out, at least for algebra tests and personality. The result was a few correlations around .10 and many Irish correlations, as John Darley once termed correlations of .02, .05, .06, and .08. For a history test, the correlations between response sets and scores on standardized personality tests were higher, but not much higher. There seemed to be several difficulties. One was that response biases appear more frequently as the stimulus situation is unstructured, and I was using tests with a high degree of structure. Another difficulty was that the algebra test was entirely, and the history test partially, composed of multiple-choice items, and the multiple-choice form in structured tests is relatively free from response set influence.

I still hold firmly the conviction that it is possible to obtain useful personality measures from algebra or history tests by means of biased responses; however appropriate items designed to elicit set will probably have to be inserted in the tests, because one cannot depend upon locating more than a few "response set" items in the usual standardized test. At any rate, since structure was a problem, I prepared a series of abstract designs of no particular significance and asked subjects to sort the designs, each of which were drawn on a 4"x 6" card, into one of four boxes labeled "like much," "like slightly," "dislike slightly," "dislike much." The idea was that with minimal structure and, with responses made on the basis of affect, bias would have ample opportunity to appear. When exploratory studies were made with small groups of subjects, it became immediately apparent that bias was present in the responses to virtually every item. This, of course, told nothing of any relationship to personality; so several groups which were operationally defined as "disparate" in personality were used for pilot studies. One group was composed of 12 accountants with five to ten years experience, another was a group of 16 real estate salesmen, and the last group was composed of nine line supervisors of machine departments.

While the groups were small and the results could be regarded only as suggestive, the analysis of the responses to the abstract designs showed biases for all groups; and the pattern of bias was discernably different for each group. This was not much to crow about, but it was enough to get 60 designs privately published as "The Perceptual Reaction Test." This permitted large scale collection of data and the recording of test responses and other information on thousands of IBM cards. This step produced a variety of findings, all of them interesting and none of them conclusive. To mention a few, neurotics tended somewhat to prefer the "dislike" and psychotics the "like" responses, homosexuals showed a response pattern of their own, normal men revealed a significantly different pattern from normal women. Indeed, with respect to the latter, it was found possible to construct a reasonably valid scale for *mf* of interest. We were doing better than had ever done before in using response biases as measures of certain characteristics of behavior, but we weren't doing nearly well enough.

In mulling over these results, it occurred to me that I had been concentrating on the wrong thing. That is, the biases we have been talking about were, of course, only biases in the normal probability sense. They were not biased in the sense of responses made by the majority of people. Perhaps I had been stupidly floundering in some semantic quagmire of normal curves, normal people, and irrationally measuring bias first in terms of one and then the other. But whatever the reason, the key to the problem seemed to lie in the departures from any established pattern of bias, not in the bias itself. That is, on the basis of probability we should expect that 50 per cent of the people should turn right and 50 per cent left when they enter a branching hallway; the same is true of picking heads or tails when a coin is tossed or of circling "true" or "false" when responding to a question to which the subject does not know the answer. The fact that such is rarely the case with human responses does indicate bias; and as we have seen earlier, such biases, in the sense of being remote from normal probability, are reflections of personality variables.

But what of the people who deviate from the established pattern of bias? What about those who rather consistently say "false" when most people say "true," who turn left when most turn right or who say "like" when most people say "dislike"? These are the truly deviant responses. It seemed on this basis, that such deviant responses were the ones to be studied. Thus we could identify a pattern of bias and then examine those subjects who revealed deviant responses in the sense of departing from the common response pattern. E. K. Strong in his Vocation Interest Blank and Starke Hathaway in the Minnesota Multiphasic Personality Inventory years before had done much the same thing when constructing their tests. They were not, of course, concerned with set or bias per se; and they were concerned with item content. But the method they used was generally suited to my purposes. Accordingly, batches of IBM cards were sorted and the Perceptual Reaction Test (PRT) response patterns of various small groups such as schizophrenics, musicians, juvenile delinquents, were each compared with the patterns of normal persons or people-at-large. These groups were small, of course, but this time it really seemed that we had data which offered more than hope. There seemed to be obvious differences in the deviant response patterns for the various groups, at least insofar as one could judge from the scanty data available.

DEVIANT RESPONSES ARE GENERAL

As I examined these data and reviewed the various researches of other workers in this field, it seemed to me that there was something general about the deviant response tendencies among the small groups of deviant subjects for whom we had data. This, it may be noted, is one of the advantages of gathering your own data, namely, the opportunity to observe peripheral but sometimes meaningful aspects of the problem being attached. But to take a specific example, we may note the behavior of schizophrenics. These patients, for the most part, experienced delusions and/or hallucinations, they were emotionally flat, and their thinking was bizarre. Such behavior, of course, explained why the schizophrenics were hospitalized, and such behavior is significant, in our society, for being placed under institutional custody. One simply does not go about talking of an alarm clock in his belly, nor asserting that an aged clergyman has been making sexual advances, etc., as these patients did. This, then, is critical deviant behavior.

Yet as I ruminated about these patients, it seemed obvious that they showed many other behavioral deviations which were essentially nonsignificant or noncritical in the sense that they would never be placed in a mental hospital if only these noncritical deviations were involved. Thus some schizophrenics grinned in a silly manner, others had a perpetual far-away look in their eyes; they used odd gestures or sat poker-faced and immobile. Most important in terms of my thinking, the schizophrenics also marked the Perceptual Reaction Test in a deviant pattern when compared to normal persons. It seemed, therefore, that deviant behavior might very well be general; hence when noncritical behavior was measured, such as deviant patterns of response on a test, these noncritical deviant responses were indicative of deviant responses in a critical area of behavior, i.e., symptomatology indicating neurotic or psychotic reactions and the like.

So we could say that deviations in one area are associated with deviations in other areas. If so, we could draw together in a general statement the results of a wide variety of researches. We may mention a few of these to indicate the range of studies which could readily be included in our general statement. In a study of 845 mental patients and 423 normal subjects, Voth found differences in the amount of autokinetic movement for schizophrenic, epileptic, anxious, etc., patients when compared to normal persons. Wallen and Altus say that the number of food aversions is related to maladjustment. Guilford used the frequency of "?" responses on three tests as a measure of indecisiveness among foremen. Although the techniques and the behavior measured differed in these studies, each of them were measuring atypical behavior in a significant area by using responses obtained in a noncritical area of behavior. While he regarded similar response patterns as a nuisance and best eliminated from tests, Cronbach would not have been surprised at these results.

Now, thus far, we have been considering behavior on a contimum of adjustment–maladjustment and measuring responses in noncritical areas of behavior to predict maladjustment in critical areas of behavior. But do we need to confine our general statement to abnormality in the maladjustment sense? After all, "abnormal" means literally "away from the norm," or, broadly speaking, it means "different or uncommon." On this latter basis, we may say that brilliant or mentally retarded persons are abnormal; we may say that, compared to men-in-general, salesmen or accountants or musicians, etc., are atypical since, after all, most men are not salesmen, etc. If this is true, and decades of experience with the Strong VIB indicates that it is certainly true for occupations, then we should be able to identify any atypical or "abnormal" group on the basis of deviant response patterns alone. We should be able to take any valid and operationally defined dimension of personality, of interest, of adjustment, and the like, and by using deviant response patterns, we should be able to measure these dimensions. Further, it seems that any type of stimulus pattern may be used for measuring noncritical behavior deviations (i.e. deviant test responses) to predict behavior deviations in the critical area under study (i.e., atypicalities, such as schizophrenia, anxiety states, creativity, mental retardation, interest in mathematics, etc.).

THE UNIMPORTANCE OF TEST ITEM CONTENT

In other words, the test item content isn't important; the deviant responses are. As we have seen earlier, a number of relatively unstructured stimulus patterns have been used, such as autokinetic movement, abstract designs, lists of foods, sway responses to spoken words, etc.;

and deviant response patterns have been identified which are capable of identifying groups which are atypical in a significant area of behavior.

What we are considering here is very serious business from the standpoint of the theory of how certain tests are constructed and how they measure whatever they are intended to measure. I am asserting that one could take the MMPI items and, by using the same technique as Strong did, prepare a Vocational Interest Blank. Conversely, one could use Hathaway's technique to make an MMPI from Strong's items. Or, as far as I can see, one could use a mixture of designs, nonsense syllables, pictures, sounds, smells, etc. and produce either the MMPI or the Strong by using the same, painstaking care in identifying the groups and in analyzing the data. In other words, E. K. Strong need not have selected items related to recreations, amusements, occupations, etc. nor need Hathaway have troubled about his 26 categories of MMPI items which ranged from general health to psychopathology. Indeed, if valid external criteria are available, either Strong or Hathaway could have used their techniques and their items to construct scales for such varied facets of deviant behavior as accident proneness, rigidity, creativity, satyriasis, scholastic overachievement, etc.

In the paragraph immediately above, I have made some predictions of what one aspect of the deviation hypothesis means. Candidly, I have run ahead of the evidence, but this is not to say that there is no evidence. Let us take the MMPI as a case in point, since we have some evidence which relates to MMPI content. Also, this test is a good example to employ, because about 800 articles dealing with the MMPI have been published; and it is certainly one of the most widely-used clinical tools. The MMPI scoring system provides that only those responses which are answered in the infrequent direction are recorded. In other words deviant responses are recorded. Barnes (1956) noticed this and reasoned that, if MMPI item content were unimportant, he should be able to take a heterogeneous group of 40 male patients and by simply counting the total number of atypical responses (X's on the MMPI record form) obtain a significant relationship between the total number of deviant responses and some of the MMPI clinical scales. It should be emphasized that Barnes merely counted all items answered in the infrequent direction without any regard for content, and his group was a mixture of diagnostic categories. He found, among other things, the total number of deviant responses correlated .93 with the Schizophrenia scale and .87 with the Psychosthenia scale of the MMPI. This is about as high as the reliability of these scales; hence correlations of greater magnitude are unlikely to occur.

In another study, Barnes (in 1955) used the results of some research which identified two major factors, neurotic and psychotic factors, in the MMPI scales. It occurred to Barnes, on the basis of the way psychotics and neurotics responded to the PRT, that atypical true answers without regard to item content of the MMPI should be essentially the psychotic factor and MMPI atypical false answers should be essentially the neurotic factor. Thus deviant sets, ignoring content, should account for the psychotic factor if they went in one direction, and for the neurotic factor if they went in the other. Barnes concluded that the simple count of atypical true answers represented a "pure factor test of the psychotic factor" and the total of atypical false answers had a heavy loading on the neurotic factor.

But while there seems to be some reason for disparaging the importance of item content per se, one may justifiably ask whether it is really possible to measure personality and the dimensions by using deviant responses alone. After all, it is reasonable to accept the results of exploratory studies described earlier and recognize that deviant response patterns could separate groups of 10 or 20 atypical subjects from "normal" or "people-in-general" on the basis of atypical responses. Yet this is considerably removed from demonstrating that valid measuring particular facets of personality or the like could be constructed from responses to stimulus patterns such as, for example, a series of abstract designs drawn with ruler and compass.

Barnes became interested in what we were doing; he took as his Ph.D. dissertation the relationship of biased test responses of pschopathology, using the abstract designs of the PRT as his test. He tested 546 deviant subjects (360 males, 186 females) obtained from neuropsychiatric settings; and as his published article (1955) reveals, he was able to construct scales for several dimensions of psychopathology, using only deviant response patterns. Also, Barnes crossvalidated his scales, showed that they had adequate reliability and prepared a diagnostic "sharpener" scale to separate psychotic from character disorder patterns. When it is kept in mind that the PRT has only 60 items, all of which are abstract designs of no particular meaning, and that it takes only six or seven minutes to administer the PRT, I feel justified in saying that Barnes' scales are remarkable. Further, we have a clear demonstration that deviant responses alone can be used to measure psychopathology in several forms.

THE DEVIATION HYPOTHESIS STATED

As we review what has been said thus far, it is apparent that the Deviation Hypothesis has two aspects which are relatively independent of each other and which may stand or fall independently when subjected to empirical test. One aspect deals with the general pervasiveness of deviant response patterns, and the other deals with the unimportance of specific content for eliciting deviant responses. The formulation of the Deviation Hypothesis may be given as follows: Deviant response patterns tend to be general; hence those deviant behavior patterns which are significant for abnormality (atypicalness) and thus regarded as symptoms (earmarks or signs) are associated with other deviant response patterns which are in noncritical areas of behavior and which are not regarded as symptoms of personality aberration (nor as indicators, signs, earmarks). The material in brackets is inserted in order to emphasize the feasibility of using deviant response patterns to identify occupational groups, interest patterns, morale level, accident proneness, etc. The remaining aspect of the Deviation Hypothesis may be stated as follows: Stimulus patterns of any type and of any sense modality may be used to elicit deviant response patterns; thus particular stimulus content is unimportant for measuring behaviors in terms of the Deviation Hypothesis. This means that, by the usual analysis, we should be able to produce a Bernreuter Personality Inventory, an MMPI, a Strong VIB, etc., by using sights, sounds, tastes, smells, etc., in any combination for item content.

The Deviation Hypothesis is regarded as rather broad in scope with respect to human behavior. The implications are myriad, and we have space to mention but a few of them. For example, when an emotionally disturbed client comes in for counseling, his behavior is deviant in a critical area and we should expect that his behavior would be deviant in noncritical areas, such as his speech, perhaps. He would be expected to talk slower or faster than normal, possibly with odd intonation and pitch; or he might, and this has been studied for one case, use many ego words such as *I, me, mine* and few emphatic words such as *you, we, our* as indicative of deviant speech output. Another implication and in another area is the relationship of the degree or extent of deviant responses in noncritical areas to the degree or extent of deviation in critical areas. Nothing much has been done on this problem; however, I should predict that the correspondence of deviant patterns in critical and noncritical areas is very close. Severe cases of schizophrenia should reveal more marked deviations in noncritical areas when compared to mild schizophrenics. Similarly, serious accident-prone persons should show greater frequency of noncritical deviant responses than those who were only mildly accident-prone. Yet another problem is the difficulty of measuring structure in stimulus patterns. Do nonsense syllables have more structure than interlaced triangles? This is not a silly question:

for response sets are more readily elicited when structure is less definite. There are many other unresolved issues, such as the problem of drugs in relation to possible reduction of deviant responses in noncritical areas, the thorny question of psychological distance measurement for points of scales of affectivity, and a host of other specific problems.

There is some progress on other issues, however, which can be reported. Mentally retarded children, for example, show deviant response patterns in noncritical areas when compared to normal subjects, and their pattern is also different from psychotic patterns. A graduate student at Louisiana State University, Otho Hesterly, is studying PRT response biases in terms of several age groups with the eventual aim of constructing a maturity scale based upon deviant response patterns in noncritical areas. Thus far, he has hopes but no evidence one way or the other.

I wish I could close on the happy note that the Deviation Hypothesis was the center of an academic teapot tempest; for to my admittedly prejudiced mind, the Deviation Hypothesis contains some rather eyebrow-raising assertions and predictions, all of which are easy to test or, if tested, are not 100 percent substantiated. To date, no words have flown, all is calm, all is bright. The issue of whether particular content is essential for personality, interest, etc. tests, I wryly note, sleeps in heavenly peace.

*   *   *   *   *

For an interesting test of the Berg Deviation Hypothesis, using college freshmen, the reader should consult Grigg and Thorpe (1960) where deviation scores, obtained from an adjective checklist, were found to differentiate students seeking private psychiatric care or personal counseling for emotional problems as against students requesting vocational counseling or no help at all. McGee has published (in 1962) a valuable review and critique of this whole problem of response style.

In 1963, Sechrest and Jackson published a critical analysis and a review of issues raised by the studies of Berg and others concerning the Deviation Hypothesis in the hope of explicating certain issues clearly associated with this hypothesis (such as the problem of generality, response styles and deviation, measurement and interpretive problems). These authors feel the hypothesis is altogether too broad and lacking in clarity to permit differential predictions, especially when it is suggested that "psychotics, lawyers, cardiac patients, transvestites, young normal children, character disorders, the obese, the feebleminded, psychoneurotics and persons suffering from constipation, among others, represent deviant groups which might be expected to manifest their particular propensities toward deviation not only in a modality relevant to their particular symptoms and to items with relevant content, but also in response to one or more of the following: preference for abstract drawings, food aversion questionnaires, stimuli for conditioned responses, autokinetic and spiral aftereffect situations, vocabulary test items, figure drawings, musical sounds, and olfactory stimuli" (Sechrest & Jackson, 1963, p. 34). Regardless, these authors recognize that Berg has performed a valuable service in emphasizing the importance of studying these deviant response patterns.

Other writers are far more negatively critical. Norman (1963), in a hard-hitting attack on the Deviation Hypothesis, produces additional test data to show that different classes of test stimuli clearly do make a difference and that test item content is relevant and crucial. His results, comparing test item content varying in relevance for the criterion groups used, rather clearly indicate that test item content is important when one is constructing valid empirical scoring keys. Norman feels that the theoretical or explanatory value which Berg ascribes to the Deviation Hypothesis is, at best trivial; at worst, such a stand leads to an orientation concerning personality assessment of a most militantly theoretical variety.

In a recent and highly controversial book which is critical of all objective testing, the Deviation Hypothesis (although un-named) is treated to a witty exaggeration. A hypothetical example is given where the statistics show that 90% of college freshmen earning high grades believe that Shakespeare wrote Omelet *rather than* King Lear. *Under these conditions the author then says that the "best" answer will have to be* Omelet. *Surely this is to condone the wedding of science and democracy where honor is done to neither" (Hoffmann, 1962, p. 85).*

As a follow-up to the more general statement of the Deviation Hypothesis in the previous paper by Berg, we now present a research report designed to test certain of these formulations. Yea–saying and nay–saying here take the center of the stage in the study of personality.

Although the research presented here only concerns itself with nay-saying, Couch and Keniston (1960) have more recently presented an extensive summary of personality findings based on response set measures intensively studied both by objective test items as well as by clinical methods, tracing these tendencies back to different resolutions of anality during the early socialization period. These authors feel that the importance of response set in the area of psychological tests is very far-reaching and that the agreeing response tendency is based on a central personality syndrome. Their paper is far too long for reproduction here; therefore a shorter research report has been selected for inclusion.

Asch's report is clearly an outgrowth from Berg's published statements. His report, of which this is a condensation, originally appeared in the Journal of Counseling Psychology, 1958, Vol. 5, pp. 206–210, *which in turn was adapted from his Ph.D. dissertation at Syracuse University. Dr. Asch, at the time this research was done, was with the VA Regional Office in Boston, Massachusetts. He is now a Counseling and Clinical Psychologist on the staff of the Hines VA Hospital in Illinois.*

Negative Response Bias and
Personality Adjustment

Morton J. Asch

An approach to personality appraisal that has appealed to social scientists with diverse specializations is that which involves the yea-saying and nay-saying tendencies in man.

The American culture, in particular, is depicted as one which strives to "accentuate the positive and eliminate the negative." The citizens of Harold Laski's "American Democracy" value most highly the "booster" and shun the "knocker." David Riesman's "other-directed" man looks with suspicion at the nonconformist. The "neurotic personality of our time" as described by Karen Horney is basically hostile and negative in orientation.

More people turn to the right rather than the left on entering a museum; the probability is .80 that we will call the first toss of a coin "heads" rather than "tails"; most students, when in doubt, tend to judge statements to be true rather than false. These are illustrations of positive response sets, tendencies which have been shown to be fairly stable and possibly reflective of a more basic generalized life pattern.

The concern of this paper is with the less popular negative response sets. It represents an attempt to study Berg's deviation hypothesis utilizing the concept of negative response bias. For experimental purposes, negative response bias is defined as a type of response set whereby a person tends to answer "disagree" on test items when in doubt.

PROBLEM

In order to study whether this type of response set is related to more critical personality patterns, three hypotheses were framed for testing with a normal population. It was felt that negative response bias might be symptomatic of a more fundamental negativism. As individuals get older many find that the superficial positive reaction yields greater social rewards than the affective "no." In spite of this, or perhaps because of this, the seemingly acquiescent adult often harbors within himself intense hostility which shows itself in more subtle ways than it did when he was three years old. Conflict with the environment manifests itself readily, however, when conditions are such as to favor the safe expression of repressed impulses.

A technique was developed, The Speed of Decision Test, which would identify the quality of the underlying response pattern. This is a specially constructed preference inventory designed to assess response bias which is independent of content variables. In the present study, this test was administered to male veterans of World War II and the Korean conflict at Veterans Administration guidance centers in the Commonwealth of Massachusetts. Those men whose scores on the Speed of Decision Test indicated negative response bias and lack of response bias were compared on performance on the Rorschach, Minnesota Multiphasic Personality Inventory, and Draw-A-Person tests.

The first two hypotheses tested were a direct outgrowth of previous research studies. Item analyses and item counts of the MMPI suggest that neurotic-tending people have a tendency to respond negatively to personality inventory items; psychotic-tending persons have a tendency to respond in the acquiescing direction to these same items. In a recent article describing the formulation of the deviation hypothesis, Berg summarizes studies utilizing the Perceptual Reaction Test, an instrument requiring an affective response to abstract designs. The general findings indicate that individuals who do not demonstrate response bias tend to be less anxious and maladjusted than those who give deviant responses.

In an attempt to explore these questions further with a sample of young veterans, these hypotheses were developed:

1. Subjects who do not demonstrate response bias are judged, on psychological tests of personality, to be better adjusted than those who demonstrate negative response bias.

2. There is a significant relationship, in the positive direction, between neurotic-tendingness and negative response bias.

The third hypothesis of the present study stems from a consideration of psychoanalytic theory. The obsessive-compulsive personality is seen by the Freudians as one fixated at the anal retentive level. Such a person continues his battle against conformity by adult cantankerousness and petulance. Unlike the three-year-old, who responds to almost every request by a direct repetitive "no," the adult quibbles, begs to differ, and in still more subtle ways expresses his need for interpersonal conflict. The hysteric, on the other hand, is viewed as one regressing to the stage of avoiding the Oedipus conflict by a symbolic closing of the eyes. It was felt that the obsessive-compulsive, directing his psychic energy towards the environment, might be expected to demonstrate more negative bias than the conflict-avoiding hysteric whose energy is bound to his symptoms.

The third hypothesis therefore reads:

3. Subjects characterized by obsessive-compulsive trends demonstrate significantly more negative response bias than those whose predominant patterns of adjustment are hysteroid.

The primary concepts used in connection with this study were defined as follows:

Normal—a normal person is one who is not hospitalized and is not classified as a deviate in any available official record.

Maladjusted—a normal person who, on psychological tests of personality, performs similarly to individuals with established psychiatric disabilities.

Neurotic-tendingness—a tendency on the part of normal persons to demonstrate behavior on psychological tests of personality similar to that demonstrated by neurotics.

Obsessive-compulsive and hysteroid trends are defined operationally in terms of clinical judgment of personality test performance of normal persons.

THE SPEED OF DECISION TEST

The SDT had the advantage of being similar in appearance to many inventories in common usage. It could therefore be described to the subject as an attitude or interest or decision-making test. The items of the inventory could also be incorporated as part of a standard psychological test without the subject being aware of this. A new response bias instrument was also developed.

Three fundamental criteria were set up for the items to be included in the new inventory. They were to be subtle, neutral, and innocuous. Test items were considered to be subtle if their purpose was not apparent to the subject. A testee anxious to please an examiner or to create a favorable impression would experience difficulty in discerning what responses would accomplish such a purpose. They are neutral to the degree that each item tends to provoke a positive response as frequently as a negative response among the general population. They are innocuous to the extent that they appear to be harmless and would not cause a pathological subject to respond differentially from a normal because of the content.

An exploratory tryout of a 75-item test was conducted with veterans and college students. On the basis of these trial runs the test was changed to isolate more effectively response bias as the factor being measured. (Example: "Forced to choose one, I would agree that Fillmore was a greater president than Buchanan.")

The directions given to the subject for taking the test and the fact that he is aware of his being timed encouraged the subject to think of this as a speed-of-decision test. Individuals whose score indicated that more than half of the items were checked in the "disagree" column might be assumed to be demonstrating negative response bias.

Three judges were used to establish that the items on the inventory met the criteria of being subtle, neutral, innocuous, and having reversal-paired statements. The final form consisted of 120 items. This form was tested on 100 college undergraduates, and a bell-shaped curve was obtained. Tentative limits, within which members of the experimental and control groups might be expected to fall, were set up as a result of an analysis of the pilot study.

Validity of the test had been established by expert judgment of test forms. Reliability was established by the split-half technique (.75 using the Spearman-Brown formula).

PROCEDURES

As part of the regular testing process at two VA guidance centers in Boston, Massachusetts, 500 normal male veterans were administered the SDT. None of these veterans had a history of any form of mental illness or a serious physical condition, such as tuberculosis or blindness, where significant psychological concomitants might be anticipated. Their mean average age was 23 years; their mean educational level was 12 years. Those men who received scores of 60 (i.e., no response bias) or scores of 54 or lower (i.e., negative response bias) were invited to participate in a study dealing with counseling techniques. There were very few men who expressed a reluctance to cooperate. This can be understood in view of their being predominantly veterans who had requested counseling and testing to help them in career planning.

The 50 men with the lowest scores on the Speed of Decision Test and the first 50 with scores of 60 were compared in terms of their performance on the three criterion instruments—the MMPI, the Rorschach, and Draw-A-Person test.

Three judges reviewed the MMPI profiles, three considered the Rorschach material, and one judge studied the D-A-P data. Only code numbers identified the subjects on these protocols. Each judge was asked to give three ratings for each of the 100 subjects on the factors of level of adjustment, presence or absence of obsessive-compulsive and hysteroid trends, and neurotic-tendingness. Judges were selected in terms of their special competency with the instrument used. They were encouraged to use whatever method was most meaningful to them in interpreting the test results to make the called-for ratings.

The majority or average opinion of the three judges on each rating for the Rorschach and MMPI was recorded as the Rorschach and MMPI diagnosis for each subject. With the D-A-P the opinion of the sole judge was accepted. Then a combined MMPI-Rorschach-DAP diagnosis was derived by finding the diagnosis based on maximal agreement at each level. It was recognized that this Composite Index, based upon evaluations of the individual tests, could very well differ from that which one might expect if the judges considered all of the tests together in acquiring a single diagnostic impression. The latter approach would have proved to be impracticable from the point of view of the time demands imposed upon the judges. Moreover, it is believed that the composite diagnosis which was used gave a more reliable impression, inasmuch as judges were dealing with the instrument with which they appeared to have most proficiency.

In testing the first hypothesis, the chi-square was used to examine the control and experimental groups in terms of the frequencies with which they were placed into the categories: "markedly maladjusted," "moderately maladjusted," and "not maladjusted." Hypothesis 2 was tested by using the chi-square to examine the relationship of the "no response bias" groups and the "negative response bias" group to the diagnostic categories of "highly similar to neurotic records," "moderately similar to neurotic records," and "not similar to neurotic records."

The third hypothesis was studied statistically through the use of a nonparametric method. Of the 100 subjects, the 29 who were judged to be clearly demonstrating obsessive-compulsive trends were compared with 13 who were judged as most clearly demonstrating hysteroid trends. It was predicted that the median score of the obsessive-compulsive group on the SDT would be significantly lower than the median score of the hysteroid group.

RESULTS AND DISCUSSION

The experimental findings may be summed up as follows:

1. Within the limitations imposed by the design of the study, the first hypothesis is confirmed. Negative response bias is associated with maladjustment. That this association is real and not a result of chance errors is attested to by the very significant chi-square values obtained with Rorschach, MMPI and Composite Index ratings. The D-A-P results approach statistical significance in the direction predicted by the first hypothesis.

2. Using the MMPI and Composite Index as criteria, the experimental results favor the second hypothesis. The Rorschach test and D-A-P ratings individually did not yield discriminations between experimental and control groups that were statistically significant.

3. Comparing the obsessive-compulsive and hysteroid subjects, differences were found in the direction predicted by the hypothesis. But these differences did not establish themselves as significant at the one per cent level set up for this study.

These experimental results tend to be consistent with those of similar and related studies on the negative response sets. They suggest the practical value of a subtle-items inventory, such as the SDT, as a group screening device for maladjustment. They underscore the importance of using several indicies of emotional status in making individual diagnoses. Finally, they generally support what appears to this writer to be a most pregnant hypothesis for research in the fields of counseling and clinical psychology: "Deviant response patterns tend to be general; hence those deviant behavior patterns which are signficant for abnormality and thus regarded as symptoms, are associated with other deviant response patterns which are in noncritical areas of behavior and which are not regarded as symptoms of personality aberration" (Berg).

SUMMARY

The aim of this study was to investigate certain aspects of the nature of negative response bias as it relates to personality adjustment. For experimental purposes, negative response bias was defined as a type of response set whereby a person tends to answer "disagree" on test items when in doubt.

A subtle items inventory, the Speed of Decision Test, was developed to measure the presence or absence of response bias in adults. This test was administered to 500 normal male veterans. The 50 men with the lowest scores constituted the experimental "negative response bias" group. The 50 men whose scores indicated lack of response bias were the control subjects. These 100 subjects were given three personality tests used as criterion instruments: the Rorschach, MMPI, and Draw-A-Person test.

The test protocols were examined by expert judges. They rated the material on three personality dimensions: adjustment, diagnosis, and dynamics. An analysis of the ratings indicated a definite association between negative response bias and maladjustment. The results also suggest that negative response bias is associated with personality traits defined as neurotic-tendingness and obsessive-compulsive trends.

PART FIVE

RELIABILITY

Many psychological tests impose time limits with the result that speed of performance is stressed. Speed should not, however, be thought of as independent from the test task that is given. Dr. Wesman, who is Treasurer and Associate Director of the Testing Division of the Psychological Corporation in New York City, urges that one think of speed in terms of a dimension rather than a trait. This article originally appeared in Educational & Psychological Measurement, *1960, Vol. 20, pp. 267–274.*

Some Effects of Speed in Test Use

Alexander G. Wesman

If we are to understand the nature of speed as a variable in psychological testing, we must first understand that speed is a dimension rather than a trait. In all too many instances, we find a tendency to reify speed —to think of it as a kind of unitary skill, like strength of grip, which we may expect will function similarly whenever called upon. This way of thinking about speed has led to the inclusion of inappropriate tests in selection batteries and misinterpretation of data in research aimed at investigating the nature of tests. It is our present purpose to illustrate, by examples, how speed is a quite different phenomenon from one setting to another.

Consider the situation in which an industrial organization sets up a test battery for selection of administrative or sales personnel. The first component is usually a test of general mental ability, intelligence, learning capacity (or whatever designation one prefers). Very often this test is one in which speed plays an important role. One reason for choosing a speeded test is, of course, the reluctance of industry to spend any more than minimum time on testing. Another reason frequently offered is that the firm wants men who can think quickly and can make rapid decisions. The implicit assumption is that speed as represented in the test and speed as represented on the job are one and the same. It is a dubious assumption at best. If the test proves valid, it is more likely to be because the test is easy for the bright candidates and difficult for the less able. It is primarily knowing more, not thinking faster, that distinguishes the high scorers from the low. For example, Bennett and Doppelt (1956) matched two groups of applicants to schools of nursing on a vocabulary test. One group was then given a set of easy vocabulary items from an alternate form while the other took a set of difficult items. The experimental tests were administered under speed conditions. The research showed that the less able applicants worked equally slowly on easy and hard items; the more able answered a larger number of the easy items than of the difficult ones. Bennett and Doppelt concluded that there was a definite relationship between the examinee's vocabulary knowledge and her rate of responding to vocabulary test items.

An experiment by McGehee (personal communication) provides similar evidence in a very different setting. A newly-employed group of embroidery punch operators in a textile plant were administered a job-sample test—on which very closely duplicated the job for which they were hired. Shortly after the hiring, production (piece) rates of high and low scorers were obtained; the job-sample test was found to have very considerable validity. However, at the end of a month, production records of high and low scorers were again compared. Group differences in performance on the job had decreased to the point of vanishing, and validity was accordingly approximately zero. Apparently those who scored high on the job-sample test were the people with prior experience as embroidery punch operators. Those who were not previously experienced did poorly on the test and on the job because they had not yet learned the necessary skills. These skills they learned relatively quickly on the job, and the acquisition resulted in performance equal to that of the previously more experienced employees. Thus, it was the knowledge and skill of both groups of employees which determined the speed at which they performed.

A third example demonstrating the effect of ability or knowledge on speed is chosen from the new Davis Reading Test. This test provides two scores: Level of Comprehension, based on the first 40 items, which almost everyone answers; and Speed of Comprehension, based on all 80 items, which almost no one completes. In the investigation of test-retest reliability, data were gathered which included scores from alternate forms of each of the two tests administered to the same students. From these data, correlation coefficients were obtained to show the relationship of Level of Comprehension scores from form to form, and of Level of Comprehension scores on one form to Speed of Comprehension scores on an alternate form. These coefficients were obtained separately for eleventh- and twelfth-grade students, and for college freshmen. In each grade, the average correlation between Level of Comprehension scores from alternate forms was exactly the same as the average correlation between Level of Comprehension on one form and Speed of Comprehension on another. Once again, the conclusion seems apparent; speed of performance is determined very largely by the knowledges and skills of students.

The above examples are illustrative of instances in which knowledge or skill is intimately related to speed. Let us now look at some situations in which the opposite is the case. The Differential Aptitude Tests consist of seven tests which are essentially power tests, and one test (Clerical Speed and Accuracy) developed specifically as a measure of speed of perceptual and motor performance. The task of the student who takes the Clerical test makes so little demand on the intellect that very few errors are made by the majority of examinees. The median correlation coefficient between Clerical scores and scores on the other seven Differential Aptitude Tests, for grades eight through twelve, is .13 for boys and .16 for girls. Thus, there is very little relationship between speed of performance on a task which requires little understanding and scores on tests which make intellectual demands on the student.

The chief characteristic of the DAT Clerical Speed and Accuracy Test is that so few errors are made. This characteristic is not, however, limited to clerical tests. Some respected intelligence tests have components which seem almost as simple as the simplest clerical test. Since the original Army Alphas, through the Chicago Non-Verbal and down to the current Wechsler intelligence scales, the digit-symbol test has been an accepted subtest for measuring intellectual power in children and adults alike. Yet the substitution of a digit for a geometric design, with the key constantly before the examinee, is hardly a complex process. The simplicity of the digit-symbol task accounts for the fact that the number of items attempted under the usual speeded administration is almost as good a score as the number of items correctly done. The word "almost" must be used because a very small number of subjects may misunderstand directions or may find even this kind of task challenging their limited mental ability. Thus, Cassel (personal communication) recently made available data on the digit-symbol subtests (I and X) of the Chicago Non-Verbal Examination for 145 boys in a state institutional school. All of these students were classified as having IQ's above 84, and their mental ages ranged from 6.1 to 10.9. On Sub-test I, only nine of the 145 boys marked as many as seven items incorrectly; all nine of these earned scores of 0–3 where the total distribution encompassed scores up to 59, with a median of 27. The results for Subtest X were very similar. Clearly, then, we have here a test which is permitted to contribute importantly to the measurement of intelligence but which is basically a perceptual speed test for a very large proportion of appropriate examinees.

Interestingly enough, although the digit-symbol substitution process does not seem to be much more demanding than is the DAT clerical task, there appears to be a real difference between these tests in their relation to more cognitive tests. In contrast with the average correlation of .13 cited above between DAT Clerical and the other Differential Aptitude Tests, the digit-symbol test (officially called "Coding B") in the Wechsler Intelligence Scale for Children has for 10-year-olds a median intercorrelation of .30 with eleven other subtests in WISC; the coefficient of correlation with the Vocabulary test is .41. These coefficients probably support the inclusion of the digit-symbol subtest in an instrument aimed at measuring general mental ability. The difference in behavior between these two simple perceptual tasks makes it difficult to generalize concerning the nature of speed as a variable.

Another way in which speed behaves is as a personality or work-habit variable. In the development of simple perceptual tests like the DAT Clerical, we are likely to assume that students will work as rapidly as perceptual and motor skills permit. This is undoubtedly so for many pupils, perhaps true for most, but certainly not true for all. Early in our experience with the DAT we found that counselors were perplexed by students who scored very well on the verbal, numerical, and abstract reasoning tests, but very poorly on the clerical test. We hypothesized that these were students who were used to checking their test answers carefully to avoid making mistakes, displaying an attitude of stress on correctness often inculcated by teachers. Accordingly forty such youngsters in one school system were retested with an alternate form, and with modified directions which were devised to counteract the hypothesized caution of the pupils. The increases in score were far greater than could be accounted for by regression or practice effect. The group as a whole went from about the fifteenth percentile to well above average; the most dramatic change was that of a boy who scored at the fourth percentile on the first test and at the eightieth on the retest. The test may have been measuring work habits or caution in these pupils, as originally administered; it does not appear to have been measuring the kind of perceptual-motor skill it was intended to tap.

As a related thought, one is reminded that many personality inventories stress that the respondent is to answer each item quickly, or with the first response that occurs to him. It would be interesting to know whether there is accompanying research to demonstrate the validity of this procedure. It seems appropriate to wonder whether, with some such inventories, different responses might be given if directions permitted unhurried, considered answers, and whether those responses might result in different personality trait scores. The writer is unaware of definitive research on this question; he recognizes that as inventories run into hundreds of items there may be discomforting practical consequences in asking the respondent to give full consideration to each and every item. Still, he cannot help wondering.

The field of achievement testing is another in which there have been more assumptions than well-directed research with regard to the behavior of speed as a variable. This topic has been discussed by Cronbach (1949) as follows:

> Another variable which reduces validity of achievement tests is the speed factor. Time limits are often needed for administrative convenience, but when speed becomes a major element in determining a person's score, the score is likely not to represent his attainment accurately. Speed is a legitimate element in achievement tests only when speed is an objective of the course. Speed is relevant and important in tests of typing attainment or reading facility, or tests of arithmetic for use in hiring cashiers. Speed is irrelevant if we wish to know how large a pupil's vocabulary is, how much science he knows, or how accurately he can reason. In most achievement tests a speed loading can be justified only if the test is to be used empirically to predict success in a task where speed is helpful, or if data are available to prove that scores on the speeded test correlate very highly with scores on the unspeeded test. Speed tests have limited validity for describing the knowledge of individual pupils, since a few well-informed pupils are slow workers.

For our purposes, one might wish that Cronbach had spelled out these principles in greater detail. Thus, one sentence might be expanded to read, "Speed is a legitimate element in achievement tests only when the same kind of speed which the test is measuring is an objective of the course." Similarly, he might well have said, "Speed is relevant and important in . . . tests of arithmetic for use in hiring cashiers if the kind of arithmetic problem is one in which it is necessary for cashiers to be able to operate with speed." Unless we have clear experimental evidence to the contrary, we might well assume in any specific situation that speed in the test is justifiable to the extent that the test is a genuine job-sample of the course or job activities for which the test is intended. There are probably satisfactory cashiers in many stores who cannot solve arithmetic reasoning problems with appreciable dispatch.

In any test which is a combination of speed and power, the role which speed plays may be a very confusing one. Let us look at one or two illustrations. As a first example, take the situation in which a vocabulary and reading comprehension test are given with a single time limit. The student who finishes the vocabulary items quickly has more time to spend on the reading passages than the student who works more slowly on vocabulary. The performance of the two students on the reading comprehension section is consequently not truly comparable. As a second example, let us consider a test of "general mental ability" consisting of verbal and numerical items presented in alternating groups. Two students with equal strength in verbal ability and equal weakness in numerical ability may obtain very different scores. The first student may achieve a relatively high score by skipping the numerical items, racing through as many verbal as he can within the time limit; the second student, permitting himself to be slowed down by the more time-consuming numerical items, may earn a much lower score. Seldom will the difference in approach of these examinees bear valid relation to the criterion.

That speededness is incompatible with item analysis has been demonstrated theoretically, logically, and experimentally. As an example of the latter, Wesman (1949) showed that if the seventieth item of a speeded test given to one group of high school graduates had been "write your own name," the item-test coefficient would have been at least .84 and the per cent passing the item no greater than 50 per cent. It is now equally recognized that reliability coefficients based on highly speeded tests are of little or no value, except perhaps to delude the unsophisticated. We know, too, that tests with very short time limits put an extremely heavy premium on exact timing in test administration; a half-minute error will have far greater effect on scores on a two-minute test than on a 30-minute test. In one midwestern high school, inattention by the administrator to timing on a three-minute test resulted in 99th percentile scores for almost every student in the class.

One of the basic questions to which we do not as yet have satisfactory answers is that of the quotidian variability on different kinds of mental tests from individual to individual. Does the speed with which an individual attacks a test depend on whether the test is easy or difficult for him? On easy tests, such as involve clerical or simple coding tasks, is an individual consistent from day to day, as he usually is on power tests? How much greater is the variability among examinees on such simple tests than is the day-to-day variability within the examinee?

Other basic questions concerning the nature of speed will occur to the psychometrician who seeks to use it as a variable. Questions will be more likely to occur if the assumptions concerning speed are kept to a minimum, and if the experimenter remembers that speed is not itself an ability, but a dimension.

One hears typically about reliability in connection with aptitude tests. A little reflection on the student's part will show that this is an important problem in all types of measurement. Experimenters who ignore such essential checks do so at some peril. The following report discusses this problem of reliability (rather, the lack of it) in an experimental area of research quite outside the typical tests and measurements field: the "new look" experiments in perception. Reliability is just as vital in these areas as with aptitude tests.

The original report appeared in the Psychological Bulletin, *1962, Vol. 59, pp. 70–73. Both authors, at the time of writing this report, were at the San Francisco State College.*

The Reliability of a Response Measure:

Differential Recognition-Threshold Scores

Donn Byrne and Joan Holcomb

The problem of reliability of measurement is a familiar one in the context of test construction and test evaluation. In other types of investigation, however, responses frequently are measured in a variety of ways by a variety of scoring procedures (often a priori ones) without evident concern about measurement. Although psychometric issues appear to be foreign to experimental methodology, any specified set of stimuli may be conceptualized as a test and the quantification of subjects' responses as test scores. Viewed in this way, such scores should be evaluated according to accepted standards for psychological tests.

An investigation of the validity of a response measure is usually implied in the design of an experiment; reliability, however, is often ignored. Whether results are postive or negative with respect to one's hypotheses, reliability of measurement can assume great importance. Psychologists have the disconcerting tendency to create a new methodology for each experiment. In work on perceptual defense, for example, it is difficult to find any two studies in which the same stimulus is presented in the same way to evoke responses which are quantified in the same manner. It seems reasonable to hypothesize that some of these stimuli presented to subjects in a particular way are going to yield more reliably-measured response dimensions than others. With a heterogeneous methodology and unknown reliability coefficients, it should not be surprising to find some degree of inconsistency across experiments not attributable to theoretical weaknesses. Thus, generally positive results mixed with some negative results may reflect differentially reliable "tests." Even the positive results are no guarantee that reliable measures have been employed. In addition, it would seem logical to construct reliable measuring techniques as a preliminary step in experimental work rather than as an afterthought.

DIFFERENTIAL RECOGNITION THRESHOLDS

As an example of inadequate measurement techniques, some of the "new look" experiments in perception of the past decade will be briefly reviewed. In studies of perceptual defense, differential recognition thresholds for emotionally toned vs. neutral stimulus material have frequently served as the dependent variable and as a measure of individual differences in defensiveness.

All four types of reliability should be considered in utilizing a differential recognition-threshold score. First, if any subjectivity is involved in the scoring process, there should be some determination of the extent to which independent judges are able to arrive at approximately identical scores. Interscorer agreement is a necessary, but not sufficient, condition for reliability of measurement. Unfortunately, many investigators determine only the reliability of the scoring procedure rather than of the scores themselves. Second, if a series of discrete, presumably homogeneous responses are combined to form a total score, it is important to determine the extent to which this score is internally consistent. Third, if the score is considered to be indicative of an enduring personality characteristic, it is essential to know the extent to which this score is stable over time. Fourth, if a different but theoretically equivalent set of stimuli is employed to elicit responses, the equivalence of the two sets of scores should be determined.

A review of perceptual defense and related studies which have used a differential recognition threshold suggests that a thorough examination of reliability is unusual. As might be anticipated, the reliability coefficient which is most frequently reported is that of interscorer consistency, and the results are generally quite good. Internal consistency is less frequently investigated, and the reported coefficients range from good to mediocre to unsatisfactory. Holtzman and Bitterman (1956) reported that perceptual thresholds for taboo and neutral words were unreliable measures; therefore, they were eliminated from a factor analytic study. An investigation of the stability of differential recognition thresholds over time was not reported in any of the studies reviewed. The majority of the studies using a differential threshold score as a variable, report no reliability information.

AN UNRELIABLE SCORE

The senior author planned to use the differential recognition threshold for hostile vs. neutral words presented tachistoscopically as a criterion measure for a new test designed to measure repressing and sensitizing defenses. It should be confessed that the reliability investigation was undertaken only when certain difficulties were encountered.

Twenty pairs of hostile and neutral words were each matched for length, initial letter, and frequency of occurrence in one million words according to the Thorndike-Lorge (1944) word count. Hostile words were defined as those representing behavior involving the derogation, injury, or destruction of either animate or inanimate objects. Neutral words were defined as those which were not emotionally toned. A word was assigned to either category on the basis of the unanimous agreement of three independent judges. The 40 words were placed on slides and arranged in random order.

The slides were used with a Keystone Overhead Projector equipped with a Flashometer. Following a demonstration with a neutral practice word, each stimulus word was presented at 1/100, 1/75, 1/50, 1/37.5, 1/25, 1/10, and 1 second. After each trial, the subject responded by writing down his best guess as to the word presented. Subjects were seen in small groups.

The threshold for each word consisted of the first trial on which that word was correctly recognized. Scores ranged from 1 (correct recognition at the 1/100 presentation) through 8 (failure to recognize the word on any trial). A subject's mean threshold on the 20 neutral words minus his mean threshold on the 20 hostile words yielded a defense score. Presumably, a positive score would indicate a sensitizing reaction and a negative score a repressing reaction.

Disappointing results in cross-validating the test that was being developed led to a belated investigation of the reliability of the criterion. Differential thresholds were obtained for almost 600 subjects, men and women enrolled in general education courses at San Francisco State College. From this total, a sample of 50 was drawn. Because some subjectivity enters into the determination of the trial on which correct recognition first occurs, the authors scored these protocoles independently. The defense scores had respectable interscorer consistency as shown by a correlation of .91.

The second type of reliability considered was internal consistency. When differential thresholds are obtained, it is assumed that there is some response homogeneity with respect to stimulus content. In this study, responses to 20 of the projected words should have been determined in part by their common reference to hostility, and these responses should to some extent differ from those evoked by the 20 non-hostile words. Therefore, split-half reliability was determined by dividing the hostile words into odd and even groups and computing the differential threshold scores for these two groups compared to their matching neutral words. The coefficient of internal consistency was .00. It was not deemed essential to apply the Spearman-Brown correction formula.

Thus, independent judges agreed about the nature of the stimulus material and about the scoring of the subjects' responses. Nevertheless, the resulting scores were unreliable. In view of this finding and the considerations discussed earlier, it is suggested that, whenever possible, any study should include a report of the reliability of its response measures.

PART SIX

FACTOR
ANALYSIS

Factor analysis is a statistical technique that appears forbidding to most students. It is essential, however, that a student of psychological tests be familiar with the rudiments of this, since whole new test batteries are now appearing on the scene which are the product of factor analytic approaches—multifactor test batteries. The following two articles should be very helpful to the student in that they present the topic of factor analysis in nontechnical language.

The first of these papers, by Dr. French, is a lucid exposition of the technique and some of the technical language employed. He also reproduces a sample factor analysis and encourages the student to follow through on the interpretation of this. Dr. French is well known in the area of psychometrics, and for many years he has been Research Associate at the Educational Testing Service in Princeton, New Jersey. The original report appeared in The College Board Review, March, 1950, No. 10, pp. 129–131, *and is here reproduced in its entirety.*

What Is Factor Analysis?

John W. French

Are you good at figures, or do you excel at writing? The psychologists of old asked themselves and other people these questions. They pondered over the many ways in which people differ from one another and attempted to list all the traits or faculties of the mind. They introspected. They thought about how they themselves differed from other people; they thought about the differences among their acquaintances. Some of them came up with a list of a half dozen or so basic faculties; others listed hundreds of ways in which people differed.

As psychology evolved into an experimental science, this "arm chair" method of forming theories was greeted with sneers. "Faculty" psychology became a taboo. It was an example of how not to do research.

NEW METHODS DEVELOPED

Time passed and the methods for measuring human differences developed. The IQ test showed that you had a little intelligence or a lot of intelligence. It showed differences in quantity between people; no differences in quality—no faculties.

We taught students Latin, and algebra, and drawing, and we constructed tests to measure how much of each subject the students learned. However, the students who learned anything fast were thought to have a high IQ; those who learned slowly in general were thought to have a low IQ—no faculties.

Now the psychometricians have come up with "factor analysis." This is a mathematical method for helping us deduce what our tests are measuring. The procedure is to give a lot of tests to a lot of students. The results will show that the tests were measuring several "factors." By using some arm chair work, not too much, we can name these factors, say, "Number Factor," "Verbal Factor," "Spatial Factor," and "Deduction Factor."

LOADINGS INDICATE FACTORS

Numbers called "loadings" will indicate how closely related each test is to each factor. The higher the loadings, the better the relation; loadings are the same as correlation coefficients. For example, an addition test might have a loading of .80 on the number factor and loadings of close to zero on the others. In some analyses, arithmetic reasoning tests have loadings of about .40 on the number factor, .40 on the deduction factor, and .40 on the verbal factor. To some extent, then, addition and arithmetic reasoning measure the same thing, the number factor. The addition test is said to be a pure test of the number factor. The arithmetic reasoning test measures three different things at the same time. Since a student will need deductive reasoning ability and verbal ability as well as number ability in college, the arithmetic reasoning test would be a better college entrance test than addition. If we are right about the factors, the arithmetic reasoning test could be replaced without loss by separate pure tests of the number, deduction, and verbal factors.

What are factors? Presumably they are traits that have some stability in our culture. They are scientifically-determined faculties. The more obvious ones resemble the faculties of old, but many of them do not. We can now do more than think deeply in our arm chairs about the structure of the mind: we can think and also use machines—we think that is better.

Factor analysis is a lot of work. Long columns of numbers must be multiplied together or squared and summed, matrices of many hundreds of numbers must be processed again and again, number by number. Machines help, but it is still a tedious process. In spite of cost and time, several hundred analyses have been published, each one covering more or less well some group of mental or physical functions. As in most new fields there is much disagreement as to procedure and findings.

After reading numerous analyses to find out where the factors were, I became greatly confused. Therefore, it seemed to me that an appropriate research project would be to compile a survey, cataloguing factor analyses and making comparisons between them to find out whether or not they agreed on anything. This rather voluminous survey has been completed and has been published as a psychometric monograph, entitled "The Description of Aptitude and Achievement Tests in Terms of Rotated Factors." The conclusion is that many factor analyses do agree.

FACTOR STUDIES AGREE

Here is an example: One analysis found two tests with high loadings on the same factor: (1) a test of learning the initials that go with a list of family names, and (2) a test of learning to associate certain numbers with certain words. Another analysis found the following two tests had high loadings on a factor: (1) a test of learning to associate certain numbers with certain words, and (2) a test of learning to associate pairs of Turkish and English words. It was not hard to see that these two analyses had found the same factor, one that could be called "associative memory." Since a number of other analyses also find a factor that seems to be associative memory, we can conclude that this is a consistent function of the mind, and we know what tests are the best measures of it.

All the factors are not easy to recognize. There seems to be a factor of integration: integrating many facts in your mind in order to make an appropriate response. Another one seems to be a factor of planning: reacting to certain facts in advance of action, so that your action will be appropriately planned. These sound very interesting, but the evidence for them is based on a few Air Force tests that we don't know much about. One of the integration tests named "Signal Interpretation" called for keeping in mind a number of rules and signals in deciding from which drawing of an aircraft carrier planes would next rise.

I look forward to the ideal situation where all the factors of importance to us will be established and where we can have a file of tests for each. When we would suddenly be asked to build a test for, say, tin-can label writers, we could select appropriate factors for the job and pull tests from the files to measure them. There would be no scramble to make up a test that would partly resemble a writer and partly resemble a tin can. Appropriate research would be to obtain ratings in success on the job of tin-can label writing and to make an analysis indicating which factors are important and how they should be weighted in the predictive battery.

We are considering proposals for the development of a battery of tests that could be given at schools and colleges. Such a battery would give us the students' scores on each of fifteen or more well-established factors. It would be used to help counselors and students in choosing major fields of study and occupations.

A SAMPLE FACTOR ANALYSIS

Now you have some idea about factor analysis, its limitations and its yearnings. How would you like to try your hand at interpreting a factor analysis? It's not complicated; try it.

In the table below you will find the loadings for each test. These indicate how closely each test is related to the Factors A, B, C, D, E, F, and G. Look at the tests that are highly related to Factor A: *Addition* and *Multiplication*. But the *Arithmetic Reasoning* test has a low loading.

Therefore, this factor (A) does not represent the principal ability needed for mathematics, but only the ability to handle numbers. It has been called the "number factor."

Can you name the other factors?

TABLE 2

C. H. GOODMAN'S ANALYSIS OF THURSTONE'S PRIMARY MENTAL ABILITIES TESTS

Tests	Factors						
	A	B	C	D	E	F	G
1. Identical Forms. Speed in spotting similar figures.	.12	.30	.36	.03	.27	—.24	—.16
2. Verbal Enumeration. Speed in spotting given type of word.	.05	.29	.06	.21	.44	—.31	.13
3. Addition. Speed at adding 2–digit numbers.	.80	—.12	.16	—.08	.37	.08	.03
4. Multiplication. Speed at multiplying by single–digit numbers.	.77	.08	.13	.12	.30	—.12	.16
5. Completion. Give words to fit definitions.	—.02	.22	.06	.22	.69	.28	—.02
6. Same–Opposites. Select synonyms or antonyms.	.01	.13	.04	.25	.72	.11	.19
7. Cards. Select drawings of cards rotated but not turned over.	.10	.38	.76	—.10	.16	.12	.01
8. Figures. Select drawings of figures rotated but not turned over.	.19	.13	.77	.23	.05	.18	.32
9. Word–Number. Recall numbers associated with words.	.07	—.01	.19	.50	—.03	.07	.25
10. Initials. Recall initials associated with names.	.00	—.05	.37	.52	—.12	.14	.08
11. Letter Grouping. Check set of letters not like other sets.	.20	.48	.10	.19	—.03	.27	—.17
12. Marks. Find rule for the location of a mark in patterns.	.07	.50	.20	—.05	.02	.06	.13
13. Number Patterns. Find rule to complete number squares.	.30	.41	.14	.15	.09	.10	—.14
14. Arithmetic Reasoning.	.21	.34	—.01	—.06	.17	.52	.15
15. Number Series. Fill in blanks in number series.	.23	.18	.25	.03	.14	.59	.05
16. Mechanical Movements. Questions about movement in drawings.	.22	.40	.26	—.25	.21	—.07	.19

In this paragraph I will give you the interpretations of those factors made by the man who carried out the analysis, Dr. Charles H. Goodman, research psychologist of the Adjutant General's Office, Department of the Army. Following the number factor is one featuring tests 11–13, all tests requiring the formation of generalized rules; call it "induction." Factor C features *cards* and *figures,* two tests of spatial relations; call it "space." Factor D features two tests concerned with memorizing associations: associative memory. Factor E: good old "verbal," but what is verbal about addition? Be happy that you have no worse problem.

Factor F: *arithmetic reasoning* problems and *number series* problems call for the application of principles to specific problems, a kind of reasoning, probably deductive. Factor G: this is called a residual factor; nothing there but a residue after everything else—all the identifiable factors—has been taken away.

Factors A–F are fairly well established. A number of other analyses have found factors that can be identified as the same ones as these. The Scholastic Aptitude Test measures the deductive reasoning factor and, to some extent, the number factor by the Mathematics section. The verbal factor is measured by the Verbal section. We have a spatial relations test. These are related to college success, but how about induction? How about many other factors that have been found and will be found? These, too, must be studied so that useful measures can be constructed.

The second report on factor analysis comes out of the Thurstone's psychological laboratory at the University of Chicago. Both the Thurstones are famous for their pioneering work on Primary Mental Abilities. During their tenure at Chicago, a series of reports would be issued from time to time; the material reprinted here is a condensation of two of these reports (Nos. 44 and 50 for 1947–48). The reader should keep in mind these relatively early publication dates. For a more recent analysis of cognitive functioning, again in terms of factor analysis, the student should consult Guilford's paper, "The Structure of Intellect" (1956), a highly condensed version of which follows this Thurstone paper.

Primary Mental Abilities and

Psychological Implications

L. L. Thurstone

The purpose of this paper is to summarize briefly the principal facts that have been learned in the last twenty years about the mental abilities. Everyone is naturally interested in his own mental abilities because they represent his potentialities and limitations in mental endowment. They do not in themselves determine success or failure which depend as well on other things such as health, encouragement, and opportunity. But a man's mental profile indicates the potentialities and limitations within which he can expect his efforts to be most fruitful.

Before introducing recent ideas on this subject, it may be useful to take a brief look at the history of this problem so as to get the setting for more recent work. For centuries it was the privilege of every writer in this field to speculate on mental endowment and to make his own preferred list of abilities. Such writing has been found to be an unstable guide for scientific work because here, as in other pre-scientific speculation, there was more error than fruitful insight. In the scientific study of this problem we do not accept any authority whatever as to what the human abilities are, or should be, unless it is supported by experimental demonstration of the distinctness of the different abilities that may be presented for our approval.

The first sustained attempt in modern times to appraise the mental endowment of individuals can be credited to Sir Francis Galton. In 1885 he started a laboratory in London for testing individuals as to intelligence. While his early tests were not considered successful for estimating the mental endowment of individuals, he deserves credit for introducing experimental methods in this field.

At a later time the problem reappeared in extensive studies of school children. These studies were based on the hypothesis that a child's school progress depends in large part on his mental endowment, and it was believed that a child's intelligence could be adequately described by a single index. It was of course recognized that his school progress was determined partly by his native intelligence and partly by the conditions in his home and school environment. Best known were the Binet tests of intelligence which were translated into many languages and which have been used all over the world in appraising the intelligence of children.

The total performance of a child on a Binet test is stated in terms of his so-called mental age. A mental age of 10 years, for example, represents the average performance of ten-year-old children, and similarly for the rest of the scale. If a child attains a mental age of 10 and if he is actually eight years old, then he is two years accelerated. Children are frequently described in this way as to their degree of mental acceleration or retardation, and this classification is of practical use in the schools. For example, when a child is failing in school, it is important to determine whether his failure is due to deficiency in native intelligence or lack of motivation. If the test indicates that the child is bright, then he must be motivated in some way. He might even be put in a more advanced class to challenge his abilities. If he is found to be mentally deficient, then he should not be expected to progress as fast as the average child of his age.

Another index that has been widely used is the intelligence quotient, the so-called IQ which is merely the ratio of the mental age to the chronological age. These indices of mental age and intelligence quotient have been useful in dealing with school children, but these measures run into logical absurdities when they are applied to adults. Consider, for example, a man who is brighter than the average of the general population. There exists no age for which his test performance is an average and consequently, by definition, there exists no mental age for him. Since the intelligence quotient is dependent on the mental age, his intelligence quotient cannot be determined. Although the mental age and the intelligence quotient have been very useful in dealing with school children, these measures are gradually being replaced by more comprehensive indices that are not limited to any particular age group.

In experimental work with intelligence tests it is customary to start the analysis by determining the correlations between the various tests. If two tests of intelligence are given to a group of people, you might expect that those who excel in one of the tests would also excel in the other. This would be the case if the two tests were measures of the same underlying trait or ability and if the results were otherwise unaffected by experimental error. The degree of association between two tests is represented in statistical work by the coefficient of correlation.

At the beginning of the century, quite a number of studies were made to determine the correlations between different tests of intelligence, and it was soon found that they were far from perfect. Two inferences were drawn from these simple observations. First, it was concluded that no test is in any sense a pure measure of the postulated general intelligence and that an appreciable part of a test performance is subject to fortuitous experimental error. At this time there also began to be considerable speculation as to whether general intelligence could be postulated as a single general function. The alternative was to consider intelligence as a complex of many distinct abilities. A third possibility which has some defenders is that intelligence is determined by thousands of factors that function without any pattern or groupings.

It was in 1904 that the British psychologist Spearman wrote a simple but epoch-making paper on the correlations of psychological tests, and he showed that under certain conditions they did indicate the existence of what he called a single intellective factor and which he denoted by the letter "g." This was the starting point for a series of lively controversies. Until 1930 the central theme in these controversies was nearly always the question whether Spearman's general intellective factor did exist. It was found that even with the best available controls, the postulated general intellective factor of Spearman was inadequate to account for the observed correlations among experimental tests. It was found necessary to acknowledge the existence of other abilities in addition to a general intellective factor. Until about twenty years ago the main scientific interest was directed at the question whether general intellective ability should be postulated in addition to the various special abilities.

In 1930 investigations were begun with a different emphasis. Instead of asking whether the experimentally-observed correlations between tests could be accounted for by a single intellective factor, the question asked was how many factors or abilities were implied in the observed correlations. For every set of tests that were given to an experimental population, the problem was to determine how many abilities were required to account for the experimental results and to identify the nature of each of the abilities that had been isolated. This was the beginning of the development of multiple factor analysis, which is a new scientific method that was designed for the solution of this psychological problem. It has since been found that the multiple factor methods are applicable also to problems in other sciences.

In recent studies, a number of primary mental abilities have been isolated by the multiple factor methods. It is assumed that the mental endowment of an individual cannot be adequately described in terms of a single intellective factor, and that a single index such as the mental age or the intelligence quotient is inadequate for the description of a person's mental abilities. Instead we need a profile of his abilities. The mental profile is a diagram showing an individual's ratings in each of the primary mental abilities. Such description of abilities is consistent with the experience of teachers and employers. Two men may be of the same general level of mental endowment and yet they may be entirely different. One of them may excel in verbal and persuasive types of work while the other excels in solving scientific or mechanical problems. The fundamental task, according to this view, is to identify the different mental abilities and to appraise them separately so as to describe each individual with a mental profile.

We turn next to a brief description of some of the primary mental abilities that have been isolated so far.

One primary ability that was isolated in the early experiments with the multiple factor methods is the ability to visualize objects in space. It is called the space factor and it is denoted by the letter "S." Most people who are intelligent are fairly well endowed with this factor, but there are many highly intelligent people who are conspicuously poor in this primary ability. Relatively few such people are found in the sciences. It is a safe prediction that a boy who is a poor visualizer would not be happy as an apprentice in a drafting room. In recent studies for the Army Air Forces it has been found that there are several visualizing factors whose psychological characteristics have not yet been completely ascertained. This group of primary abilities associated with visualizing was probably involved in Sir Francis Galton's early experiments in which he tried to distinguish between people who are visually minded and those who are auditorily minded.

Another factor that was isolated early in the factorial experiments was the number factor "N." This factor represents facility in doing simple arithmetical tasks but it is rather narrow. The number factor is not heavily involved in arithmetical reasoning or in mathematics. In fact, it would not be surprising to find good mathematicians who are relatively poor in this factor. On the other hand, a cashier would soon quit his job if he were poor in the number factor. We have been puzzled about the underlying nature of the number factor. If we are dealing with differences in native endowment, then it should be possible to describe the nature of this factor in terms of fundamental processes rather than in such terms as "number," which is a cultural concept. Eventually, when the nature of this factor is more completely understood, it may turn out to be merely a historical accident that the factor was identified in tests that happened to be numerical in character. This is a question for the future to answer.

In considering each of these factors of mental endowment, we should keep in mind that the correlations between most of them are low and positive. Consequently a person's mental endowment cannot be adequately described in terms of a single index. Each person should be appraised separately as to the different factors so that the description is in terms of a mental profile.

One of the most socially important primary mental abilities that have been isolated is called "verbal comprehension" and it has been denoted "V." It is represented rather well by tests of vocabulary or tests of verbal reasoning, as in the interpretation of proverbs or the comprehension of difficult prose. There are several related factors concerned with verbal thinking. Another verbal factor is the word-fluency factor, "W." At first it was difficult to see just why these two factors which are both verbal should nevertheless be so clearly separated in the multiple factor analysis. Closer examination of the tests by which these two verbal factors were identified revealed an interesting difference. The word-fluency factor "W" is involved in those tasks in which the individual must produce the words himself in some restricted context, whereas the verbal comprehension factor "V" is involved in understanding the verbal material that is given to him. A simple test for the word-fluency factor is to ask the subject to write as many boys' names as he can think of in a few minutes. The nature of the task can be varied considerably with the same result. Some people can do this kind of task with ease whereas others stumble and hesitate when the associations do not come readily. These two primary mental abilities are distinct in the sense that a man may be verbally fluent, even though he has a limited vocabulary; and another man may have an extensive vocabulary and be capable of profound verbal comprehension, even though he is not verbally fluent. The social and educational implications of these differences are self-evident. In studying patients with amnesic aphasia, separate consideration should be given to these two verbal abilities because the patient may be able to comprehend verbal material without being able to think of the words himself. This indicates that the factor "V" is intact, whereas the factor "W" has suffered deterioration or loss. It is reassuring that such different approaches to the same problem show agreement as to what constitutes the primary mental abilities. A third verbal factor has been isolated that is concerned with fluency in sustained discourse.

It is a commonplace observation that some people have good memories and that others have poor memories. The results of factorial studies sustain this popular impression. The ability to memorize is a primary ability that is relatively independent of other abilities, although all of them are somewhat positively correlated. A man who is of superior mental endowment may or may not be fortunate enough to have a good memory. There are indications of several distinct memory abilities. For example, there seems to be a differentiation between the ability to memorize and the ability to recall past experience which you did not at the time intend to recall. The memorizing factor seems to transcend the content so that it is applicable to numerical, verbal, or visual material. Actual performance in memorizing is affected, however, by the different kinds of imagery that are specifically involved.

One of the most interesting of the primary mental abilities is the ability to discover the rule or principle in the material that one is working with. This primary ability has been called "induction." It also transcends the nature of the material and it is not limited to any of the sense modalities. Consequently it must be mediated by central processes. It is natural to ask whether this ability is associated with originality or creativeness, but on that question the factorial experiments have not yet given any answer.

There has appeared in several studies a factor that seems to be associated with the ability to carry out restrictive thinking. This is the ability to reason with problems in which there is a definite answer, as distinguished from those in which the effective solutions are not unique. The underlying nature of this factor is not clear.

In the field of perceptual dynamics it has been found that speed of perception is a primary factor that is independent of visual acuity in the usual sense. It is probably centrally determined. In separate studies of visual and auditory tests, several factors have been identified with perceptual closure. One of these is called speed of closure and it is concerned with the ability to fuse the perceptual field into a single percept. It is not yet known whether speed of closure for vision is the same as speed of closure for hearing. In order to answer such a question it will be necessary to conduct both visual and auditory tests on the same subjects. The question has also been raised whether speed of closure is related to induction, which is a similar function at the conceptual level. This question is now being investigated experimentally. A practical example of the effects of the closure factors can be seen with two individuals who have the same degree of deficiency in hearing as determined by audiometer tests and who differ in speed or flexibility of auditory closure. One of them will be able to get along fairly well in understanding what people say. He can fuse the inadequate auditory stimuli into meaningful speech, whereas the other individual is unable to do so. The closure factors are abilities quite independent of purely sensory functions.

The question is often raised whether the isolation of a number of distinct primary mental abilities has a bearing on the old controversy about Spearman's postulated general intellective factor. This old problem has taken a new form. The primary mental abilities are correlated so that those individuals who have a high rating in one of the primaries show somewhat higher than average ratings on other primaries. The correlations among primary abilities have themselves been subjected to multiple factor analysis, and it has been found that these correlations can be accounted for by what are called second-order factors. One of these which is rather prominent seems to be the same as Spearman's general intellective factor. It is rather well represented in such primary factors as induction, the space factor, and verbal comprehension, and it is rather low in memory, perceptual speed, and perceptual closure. This finding agrees with the general conception about the intellective factor.

Here we have a clue to an interpretation that may unify the early work of Spearman and the later work with multiple-factor analysis. The interpretation that seems plausible at this time is that the primary factors represent different kinds of mental facilities such as several kinds of memory, several kinds of perceptual closure, several visualizing factors, and several verbal factors. These primary abilities may be regarded as media for the expression of intellect, and people differ markedly in the effectiveness with which they can express themselves in these different media. The second-order factors may represent parameters that are more central in character and more universal in the sense that they are not determined by the efficiency of each modality or imagery type. The first-order primary factors may be regarded as separate organs, in a general sense, while the second-order or general factors represent parameters which influence the activities of the several organs or primary factors. The general factors may then be expected to have no particular locus, whereas some of the primary factors may eventually be rather definitely localized.

Experiments have been carried out at different age levels with the multiple-factor methods. These included groups of college students, several groups of high school students, eighth grade children and finally a group of kindergarten children who could not read and for whom special tests in pictorial form had to be devised. In all of these groups the primary abilities were isolated. Essentially the same factors were found at the different ages. Some abilities mature much earlier than others. The perceptual closure factors mature at about eight or nine, whereas the verbal comprehension factor matures rather late. Some of the primary mental abilities can be appraised even at the kindergarten age before the children have learned to read. The fact that the space factor and the number factors often mature rather early raises a question about revision in the school curriculum. It may be that arithmetic and geometrical thinking should be introduced earlier than they are at present in American schools.

Experiments are in progress to determine whether the children of different mental profiles have differential abilities in learning to read. If this should be the case, then the problem will be investigated whether the method of teaching reading should be selected with reference to the mental profiles of the first grade children. It is conceivable that the teaching method which is best for one mental profile is not necessarily the best for a pupil with a different mental profile.

One of the important educational problems in the first few grades is that a certain proportion of children have difficulty in learning to read. In many cases this difficulty does not seem to be associated with low intelligence, but it seems to be more specific. Studies have been initiated in order to relate the mental profiles at the kindergarten age with subsequent performance in reading. There is a possibility that the methods of teaching reading should be readjusted to the mental profiles of the children. If it should be found that children of different mental profiles profit by different methods of teaching reading, then the same type of problem can be raised at all subsequent ages. It may be specially important to adjust the teaching methods at the early ages to the mental profiles of the children.

The isolation of primary mental abilities has reopened in modern form the old controversies about the mental faculties and about formal discipline. It is natural to ask whether the primary abilities can be trained. Our answer to this question is in the affirmative. If two boys who differ in one of the primary abilities were given one hundred hours of drill in that ability, we should expect the gifted boy to profit more than his less gifted partner. Both of them would no doubt improve but their difference would probably be greater after practice than before. However, every child is entitled to an opportunity for training in his mental abilities and especially in those which constitute his best mental assets.

Experiments are under way with a one-year curriculum that has been prepared for the training of mental abilities of five- and six-year-old children. It consists of a new game each day, the games being designed so as to train young children in space and perception, verbal comprehension, and inductive reasoning. Young children of this age are better in reasoning than we ordinarily believe. Adults carry out most of their reasoning in the verbal medium, which is not well developed in young children.

One of the most frequently occurring questions is whether the primary mental abilities are inherited. It is our belief that the mental abilities are genetically determined and that the actual overt performance of an individual is also determined by his opportunities and motivational conditions. No amount of opportunity and encouragement will produce outstanding results if they are wasted on an individual of limited mental endowment. A study was recently made of 150 pairs of identical and fraternal twins who were given 40 psychological tests of different primary abilities. The identical pairs of twins were more similar in these tests than the fraternal pairs, which was the expected result.

There are interesting relations between the mental profiles of students and their professional interests. For example, students whose profiles are highest in the several verbal abilities are usually interested in some linguistic occupation, such as writing or journalism. Students whose profiles are highest in reasoning and in visualizing are usually interested in physical science or engineering. Sometimes a mental profile shows an outstanding ability which the subject has not been aware of. In advising students about occupational choice, the mental profile should be used with discretion. For example, it would be an unfortunate policy to send each person into that occupation for which his mental profile is the most typical. That would tend toward the maximum of mediocrity. Some students want to enter a field for which their profiles are unusual. Such a combination sometimes leads to outstanding achievement. On the other hand, if a student who is low in the visualizing functions wants to enter engineering or physical science, he should be warned that he will probably have trouble with certain subjects such as descriptive geometry and machine design.

There are hundreds of interesting case histories that show the relation between the mental profile and the ways in which a person tries to solve his personal and emotional problems. A study was recently made of the primary abilities of patients who had been admitted to a mental hospital. These patients were studied with reference to the relative dominance of the visualizing functions and the verbal functions. It was reported that these two groups of patients showed strikingly different symptoms. For example, none of the patients in whom the visualizing functions were dominant showed any hallucinations. This is a very challenging field for exploration with the primary abilities.

Mental profiles have been determined for over half a million high school children in Chicago, and it has been found that all possible combinations occur in the profiles. The records show many interesting case histories. A boy who was a poor reader was considered a dunce by his teachers. His mental profile showed that the highest score on space and reasoning was his and that he had high scores in all other factors except the verbal factor, "V." His teachers changed their attitudes when they saw that his handicap was quite specific. An amusing case was a girl who talked herself out of a number of situations involving truancy and misbehavior by fantastic but plausible stories. When her lies were eventually discovered, it was also found that her mental profile was very low in all factors except one, namely, verbal fluency. If the profile had been seen earlier, her teachers would have been warned about the possibilities of such a strange profile. It requires often considerable insight of the examiner to relate the mental profile to the circumstances of each case, but there is no question that the profile is more helpful than the IQ in the interpretation of educational and behavior problems.

Multiple factor experiments have been carried out for the United States Navy to isolate the primary mental abilities in the complex that is known as "mechanical aptitude." There is a rather common misconception according to which mechanical aptitude is assumed to consist of dexterity in the finger tips, combined perhaps with a willingness to get one's hands dirty. Mechanical aptitude is mostly in the head. It is not a single factor but a group of primary factors of abilities. It is known that the space factor is one of the abilities in this complex.

Several primary abilities have been isolated in this field and they are now being studied for psychological interpretation. The educational misconceptions in this field are rather serious. There seems to be relatively little recognition of the fact that superior mental endowment does not always show verbal excellence. This is an important problem in the appraisal of mental endowment as a national asset, especially in a culture which is essentially defined by its science and technology.

It is our belief that artistic talent and musical talent are also in the nature of complexes of primary abilities that can be identified by multiple-factor experiments.

The central idea in this work is that the human intellect consists of a finite number of distinguishable functions which are called primary factors or abilities. It has been shown that these functions can be isolated by analyzing the differential performances of groups of human subjects in specially designed experimental tests. These experimental and analytical studies lead to the description of each individual in terms of a profile which represents his differential performance on the different primary factors. It seems self-evident that the description of each person in terms of a mental profile will be more useful than the attempt to compress each individuality into any single measure or index. We have barely started in a field of investigation that will enable the next generation to be more rational than we have been in planning the education of children and in selecting people for each kind of work. Even at the present time we can do much better in appraising the mental abilities than was possible ten years ago.

One of the recent and productive applications of the technique of factor analysis to the understanding of what intelligence is comes from the work of Guilford and his associates at the University of Southern California, who are engaged in studies on "high-level personnel." This research is largely an outgrowth of the well known Army Air Forces Psychology Research Program in World War II. Not only have these factor analytic studies brought organization into the interpretative field—resulting in what Guilford has elected to term "the structure of intellect"—but such studies have also indicated some real gaps in our knowledge and pointed up areas where new types of tests will need to be developed. Such research has shown that intelligence is a many-faceted thing, something far more complex than the earlier Spearman formulation of "g" and "s."

Professor Guilford has published a series of articles dealing with the structure of intellect, all too detailed for presentation here. The following brief report of this work appeared as one section of a larger chapter devoted to tests of intellectual and special aptitudes, which appeared in the Review of Educational Research, *1959, Vol. 29, pp. 26–30.*

The Structure of Intellect

J. P. Guilford

The conception of fundamental differential aptitudes and the basic research aimed at their discovery were not taken seriously until Thurstone proposed his theory of multiple factors and carried out the first comprehensive factor-analytic study from this point of view, a little more than two decades ago. Since that time there has been substantial development along this line in the further work of Thurstone and his associates and in the Air Force wartime research on classification tests. By the end of the war, about 25 primary mental abilities (not all of them in the general intellectual area) had been found by Thurstone's methods of analysis. Many of them were demonstrated to have some importance in the selection and classification of aircraft pilots, navigators, bombardiers, and other aircrew personnel.

Since the war, the highest concentration of research along the same lines has been in connection with the project on "Aptitudes of High-Level Personnel" at the University of Southern California. In this project, the prevailing technique has represented a wedding of factor analysis with experimental method. The kinds of tasks or tests have been varied systematically, both qualitatively and quantitatively, according to hypotheses generated concerning the existence of certain primary intellectual abilities and concerning their properties. The batteries of tests have been administered to military personnel who were entering upon courses of training that in most cases led to the status of commissioned officers. The intellectual abilities under investigation were included under the heuristic categories of reasoning, creative thinking, evaluation, planning, and problem solving. Since the initiation of the project in 1949, a dozen major factor-analytic studies have been carried out.

One of the obvious consequences of these studies is the continued indication that human intellect is a very complex phenomenon. The possibility that there is a unitary trait of intelligence, at least at adult levels, grows more remote. This is not a necessary consequence of the use of multiple-factor analysis. The results of an analysis are determined by the intercorrelations of the test scores. When tests are varied sufficiently in kind, zero correlations are numerous. The strongest logical support for the belief in a general intellectual factor has been the assertion that tests of intellectual abilities universally intercorrelate positively. This assertion is definitely not consistent with the facts.

Another consequence has been the discovery and verification of primary abilities in new areas such as creative thinking and planning. This is partly attributable to the use of new varieties of tests, but especially to a willingness to utilize tests of the completion or open-end type, tests that even require some subjective judgment in scoring. It does not seem to be possible to measure some of the more obviously creative talents by means of multiple-choice tests or other types of tests in which responses are not produced by the examinee but are presented to him. One implication of this is that an overwhelming emphasis upon completely objective testing could have serious educational consequences. Achievement tests, particularly, embody educational objectives and implement an educational philosophy, expressed or unexpressed.

Perhaps the most significant consequences have been the implications of the intellectual factors (a) for the assessment of individuals, (b) for the education of children and youth, and (c) for an understanding of intellect itself. Since the first two of these follow from the third, the picture of the nature of intellect that grows out of the studies will be presented briefly. From this picture, other implications may be readily deduced.

With the growing numbers of primary abilities discovered, it became increasingly important to attempt to find some unifying principles that would make possible an easier comprehension of the total list. Attempts to classify the factors have proved to be moderately successful, and in the process some significant principles of organization have emerged. This would not have been possible without the available knowledge of a sufficient number and variety of factors. The result of these attempts has been called a "structure of intellect." Although the organization of intellectual factors in a unified system, like most general theories, will probably undergo many changes as new information accumulates, in its present form it has proven very helpful in guiding further factorial research, and it seems to offer concepts that will be useful to the experimental psychologist as well as to the educator.

The first and most obvious principle regarding the structure of intellect is that primary abilities differ according to the kind of material or content dealt with by the individual. For a long time we have had the recognition of a distinction between verbal and nonverbal tests. There proved to be verbal and nonverbal factors of intellect. But the nonverbal category subdivides into two classes of abilities. There are abilities to deal with "figural" material (concrete, perceived forms, and properties) on the one hand, and abilities to deal with "symbolic" material (composed of letters, numbers, and the like) on the other. In the verbal category are abilities for dealing with concepts or meanings; hence, the third class of factors has been called "semantic." There are parallel abilities for dealing with the three kinds of content—figural, symbolic, and semantic.

Within each of the three categories as to content, factors differ with respect to the kinds of operations performed on the material. There are basically five kinds of operations as indicated by five kinds of factors. One operation is that of cognition, which simply has to do with knowing information. We discover or recognize perceived objects and their properties, we discover or recognize symbolic units, such as words and other expressions, and we discover or recognize meanings. A second kind of operation is that of memory or retention. An individual's memory is not equally good for all kinds of material or all kinds of information.

The third and fourth kinds of operations have to do with productive thinking. Productive thinking is involved when from given information some other information is generated. But it makes a difference whether the conclusion or other outcome is a unique one that is essentially determined by the information given or whether the generated information can be varied or must be varied, alternative outcomes being not only possible but also sometimes demanded. The former pertains to convergent thinking—thinking that converges upon the unique consequence. The latter pertains to divergent thinking—thinking that goes searching, changes route, and yields multiple answers. It is in the divergent-thinking category that we find the abilities most clearly associated with creative performance—fluency of thinking, flexibility of thinking, and originality.

The fifth kind of operation is evaluation. We are perpetually checking and rechecking our information, our memories, and our productions, convergent or divergent. In this connection we make use of feedback information that helps us to arrive at decisions as to the correctness, goodness, appropriateness, or suitability of our cognitions, memories, and conclusions. There is a set of evaluative abilities parallel to the productive-thinking abilities, memory abilities, and cognitive abilities.

The third major principle of classification of the primary intellectual abilities is in terms of the kinds of products achieved by the different kinds of operations applied to the different kinds of contents. We are not certain, as yet, that the same list of kinds of products applied in the case of every kind of operation and every kind of content, but enough is known to suggest that this may be so.

Six kinds of products have been recognized, and each kind results from the various kinds of operations. The kinds of products are units of information, classes of units, relations between units, patterns or systems of information, transformations, and implications. A few examples will show how operations, contents, and products combine in connection with factors. We cognize units of information in figural form. We remember related (associated) units of information in semantic form (ideas). A flexible thinker readily transforms information that comes to him in symbolic form, which suggests that he might be indulging in mathematical thinking to produce or to arrive at new information.

A COMPREHENSIVE THEORY OF INTELLECT

With three kinds of content, five kinds of operations, and six kinds of products involved in intellectual performances, there should be 3 x 5 x 6, or 90, primary intellectual abilities. About 50 of the primary intellectual abilities are now known through factorial investigations. It might thus seem that more than half of the possible intellectual factors are known, but there are other considerations that suggest that more than 90 potential factors exist.

There is much empirical evidence of a nonfactorial nature concerning an area of intellect that is sometimes called "social intelligence" and more often recently called "empathy" or "empathic ability." As commonly conceived and investigated, this area of abilities pertains to the cognition of the thoughts, feelings, and attitudes of perceived individuals. If we think by analogy to what is known about recognized intellectual abilities, we may suppose that in the area of empathy we are dealing with a fourth kind of content, namely, a kind of material that may be designated as "behavioral."

Carrying the analogy further, we may hypothesize that the abilities for dealing with behavioral content are parallel to those already known (or predicted) in connection with the other kinds of content. The same operations theoretically apply, so that besides abilities to cognize the behavior of others we have separate abilities for remembering behavior, for doing productive thinking about it, convergent and divergent, and for evaluating our cognitions and conclusions about it. Products of behavioral intellectual operations would be expected to fall in the same six categories—units, classes, relations, systems, transformations, and implications.

With the category of behavioral intelligence added, the comprehensive theory of human intellect, which has been elaborated in sketchy form, can be illustrated by means of a geometric model as in Figure 1. The three principles of classification of the primary abilities are represented by the three dimensions of the cubical model. The order of the categories in each dimension is logical but not firmly fixed, since we lack the criteria for establishing unique orders. There is little doubt that some of the intellectual factors have common linkages within individuals and would, therefore, exhibit some positive intercorrelations in populations. A reasonable, general prediction would be that correlations between factors are in direct proportion to proximity within the system when the orders of the categories are properly arranged.

Besides providing the basic variables along which individuals should be evaluated for various purposes, the structure of intellect suggests certain general implications for education. It may become popular, once again, to speak of education as development of the mind or of intellect. Knowing the intellectual abilities in all their variety and knowing their properties, we are in a much better position to suggest the course content and the procedures of instruction that should promote their improvement to the extent that they can be improved. In terms of learning

FIGURE 1
THEORETICAL MODEL FOR THE COMPLETE STRUCTURE OF INTELLECT

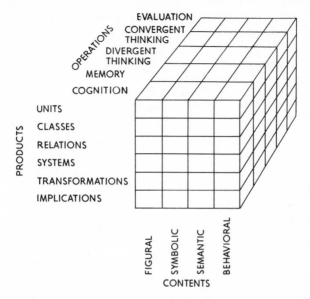

theory, the implication definitely favors a cognitive bias in preference to the present stimulus-response bias. According to the cognitive view, the organism is an agent that discovers information, remembers information and uses information in productive thinking and in evaluating any of its intellectual products. Such a view should have its consequences in the modification of philosophy of education, with potentially far-reaching effects.

*   *   *   *   *

The above is a very brief abstract of the entire theoretical structure, generated by factor-analytic methods. The interested reader should consult the earlier and more detailed presentation of the theory (Guilford, 1956). At the time of writing, the latest revision of the model is that presented by Guilford and Merrifield (1960). The Psychological Laboratory at the University of Southern California continues to issue bulletins which elaborate and fill-in certain gaps in the model. A very recent publication (Gershon, Guilford & Merrifield, 1963) from this laboratory shows that the model continues to lead to undiscovered, differentiable intellectual abilities.

PART SEVEN

VALIDITY

The General Aptitude Test Battery (GATB), the product of years of research by the U.S. Employment Service, is possibly the most successful of the various multi-aptitude test batteries currently in use. Its origins go back to the work of the Minnesota Employment Stabilization Research Institute during the depression years (Dvorak, 1935). Extensive validity data, both concurrent and predictive, are available, and this research is a continuing process. For general description of these tests, consult Dvorak (1956). Research with these tests is especially significant since aptitude patterns have been developed, which has resulted in a psychological classification of occupation groups into "families." Recently the test norms have been extended downward to ninth grade groups (U.S. Dept. Labor, 1959) so that now this battery covers a very wide range of talent.

Dr. Dvorak is Chief of the Testing Division, U.S. Employment Service, Department of Labor, and it is she who has largely been responsible for the general direction of GATB research. The following material has been abstracted and condensed from Section III of the GATB Manual (U.S. Dept. of Labor, 1958). This manual, together with that of the Differential Aptitude Test Battery, is a model of completeness, especially in regard to the presentation of extensive validity data.

Development of Occupational Norms

Beatrice J. Dvorak

The basic assumption underlying the GATB is that a large variety of tests can be reduced to several factors, and that a large variety of occupations can also be clustered into groups according to similarities in the abilities required. It is assumed that occupations differ from each other in varying degrees and that occupations can be grouped into families on the basis of similarities in the abilities required. One of the major efforts of this research has been to show that these are differential ability patterns among workers in various types of occupations, and that these patterns have validity. The GATB may then be accurately described as a "multipotential" test battery.

Since the GATB has been designed for use primarily in everyday employment situations, the emphasis has been placed on empirical and predictive validity (although other types of validity have not been ignored). The GATB is the only multi-aptitude test battery currently available which is based on such extensive "working population" norms. For this reason, the GATB treatment of validity is all-important. The discussion of validity has, therefore, a thoroughly realistic base in the world of occupations.

Since a suitable criterion is essential to the successful conduct of a test development study, the determination of the availability of the needed criterion, or measure of job performance, is made early in the process. It is important here that the criterion be a measure of an important phase of the job which involves the essential job performance abilities, rather than a measure of general job success. For example, although factors such as cooperativeness, dependability and diligence are important determinants of general job success, these factors are not measured by aptitude tests and should not be reflected in a criterion to be used for test development purposes. A suitable criterion for aptitude test development purposes should be a reliable and valid measure of each worker's job proficiency with respect to quantity and quality of production; it should be a good measure of the performance that we wish to predict with the aptitude tests.

Types of Criteria. In broad terms, criteria can be classified into two main categories: objective and subjective. An objective criterion is a quantitative measure of quantity and/or quality of production. "Production records" is a general term used to denote a variety of objective criteria. The actual records may be expressed as "units produced," "percent of production standard achieved," "piece-rate earnings," or some other comparable measure to reflect quantity of production; or they may be expressed in terms of the number of errors made or the number of items rejected to reflect quality of production. Sometimes the two types of records may be combined statistically to obtain a single measure of both the quality and quantity of production for each worker. In addition to production records, work samples, such as proficiency tests in typing and stenography, may be used as objective criteria. It is possible to obtain separate or combined measures of speed and accuracy with work-sample criteria.

Subjective criteria involve a judgment of performance, usually made by somebody who is in a good position to rate the performance of each individual in the sample, such as a foreman, supervisor, or instructor. The rating technique might involve one of a variety of procedures, such as broad category or group ratings, rank-order ratings, paired comparison ratings which yield a rank-order distribution, or the use of a descriptive rating scale. Regardless of the type of rating procedure employed, the objective is to place each individual in the experimental sample in the correct relative position with respect to his job performance ability.

School grades are also used as criteria for test development studies. These may be primarily objective, or to a large extent subjective, depending upon the grading system used in the school. For example, school grades would be considered as objective if the final grades for each course were based solely upon examination marks made by the students. However, school grades become relatively subjective when an instructor uses the examination marks as a guide and assigns final grades in accordance with his judgment of each student's total performance.

Even though traditionally it has been customary to classify criteria as either "objective" or "subjective," it should be borne in mind that there seldom is a clear-cut line between these two types of criteria. There often is an element of subjectivity in a criterion that is expressed in units which appear to be completely objective. For example, when records of the number of rejects are employed to evaluate the quality of workers' performance, the criterion appears to be completely objective. However, there must necessarily be subjective factors involved in setting the standards of acceptability for the items being produced, as well as in the evaluation of finished products in terms of the established standards to determine if they should be accepted or rejected. Similarly, there are subjective elements involved in criteria based on quantity of production. Subjective determinations are made of factors, such as the method of measuring quantity of production and the rate of production considered to be satisfactory.

At one time objective criteria were generally regarded as more dependable measures of job performance than subjective criteria. In the early years of the Employment Service test development program, attempts were made to use only objective criteria for test development purposes. However, objective criteria were just not available for many occupations, and for many jobs for which objective criteria were available, it was not possible to obtain comparable measures on samples of sufficient size for test development purposes. It was also found that objective criteria usually covered only one facet of job performance, such as quantity of production. These factors led to the employment of subjective criteria in test development studies. Experience has since shown that it is often advisable to obtain both objective and subjective criterion data for the same sample. Each criterion correlated separately with the test scores can contribute data for meaningful interpretation. In a test development study on the occupation of tile paster, a job in the production of ceramic products, both production records and supervisory ratings were obtained as criteria. The production records showed significant correlation with measures of manual dexterity and motor speed, whereas the supervisory ratings showed significant correlation with measures of form perception as well as with measures of manual dexterity and motor speed. Further study showed that the production records were based solely on quantity of production, whereas the supervisory ratings reflected both quantity and quality of production. The job analysis data indicated that although form perception was involved in quality of production it was not a determinant of quantity. In this instance the subjective criterion data not only served to substantiate the findings of the objective criterion, but also revealed a significant relationship between job performance and measures of form perception that could not have been made evident through use of the objective criterion alone. On the basis of experiences similar to the one cited immediately above, it is believed that we should not generalize with respect to the superiority of one type of criterion over another. Both objective and subjective criteria have their specific uses. When both types of criterion data are available, the choice to lean more heavily on either one or to make equal use of both for purposes of test validation must necessarily vary in accordance with the pertinent factors to be considered in each specific situation.

Quality of Criterion.   The success or failure of a test development study can be determined by the quality of the criterion that is obtained. Therefore, it is of extreme importance to evaluate the criterion data in every way possible. As already stated, it is important that the criterion employed for a test development study be primarily a measure of each worker's job proficiency and that other determinants of general job success, such as cooperativeness and dependability, be excluded from this criterion. Data should be collected which enable a statistical evaluation of the reliability and validity of the criterion. The reliability of a criterion can be measured by obtaining two or more sets of criterion data covering different periods of time and correlating them, or by correlating the ratings on the same people made by different supervisors or foremen.

The validity of the criterion is extremely difficult to measure and usually can be measured only indirectly. For example, we can determine the extent to which other factors than job performance might be influencing the criterion. Significant correlation between the criterion and variables such as experience, age, and education are sometimes indicative that the criterion is not a true measure of job performance. In some instances, it might be possible to apply a statistical correction to nullify the effects of these extraneous factors. Or this objective might be achieved by applying some type of experimental control, such as excluding from the sample those individuals at the extremes of the distribution of the variable that is unduly influencing the criterion. For example, if an analysis of the data has revealed that length of experience on the job has biased the job performance ratings assigned to workers, the experience factor can be held relatively constant by excluding from the sample those workers who have either extremely high or low amounts of experience relative to the other workers in the sample. Sometimes, however, no statistical correction or experimental control technique is applicable and we either have to discard the criterion, or use it with caution and interpret our results with reservations.

It should also be pointed out that in some instances, a criterion may be a valid measure of job performance even though it does exhibit significant correlation with variables such as age, experience, and education. It is difficult to determine when these correlations are indicative of spurious relationships which call for some correction to be made or for the data to be discarded, or when job performance really does have a true relationship to these other variables. Every effort should be made to obtain as much information as possible which might enable a meaningful interpretation of the obtained relationships. For example, in a particular experimental sample the workers who have been on the job longer may actually be the best performers or they may have been given the higher ratings only because the supervisor is better acquainted with them. Sometimes a thorough examination of the experience and criterion data may yield some meaningful clues. The observation that none or very few of the less experienced workers have been placed in the high part of the criterion distribution might be indicative that the ratings are unduly biased. If all workers in the sample have completed the training period, and there has been no significant change in the labor market or company hiring procedures between the time that the more and less experienced workers were hired, then it is unlikely that there would really be a marked preponderance of proficiency among the more experienced workers.

It is important to make certain that objective criterion data are comparable for all workers and are not influenced by working conditions rather than by each worker's job performance ability. Production records as a measure of proficiency are considered a good criterion if each worker has an equal opportunity to produce as many units as he can and production is measured uniformly for all workers. If because of the nature of the job, the flow of work is subject to fluctuations, or if a machine controls the speed of production, production records would not make a suitable criterion. Factors such as lighting, age of machines, availability of materials and additional duties performed by workers must be taken into consideration when the use of production records as a criterion is contemplated in order to insure comparability.

Treatment of Criterion Data. In order to make use of the criterion for purposes of statistical analysis, it is necessary for the data to be in a form which enables us to determine the relationships between the criterion and test performance. Usually objective criteria are expressed in units already forming continuous distributions which can be readily correlated with the test results. Sometimes, for the sake of convenience of computation, some conversion of the units might be desirable.

Subjective criterion data usually require conversion to form which enables correlation with the test results. For example, rank-order ratings, which place each individual in his correct relative position, space each person an equal distance from the next, which tends to indicate that the job performance of each individual in the sample varies by an equal amount from the next better and poorer workers. This, we know, is not the case, because job performance tends to be normally distributed. Therefore, before using rank-order ratings to compute product-moment correlations, we convert the ranks to linear scores, which are a better representation of the true differences in job performance between each worker and the next. Items on a descriptive rating scale are usually weighted and summed to obtain a numerical score for each person in the experimental sample. Broad category or group ratings, which might merely designate each worker in the sample as either above average, average, or below average, are converted to quantitative values on the basis of the normal distribution curve. These data can then be used to compute product-moment correlation coefficients corrected for broad categories. When ratings are expressed in two categories, such as satisfactory or unsatisfactory, biserial correlation coefficients can be computed.

Since norms on Employment Service test batteries are established for use with the multiple cutoff method, and scores are regarded as either "qualifying" or "nonqualifying," a technique which enables the correlation of a dichotomously expressed variable is employed to evaluate the norms. The criterion, regardless of its original units, is also dichotomized and tetrachoric correlation coefficients are computed. The question arises with respect to the point at which the criterion should be dichotomized, or where should the criterion cutting score be set?

When the criterion is to be dichotomized, it is desirable to find the "true" point of demarcation between the high and low criterion groups whenever possible. This point is not constant for all groups but varies from one study to another. Experience in conducting test development studies and consultation with foremen and supervisors have indicated that, in general, a valid division is obtained by placing approximately one-third of the experimental sample in the low criterion group and approximately two-thirds in the high criterion group. However, this does not mean that the criterion should always be dichotomized with approximately one-third of the sample placed in the low criterion group. To make the best determination of the division point, it is necessary to consult with the foremen, supervisors, or instructors who are familiar with the performance of everybody in the sample and who are in the best position to specify where the line of demarcation between satisfactory and marginal performance falls. It is often difficult for this determination to be made even by foremen or supervisors who are thoroughly familiar with the performance of everybody in the experimental sample. Greater difficulty in making this determination is experienced when there are no established quantitative standards available. On the other hand, if production records are available and it is known that production below a specified level is regarded as unsatisfactory by the company, then determining the criterion critical score is not a difficult matter; or if school grades are the criterion and it is known that the passing grade is at a certain point, there is not much difficulty.

It should be recognized that in some samples, where there has already been some restriction in the range of ability, there may not be a "true" unsatisfactory or low criterion group. This would be particularly true for groups of college seniors or samples of experienced workers which include only those individuals who have demonstrated satisfactory performance, and from which those people who have not performed satisfactorily have dropped out. For samples of this type, in which everybody exhibits satisfactory performance, even though some people are better than others, it is necessary to establish high and low criterion groups on a relative basis by setting a criterion critical score at some arbitrary point which divides the most proficient from the less proficient people in the sample.

Experimental Battery. After a suitable and reliable criterion has been obtained, the next step is to select the experimental battery. When the United States Employment Service (USES) first began its test research program in 1935, about 15 suitable tests were selected for tryout in a particular study by inspecting the job analysis information to see what abilities might be involved, and by considering the results of previous studies of the same or a similar occupation. Over a period of time a large number of tests were constructed, and by a process of factor analysis, it was found that they grouped themselves into ten families or groups of tests. These were measuring ten significant vocational abilities. Fifteen tests were selected which provided a good measure of all 10 of these abilities. These constitute the first edition of the USES GATB, B–1001. From 1945 to 1952 this battery has been used as the standard experimental battery in every test development study that has been undertaken to develop occupational norms. However, in the fall of 1952 another edition of the GATB, the "Separate-Answer-Sheet Form," B–1002, was introduced to the State Employment Services for use also in operational activities and in test development studies. The entire General Aptitude Test Battery is usually administered to every experimental sample.

Experimental Sample. In the USES test development studies, the sample may consist of applicants, employees, trainees, apprentices, or students. The objective is to have the sample large enough to be truly representative of the population from which it is drawn, and to be chosen without bias in regard to the proficiency of the good, mediocre, and poor individuals comprising the sample. It is desirable to include in the experimental sample all the people in the occupation being studied who meet the requirements with respect to factors such as job duties performed, age, education, experience, criterion of job performance, and availability for testing. As the size of the sample increases, the dependability of the statistics computed on the basis of the sample increases.

When a sample of employed workers is tested for test development purposes, it is desirable for the final sample to include at least 50 workers, preferably more, who are all performing the same kind of work and who have survived the training period on the job. It is recognized that some plants may not have as many as 50 workers all performing the same job duties, or perhaps, the management cannot see its way clear to make all the workers on a particular job available for experimental testing, because this would interfere too much with the plant's production. In such instances the study is conducted on a sample of fewer than 50 but no less than 30 workers. Experience in conducting experimental studies has shown that after the data are collected, some workers are excluded because of the incompleteness or inadequacy of the data, or because they are not representative of the workers generally found in the occupation being studied. Thus to have at least 50 workers remaining in the final sample, it is sometimes necessary to include 70 or more workers in the sample initially selected for testing.

When a sample of students, trainees, or apprentices is tested for test-development purposes, the size of the experimental sample depends upon the objective of the study and the time when testing occurs. If the objective is to develop norms for a vocational course, such as machine shop or radio, or for a college or university area of specialization, it is desirable for the final sample to include at least 50 students. If the testing is done at the beginning of a course, it is desirable to include a much larger number of students, since some will drop out before the completion of the course.

When a sample of students, trainees, applicants, or apprentices is tested, the "longitudinal" experimental design is often used. A criticism frequently made by people interested in test research is that little, if any, follow-up work is done to evaluate the operational efficiency of test norms resulting from test development studies based on experimental samples of employed workers. It is generally conceded that ideally it would be preferable to establish occupational norms based on samples as similar as possible in respect to age, education, and experience to the group on which it is expected the test norms will be used; that such samples should be tested prior to hiring; and that such hiring should be done without regard to test results. However, in fact, it is not often possible to achieve this ideal in practice. Similarly, it is difficult to obtain follow-up data showing the predictive value of the established norms in terms of data which readily lend themselves to statistical interpretation. Notwithstanding these difficulties, the USES has obtained data from a number of studies using the longitudinal experimental design in the development of occupational norms. In this type of design the tests are administered to all applicants for a job rather than to those who are already employed in the job. This experimental design is particularly apropos when a new plant is being staffed and hence no workers are available for study. In this design the entire GATB is administered to all applicants that are referred to an employer, but the test scores are not used in making selections. Only regular interviewing methods are used. After the workers have been on the job a sufficient length of time to reach normal production, criterion data are obtained. Criterion data are also obtained on those individuals who did not complete the training period because of inability to perform the job duties satisfactorily. Studies of this type have the advantage of sampling a relatively wide range of ability with respect to both test and job performance. The longitudinal design has the advantage also of using test scores that have not been influenced by training.

The Employment Service makes it a point to utilize the longitudinal design for test development purposes whenever possible. However, all too often it is not feasible to use this type of experimental design because a waiting period which may vary from several weeks to several years is required before test norms can become available for operating purposes. In instances where test norms are required as soon as possible for a particular occupation, the concurrent validation experimental design must be used. The correlations obtained between test results and the criterion in studies of this type are regarded as measures of descriptive or concurrent validity. When studies which yield measures of descriptive or concurrent validity have been conducted, an effort is made to conduct check studies by using the longitudinal design in order to obtain correlations between test results and the criterion that can be regarded as measures of predictive validity.

Analysis of Data. After the tests have been administered to an experimental sample and the criterion data have been collected, the data are analyzed to determine the group of tests having maximum validity for the occupation. Various methods for analyzing such data have been used. In the early years of the test research program, when the USES was interested merely in developing one specific battery at a time, the Wherry-Doolittle Multiple Correlation Technique was used to arrive at the combination of tests with maximum validity for the occupation. When the use of the General Aptitude Test Battery was inaugurated, however, the methods of analyzing the data were changed somewhat because the objective became somewhat different. The USES is now interested not only in establishing test norms for a single occupation but also in relating a given set of occupational norms to the norm structure for groups of occupations, so that a single battery of tests can be scored for a large variety of occupations. This means an interest in occupational differentiation as well as in differentiating good from poor workers within an occupation. A shift was made to the multiple cutting-score method. All the aptitudes regarded as significant are considered for inclusion in the final test norms. The data are further analyzed to determine which combination of significant aptitudes and cutting scores will yield the best selective efficiency in terms of the criterion of the experimental sample.

Establishment of Test Norms.   Norms on Employment Service test batteries are established for use with the multiple cutoff method, and scores are regarded as either "qualifying" or "nonqualifying." A critical or minimum qualifying score is set on each aptitude included in the final battery for subsequent use in the selection of new workers or the counseling of applicants by means of the multiple hurdle method. In other words, an individual is considered qualified only if he meets the minimum score on *each* of the key aptitudes. There is no total weighted score to be obtained.

Since Employment Service test norms indicate whether an individual is "qualified" or "nonqualified," a technique which enable the correlation of a dichotomously expressed variable is employed to evaluate the norms. Therefore, the criterion is dichotomized and tetrachoric correlation coefficients are computed between trial set of norms and the criterion. The trial norms consist of various combinations of significant aptitudes and minimum scores; the combination which yields the best selective efficiency is established as the final norms or test battery for the specific occupation being studied.

Minimum scores on Employment Service test norms are set so that the proportion of the experimental sample in the nonqualifying test score group approximates the proportion in the low or unsatisfactory criterion group. This usually tends to maximize the tetrachoric correlation coefficient and results in the test norms qualifying the maximum number of satisfactory individuals and screening out the maximum number of unsatisfactory individuals. Of course, factors such as the composition of an experimental sample, labor market conditions, production requirements of a particular plant, caliber or supervisory personnel, training techniques and production methods are determinants of the proportion of a sample placed in the low criterion group as well as the proportion that it is expedient to screen out on the basis of test results. Since it has been found that these proportions frequently approximate one-third of the sample, setting the minimum score on each significant aptitude approximately one standard deviation unit below the mean obtained for the experimental sample usually screens out the desired number and results in good selective efficiency. The number of aptitudes included in the final norms also affects the points at which minimum scores are set, because as the number of aptitudes included in the norms is increased, it is usually necessary to lower the points at which minimum scores are set in order to screen out the desired proportion. In general, if the final test norms include only two aptitudes, minimum scores are usually set at 5-point score levels slightly higher than one standard deviation unit below the sample mean on each aptitude; if the norms include three aptitudes, minimum scores are usually set at 5-point score levels close to one sigma below the mean; and if the norms include four aptitudes, minimum scores are usually set at 5-point score levels slightly lower than one sigma below the mean. Minimum scores are set at 5-point score levels in order to avoid taking undue advantage of chance fluctuations, to effect greater comparability of the results of various studies, and to facilitate use of the norms for operating purposes.

We noted that often there seemed to be a relationship between test scores and job proficiency only to an optimum point. Since there was not a straight-line relationship throughout the entire range, the Wherry-Doolittle Multiple Correlation Technique did not yield that ability in the final norms. For example, finger dexterity might be a crucial ability for some jobs; without a minimum amount of it, persons would not be able to perform successfully on the job; but, beyond a certain point, additional increments of finger dexterity would not be associated with additional production on the job.

Even when a crucial ability does show a straight-line relationship between test scores and success, the method of multiple regression weights permits the possession of other abilities to compensate for a low amount of a crucial ability. In our experience, an employer is not satisfied with a worker who is awkward with his fingers in a certain job, even though he may have an unusually high amount of other abilities required by the job. Hence we use the multiple cutoff method which does not permit such compensation of some abilities for others required by the job.

Determination of Validity of Battery. The validity of the test battery composed of the key aptitudes and cutting scores is determined by means of a correlation coefficient showing the relationship between the norms and the criterion. Usually the tetrachoric correlation coefficient is used to indicate this relationship. In the USES studies, a tetrachoric correlation coefficient is not regarded as significant unless it is at least twice its standard error.

The following are two examples of test-development studies. That for mounter is an illustration of the concurrent validation experimental design in which the minimum qualifying scores eliminate approximately one-third of the experimental sample. The study for file clerk is an illustration of the longitudinal design in which the minimum qualifying scores eliminate approximately 30 per cent of the experimental sample.

Study of Mounter I (DOT code: 7–00.016): Assembles radio tube mounts and stems of cathode grids and plate by positioning and connecting very small and medium sized parts and wires either manually or with tweezers; spot welds parts in place. Experimental sample of 65 workers with criterion of piece-rate earnings. Statistical results: Table 3 shows that the aptitudes with high mean scores relative to the general population and to each other aptitude are spatial, form perception, aiming, and finger dexterity; the aptitudes with low standard deviation relative to the general population and to each other aptitude are numerical and aiming; aptitudes with correlations significant at the .01 level are finger dexterity and manual dexterity.

TABLE 3

STATISTICAL DATA FOR 65 MOUNTERS AND GATB SCORES

Aptitude	Mean	σ	r	σ_r
G — Intelligence	106.9	15.3	—.075	.123
V — Verbal Aptitude	102.2	14.7	—.061	.124
N — Numerical Aptitude	105.8	13.3	.064	.124
S — Spatial Aptitude	109.3	16.6	—.009	.124
P — Form Perception	111.8	15.6	.015	.124
Q — Clerical Perception	106.2	15.9	.097	.123
A — Aiming	107.1	13.9	.229	.118
T — Motor Speed	103.6	15.5	.191	.120
F — Finger Dexterity	109.5	18.4	.437	.100
M — Manual Dexterity	98.7	20.7	.353	.109

The job analysis data for this occupation showed that the aptitudes of form perception, aiming, finger dexterity, and manual dexterity appeared to warrant consideration for inclusion in the test norms. Considering this together with the statistical results, the aptitudes of form perception, aiming, finger dexterity, and manual dexterity were selected. The critical scores were set at 85, 85, 90, and 85, respectively.

To check on the effectiveness of these norms, analysis showed that 14 of the 26 poorer workers (54 per cent) failed to achieve the minimum scores established as cutting scores for these norms. Of the 42 workers who made qualifying test scores, 30 (71 per cent) proved to be good workers. This indicated that if the norms had been used for selection, 54 per cent of the poorer workers would not have been hired and 71 per cent of those hired would have been good workers. In statistical terms, this represents an r_{tet} of .49 with standard error of .20.

Study of File Clerk (1–17.02). Experimental sample here involved 50 workers, tested before they were hired, and who were selected without regard to test scores. Criterion: supervisory ratings (group ratings in fifths). Test results showed aptitudes with high mean scores relative to the general population and to each other aptitude were: *G, V, S, Q, A,* and *F* (see previous table for identification of these symbols). Aptitude with low standard deviations relative to the general population and to each other aptitude were *G, P,* and *Q.* Aptitudes with *r*'s at the .01 level are *G, V,* and *Q.* In the determination of occupational norms, the job analysis showed that *G, V, Q,* and *F* warranted consideration for inclusion in the test norms. Taking this into consideration, together with the other statistical results, *G* and *Q* were selected, and the critical scores were set at 100 and 95 respectively.

Regarding the effectiveness of these norms, one study showed that 12 of 17 poorer workers (71 per cent) failed to achieve these minimum standards. Of the 36 workers who made qualifying test scores, 31 (86 per cent) proved to be good workers. This indicated that, if test norms had been used for selection, 71 per cent of the poorer workers would not have been hired and 86 per cent of those hired would have been good workers. Statistically these data can be summarized by an r_{tet} of .90 with a standard error of .24.

Check Studies. The USES people are well aware of the necessity of cross-validation studies. It is always unwise to accept the results of any one study as "true" or "final." Whenever possible such studies are conducted, typically with good results. The interested reader may refer to the GATB Manual (U.S. Dept. of Labor, 1958, Sect. III).

The research literature is replete with careful studies where item analysis procedures have resulted in excellent measuring devices—but, as it turns out, only for the group on which the particular item analysis was done. Cross-validation here becomes all important. The following paper by Dr. Cureton is reprinted here not only because he makes a strong point, but also because of the humorous note in it all—something which is rather infrequent in professional psychological journals. Dr. Cureton is Chairman of the Department of Psychology at the University of Tennessee and has long been known for his work in test construction and test theory. The paper, reproduced in its entirety, originally appeared in Educational & Psychological Measurement, 1950, Vol. 10, pp. 94–96.

Validity, Reliability, and Baloney

Edward E. Cureton

It is a generally accepted principle that if a test has demonstrated validity for some given purpose, considerations of reliability are secondary. The statistical literature also informs us that a validity coefficient cannot exceed the square root of the reliability coefficient of either the predictor or the criterion. This paper describes the construction and validation of a new test which seems to call in question these accepted principles. Since the technique of validation is the crucial point, I shall discuss the validation procedures before describing the test in detail.

Briefly, the test uses a new type of projective technique which appears to reveal controllable variations in psychokinetic force as applied in certain particular situations. In the present study the criterion is college scholarship, as given by the usual grade-point average. The subjects were 29 senior and graduate students in a course in Psychological Measurements. These students took Forms Q and R of the Cooperative Vocabulary Test, Form R being administered about two weeks after Form Q. The correlation between grade-point average and the combined score on both forms of this test was .23. The reliability of the test, estimated by the Spearman-Brown formula from the correlation between the two forms, was .90.

The experimental form of the new test, which I have termed the "B-Projective Psychokinesis Test," or Test B, was also applied to the group. This experimental form contained 85 items, and there was a reaction to every item for every student. The items called for unequivocal "plus" or "minus" reactions, but in advance of data there is no way to tell which reaction to a given item may be valid for any particular purpose. In this respect, Test B is much like many well-known interest and personality inventories. Since there were no intermediate reactions, all scoring was based on the "plus" reactions alone.

I first obtained the mean grade-point average of all the students whose reaction to each item was "plus." Instead of using the usual technique of biserial correlation, however, I used an item-validity index based on the significance of the difference between the mean grade-point average of the whole group, and the mean grade-point average of those who gave the "plus" reaction to any particular item. This is a straightforward case of sampling from a finite universe. The mean and standard deviation of the grade-point averages of the entire group of 29 are the known parameters. The null hypothesis to be tested is the hypothesis that the subgroup giving the "plus" reaction to any item is a random sample from this population. The mean number giving the "plus" reaction to any item was 14.6. I therefore computed the standard error of the mean for independent samples of 14.6 drawn from a universe of 29, with replacement. If the mean grade-point average of those giving the "plus" reaction to any particular item was more than one standard error above the mean of the whole 69, the item was retained with a scoring weight of plus one. If it was more than one standard error below this general mean, the item was retained with a scoring weight of minus one.

By this procedure, nine positively weighted items and 15 negatively weighted items were obtained. A scoring key for all 24 selected items was prepared, and the "plus" reactions for the 29 students were scored with this key. The correlations between the 29 scores on the revised Test B and the grade-point averages was found to be .82. In comparison with the Vocabulary Test, which correlated only .23 with the same criterion, Test B appears to possess considerable promise as a predictor of college scholarship. However, the authors of many interest and personality tests, who have used essentially similar validation techniques, have warned us to interpret high validity coefficients with caution when they are derived from the same data used in making the item analysis.

The correlation between Test B and the Vocabulary Test was .31, which is .08 higher than the correlation between the Vocabulary Test and the grade-point averages. On the other hand, the reliability of Test B by the Kuder-Richardson Formula 20, was −.06. Hence it would appear that the accepted principles previously mentioned are called in question rather severely by the findings of this study. The difficulty may be explained, however, by a consideration of the structure of the B-Projective Psychokinesis Test.

The items of Test B consisted of 85 metal-rimmed labelling tags. Each tag bore an item number, from 1 to 85, on one side only. To derive a score for any given student, I first put the 85 tags in a cocktail shaker and shook them up thoroughly. Then I looked at the student's grade-point average. If it was B or above, I projected into the cocktail shaker a wish that the student should receive a high "plus" reaction score. If his grade-point average was below B, I projected a wish that he should receive a low score. Then I threw the tags on the table. To obtain the student's score, I counted as "plus" reactions all the tags which lit with the numbered side up. The derivation of the term "B-Projective Psychokinesis Test" should not be obvious.

The moral of this story, I think, is clear. When a validity coefficient is computed from the same data used in making an item analysis, this coefficient cannot be interpreted uncritically. And, contrary to many statements in the literature, it cannot be interpreted "with caution" either. There is one clear interpretation for all such validity coefficients. This interpretation is—

"BALONEY!"

The Cureton article was a humorous and hard-hitting statement of the necessity of cross-validation. Here, in the Kirkpatrick report, is an actual empirical demonstration in an industrial setting. This study is here included largely because of its demonstration of methodology. The author's main point is to show that, without "hold out" or cross-validation procedures, data which look very promising may in actual fact vanish into the limbo. For many years, psychological research in the measurement area did not take this essential and "next" step; currently, however, it is generally assumed that all new data of the type Kirkpatrick reports here be cross-validated.

The Jurgensen Classification Inventory, the personality measure with which this research was done, is itself of interest. The test is published with neither norms nor standardized scoring keys. It was developed primarily for industrial and business use. The absence of a standardized scoring key was deliberate, since this then forced each organization which employed the test to develop its own local norms.

At the time Dr. Kirkpatrick wrote this article, he was a staff member of the Psychological Services Center at Syracuse University. He is now Vice President and Director of the Industrial Division of Byron Harless & Kirkpatrick Associates, a management consulting firm in Tampa, Jacksonville, and Atlanta. The following article is a condensation of the original which appeared in the Journal of Applied Psychology, *1951, Vol. 35, pp. 413–417.*

Cross-Validation of a Forced-Choice

Personality Inventory

James J. Kirkpatrick

The need for a personality test designed specifically for personnel selection has long been recognized. There is general agreement that an individual's personality attributes are important determinants of his vocational or scholastic success. It is probable that the effectiveness of many of our selection programs could be considerably improved if we had a satisfactory technique for personality evaluation. Unfortunately, owing to the complex and intangible nature of personality itself, only modest progress has been made in the development of personality tests which are actually predictive of later performance. A personality test that could be validly used for personnel selection would be an invaluable contribution to many testing programs. It is the purpose of this paper to evaluate one attempt to devise such a test.

THE CLASSIFICATION INVENTORY

In 1944, Jurgensen reported on a personality test that he had developed which he called the Classification Inventory. In addition to being one of the few tests of personality designed primarily for personnel selection, it is rather unique in utilizing a modified forced-choice technique. The success of the forced-choice method in the related area of personnel rating indicates that this approach may be a partial answer to the difficulties which are inherent in the complex problem of personality assessment in the selection situation.

In order to avoid certain difficulties encountered when using the conventional personality test of the questionnaire type, Jurgensen set up the following commendable requirements for his Classification Inventory:

1. The applicant must not be able to predict the "right" answer in order to gain favorable consideration.

2. It should be possible to give an answer to the items. Responses should not be forced into a "yes" or "no" dichotomy, and there should be no ambiguous "?" category.

3. The test should be analyzed and validated on particular jobs rather than on traits, which lack precise meaning.

4. The validation sample should be comparable to the population for which the test is to be used eventually as a selection instrument.

The Classification Inventory Test, in its present 1947 edition, consists of 288 items, of which 216 are in triad form and 72 are in paired form. In each triad the examinee is required to select his first and his third choice, and in each pair he indicates his preference. Testing time is approximately 45 minutes, and the test is suitable for group administration.

As indicated in the last two requirements mentioned above, Jurgensen recommends selecting items on the basis of an item analysis and validating the test for specific jobs on representative samples. However, it is in this connection that Jurgensen's actual procedure leaves much to be desired. While he reports several validity coefficients ranging from .67 to .81, these values are based on two small samples, one consisting of 40 salesmen and the other composed of 30 graduate students. In addition, these validity coefficients were not obtained from holdout groups, since the subjects in the corresponding item analysis groups are the same 40 salesmen and 30 graduate students. Failure to cross-validate is a deficiency found all too frequently in the psychological literature.

OTHER VALIDITY STUDIES OF THE CLASSIFICATION INVENTORY

Subsequent research dealing with the Classification Inventory has yielded rather contradictory results. In an investigation of the test as a predictor of college achievement, Adams obtained validity coefficients ranging from −.01 to .06. The total number of students used in this study was 585. With an industrial sample of 176 subjects, Pred also obtained negative results in an investigation of the validity of the test in distinguishing between "good" and "poor" industrial supervisors. Both of these studies utilized cross-validation procedures. (Both of these studies are unpublished M.A. theses, Purdue University.)

More favorable conclusions regarding the Classification Inventory were reached by Knauft (1949) in an investigation designed to predict managerial success. Although he reports a correlation coefficient of .64 between test scores and a composite criterion of job success for 79 subjects, he warns that this value must be interpreted with considerable caution since 54 per cent of the sample on which this coefficient is based was used in the item analysis. However, Knauft did carry out a cross-validation study on 32 cases, obtaining a t ratio significant at the 5 per cent confidence level, based on the difference between the mean test scores for the 16 highest on the criterion and the 16 lowest.

THE PRESENT STUDY

This study is concerned with the validity of the Classification Inventory as a predictor of college achievement. In addition, an attempt is made to throw some light on the question of cross-validation.

The test was administered in group situations to 261 male students enrolled in introductory and advanced psychology courses at the University of Tennessee. The nature of the Classification Inventory was explained, and the subjects were informed as to their role in this experiment designed to evaluate the test. The subjects were encouraged to fill in the inventory as accurately as possible.

Rather than developing scoring keys on the basis of assumed personality traits, Jurgensen recommends the use of a criterion of job success, since, from an operational standpoint, the objective is to differentiate among persons exemplifying varying degrees of job proficiency. Therefore, in this study, the criterion of job success which seemed appropriate was grade point average, since this offers an objective index of success in an important aspect of student life.

For the purpose of developing scoring keys for the Classification Inventory, an item analysis was performed on a sample of 179 subjects selected randomly from the total group of 261 male students. The remaining 82 subjects were used in the validation of the test. Of the 179 subjects in the item analysis sample, the top 50 on the criterion were selected as the upper group, and the lowest 50 were selected for the lower group. Thus, the upper and lower groups each represented approximately 28 per cent of the total item analysis sample.

Jurgensen recommends selecting items which are found to discriminate between upper and lower groups at a level of significance of .10, assigning increasing weights for individual items in proportion to the significance with which they function. While such a differential weighting system is generally considered an unnecessary refinement, this procedure was followed for the first scoring key by assigning a weight of one to those items which, on the basis of the item analysis, discriminated at the .10 level of significance up to the .02 level, a weight of two for those items from .02 up to .002, and a weight of three for those items at .002 and above. Both positive and negative weights were used, a positive weight being assigned when the upper group was found to have the larger frequency of response to a given item, while a negative weight was assigned when this situation was reversed. This first key is termed the weighted key. A second scoring key was derived without differentially weighting the items, and this will be referred to as the unweighted key.

The validation sample was composed of the hold-out group of 82 male subjects. Their tests were scored by both of the keys derived from the item analysis. A constant of 100 was added to each score for the purpose of avoiding negative values. The relationship between test scores and the criterion of grade point average was then estimated by computing Pearson correlation coefficients. For the weighted key, a validity coefficient of .16 was obtained, while the unweighted key yielded a validity coefficient of .12. Neither of these correlation coefficients is significantly greater than zero at the 5 per cent level of confidence.

Therefore, the results of this validity study of the Classification Inventory are essentially negative. At least for the population for which this student sample is representative, the test has not been demonstrated to possess satisfactory validity as a predictor of scholastic achievement. However, it is possible that the test may be of value in some situations, while being invalid in others. In the study mentioned previously, Knauft does present some evidence for its validity, based on a holdout group of 32 cases.

A tentative explanation of the negative results obtained with the Classification Inventory as a predictor of academic standing is suggested by a consideration of the factors that go into grade point average. That intellectual factors are of much import is indicated by the relatively high relationship often found between intelligence test scores and college grades. On the other hand, the influence of personality factors on grades has not been clearly established. It may well be that the personality attributes measured by this test are relatively insignificant, as compared with intellectual factors, in accounting for the variance in college grades. To the extent that this is true, these personality trends tend to be obscured upon cross-validation. Therefore, the low validities found in this study do not indicate that the test may not be of value in other situations and in comparison with other types of criteria, nor is the value of item analysis questioned by these results. However, the evidence presented in this study points to the fact that if the validity of a test is not determined on a hold-out group, the results are likely to be misleading. Validity cannot be created by item analysis. However, the impression of validity may be created by failing to follow cross-validation procedures.

When hold-out groups are not used, validity coefficients will be spuriously high. Just how much error is involved is a moot question. A secondary purpose of the present study is to present empirical evidence to illustrate the extent to which the failure to cross-validate introduces error into a validation study. In line with this objective, the weighted key, which yielded a validity coefficient of .16 on the hold-out group, was used in scoring the tests for the 100 subjects in the upper and lower item analysis groups. In other words, scores were obtained on those individuals whose answer sheets were previously used for selecting and weighting items in the development of that scoring key. When these scores were correlated against the grade point average criterion, a tremendous increase in the validity coefficient resulted: i.e., from .16 to .76.

The aforementioned Pearson correlation coefficient of .76 may be somewhat questionable on the basis that it was computed on the 100 subjects in the two tails of the distribution, each of which included approximately 28 per cent of the sample. To investigate this possible source of error, a biserial r for widespread classes was computed. This value was found to be .70, which again emphasizes the amount of error introduced when cross-validation procedures are not employed. It is interesting to note that the regular product moment r and the biserial r are in close agreement, both being computed from the same data. The biserial r for widespread classes is probably the better estimate of the validity coefficient in this particular situation and will be referred to in the following comparison with the cross-validation coefficient.

Although the increase in the validity coefficient from .16 to .70 is large enough to be convincing, a test of the significance of the difference between these two r's was made. Using Fisher's z transformation, a critical ratio of 4.66 was obtained, leaving little doubt concerning the existence of a real difference.

Admittedly, it is often difficult to secure samples of sufficient size in the practical situation, particularly in the case of studies requiring both item analysis and validation. It is recognized that the size of the groups used in the present study is not all that might be desired. Katzell (1951) offers a possible solution to the dilemma confronting the psychologist who has available a sample of limited size upon which to determine the validity of a test that requires a preliminary item analysis. This suggested procedure involves the selection of two relatively small random samples, deriving two separate scoring keys, and performing a double cross-validation. Items for which the composite validities are significant are retained for the final key. This technique seems to be promising, for it apparently would extract the maximum information from a given set of data. Of course, it would be desirable to have a formula which would allow one to validate on the same sample used for the item analysis, and then step down the obtained validity coefficient to an estimate of its size had it been obtained on a hold-out group. A formula for this purpose unquestionably would be of great value to the psychologist, who often is unable to secure samples of adequate size. While such a formula may not be impossible to derive, it has not been derived so far. Until such a formula is developed, the recommendation to follow cross-validation procedures cannot be made too emphatic. It is not sufficient merely to comment that results obtained without cross-validation should be interpreted with caution; there is no legitimate interpretation of such correlations.

SUMMARY

This study was designed to investigate the validity of the Jurgensen Classification Inventory, a personality test designed for personnel selection as a predictor of academic achievement of college students. The test was administered to 261 male students. Using grade point average as the criterion of scholastic success, an item analysis was completed on 179 subjects selected at random from the total group. Two scoring keys were derived, and their validities determined on the hold-out group of 82 students by computing Pearson correlation coefficients between test scores and the criterion. For both scoring keys developed, validity coefficients were positive but lacked statistical significance. The higher correlation coefficient was found to be .16. As a result of this investigation, it may be concluded that for this population, the Classification Inventory has not been shown to be sufficiently valid to warrant its use as a selection device. The fallacy of failing to use a hold-out group for test validation was illustrated by computing a validity coefficient on the same subjects used in the item analysis group, with the result that the correlation coefficient jumped from .16 to .70.

Many people, especially those who do not work in the field of performance prediction, take a very naive view of criterion problems. Criteria are rarely "just lying around" and, instead, must be made the subject of very careful plans. The author of the following article indicates that it took the experience of the last war to show psychologists that inadequate criteria were often the cause of poor prediction. The article was originally written in response to an editor's invitation to Dr. Jenkins to comment on significant developments in psychology in World War II. Instead of trying to catalog the work of some 90 psychologists who worked in naval aviation, he elected to discuss the topic of validity to which so many members of this group made signal contributions. The article should also be read in conjunction with the Flanagan report on psychological research in AAF on aircrew selection (pp. 163–170). What follows is a condensation of Dr. Jenkins' original report which appeared in the Journal of Consulting Psychology, 1946, *Vol. 10, pp. 39–98.*

Validity for What?

John G. Jenkins

The events of World War I taught American psychologists the necessity of validation. The experiences of the next two decades taught them much about the technique of validation. It remained for World War II to drive home to psychologists at large the necessity of devoting much time and thought to the basis for validation.

The necessity of validating predictor batteries has so long been accepted in this country that our younger colleagues often express surprise on learning that validation was ever regarded as anything but mandatory. Yet a review of German test literature of the years 1920–1940 will show that the German tradition has been to spend much time on test construction and then to ignore the problem of checking to learn whether the predictors do in fact predict. Enough has been learned about testing in the Luftwaffe and in the Reichswehr to make us sure that face validity, rather than measured validity, was regarded as adequate by the Germans even in war time. By way of contrast, tests developed and published without validation have never had any considerable acceptance in the United States.

Having accepted the obligation to validate, American psychologists made great strides, during the years 1920–1940, in learning how to validate. The advanced graduate student of 1940 had at his fingertips a variety of techniques which were completely or partially unknown to the expert of 1947. Item analysis was a commonplace. Factor analysis was available to many. Correlational measures of various sorts were familiarly used in every quarter. Textbooks provided correctional formulae by which the most pedestrian student could take care of truncation of range, attenuation, and other shortcomings of the standardizing sample. Techniques for combining predictors in the interest of maximal predictive efficiency were available for everyday use. Given a criterion, the psychologist of 1940 was prepared to do a very accurate job of predicting it.

It required the events of World War II to show many psychologists that the phrase "given a criterion" lies at the source of much inadequate prediction. Prior to the war—if the publications in our journals are any indication—psychologists in general tended to accept the tacit assumption that criteria were either given of God or just to be found lying about. They had earlier appeared to believe that little time need be devoted to what they were trying to predict, provided only that enough time were spent on the accurate combination of predictor items, selected in the light of whatever criterion expediency might provide. These assumptions proved to be inadequate, when organized psychology launched itself upon the task of helping to select men for a war which the country appeared, for a considerable time, to be in serious danger of losing.

Any reader who feels that the above account is a caricature of the facts has only to turn to the published literature of 1920–1940. He will find many hundreds of articles dealing with the construction of predictors. When he comes to look for systematic treatments of the criterion-to-be-predicted, however, he will find the index strangely silent. During the 20 years immediately preceding World War II, the literature contains only a handful of titles dealing with the criterion and thoughtful enough to withstand critical scrutiny.

Psychologists working in naval aviation in World War II soon found that their criterion was not "given." Asked to help in forwarding to the combat areas as many "good" pilots as possible, they began to inspect and to discuss the whole problem of obtaining adequate criteria. By the end of the war, they had made certain advances in establishing criteria more nearly adequate to the demands of the sponsor. However, the greatest advance, in the opinion of the writer, was in the thinking and discussions about criteria which led this group toward the formulation of certain principles regarding the selection and development of criteria. This paper attempts to formulate briefly certain major outcomes of these discussions.

The basic postulate of adequate validational procedures may be stated as follows:

Satisfaction of the needs of the sponsor can be expected only if the criterion employed is both reliable and valid in terms of the task set by the sponsor.

Reliability and validity of predictors is an old familiar topic to all readers of this journal. Applying the concepts of reliability and validity to the criterion is believed to be novel enough to warrant the discussion given below.

A somewhat more detailed statement of the basic postulates may be given in this form:

I. Criteria may be inadequately reliable because of:
   A. Instability inherent in the criterion performance itself.
   B. Disagreement between allegedly competent judges on reviewing the same or successive samples of the same performance.
   C. Administrative procedures leading to the making of critical entries by clerical personnel who did not observe the performance or who were inadequate to judge it.
   D. Failure to secure a sufficient number of samples of performance or to observe the individual sample long enough to make a stable judgment.
II. Criteria may not be adequately valid to the task set by the sponsor because of:
   A. Failure of the criterion-measure to comprise a large and significant part of the total field performance desired.
   B. Failure of performance in training to forecast later field performance.
   C. Intercurrent changes in training-performance due to
      1. Advice given by the psychologist following his job-analysis or other observations.
      2. Administrative or other extrinsic pressures.
      3. Changes in the field performance itself.

These statements may be reviewed and illustrated in some detail. Most of the illustrative material will be drawn from naval aviation; much illustrative material could be presented from outside navy sources.

RELIABILITY OF CRITERION DATA

Instability Inherent in the Criterion Performance.   Various predictive efforts in World War II have failed because the very performance that was to be predicted has proved to be inherently unstable. Number of hits scored by an aircraft gunner on a towed sleeve is a criterion possessing a delightful degree of objectivity. All studies of this criterion known to the writer, however, find the individual scores so low in reliability as to be without value in placing individuals in any sort of continuum. Certain physiological measures encountered in naval aviation give high split-half reliabilities and very low test-retest reliabilities. Raymond Franzen, in comments made at professional meetings, has spoken of such measures as describing a biological instant in the life of an individual rather than the individual. It remains to be seen whether certain "personality" traits do not belong in this class. Certainly some of the research literature suggests a degree of inconsistency in these types of behavior which bodes ill for efficiency of prediction. It would not be surprising to find that here, as in the performances named above, we are dealing with criterion-reliabilities so low as to preclude the possibility of validities high enough for practical usefulness.

Disagreement between Judges.   Student pilots pass or fail in aviation training on the basis of judgments by instructors and/or check pilots. In one good-sized sample of navy cadets, it was found that immediately successive check-flights, given by two experienced instructors, yielded a reliability of grading of approximately .00. (Actually the coefficient of correlation was slightly negative!) It is apparent that successive gradings cannot be predicted at this level of reliability. Research in categories of aviation training outside the Navy is known to have given similar results. In this situation, one either accepts the word of some one instructor and uses this as a criterion, knowing that other instructors would not agree; or one attempts to work with instructors to obtain improved agreement.

Entries by Clerical Personnel.   Navy instructors were required to fill out a detailed form, giving critical comments on various phases of each flight completed by each student. In actual practice, it was found that certain instructors (who were conscientious in the actual instruction of their students) gave only a general grade, leaving the detailed grading to a clerk. The clerk, who had not seen the flight and could not have judged it acceptably if he had seen it, supplied the detailed grades in a fashion which gave an overall distribution of conventional form. Yet, here, the psychologist initially attempted to predict detailed entries in regard to coordination, judgment, observance of traffic rules, attitude toward flying, and the like. In view of the fact that the original entries were made as they were, one is tempted to describe them in terms of the concept of "Test-No-Test Reliability." The concept will be familiar to anyone who has reviewed thousands of physical examination forms only to find body temperature invariably set down as "98.6."

Inadequate Sample of Performance.   Early in the war, psychologists were invited to predict "failure" in the low-pressure chamber. They were confronted with the observable fact that certain men, when brought to simulated altitudes of 15,000 feet and above, either fainted or asked for discontinuance of the run. Research was to show that such "failure" was highly unreliable. To obtain a dependable sample of those who could not tolerate altitude—among the young subjects in question —it was necessary to make repeated runs. Ultimately one ended up with a population consisting of those who failed consistently in repeated runs. Unfortunately, from a statistical point of view at least, this proved to be a minute portion of the sample. There is real reason to believe that failure in flight training, if subjected to the same procedure, could be made to yield a final (and quite possibly minute) population of "real" failures. The fact remains that, while flight failure is stable enough to predict, no battery has yet been found which significantly predicts one-time "failure" in the low pressure chamber.

VALIDITY OF CRITERION DATA

Criterion Only Part of Field Performance.   Viteles tells the tale of how he set up a battery to predict the manual operations of a substation operator, only to find that the operator would be discharged if he failed to keep his station acceptably clean. The tale finds many parallels in the armed services. There is always the danger that the investigator may accept some convenient measure (especially if it be objective and quantifiable) only to find ultimately that the performance which produces this measure is merely a part, and perhaps an unimportant part, of the total field performance desired by the sponsor. For example, the skilled aspects of piloting can be objectively recorded. Pilots could be selected on the basis of such criteria. To make such a selection, however, would be to ignore the importance of judgment and of emotional adjustment in piloting. We might, in other words, pick pilots who would do the right thing at the wrong time and in a state of emotional collapse—a selection which the sponsor would soon indignantly reject. Experience shows that the researcher must devote much time and thought to determining that the performance he selects as a source of criterion data is an adequate representation of the total field performance desired by the sponsor.

Lack of Relation between Training and Field Performance.   Performance in training has been a common criterion, chiefly because of its availability. As far as this writer knows, it has been the primary criterion for the validation of pilot-selection tests the world over. Granted that pilots who fail training cannot ever get into combat, we have no assurance that those who do well in training will do well in combat. There is at least a theoretical possibility that there may be a negative relation between training-performance and combat-performance. For example, by selecting for ability to pass training, we may be selecting conformers and rejecting the less conventional males, who might be our best bets in lethal air-assignments. Procedures to obtain data on this question have long been under way. In the meantime it seems to be incumbent on all of us to determine empirically whether, by using outcome of training as a criterion, we may be depriving our sponsors of able field-performers. This would appear to be a problem in the industrial and professional fields as well as in military occupations. It may be added, parenthetically, that surveys of this nature inevitably raise interesting questions as to the validity of the training procedures themselves.

Intercurrent Changes in the Criterion. This may be regarded as involving either the validity of the criterion or its reliability, according to the definition given by the reader. It is here placed under validity simply because these changes imply that the performance that one predicts is inadequate to the task set by the sponsor as the sponsor currently conceives this task. Sometimes this comes about through the efforts of the psychologist himself. For example, the psychologists who were invited to work with the selection of aircraft gunners became convinced that the training was over-intellectualized. When appropriate changes were made at their suggestion, the intelligence test which had contributed heavily to the prediction of the earlier grades dropped to approximately zero predictive efficiency. At other times, administrative changes in the curriculum have been enough to upset the matrix of predictors. Flight training during the war proved to be particularly fluid, involving changes both in the items taught and in the method of appraisal. Such changes always held the threat that we might be predicting what the sponsor desired yesterday rather than what he desired today. Finally, as the nature of the war changed from defensive, through defensive-holding, to all-out offensive, there was real reason to believe that the qualities desirable in combat aviators were themselves subject to change. Adequately meeting the desires of the sponsor would imply that prediction was adjusted to meet the ultimate changes in the field situation. Some evidence, presented before the war, suggests that the same may hold true in industry as a given concern shifts over from a period of dynamic expansion to a period of conservative and steady operation.

The materials presented above, even in necessarily abbreviated form, may be enough to indicate increased sophistication in regard to that which psychologists are trying to predict. They may be enough to suggest that the psychologist who readily accepts any convenient measure is guilty of inadequate devotion to his technical responsibility. They should certainly be enough to demonstrate that validation is not a simple technical problem and that the criterion itself may provide the psychologist with as great a technical challenge as the procedures incident to the assembly of good predictors. There is much more to be written on the subject. If this brief paper serves as a stimulus adequate to bring out pertinent discussion from those who have encountered the basic problem in the armed services, in industry, and in education, it will have served its purpose.

All textbooks, both in the area of aptitude testing and in statistics, talk of the lowering of validity coefficients when the range of talent of the group tested is restricted. One of the most famous projects, wherein large efforts were made to secure a heterogeneous experimental sample—and despite the knowledge of the authorities that most members of the experimental group would fail—was the Army Air Force's Aviation Psychology Research Program, of which Dr. John C. Flanagan was the director. The usual procedure, where such an original heterogeneous group is not available, is to make some sort of statistical correction for the restricted range of talent being dealt with. In a research project not likely to be equaled anywhere else, the AAF chose the harder way. It should be remembered, however, that all the failures involved (about 75 per cent of the cases) were not eliminated from the AAF entirely, since these men could usually be shifted to many other useful AAF specialties and so were not "lost" to the service. But it is only with a huge and highly diversified organization, such as the AAF, where such personnel procedures can effectively work.

As one example of how the size of the validity index drops when it is computed on a restricted (qualified) group, take the instance of the Mechanical Principles Test, which is treated in the accompanying article. Here the biserial correlation for a small qualified group is a mere .18, whereas the corresponding statistic obtained from the total or more heterogeneous group is .44.

The AAF test battery was an extensive one, involving almost an entire day of paper-and-pencil tests followed by approximately two hours of apparatus testing. A final composite score on all of these tests, after determination of best weights, was then converted into a "pilot composite" or "stanine" score—another form of a standard score—with a stanine of nine as top and that of one as bottom. Similar stanine composite scores were also computed to predict success in navigator and bombardier training and, later, gunner. Thus the same test battery, but with different statistical weights for the individual tests, had multiple uses for the AAF.

The following article is an abstract, considerably reduced from the original report which appeared in Educational & Psychological Measurement, *1946, Vol. 6, pp. 445–466.*

The Experimental Evaluation of a

Selection Procedure

John C. Flanagan

A common problem for research workers concerned with the development and improvement of procedures for the selection and training of personnel is the adequate evaluation of procedures after they have been established. Educational institutions, business and industrial concerns, and government organizations, having once accepted certain procedures are generally opposed to suspending the use of these procedures for a large enough group to obtain an adequate evaluation of them. This makes it very difficult to refine and to further improve the procedures.

Because of the very large numbers of men involved and the great importance of the procedures for the selection of aircrew in the Army Air Forces, such an evaluation of these procedures appeared especially desirable. It was believed that a check on the value and inter-relation of both the initial screening procedures and the procedures for qualifying men for pilot training on the more comprehensive Aircrew Classification Tests should be made. This could be accomplished by examining a large enough sample of applicants with these tests and by sending all of the men tested into training, regardless of the test results. Accordingly, a memorandum was prepared entitled "Experimental Study of Eligibility Requirements for Aviation Cadets" by the present writer in his position as Chief of the Psychological Branch in May, 1943.

A variety of objections to this proposal were eventually overcome and, in June of 1943, the argument that the procedures were not perfect and that further improvement depended on this type of evaluation won out. The only restriction was to require the regular physical examination of all recruits; no one was to be rejected from this experimental group except for purely physical reasons. Some forty boards, representing all nine service commands, were authorized to recruit the personnel, and each Board was given a definite quota. Total N was set at 1,450 men.

RECRUITING THE GROUP

To insure that the personnel of the boards should understand the general plan and the specific procedures to be followed, an officer from the Psychological Branch, Research Division, Office of the Air Surgeon, was sent during the month of July to each of the boards which had been given a quota. At the time these men were being recruited, the normal procedure was to be sent to basic training centers for six weeks' basic training, then to college for approximately five months pre-aviation cadet college training, and after that, to preflight school for about two months. Following this the individual was sent to primary flying or to one of the other aircrew specialty schools.

Since it was desired that the results of this experiment should be available as quickly as possible, it was decided that the pre-aviation cadet college course would be omitted for these men. Accordingly, beginning about August 1, 1943, all applicants at the authorized boards were given a statement to sign. This statement said, "I wish to enter pilot training. If I am found qualified by the Examining Board, I agree (1) to enter pilot training after a shortened period of basic military training without first taking the pre-aviation cadet college training course, and (2) to volunteer for induction within ten (10) days following the day on which I am found qualified by the Examining Board." For enlisted men a similar blank form was provided, except that it had no reference to basic military training or to volunteering. The examiner also read a statement to the men, pointing out the advantages to them of becoming aviation cadets five months earlier, of having the opportunity to earn pilot ratings and of becoming officers that much sooner.

All applicants who signed the waiver were given the AAF Qualifying Examination, and regardless of their score on this test were given a physical examination and an interview by the board. If they were found physically qualified and had no criminal record, they were qualified by the board for aircrew training. Records on these specially-recruited men were sent directly to the War Department. In Washington special orders were written, sending a large group of them at one time to a basic-training center with special instructions for their disposition.

From the basic-training center they were sent to a classification center where the Aircrew Classification Tests were given them. If found physically qualified, they were sent into pilot preflight school, regardless of the scores made on the Aircrew Classification Tests. The orders assigning these men to classification centers indicated that they were members of the experimental group. Upon completing their classification processing, they were sent along with other aviation cadets to preflight schools with no designation as to which ones were members of the experimental group.

At the conclusion of this recruiting process, and after the physical examination and the psychological testing, plus inevitable losses and mistakes in such a large undertaking, a total of 1,143 men were assigned to pilot preflight schools. This constituted the primary sample on which the study was based.

DESCRIPTION OF THE SAMPLE

It is believed that the sample comprising the basic group for this experiment was thoroughly typical of applicants for aviation cadet training. The average was a little more than twenty-one years, with approximately 30 per cent of the group 18 and 19 years old. By far the largest age group was 19, and 10 per cent were more than 26. From the standpoint of education, 2 per cent were college graduates, an additional 16 per cent had had some college training, 58 per cent were high school graduates, and the remaining 25 per cent had not finished high school, including 1 per cent who had never attended high school.

Approximately half of them were recruited from the Army and half from civilian status. With regard to previous flying experience, nearly 5 per cent had flown solo and an additional 4 per cent had had previous instruction. About 58 per cent had been passengers in a plane but had received no instruction, and 33 per cent had never been passengers in a plane. In this group, 25 per cent were married, 74 per cent single, and 1 per cent widowed, divorced, or separated.

Their average score on the Army General Classification test was 113.0, with a standard deviation for the group of 13.8. Approximately 10 per cent of the group achieved Army General Classification Test scores above 130, which placed them in Category 1, and approximately 10 per cent obtained scores below 95.

In this original group, 58 per cent obtained scores which would have normally passed them on the AAF Qualifying Examination, and 42 per cent made scores which would have caused their rejection. The average score was a few points higher than the passing mark, and the standard deviation was approximately that which had previously been found for unselected applicants.

It is clear from their educational background, their Army General Classification Test scores, and their scores on the AAF Qualifying Examination, that this group does not represent a random sample of men of Army age. Rather, it represents approximately the usual amount of self-selection which can be expected in a group of applicants who have chosen to compete for a highly desirable job for which the requirements are relatively high, both in terms of the examinations at the time of entrance and of the standards for retention in and graduation from the training schools.

THE RESULTS

Of the 1,143 men who were assigned to pilot preflight schools, 582 were eliminated in primary flying training schools, 83 were eliminated in basic training schools, and 24 eliminated in advanced flying schools. The remaining 265 graduated from advanced flying training and were rated as pilots. Of the 878 men eliminated, 99 were eliminated for academic deficiencies in preflight school, 591 were eliminated for flying deficiency at one of the three phases of flying training, and 65 were eliminated at their own request or because of their fear of flying. The remaining 122 men were eliminated for administrative reasons, including physical disqualification. Approximately half of these were eliminated during preflight school.

Thus in this group of applicants who were allowed to enter pilot

FIGURE 2
EXPERIMENTAL GROUP
VALUE OF AUGMENTED PILOT STANINE FOR PREDICTING
GRADUATION OR ELIMINATION FOR ALL REASONS FROM
PILOT TRAINING-PREFLIGHT THROUGH ADVANCED

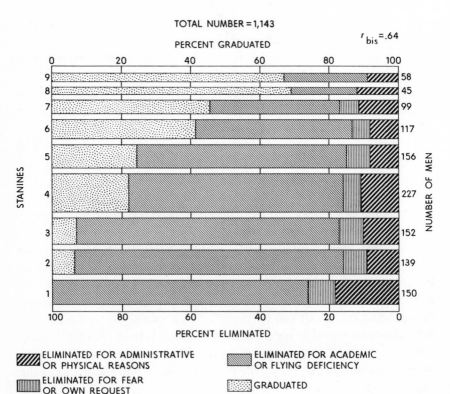

TOTAL NUMBER = 1,143

PERCENT GRADUATED

$r_{bis} = .64$

ELIMINATED FOR ADMINISTRATIVE OR PHYSICAL REASONS

ELIMINATED FOR FEAR OR OWN REQUEST

ELIMINATED FOR ACADEMIC OR FLYING DEFICIENCY

GRADUATED

training without any screening for aptitudes, interests, or ability, only 23 per cent were successful in completing the course of pilot training and becoming rated pilots. The question which the experiment was designed to answer was, "How well did the initial screening test results, the various classification test scores, and the pilot stanine predict which one of this group would succeed?"

Figure 2 shows the success of the pilot stanine in predicting which of these applicants would be successful. Very few of the 8's and 9's were eliminated in the training schools, and of those that were, many were eliminated for physical or administrative reasons which the tests were not designed to predict. Nearly half of the 7's were successful in completing training, but only a quarter of the 4's and 5's and only

FIGURE 3
VALUE OF PILOT STANINE FOR PREDICTING GRADUATION OR ELIMINATION
FOR FLYING DEFICIENCY, FEAR OR OWN REQUEST FROM FLYING TRAINING,
PRIMARY THROUGH ADVANCED, EXCLUDING CASES WITH CREDIT FOR
PREVIOUS FLYING EXPERIENCE

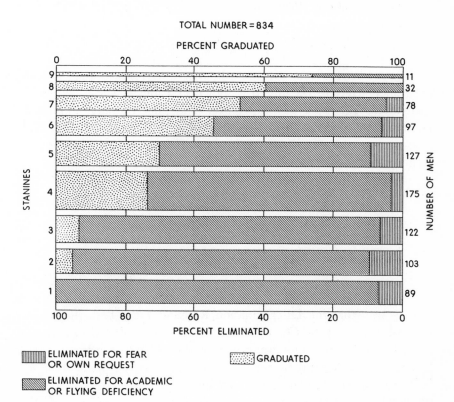

TOTAL NUMBER = 834

PERCENT GRADUATED

ELIMINATED FOR FEAR
OR OWN REQUEST

ELIMINATED FOR ACADEMIC
OR FLYING DEFICIENCY

GRADUATED

a very small percentage of the 2's and 3's. None of the 1's were successful in completing pilot training.

Figure 3 presents a similar study. It includes only those cases with no previous flying experience (no pilot credit) who graduated from preflight school and entered elementary flying schools. It also excludes from consideration men who were eliminated for any reason other than flying deficiency or fear of flying. This chart also indicates the marked success of the pilot stanine in predicting which men would graduate from flying training.

When one evaluates the validity of the individual tests, it is of interest to note that the two best tests, by quite a large margin, were the General Information Test and the Instrument Comprehension Test II (biserial r, respectively, of .50 and .48 against a pass-fail criterion). These two printed tests were also found to be superior to any of the apparatus tests in predictive value. Both of these tests represented novel ideas developed within the Aviation Psychology Program. The other printed tests also showed substantial predictive validity: Mechanical Principles ($r_{bis} = .43$) and Spatial Orientation Test II (.40).

THE SPATIAL ORIENTATION TESTS

The predictive value of the six apparatus tests at the time the experimental group was tested is shown in Table 4. These are biserial correlations against a pass-fail criterion in pilot training. Elmination from the group was for flying deficiency, fear or at the individual cadet's own request; the time span involves pre-flight through advanced pilot training.

TABLE 4
PREDICTIVE VALUE OF APPARATUS TESTS FOR SUCCESS IN PILOT TRAINING

Discrimination Reaction Time	.42
Rudder Control	.40
Complex Coordination	.41
Two-Hand Coordination	.36
Rotary Pursuit	.31
Finger Dexterity	.18

It is seen that the Discrimination Reaction Time Test, the Rudder Control Test, and the Complex Coordination Test all have substantial predictive value for pilot training. The Two-Hand Coordination Test had somewhat less predictive value and the Rotary Pursuit Test still less for this sample. The Finger Dexterity Test was not weighted for prediction of success in pilot training (but it did help in the prediction of success in other AAF specialties such as navigator, and so was retained in the battery).

A number of statistical studies were made to evaluate the effectiveness of this test battery. Intercorrelations among all variables were computed and best weights for individual tests were studied. In calculating these coefficients, men eliminated for physical and administrative reasons were excluded from consideration. The two categories consisted of 262 men who graduated from advanced training and 755 who were eliminated in preflight, primary, basic or advanced schools because of academic failure, flying deficiency, or fear of flying. The results of these analyses are reproduced in Table 5.

TABLE 5

PREDICTIVE VALUE OF VARIOUS COMBINATIONS OF TESTS FOR
SUCCESS IN PILOT TRAINING AS DETERMINED FROM AN
EXPERIMENTAL GROUP OF 1017 MEN

Combination of Predictions Used	Correlation Coefficient with Pilot Training Graduates—Eliminees (academic and flying deficiency and fear of flying)
Pilot stanine	.660
Best-weighted combination of aircrew classification tests for this sample	.690
Best-weighted combination of printed tests in aircrew classification battery for this sample	.641
Best-weighted combination of apparatus tests in aircrew classification battery for this sample	.578

As it is indicated in the table, it is also possible to predict success in pilot training with printed tests alone with an accuracy only moderately diminished, a correlation efficiency .05 smaller, than with the complete battery. Using the apparatus tests alone, the corresponding reduction in the coefficient is .11.

A type of problem frequently encountered in selection research is the question of the effect of selection on the basis of one variable on the predictive value found for a second set of scores. To make an empirical check on this, biserial correlation coefficients were computed excluding all of those individuals who would have normally been rejected on the basis of the AAF Qualifying Examination score. The correlation coefficients obtained for this group of 540 men were compared with those obtained for the uncurtailed group of 1036 in predicting success in preflight and primary training schools. It was found that the average coefficient was approximately .05 lower in the restricted group. The validity of the pilot stanine was also .05 lower in this curtailed group.

A special study was made of the aircraft accident records of this group. Of the total group of about a thousand men, twenty had aircraft accidents in training planes in the AAF Training Command. There were five accidents that involved pilots with pilot stanines of 7, 8, or 9. These higher stanine groups produced approximately a hundred of the graduates from pilot training. The lower stanine groups, which produced 150 graduates, had a total of 15 accidents.

Four of the accidents were fatal, and these all involved individuals in the lower stanine groups. For the four men involved in fatal accidents, the stanines for bombardier, navigator, and pilot training were, in that order, 324, 636, 445, and 996. The first three were all violating flying regulations at the time of the accidents. The fourth individual overshot his turn from baseleg to final approach in lining up with the runway. In trying to bring the plane back, he stalled out and went into a half-snap. The instructor then took over but the plane hit on the left wing and cartwheeled.

IMPLICATIONS

This study of 1,000 applicants and their success in pilot training in relation to their scores on the selection and classification tests has clearly demonstrated the effectiveness of these procedures when applied to groups of men recruited from civilian life or from the Army. Of 405 men who failed on the AAF Qualifying Examination and were subsequently sent into pilot training, only 12 achieved pilot stanines of 7, 8, or 9, and only four of these and 41 others of the more than 500 men who failed the Qualifying Examination were graduated from pilot training.

The value of the second screening by the Aircrew Classification Tests was dramatically demonstrated by the graduation of only 16 men out of 442 with pilot stanines of 1, 2, and 3 sent into preflight training. At the same time, 113 men graduated of the 199 with pilot stanines of 7, 8, and 9 sent into preflight training.

The correlation coefficient of .66 obtained between pilot stanine and success in pilot training compares favorably with the best predictions which have been obtained in educational and industrial work. It now appears that further improvement of instructional techniques and procedures for passing and failing students needs to be made before a substantial amount of further refinement in the selection and classification procedures can be expected.

In the preceding paper by Dr. Flanagan concerning AAF aptitude test batteries for Air Force technical occupations, the author noted that attention should probably be given to instructors and their ratings of pass and fail—that possibly predictions might be increased still more if training were given in the assignment of grades. The following report analyzes one aspect of this situation with pilot instructors.

Dr. Krumboltz served with the AAF as research psychologist in 1955–57 and is now Associate Professor of Education and Psychology at Stanford University. Dr. Christal is Supervisor of Aircrew Selection and Classification at the Air Force Personnel & Training Research Center. This study was conducted at the Lackland Air Force Base in Texas under ARDC Project No. 7719, Task No. 17009. What is reproduced here is a condensation of an article which appeared in the Journal of Applied Psychology, 1957, Vol. 41, pp. 409–413.

Relative Pilot Aptitude and Success in

Primary Pilot Training

John D. Krumboltz and Raymond E. Christal

If a cadet with medium aptitude for flying is placed in a group of high aptitude cadets, would he be more likely to fail than if he had been placed in a group of low aptitude cadets? The question may be put another way. Does a flying instructor have an absolute frame of reference in judging which cadets pass and which fail, or does he have a relative frame of reference so that his standard of what is acceptable varies with the quality of students he is instructing? It might be that an instructor would fail the worst student in his group, even though the worst student in his group might have been the best student in some other group had the groups been formed differently. This problem is especially acute in pilot training, since each instructor usually has only four students. If the four students are randomly assigned to instructors, and if a relative frame of reference operates, then chance factors would contribute to the probability of passing. One student grouped with highly talented fellow students might fail while another student of equal or even less ability might pass because he had happened to be placed with students of low ability. If such a condition prevails, the Air Force is not getting the best possible pilots; deserving men are failing; and the true validity of the pilot stanine is not being estimated accurately. The present study was designed to determine whether such a phenomenon exists.

It seems reasonable to suppose that one's frame of reference shifts in accordance with the quality of the material to be judged. Such a supposition has been confirmed by psychological research dealing with adaptation levels and frames of reference. The generalized result of a number of studies is that individuals tend to form their standards of judgment from the nature of the objects to be judged. The beauty of a picture, the wickedness of a crime, the pleasantness of a color, and the loudness of a sound are just a few examples of how judgments are subject to the frame of reference of the observer.

There is already some evidence that instructors in primary pilot training do not possess an absolute frame of reference in judging the quality of student pilots. Boyle & Hagin (1953) found that 70 per cent of the students with no previous flying training passed when they were grouped with each other, but only 49 per cent passed when they were in groups with students who had prior light plane training.

PROCEDURE

The records of one primary pilot training school over a six-year period of time were utilized to obtain cases for the present study. To achieve a relatively homogeneous sample, the only cases included in the study were aviation cadets in instructional groups of four. Any group containing a cadet held over to a later class was excluded from the study. Instructional groups containing one or more student officers (AFROTC graduates) were not analyzed because of a possible instructor bias for or against student officers. Groups containing student officers only were not numerous enough to justify extensive study. A total of 54 instructional groups containing 216 aviation cadets met the requirements for this study.

The criterion of success consisted of the dichotomy of "pass" or "fail" in primary pilot training. All men eliminated from training and not held over to a later class were classified in the "fail" category, regardless of the stated reason for their elimination.

Each student's relative pilot aptitude (RPA) score was determined in the following manner. Students' names and their pilot stanine scores were first arranged in accordance with the actual instructional grouping that had occurred during primary pilot training. Then for each man the mean pilot stanine of the other men in his group was calculated. Each man's own pilot stanine minus the mean stanine of the other men in his group, plus a constant of ten (to eliminate negative members) constituted his RPA score. A high score, therefore, indicated that a man had relatively more aptitude than the average of the other men in his group. A low score indicated that he had relatively less aptitude than others in his group.

Within each stanine level the men were ranked by RPA scores and divided according to whether they passed or failed in pilot training. The distribution of RPA scores was split approximately at the median for each stanine level. Therefore, the men of each stanine level were divided into four categories: high RPA and "pass," high RPA and "fail," low RPA and "pass," low RPA and "fail."

It was hypothesized that within each stanine level, cadets with high RPA scores would be more likely to pass than cadets with low RPA scores. Furthermore, it was hypothesized that this would be more true in the middle range of talent than at the extremes. For purposes of statistical analysis, these hypotheses were translated to statistical null hypotheses as indicated below.

The primary null hypothesis was that within each stanine level the proportion of passing cadets in the high RPA group is the same as the proportion of passing cadets in the low RPA group.

The second null hypothesis was that there is no difference in the proportion of passing cadets among stanines. This hypothesis, as stated, was not basic to the study but was included to provide for a test of an interaction effect—the third hypothesis.

The third hypothesis was that there is no interaction between stanine level and RPA scores. That is, the proportion of passing cadets in the high and low RPA categories is the same for each stanine level.

In 1956, Wilson described a method for computing tests of analysis of variance hypotheses with nonparametric data. This technique was utilized for testing each of the above hypotheses. The .05 level of confidence was chosen for rejection of the null hypotheses.*

RESULTS

The number of cases falling in each RPA and "pass-fail" category by stanine is presented in Table 6.

The relative pilot aptitude of a man within his instructional group was found to be significantly related to his chances for success in primary

---

*Dr. Krumboltz, in a personal communication to the editor, comments that despite the fact that this Wilson test lacks "power" (McNemar, 1958), the findings of this study, significant in spite of this inefficient test, remain unaltered.

pilot training. In general, a cadet had a better chance of success if he was grouped with cadets of relatively lower aptitude than himself rather than with cadets of relatively higher aptitude. The first hypothesis is therefore rejected.

The second hypothesis was accepted, since the proportion of cadets passing in each stanine did not differ sufficiently to reach the required significance level. It should be noted that the test of this second hypothesis was not a sensitive one: It failed to take into account the linear trend for higher stanine levels to be associated with greater proportions of passing cadets. The validity of the pilot stanine itself is revealed by the biserial correlation of the stanine with the pass-fail criterion which is reported in Table 6. The second hypothesis was included in the analysis to isolate the source of variation due to stanine level and to provide for a test of the interaction between RPA categories and stanine levels.

TABLE 6

NUMBER OF AVIATION CADETS FALLING IN EACH RPA AND PASS-FAIL
CATEGORY BY STANINE

	Stanine														
	9		8		7		6		5		4		3		Total
RPA Score...	Pass	Fail	Pass	Fail	Pass	Fail	Pass	Fail	Pass	Fail	Pass	Fail	Pass	Fail	Pass	Fail
High...	6	1	7	3	13	3	14	2	19	5	10	5	6	5	75	24
Low ...	5	1	9	2	11	5	14	7	14	10	7	10	8	9	68	44
Total...	11	2	16	5	24	8	28	9	33	15	17	15	14	14	143	68

Note: Three cadets with stanine 2 scores and two cadets with stanine 1 scores are not included in this table because of the low frequencies involved. All five failed in primary pilot training.

No significant interaction was observed. It was originally hypothesized that a cadet's relative pilot aptitude would have more effect on cadets in the middle range of aptitude scores than on cadets toward either extreme. A tendency in this direction can be noted. Inspection of Table 6 reveals that the effect of RPA standing on success is more pronounced in stanines 4, 5, 6, and 7 than it is in stanines 3, 8, and 9. In fact, there is a slight reversal in direction in stanine 8. However, such differences in the effect of RPA standing at different stanine levels were too slight to produce a significant interaction effect.

The biserial validity of the RPA scores against the pass-fail criterion was .412, while the validity of the pilot stanine was only .348. It is obvious that the validity of the pilot stanine was attenuated by the instructors' relative frames of reference which introduced irrelevant variance into the criterion. Without this attenuation, the validity of the pilot stanine would be identical to the validity of the RPA scores. This is true since the RPA scores are in reality nothing more than pilot stanines adjusted for differences in group means.

The RPA score can be analyzed in another manner by breaking it into its components: (a) the pilot stanine score, and (b) the mean pilot stanine of the other three men in the group. Table 7 reports the intercorrelation of these two components, along with their validity for the pilot training pass-fail criterion. Although the second component has a validity of only −.134, it raises the validity of the pilot stanine from .348 to .414 when the two components are combined in a multiple correlation formula. It may be observed that this multiple correlation is identical to the validity of the RPA score itself.

TABLE 7
INTERCORRELATIONS OF RPA WITH PASS-FAIL IN PRIMARY PILOT TRAINING
(N = 216)

Variable	Variable			Mean	SD
	1	2	3		
1. Pilot stanine		.240	.348[a]	5.51	1.81
2. Mean of other three men	.240		−.134[a]	5.50	1.22
3. Pass-Fail	.348[a]	−.134[a]		.66[b]	.47[b]

a Biserial correlations
b Pass = 1, Fail = 0

There is some evidence of homogeneous grouping by aptitude in this sample. A simple analysis of variance revealed that the mean pilot stanines of the instructional groups varied more than might be expected if there had been no homogeneous grouping. Inspection of the groupings revealed that most of the groups were arranged alphabetically, but that a few groups did have considerable restriction in variability. To the extent that homogeneous grouping did occur, one would expect attenuation in the validity of RPA scores. If no homogeneous grouping had occurred in any of the groups, the effect of RPA standing on success in pilot training would have been even more pronounced than it was found to be here.

IMPLICATIONS

Results of previous research studies have been confirmed in a practical situation. An instructor does not have a constant frame of reference for evaluating the performance of pilot trainees, just as subjects in other experiments lack a constant frame of reference for judging the beauty of a picture or the magnitude of a weight. To the extent that these results are generalizable to other training situations in civilian as well as military life, certain implications are apparent.

First, the true validities of aptitude tests are being underestimated when this phenomenon operates. The criterion is contaminated by irrelevant variance which is unrelated to the predictors.

Secondly, many students are being graded unfairly. Some students are given low grades or are eliminated from pilot training, not because their performance is below some absolute standard, but rather because it is below the average of the particular group in which they happen to find themselves. When this happens, the nation does not get optimal utilization of the available qualified manpower. In the Air Force, the likelihood of grading bias can be reduced by assigning cadets to instructional groups in such a way that each group would have the same mean on the pilot stanine. When the means of all groups have been made equal, then the pilot stanine would correlate perfectly with RPA scores. In civilian institutions it might be possible to assign students to sections of an undergraduate course in such a manner as to equate section means on some related aptitude score. When this is not desirable or convenient, an alternative might be to inform each instructor of the general level of aptitude in his section. He could use this information to guide his evaluations. In certain cases it might be possible to set up objective tests for measuring proficiency. In other instances, as in the pilot training program, for example, the instructors could be furnished a standardized set of case studies which contain objective and observable characteristics of persons judged to be making satisfactory or unsatisfactory progress.

A related problem has to do with the changes in grading practices over time. Grades and attrition rates in any civilian or military training program are not likely to be sensitive to fluctuations in the level of incoming talent. The standard for satisfactory performance tends to slide up and down with the ability of the group. Any method of standardizing grading practices would help alleviate this problem. Where objective and valid selection tests are employed, administrative action could be taken to vary grades and the attrition rate inversely with the level of talent selected.

SUMMARY

Does a flying instructor have an absolute frame of reference in judging which cadets pass and which fail, or does he have a relative frame of reference so that his standard of what is acceptable varies with the quality of students he is currently instructing? Based on a sample of 216 aviation cadets sampled from one primary training base over a six-year period of time, the analysis revealed that a cadet has a better chance of success if he is grouped with cadets of relatively lower aptitude than himself, rather than with cadets of relatively higher aptitude. Thus, instructors in this study tended to have a relative frame of reference. To the extent that this phenomenon operates in other training situations, the nation is denied the services of the most highly-qualified trained personnel, and the true validity of aptitude tests is underestimated. Methods of minimizing these dangers are discussed.

The last two articles have dealt with the success with psychological tests in the selection and training of military aviation specialists. The question is often posed concerning what civilian airlines do concerning these matters. After World War II, the American Institute for Research (with headquarters in Pittsburgh) made the AAF testing procedures, along with certain modifications, available to civilian airline companies. The following is a condensation of Research Report #13 *(April, 1957) by the American Institute for Research, of which Dr. John Flanagan is both President and Director of Research.*

Research on the Selection of

Aircrew Personnel

Few men bear more responsibility for lives and property than the modern air transport pilot. And few jobs require a wider range of skills and judgment than are necessary for the successful airline or executive pilot. To qualify for these advanced flying jobs, the pilot must undergo a long period of apprenticeship and formal training. He must win and maintain appropriate government licenses, and must normally pass both a physical and a flying proficiency check at least once a year.

Even with excellent training and careful evaluation, it is found that some pilots are able to perform more effectively than others. Apparently, the successful pilot has certain aptitudes and abilities which allow him to profit from his long training in a way which is not possible for men who have lesser degrees of these traits. The American Institute for Research set out to determine whether the characteristics necessary for civil transport pilot success could be identified and measured.

In the Army Air Forces during World War II, it was shown that successful pilots have a common pattern of aptitudes, and that most of these aptitudes can be measured by specially-constructed psychological tests. Standard psychological tests had limited value. But the "tailor-made" AAF tests, based on critical job elements identified by systematic study of failures in pilot training, were highly successful in estimating the likelihood that a young man would succeed as a pilot.

The AAF evidence showed that low-aptitude individuals not only had difficulty in completing formal pilot training, but also tended to be poor pilots on the rare occasions when they did manage to pass the course. Hence, it appeared that psychological tests would be useful in differentiating good and poor aircrew potential, even at advanced levels.

After the war, the American Institute for Research undertook a series of research studies on the job of the airline pilot. The first step was to determine the critical requirements of the job. Some of the requirements were essentially the same as for military pilots, but many were different. The research team then undertook to analyze the job requirements and determine the basic aptitudes and background necessary to success in airline flying. Much of this research was done in cooperation with the Civil Aeronautics Administration, under the sponsorship of the Committee on Aviation Psychology of the National Research Council. On the basis of this analysis, tests were developed to measure the potential of individuals for the job.

With the cooperation of Trans-World Airlines and the U.S. Army Air Forces, these new tests and tests developed for military flying were tried out. The first tryout was carried out in July and August, 1946, on about 400 first officers. At the same time, the research staff tabulated reports submitted on these men by the captains and check pilots with whom they had flown during the six to twelve months they had been with the company. These fitness reports and records of check flights were then compared with the test scores.

On the basis of this study, the tests were again revised. When they were considered adequate, a testing service was offered to airlines in this country and abroad. Since that time, over 7,000 applicants have been tested for various airlines.

The testing services of the Institute have also been broadened to include selection of flight engineers for the airlines, and of pilots and pilot-mechanics for business organizations which operate their own aircraft.

United Air Lines conducts an intensive training course for newly hired aircrew personnel. It has been estimated that the cost of this training is $6,000 per trainee. If, for a moderate testing cost, United can hire only those who have a good chance of completing the training course successfully, the airline stands to save training dollars as well as to maintain an effective and proficient aircrew force.

With the cooperation of the United Air Lines, the Institute checked the test scores of 568 applicants against their success or failure in training. The results of two studies have been combined in Table 8.

The higher the "stanine" score a man earns on the tests, the more likely he is to complete the training course successfully. Of course, United did not hire any individuals with stanines lower than 4. How-

TABLE 8
RELATIONSHIP OF TEST STANINE SCORE TO PERFORMANCE OF
568 PILOTS AND FLIGHT ENGINEERS IN THE UNITED AIR LINES
TRAINING COURSE

Test Stanine	% Fail	% Completing Training	N
9	4	96	56
8	4	96	74
7	13	87	109
6	22	78	143
5	20	80	159
4	37	63	27

ever, the trend of the results indicates clearly that more and more failures could be expected among stanines of 3, 2, and 1.

The results of this study are especially impressive, in view of the fact that the applicants had been carefully screened by the airline before they took the Institute's tests. The number of men who had originally applied for employment as pilots was reduced substantially through a series of interviews and, in most cases, through the administration of standard psychological tests. Only those candidates who appeared entirely satisfactory according to the air-line's previous selection procedures were sent to take the Institute's tests. But it turned out that even this select group could be divided into relatively poor and good "risks" on the job.

The value of the tests in identifying failures had also been shown in an earlier study of attrition rates. In the year before United Air Lines began to screen applicants with the selection tests, it became apparent that the number of applicants with prior training in instrument flight was rapidly decreasing. This was a cause for concern, since the failure rate among pilots without this experience was nearly three times as great as for the pilots previously trained.

The next year, the proportion of newly-employed pilots who had earned official instrument ratings dropped from 79 per cent to 26 per cent. But with the introduction of the selection tests at the beginning of that year, the failure rate actually was lowered. In the group without instrument ratings, the proportion released during training fell from 47 per cent to 18 per cent. And even in the rated group, the former rate of 17 per cent failures was cut nearly in half. As far as is known, the standards established for passing the course did not change during this time.

After more than a thousand pilots had been tested, the Institute searched CAA medical records to determine the relationship between performance on the aircrew selection tests and the extent to which applicants tended to remain in flying. The medical records indicated which of the pilots still held valid medical certificates, either Airline Transport or Commercial, and presumably were still flying in 1950. Table 9 shows the distribution of stanines of the 488 men who did not possess current medical certificates, indicating that they were no longer active in flying. It appears that the lower a man's test scores, the less likely he was to remain in commercial flying.

TABLE 9
RELATIONSHIP OF TEST STANINE SCORES TO CONTINUATION OF
1,077 PILOTS IN COMMERCIAL FLYING TWO TO FOUR YEARS LATER

Stanine	% No Longer Flying	% Still Flying	N
High (7–9)	33	67	270
Satisfactory (5–6)	42	58	372
Borderline (3–4)	54	46	313
Low (1–2)	60	40	122

When El Al Israel Airlines began using the tests, it was decided to check the tests against what airline officials already knew about their personnel. The test stanines of 24 aircrew personnel (including first officers, flight engineers, pilot trainees, and flight engineer trainees) were compared with ratings of their job performance by other members of the flying staff of El Al.

Table 10 indicates that the tests discriminate satisfactorily between pilots and flight engineers whose performance impressed their colleagues as outstanding, and those judged as average and below. Despite the factor of subjectivity involved in rating the performance of others, and despite the small number of individuals for whom both test scores and ratings were available, the results for the total group, for pilots alone, and for captains, are sufficiently clearcut that they cannot be attributed to sampling fluctuations. As a result of this study, El Al has been using the tests prior to hiring new personnel.

TABLE 10
RELATIONSHIP OF STANINES TO JOB PERFORMANCE OF 24
EL AL ISRAEL FLIGHT PERSONNEL

Stanine	Below Av on Job	Av or Above Rating	N
High (7–9)	0	100%	5
Medium (4–6)	46	54%	13
Low (1–3)	50	50%	6

It is of interest to note that none of the successful captains, most of whom had been employed by El Al for some time, had stanines below three. It may be that other pilots, with lower stanines, had tried and failed to make the grade with El Al.

Supporting evidence for this conjecture is provided by a number of studies in which the stanine scores of the pilot applicants were compared with the scores of pilots already employed. In each case, it was found that individuals who had demonstrated their abilities as aircrew members have generally high stanines, while the stanines of applicants are distributed among all levels.

It is a well-recognized fact in the psychology of individual differences that different persons show different amounts of gain in any learning task because, at the outset, they start from different levels of proficiency. Rather, then, than using "final grade in course" as the criterion against which we check the validity of the predictors used, perhaps it would be sounder, psychologically, to compute some measure of individual gain for each subject. The proper validity question would then become whether our aptitude tests are significantly related to individual gains obtained from the practice. Although this makes considerable sense, such a criterion is rarely reported on in the research literature. Drs. Manning and DuBois, both then on the staff of the Department of Psychology at Washington University in St. Louis, have reported a study where these ideas were put to experimental test. The original article, of which a condensed version is presented here, appeared in the Journal of Applied Psychology, 1958, *Vol. 42, pp. 191–194. Since that time Dr. Manning has joined the psychology staff of Texas Christian University.*

Gain in Proficiency as a Criterion in Test Validation

Winton H. Manning and Philip H. DuBois

In the validation of selection tests, final grade in a training course is often the criterion. Because of practical difficulties, on-the-job performance has been used less frequently. A third relevant criterion has been generally overlooked, namely, gain-in-proficiency or improvement through training.

Under commonly existing conditions, final grade may not adequately represent the performance of students in a training course. Consider a situation in which: (a) trainees differ in their initial level of performance, that is, their prior education and experience has led to diversity in pretraining proficiency; and (b) the training curriculum does not ordinarily result in mastery of the job, but rather develops skills fundamental to efficient learning on-the-job. In this training situation, improvement or gain-in-proficiency may constitute a more signficant dimension of student performance than does final standing.

If we should decide, on rational grounds, that a gains criterion is relevant to our training situation, there still remains the problem of measuring improvement. Past researches have typically used as the measure of improvement a crude gain score, that is, the simple arithmetic difference between scores on pretraining and post-training proficiency measures. However, when learning is measured by crude gain scores, gain appears to be not only uncorrelated with aptitude measures, but also uncorrelated with other measures of gain. There is reason to suspect that this apparent unrelatedness of gain scores is derived from a peculiarity of the crude gain measure itself.

Recently (in 1957), DuBois described an application of correlational analysis to the measurement of improvement which overcomes many disadvantages of the crude gain measure. Residual gain, which is advocated as preferable to crude gain, is defined as that portion of the measure of final status which is not correlated with initial status. Specifically, in terms of z scores, a residual gain score $(z_{2.1})$, represents the difference between actual final proficiency (z_2), and final proficiency, predicted from initial status $(r_{21}z_1)$.

The purpose of this study was to compare the predictability of three criteria of student proficiency. Two questions were of particular interest: (a) Of three criteria (crude gain, residual gain, and final status), which is most correlated and which least correlated with each of several selected aptitude measures? (b) As compared with more conventional tests, will measures obtained from a simple learning task contribute unique variance to the prediction of gain or final proficiency in a complex technical skill acquired in a classroom training situation?

PROCEDURE

The S's were 213 trainees from 13 successive classes in the aircraft ignition phase of the U.S. Navy Aviation Machinists Mates' School (Advanced). All were enlisted naval personnel with ratings of second class petty officer or above.

On the first day of training, one form of a comprehensive examination in aircraft ignition was administered as the pretraining proficiency measure. This test consisted of 60 five-choice, multiple-response questions. Following three weeks of training in aircraft ignition, an alternate form of this achievement test, also 60 items in length, was adminstered as the regular final examnation. These two tests, one administered on the first day and another on the last day of training, served as bases for computing two gain scores: residual gain and crude gain. Scores on the second test alone were used as the measure of final standing in the course.

Three Navy Basic Battery Tests and the DuBois-Bunch Learning Test (1949) served as predictors. The General Classification Test (GCT) may be regarded as a test of verbal ability. The Arithmetic Test (ARI) consists of items involving arithmetic computation and problem solving. The Mechanical Test (MECH) is made up of items involving mechanical and electrical knowledge and comprehension and application of mechanical principles. The DuBois-Bunch Learning Test is a simple perceptual learning task, adapted for group administration. It consists of ten 90-second trials with a 30-second rest pause between trials.

RESULTS AND DISCUSSION

Mean performance on the proficiency tests increased from 22.7 items correct for the pretest to 47.2 for the post-test. The standard deviation of pretest scores was 5.51; for post-test scores it was 5.89. The correlation between pretest and post-test scores was .41. Navy Basic Battery Test scores are standard scores, based upon a normative sample, with means of 50 and standard deviations of 10. Scores of S's in our sample averaged slightly higher than these theoretical values and also exhibited some restriction.

Split-half reliabilities of the three criteria were .56 for crude gain, .67 for residual gain and .77 for final status. Because the criteria differ in terms of reliability, comparisons of their relative predictability might be obscured.

There were clear differences in the predictability of the three criteria. Correlations of predictors with the crude gains criterion were generally quite low (.08 for GGT, .12 for ARI). In only one instance did the obtained validities differ from zero sufficiently to be statistically significant, and this was with Final Trial Scores (FLT) on the Learning Test (r here was .14). Correlations of predictors with the residual gains criterion were lower than those of final status, but all were of sufficient magnitude to be significant at the .01 level or beyond. These ranged from a low of .18 to a high of .34. Correlations of final status with predictors were all highly significant (range here was from .21 to .47).

Another comparison of the predictability of the three criteria may be made by inspection of Table 11. Multiple correlations between each of the three criteria and various combinations of predictors were computed, and the significance of these multiple correlations then tested by means of analysis of variance. None of the multiple correlations of crude gain was significant. All multiple R's with residual gain were significant beyond the .001 level. This was also true, of course, for multiple correlations with final status.

TABLE 11
MULTIPLE PREDICTION OF THREE CRITERIA OF STUDENT PERFORMANCE

Predictors	Crude Gain	Residual Gain	Final Status
GCT, ARI, MECH... .14		.38	.50
ILT, FLT .... .14		.28	.35
GCT, ARI, MECH, ILT, FLT................... .17		.40	.52
GCT, ARI, MECH, RGLT*...................... .16		.39	.52
GCT, MECH, FLT................................. .15		.39	.52

Note: All correlations in last two rows are significant at .001 level of confidence.
*RGLT = Residual Gain on Learning Test

Another question concerned the hypothesis that measures derived from the DuBois-Bunch Learning Test would increase significantly the multiple correlation obtainable using only the Navy Basic Battery Tests. It was felt that measures of performance from a simple learning task might increase significantly the prediction of gain in a training course beyond that obtainable by more conventional aptitude tests. The increase in the multiple correlation, .02 at best, was not significant. It is of interest to note, however, that one of the best predictors of final standing and of residual gain in the training course was the final trial score on this simple learning task.

SUMMARY

A decision concerning which criterion, gain or final grade, should be adopted in a particular training situation rests primarily upon logical considerations. However, in correlating aptitude measures with final grade, it is quite possible that overlap of nonvalid variance, such as verbal facility and test-wiseness, may in some situations lead to spuriously high validity coefficients.

In contrast to this, residual gain represents the portion of the post-training measure which is uncorrelated with initial status. As a consequence, some of the nonappropriate variance may have been removed from the criterion. In this sense, a criterion of residual gain for test validation may be more realistic than the more frequently adopted criterion of final standing, while at the same time avoiding inconsistencies encountered when the crude gain measure is used.

*   *   *   *   *

In addition to showing this use of residual gain as a criterion measure in test validation, Mayo and DuBois (1963) have recently shown the concept to be of value in measuring gain in leadership performance. Here these authors applied residual gain and related correlational procedures to an experimental group of some 200 Navy chief petty officers who were students in a five-week "military atmosphere" leadership training course (and who were compared with a control group not receiving such training). Significant differences were found when the leadership performance of the two groups was observed on the job two months after the experimental group had returned to their original duty stations. The authors feel that this concept of residual gain has much to recommend it when the researcher's aim is to measure gains in educational or psychological work.

As the previous article by Manning & DuBois has shown, selection tests may be used to predict something beyond mere success in initial learning of a task. R. L. Thorndike (1949) has written about validity also along a time dimension, distinguishing immediate, intermediate and ultimate criteria. Most validity studies confine themselves to the first two; there are few reports in the literature concerning the third. Particularly in an industrial situation, there are many practical difficulties with long-range follow-ups. The following report by Dr. Worbois, industrial psychologist for the Detroit Edison Company, presents just such data, comparing the validity of a selection battery used in 1929 and again in 1948—a longitudinal followup. The report presented here is a condensed version of the original article in the Journal of Applied Psychology, 1951, Vol. 35, pp. 15–19.

Before reading this article, the students need to know the basic facts of the multiple correlation and statistical weighting technique (i.e., Wherry-Doolittle) as against the multiple critical-score method. Cronbach (1960, pp. 339–334) has a succinct and non-technical discussion of these techniques as applied to selection problems. The former is sometimes referred to as the USA method, since it was so prominently used in the AAF Psychology Research Program in World War II. The multiple cutting-score method was favored by the British in their selection procedures (Vernon & Parry, 1949). The article by Dvorak, which immediately follows the Worbois paper, discusses this problem in connection with the GATB of the U.S. Employment Service. The Worbois and the Dvorak articles should be read in conjunction with each other.

A reference is made in the Worbois article to a study by Grimsley (1949) wherein both these techniques were compared. This research involved 500 students in elementary accounting courses at the University of Southern California. Seven five-minute tests were constructed to predict final course grades. The data were statistically analyzed both by multiple correlation and by multiple cutting-score methods. In this instance, neither method showed any significant difference in predictive efficiency. There were insignificant differences in favor of the multiple cutting-score device at the highest selection level, but the Wherry-Doolittle Technique worked better at the lower levels of selection. Grimsley points out, however, that the multiple cutting-score method has additional advantages: it required only one-third as much calculation time; it demanded minimum knowledge of psychological statistics; and it was less effected by shrinkage.

Predicting Long-Range Performance of

Substation Operators

G. M. Worbois

Selection tests are frequently validated on a criterion of success covering the first few months or years of employment. The tests may be shown to provide a reliable prediction of time to reach a production rate, progress in training for the job, or supervisors' ratings of success. To allow for chance errors, the results are checked on another, independent group.

This leaves another problem which is sometimes bothersome: Do the tests also predict performance over the entire employment period? When the initial criterion is highly related to the criterion of long-range performance, it would be expected. However, the initial criterion is not always highly related to the long-range criterion. For example, if the initial criterion is something like "learning the job," and the long-range criterion is something like "dependability," there may be little relationship between them.

The tests may be very useful in predicting the initial criterion. Perhaps that is all that should be expected from them. On the other hand, if the tests predict both initial and long-range performance, the contribution of the tests in building an efficient personnel organization will be greater.

There are also practical implications. When a battery of tests is constructed to predict an initial criterion, there is a tendency for "management" to generalize, assuming that the tests predict performance over the entire period of employment. The tests may or may not do this. Perhaps the psychologist has a responsibility to determine whether the test batteries predict long-range performance as well as the initial criterion. At least, the tests which predict the initial criterion should not be negatively related to the long-range criterion.

THE PROBLEM

In the present study, a battery of tests is compared to both an initial criterion and a long-range criterion. The tests and the job for which they were developed have been described by Viteles (1932, pp. 260–273). After the tests had been validated and installed at the Philadelphia Electric Company, they were revalidated and installed at The Detroit Edison Company under the direction of Viteles. Several criteria were used for comparison with test results. The one which showed best agreement with the tests, consisted mainly of progress in learning the job.* For the present study, this criterion seemed to be the best index of initial success covering the first few years of employment. This is called the initial criterion.

About 63 per cent of the men who participated in the original validation (1929) remained on the job to be rated again by supervisors in 1948 and are called the long-range criterion. These ratings were checked for reliability, and the correlations were above .85.

There was not much agreement between the 1929, or initial, criterion scores and the 1948 ratings, or long-range criterion, since the correlation was only .33. This raised the problem reported here: Do certain test standards developed on the initial criterion for this situation show reliable agreement with the long-range criterion?

PROCEDURES

Scores on ten tests were available for the total group of 119 employees who took the tests in 1929. A battery of five tests was selected by the Wherry-Doolittle method to give the best prediction for the initial criterion. Battery scores were computed for the 75 men remaining on the job. A check was made on the means and standard deviations between these two distributions (for the 75 and the total group of 119). No significant differences were found. These battery scores were then compared with the long-range criterion.

As another means of combining the tests, the multiple cutting-score method as described by Grimsley (1949) was used. Three tests were selected by this method to give the best prediction of the initial criterion. Comparisons of scores on this battery with the long-range criterion were made for the 75 men remaining on the job.

RESULTS

For the first method of developing the test battery (Wheery-Doolittle) the rule of "adding tests as long as there is an increase in R" was followed. In Table 12 are shown the R's as each test is added and the beta weights for each test.

---

*The criterion consisted of the sum of (1) grades in the departmental training school and (2) grades for examinations covering practical operating problems. The standard deviation for the former was 6.9, while for the latter it was 2.8. The correlation between the school grades and the examination grades was .46.

TABLE 12
Test Weights and R by the Wherry-Doolittle Method, $N = 119$

Tests	Beta Weight	R
Location	.2289	.362
Series Completion	.2151	.425
Blocks A	.1100	.449
Blocks D	.1226	.458
Directions	.1159	.464

For the second method of developing the test battery, the subjects were first separated into three groups: the 27 per cent rated highest, the 27 per cent rated lowest, with the remainder as the average group in terms of the initial criterion. Mean criterion scores and the per cent passing each standard (high, average, low, fail) were computed for each of the criterion groups. From this it appeared that the best combination of tests would be: Location, Directions, and Series Completion.

Table 13 shows the mean criterion scores for persons selected by different levels on the tests. The A level of standards on the tests is highest, and C is the lowest. The men who failed to meet the C standards on the tests are placed in the FF group. The criterion scores show how the men who passed different levels on the tests were rated.

TABLE 13
Comparison of Groups Selected at Different Levels by the Two Methods on Both the Initial Criterion and the Long-Range Criterion, $N = 75$

							Per Cent of Lowest Rated Men Passing Test Standard			
Level of Test Standard (1)	Selected Cases (2)	Common Cases (3)	Mean Initial Criterion W-D* (4)	MC-S† (5)	Mean Long-Range Criterion W-D (6)	MC-S (7)	Initial Criterion $N = 20$ W-D (8)	MC-S (9)	Long-Range Criterion $N = 20$ W-D (10)	MC-S (11)
A	11	7	12.4	11.4	11.2	10.3	5%	10%	10%	5%
B	24	17	11.5	11.0	10.7	10.2	15%	15%	15%	20%
C	35	27	10.7	10.0	10.1	9.9	25%	40%	25%	30%
FF	40	32	8.0	8.6	8.4	8.6				

*W-D = Wherry-Doolittle Battery   Initial Criterion: M=9.27, S.D.=3.07
†MC-S = Multiple Cutting-Score Battery   Long-Range Criterion: M=9.21, S.D.=3.01
Explanation: Level A as determined by the multiple cutting-score (MC-S method) selected 11 men. Of these, 7 were also among the top 11 in scores on the Wherry-Doolittle (W-D) battery. Level B selected 24 men (11 of whom also passed Level A). Of these, 17 were also among the top 24 on the W-D battery. Level C selected 35 men. The FF group includes those who failed the C level.

In columns 4 and 5 are shown the mean initial criterion scores for those who passed the various levels on the tests. Thus, the mean initial criterion score for the 11 highest men on the W-D battery was 12.4. The mean initial criterion score for the 11 men selected by Level A.

standards on the MC-S battery was 11.4. It can be seen that for both methods the men passing higher standards on the tests had higher initial criterion scores.

In columns 6 and 7 are shown the mean long-range criterion scores for the same men, and, of course, the same test standards. While there is some shrinkage for both methods, those passing higher test standards have higher criterion scores. In columns 8 through 11 are shown the percentages of the lowest-rated men who passed the various test standards. It can be noted that, in this group, either method of developing the test battery on the 1929 data would have screened· about three out of four men who over the years turned out to be poorest on the job (as judged by the 1948 ratings). This is true if the lowest standards on the test had been used. If higher standards had been used, a larger percentage of the poor men would have been screened.

Analysis was made of the signficance of differences (via *t* tests) between mean criterion scores of those who pass and those who fail the various test standards. The B (or average) level test standards shows the best discrimination between those who pass and those who fail in terms of the initial criterion; both methods of test battery development gave results at better than the one percent level of confidence. But the Wherry-Doolittle method, developed on the basis of the initial criterion, also "worked" in predicting the long-range criterion, whereas here the multiple cutting-score method would not have been as reliable.

It should be noted that the results reported by Grimsley showed equally effective predictions via both methods. However, several conditions are different in the two studies. In fact, the main similarity is that the test batteries were developed by the same methods. His study applied the test standards to the same criterion for a different group. The present study applied the test standards to a different criterion for the same group. In the following sections, the test standards are applied to a different criterion for a different group.

Results for Other Groups. Test standards developed on the initial criterion for the above group may also be applied against the long-range criterion for other groups. The next group to which they were applied consisted of substation operators who had been employees of the company in 1929 but were not given the tests during the original study. After the tests had been validated, they were routinely given to all of the substation operators. Most of these men were not included in the original study, because they had been operators for less than a year, or because they were working in "automatic" rather than "manual" substations. None of them was tested before employment. There were

98 men who were given the tests shortly after 1929, and who were rated in 1948.

The long-range criterion scores were compared for those who passed and failed the test standards. It was found that those who passed the tests at the A standard (highest) had significantly higher criterion scores. This was true for both methods of developing test standards. But those who passed the C standard (low) on the multiple cutting-score battery also had significantly higher criterion scores.

Another group to which the test standards may be applied is: those substation operators who were employed after the original study in 1929. These people were employed partly on the basis of their test scores. Accordingly, in this group there is a smaller percentage of low test scores. Relationships with the criterion, accordingly, would be expected to be attenuated.

There were 106 of these substation operators who had worked at least five years as operators, and who were rated in 1948. Their average length of service was 13.5 years.

The long-range criterion scores were compared for those who passed and those who failed the test standards. Here it was observed that at the B and C levels there is a significant difference in long-range criterion scores using the W-D battery. At the A level for the W-D battery and at each of the levels for the MC-S battery, the differences are not significant.

DISCUSSION

Test standards were developed on the initial criterion for one group and then were applied to a long-range criterion for (1) the same group, (2) a different group employed without benefit of the tests, and (3) a group selected partly on the basis of their test scores. This kind of application involves more than statistical regression found in applying test standards from one group to another comparable group. Each group in this study is different. The second group is different from the first in that they were employed at a different time and had been assigned to different kinds of substation operating jobs. The third group is different from the first in that they were employed mainly in the depression years, and low test scores were eliminated in the hiring process.

Furthermore, the criterion is different from that by which the tests were developed. The tests designed to predict the initial criterion were not necessarily designed to predict the long-range criterion. The criteria themselves are not closely related.

It might be surprising, therefore, to find much of any relationship between test scores and the long-range criterion for any of these groups. Any positive relationship found, however, is of practical concern. It would indicate predictive value for the tests beyond that for which they were originally designed. From the employment standpoint, it would show the value of the tests in selecting employees who are likely to be successful over many years of service, as well as during the first few years of learning the job.

The results for each group are not always consistent. For some groups a high standard appears preferable, for others a low standard gives better discrimination. For some groups, one method of developing test standards appears better than another. These variations of results from group to group indicate that validation of tests should be based on groups similar to those for which they are going to be used. As the employment market, nature of the job, etc., produce changes in the group, the influence of those changes may affect the predictive power of the tests. This indicates the necessity for continuous evaluation of the testing procedure.

The results also indicate that any one method of developing test standards may not always be the best one. Depending on the nature of the relationships between test scores, the selection ratio, and a number of other factors, one method may be preferable to another. As long as the relationships between test batteries are not perfect, there is a reasonable assumption that one may be better than another in a specific case.* Even though the advantage of one may be small, if it provides a real increase in predictive value, its use may be justified in better selection.

SUMMARY

Test batteries were developed for predicting the success of substation operators over the first few years of service. The test standards were then applied to a long-range criterion.

The results indicate that test standards predict performance at this job over many years of service, but that the same standard or the same method of developing the standard is not always best.

Need for adjusting test standards as the group for which they are used changes, is indicated.

---

*For all 279 men reported, the coefficient of contingency, corrected for broad categories, between the W-D and the MC-S battery was .62.

This article by Dr. Dvorak, who is Chief of the Testing Division,
Bureau of Employment Security, U.S. Department of Labor, should be
read in conjunction with the previous paper by Worbois. Here Dr.
Dvorak describes a few basic facts of the General Aptitude Test Battery
(GATB), explaining why the multiple correlation technique of treating
test battery scores was abandoned and the multiple cutting-score method
substituted. The paper has special relevance because the GATB is the
most widely validated multiple aptitude test battery. It has been vali-
dated against actual occupational or on-the-job criteria (and this despite
the mention of a student dentist group in the article). The article origin-
ally appeared in Personnel Psychology, *1956, Vol. 9, pp. 45–47.*

Advantages of the Multiple Cut-Off Method

Beatrice J. Dvorak

The U.S. Employment Service of the U.S. Department of Labor uses
the multiple cut-off method for occupational norms on test batteries. A
minimum or critical score is established on each significant aptitude.
For example, the norms for dentists are: Intelligence—120; Spatial
Aptitude—115; Form Perception—100, Finger Dexterity—90. No
total weighted score is obtained; a qualifying test score is achieved only
by attaining at least the minimum score on each of the significant aptitudes. In order to determine the significant aptitudes, we analyze the
data in four ways: we correlate all the aptitude scores on the GATB
with the criterion; we compute the mean scores for all the aptitudes
and compare them with the means for the general working population;
we compute the standard deviations for all the aptitude score distributions and compare them with the standard deviations for the general
working population to get an indication of the range of talent; we
analyze the job analysis information qualitatively. The result of this
analysis gives us the key abilities required for the performance of the
job. After the key abilities have been selected, the norms are established
in terms of minimum scores for each of the significant aptitudes. These
cutting scores are set at the point which will provide maximum differentiation between the good and the poor workers or trainees. The
predictive validity for the dentist norms shown above was .57 with a
standard error of .14. The criterion was dichotomized so that 24 per

cent of the students were placed in the low criterion group; 24 per cent of the students did not make qualifying test scores in terms of the established norms.

In the early days of our test research we used total weighted scores as occupational norms. These were derived by the Wherry-Doolittle Multiple Correlation Technique. But along about 1945 we began to abandon the method because we had noted, over a long period of time, that what seemed to be important abilities for a particular job, on the basis of the job analysis, were often omitted from the norms. There seemed to be a good explanation for this. The very ability that might be a key ability in the job would show a low standard deviation for the distribution of those test scores. This homogeneity of the group on that ability probably resulted from the fact that those workers who did not have a sufficient amount of that ability had not survived on the job. Because of this restriction in range, the correlation between these test scores and the criterion would be low. Even with applicant samples there is likely to be a restriction in range, because it is difficult to get employers to conduct adequate termination interviews and keep records on them for criterion purposes to determine whether the workers left because of inability to do the job or for personal reasons that had nothing to do with job proficiency.

Even when there was no restriction in range, we noted that often there seemed to be a relationship between test scores and job proficiency only to an optimum point. Since there was not a straight-line relationship throughout the entire range, the Wherry-Doolittle Multiple Correlation Technique did not yield that ability in the final norms. For example, finger dexterity might be a crucial ability for some jobs; without a certain amount of it, persons would not be able to perform on the job; but, beyond a certain point, additional increments of finger dexterity would not be associated with additional production on the job.

Even when a crucial ability does show a straight-line relationship between test scores and success, the method of multiple regression weights permits the possession of other abilities to compensate for a low amount of a crucial ability. In our experience, an employer is not satisfied with a worker who is awkward with his fingers in a certain job even though he may have an unusually high amount of the other abilities required by the job. Hence we use the multiple cut-off method which does not permit such compensation of some abilities for others required by the job. The multiple regression technique throws away much information because it yields a composite index.

Too often is the assumption made that worker proficiency, where aptitude measures are employed to predict such, can be described in terms of a single variable. In the following article, Dr. Ghiselli states we had better use several dimensions rather than one, which then means we deal with a criterion "space." We have also typically underestimated dynamic or changing criteria—investment salesmen, for example, who improve over a six year period. All this means that research work with any criterion problem becomes complex so that merely calculating linear correlations against a single criterion is relatively useless. Dr. Ghiselli is one of the foremost industrial psychologists in USA and has published widely. He is Professor of Psychology at the University of California at Berkeley. The following article appeared in the Journal of Applied Psychology, *1956, Vol. 40, pp. 1–4.*

Dimensional Problems of Criteria

E. E. Ghiselli

The discussions by Otis, Toops, Bellows, and Thorndike constitute the fundamental conceptual formulations of the criterion problem, yet all have been published within the last decade and a half. While others have considered matters connected with the development of criteria for use in validating selective devices, by and large their concern has been with technical details or some restricted phase. Thus the broader aspects of the criterion problem have not received the attention they deserve.

In a way it is unfortunate that the term criteria has been used to denote measurements of job success. This term refers to standards for the evaluation of something else, and the implication is that the "something else" is of greater importance than the standards themselves. In the present context, selective devices are the "something else." It is certainly true that far more attention has been devoted to the development of predictive devices than to the understanding and evaluation of criteria.

Since criteria are means for quantitatively describing workers' performance, an examination of the dimensional problems of criteria would seem both legitimate and necessary. While such an examination may raise new and as yet unanswerable questions, at least those who are concerned with the selection of workers will be in a better position to see the kinds of problems that confront them. This paper will deal with certain matters connected with the dimensionality of criteria—static dimensionality, dynamic dimensionality, and individual dimensionality.

STATIC DIMENSIONALITY

As it is ordinarily stated, the selection problem involves the prediction of a single variable—the criterion. The presumption is that the job proficiency of workers can be described completely by a single dimension. But for almost any job there are a number of dimensions on which workers' performance can be measured. Thus typists can be evaluated not only in terms of speed of typing, but also in terms of errors, neatness of product, absences, etc. When confronted with this situation, the common procedure is to select one of the criterion variables and say that it is the best, the most pertinent, or the most representative.

When there are several criterion variates for a given job, sometimes the decision is to combine all measures into a single composite. This presents a series of technical problems and also a series of theoretical ones. Mere assignment of equal weight to all components is seldom satisfactory, because other grounds, perhaps purely intuitive ones, suggest that all components are not equally important. Almost all of those who have attempted rational solutions to the differential weighting of a set of independent variables fall back upon some notion of a general factor. The objectives may be stated differently. It is frequently stated that the purpose is to maximize differences between individuals in terms of composite criterion scores and to minimize differences in scores on the different criterion variables within the individual. However, the end result is the same, and the various criterion variates are thereby weighted in terms of their principal component.

This would be a satisfactory solution if it could be demonstrated that all of the different measures of performance for any given job are determined largely by the same general factors. However, such evidence as there is suggests that if there are general factors at work, at best they are of minor importance. In other words, it would appear that workers' performance on any given job is best described in terms of several dimensions, and one dimension is not sufficient.

If the proposition is accepted that criteria are multidimensional with the dimensions being independent, or at least relatively so, then the situation is not an easy one. There is no way to combine the independent scores of an individual into a single value that will describe him uniquely. Rather it will be necessary to locate his position in the multidimensional criterion space. This can be accomplished in either of two ways:

each criterion dimension can be predicted separately and the individual's position in the space estimated, or the space can be divided into parts and that portion of the space in which the individual is most likely to fall could be estimated by the discriminate function.

These solutions require judgments as to which portions of the space contain most desirable individuals. When a single criterion variable is being predicted, the problem is simple. All that needs to be said in making a decision with respect to candidates for a job is that the higher the score, the better. But with the multidimensional situation it is necessary to define which parts of the space are the satisfactory range, indicating the persons who should be hired, and which parts are the unsatisfactory range, indicating those individuals who should be rejected. It might be argued that these people who are high on every criterion variate are successful and hence should be selected. The criterion space then would be divided into two parts, one at the upper right-hand corner containing only individuals who are high on all variables and therefore to be classed as satisfactory, and all of the remaining area of the space containing all of the rest of the individuals who would then be classified as unsatisfactory. Persons who fall into this second part would necessarily be classified as unsatisfactory even if they were high on all but one of the dimensions.

Procedures such as these clearly presume that all criterion dimensions are equally important and that a low score on any one is tantamount to complete failure. This situation may hold in certain circumstances but probably not in too many. In most cases the notion of equality among criterion dimensions cannot be supported, and compensation for low scores on one dimension must be allowed for by high scores on another.

Kurtz (1937) has provided a rational solution of a very different kind. He has proposed that when criteria are multidimensional they need not be combined, nor need the individuals' unique positions in the multidimensional space be described. Rather, predictors can be weighted so that the highest possible average of the validity coefficients with all of the criterion variates is obtained. This solution simply ignores the problem of differential importance of criteria. Yet a kind of compromise is effected which in many situations may be as good as or even better than arbitrarily combining all criterion variates into an equally weighted composite and predicting it.

Undoubtedly there are still other kinds of solutions to the multivariate criterion problem, but few have given it systematic consideration. It is obvious that new ideas are necessary and that ingenuity should be the order of the day.

DYNAMIC CRITERIA

The foregoing criteria have been called static, since in dealing with them the matter of change is not considered. For any given type of criterion, data are collected for a period of time and then merely summed. Yet it is apparent that the performance of workers does change as they learn and develop on the job. The length of time during which such change occurs generally seems to be underestimated. The tendency is to think that most improvement occurs within the first few weeks or months after the individual is placed on the job. However, increases in job proficiency have been noted over quite long periods of time. A London study reported significant improvements in the performance of bus drivers even after five years on the job. Haire and the present writer found that the performance of investment salesmen improved at a constant rate during the first six years of employment with no suggestion of a leveling-off.

The obvious thing to do is to examine the intercorrelations among criterion measurements taken at different periods of time in order to ascertain the kind of pattern that holds. For example, analysis of the intercorrelations among monthly production records for a period of several years would give some indication of the extent to which dimensionality changes with time.

Pertinent facts are few, but generalizing from the results of laboratory experiments on learning one would expect to find the intercorrelations among measures of proficiency taken at different periods fairly uniform in magnitude, with the relationships among extreme periods perhaps being somewhat lower than the relationships among near periods. Haire and the present writer found just this state of affairs holding for the intercorrelations among the monthly sales of investment salesmen for a two-year period, and for the intercorrelations among the weekly production records of taxicab drivers for an 18-week period. This uniformity in magnitude of intercorrelations is most easily accounted for on the basis of a single set of general factors equally important throughout time.

If this be the true state of affairs, it would mean that the selection problem is quite simple. When those individuals who are superior in the early phases are differentiated accurately, those who will be superior later on are thereby located, since they are the same individuals. However, even if the intercorrelations among criteria taken at different times are exactly the same in magnitude, since they will not be perfect they could be accounted for just as well by a variety of different factors changing in importance as time passes.

For the taxicab drivers described earlier, the scores earned by the men on a series of tests administered at the time of hiring were available. The scores on the various tests were correlated with production on each of the first 18 weeks of employment. If the uniform correlations among production records for the various weeks were the result of general factors of uniform importance, then the validities of the tests should be the same throughout the entire period. While for some of the tests the magnitude of the validity coefficients did remain practically unchanged throughout the period, other tests showed a gradual reduction in validity, still others a gradual increase, and one even showed regular and significant cyclical changes in validity from about zero to .40.

If this be the state of affairs with criteria, then the prediction problem is a difficult one indeed. The general predictions of job success that one desires to make, predictions of performance whether success occurs early or late in employment, would necessarily be relatively poor. To be of substantial magnitude, predictions would have to be of performance fairly close pinpointed in time.

CRITERION DIMENSIONALITY OF THE INDIVIDUAL

Some 15 years ago Otis made a most challenging statement about the criterion problem. In effect, he said that several workers on the same job might be considered equally good, and yet the nature of their contributions to their organization might be quite different. In other words, the idea is that workers on the same job might be evaluated in terms of different criterion dimensions. Thus one college professor is considered good because he is an excellent teacher, and another because his research is very significant. This is not saying that an individual is to be considered good if he is high on any one criterion variable. Rather, the notion is that while certain criterion variables are appropriate in describing the performance of some workers, they just are not pertinent in describing the performance of other workers on exactly the same job.

It would appear, therefore, that the criterion dimensionality of the individual should be investigated, just as other psychologists investigate the personality dimensionality of the individual. It is quite possible that workers assigned to the same job perform quite differently in a qualitative as well as in a quantitative sense. For example, one clerk in a department store may perceive his job as seller of the merchandise assigned to him. Another sales clerk may view his job as builder of general good will. The number of dollars the store receives as a result of the efforts of the two workers might be exactly the same, in the one case because the clerk himself sells a lot of merchandise, and in the other case because the clerk gets the customers to buy throughout the entire store. Under these circumstances, the factors leading to successful performance of the one kind would be quite different from those leading to successful performance of the other kind. It follows, then, that different types of tests necessarily would have to be used in order to predict the two different kinds of performances.

It might be argued that what is being considered here is not one job, but two. However, in an administrative sense there is just one job, and it is only in a psychological sense that the jobs are qualitatively different. Studies of criterion dimensionality of the individual are one way of determining whether different positions in the same job in fact are psychologically the same or different.

SOME CONCLUSIONS CONCERNING THE DIMENSIONALITY OF CRITERIA

The matters discussed here are merely translations and formalizations of the kinds of problems that are commonly raised in connection with criteria. They are embarrassing and confusing questions, but nonetheless legitimate, and the psychologist should be prepared to provide answers to them. The questions are termed embarrassing because satisfactory answers have not been provided, and confusing because their full implications and the possible scope of answers are not well understood.

The evaluation of selective devices merely by simple correlations with single criterion variables is insufficient. It is apparent that the description of workers' job performance is a complex matter. Satisfactory statements concerning validity, therefore, cannot be made until rational solutions are developed for the various dimensional problems of criteria.

In dealing with the problem of criterion prediction, research results are frequently cited in terms of overall validity coefficients, and these are often disappointingly low. In the following article, Dr. Fisher points out that our measures are typically more accurate in predicting non-adaptive behavior rather than "good" behavior (or absence of pathological signs). His "twisted pear" phenomenon is arrived at by inspection of scattergrams derived from diverse fields from which both theoretical and practical conclusions may be drawn. Dr. Fisher is currently Chief Psychologist at the Langley Porter Neuropsychiatric Clinic in San Francisco, and also Associate Clinical Professor of Medical Psychology at the University of California's School of Medicine. The article is abstracted from the Journal of Consulting Psychology, 1959, *Vol. 23, pp. 400–405, which, in turn, was based on a paper read at the XV International Congress of Psychology, Brussels, July, 1957.*

The Twisted Pear and the

Prediction of Behavior

Jerome Fisher

"To say that nature should conform to a Gaussian distribution is asking too much. Who is there to tell nature what the statisticians would like?" This statement, made recently by Boring in an editorial context, seems an appropriate introduction to the question and the point of view presented in this paper. It is by no means a new point of view. Rather, it is a variation on the familiar theme that organisms, whose behaviors are variously studied for purposes of prediction, do not conform to the assumed mathematical conditions which are often assigned to them in statistical manipulations of data.

In substance, the paper raises questions not only about the appropriateness of our statistical assumptions as they concern prediction problems but, also, it ventures the proposition that, because of certain biological and psychological variants, organismic behaviors are predictable in only one segment of a predictor-criterion relationship.

Several years ago, in analyzing the results of a cross-validation study involving the Rorschach, my colleagues and I noted a curious but consistent result. When the Rorschach yielded a score indicating the presence of brain disease, the agreement with independent criterion judgments of brain pathology was extraordinarily good (94 per cent). A low score, however, was not accurate in predicting the absence of brain pathology. A Pearson validity coefficient was computed and found to be a respectable, significant, but humble .32.

Next, we subjected several standard neurological procedures, such as the EEG, the lumbar puncture, etc., to essentially the same validation analysis. Except for a few minor variations, five neurological diagnostic techniques gave the same results: High accuracy in predicting pathology from positive test findings, but like the Rorschach, poor accuracy in predicting the absence of pathology from negative diagnostic signs. The over-all validity coefficients ranged from .13 to .32.

When scattergrams were plotted of the relationship between predictor scores and the criterion, a nonlinear heteroscedastic configuration was revealed which looked like a twisted pear; it is approximated in Figure 4.

FIGURE 4
SCHEMATIC MODEL OF PREDICTION IN BEHAVIOR

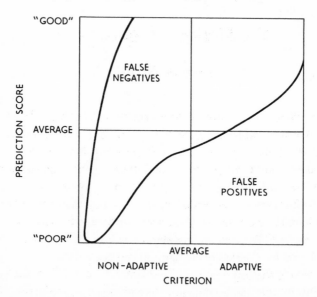

This finding raised the question: Is the twisted pear unique to these data or is it a general pattern, characteristic of prediction problems?

The diagram will call to mind many familiar observations and findings. When scattergrams from several sources are examined, where more or less known criteria are plotted against more or less standard predictors, e.g., objective tests, a linear relationship with relatively little array variance will be observable at one end of the plot. The relationship, however, becomes increasingly nonlinear and increasingly variable as it approaches the middle and upper extreme. The terms "adaptive" and "nonadaptive" are used in Figure 4 to suggest an implicit but functionalistic conception of the corresponding relationships between predictor "good" and "poor" scores and the criterion behavior of organisms. In other words, the predictor becomes decreasingly predictive of the criterion as the scores obtained increase from the "poor" to "good" extremes of the predictor. To illustrate this predictor-criterion differential, the findings of studies of intelligence, learning, personality, and pathology will be presented and discussed.

According to Figure 4, the predictive efficiency of the IQ at the "poor" extreme should be considerably better than for average and "good" (superior) IQ's. Specifically, with IQ's below, say 50, it is highly predictable that the individual will require custodial or complete protective care, and that he will not acquire any scholastic skills. With IQ's of about 50–70, there appears to be moderately good predictability that the individual will require special training and guidance, particularly at work and at school. With IQ's of approximately 70–85, and, to a greater degree between 85–110, however, vocational and scholastic limitations vs. successes become increasing difficult to predict.

Table 14 summarizes the results of several longitudinal studies of the vocational and educational achievements of male mental defectives, their controls, and, in addition, the vocational and scholastic attainments of Terman's gifted men (Terman & Oden, 1947). The latter included some 730 subjects whose childhood IQ's were 140 or higher and who were classified into two groups by raters on the basis of vocational achievement 18 years later. The A group (mean childhood IQ = 155) was the most successful and the C group (mean IQ = 150) the least successful. The C group of 150 men, therefore, was, by definition and rating procedures, an underachieving group. Table 14 reveals that as a group, Terman's gifted men, 25 years of age and older in 1940, were superior occupationally to the general male population in the U.S. Further analysis of the data (not reported in Table 14), however, discloses that 28 per cent of the C group fell at or below the median occupational level of the employed males in the U.S., as well as of those in California in 1940. Terman and Oden (1947) note that:

> On the average, those of highest IQ accomplish more and are equally well-adjusted, but one cannot anywhere draw an arbitrary IQ line that will set off potential genius from relative mediocrity. Some of our subjects who have achieved most notably did not, either in childhood or in adult life, rate above the average of the total group in tested intelligence.

TABLE 14
COMPARISON OF EDUCATIONAL AND OCCUPATIONAL ACHIEVEMENTS OF MEN WHOSE IQs WERE OBTAINED IN CHILDHOOD

Groups	Mean IQ at Time of Test	Mean Age at Time of Test	Follow-up in Years	Occupational Achievement				Educational Achievement				
				| Minnesota Occupational Scale*								
				N	VI & V	IV & III	II & I	N	8th Grade and Lower	9th–12th	Some College	College Graduation
Terman's gifted (1940)												
A (N=96)	155.0			149† ⎫				150 ⎫				
B		9.7	18	436 ⎬	10.3%	24.3%	65.3%	481 ⎬	0.0%	14.7%	18.3%	66.9%
C (N=92)	150.0			139 ⎭				150 ⎭				
Baller's (1935) control	107.8	8–9	21	113 ⎫	43.5	40.6	15.9	124 ⎫	36.0	35.3	15.5	13.1
Fairbanks (1931) control	90.0	12 (?)	17	39 ⎭				25 ⎭				
Baller's (1935) mental defectives	60.5	8–9	21	67 ⎫	77.3	22.7	0.0	113 ⎫	93.5	6.5	0.0	0.0
Fairbank's (1931) mental defectives..	68.0	12	17	69 ⎭				43 ⎭				
U.S. Census (1940)‡					44.7	41.6	13.8		60.4	29.5	5.5	4.6

*The Minnesota Occupational Scale was used by Terman for the classification of his gifted men. Because the other follow-up studies cited here were conducted and reported in the same decade (1930-1940), the Minnesota Occupational Scale was adapted and applied to them also. Roe's (1956) more recent two-way classification of occupations gives similar results. Roughly, the classifications I & II refer to professional and managerial; III & IV—skilled labor and agricultural; V & VI—semiskilled and laborer.

†The Ns of 149 and 139, respectively, as well as the Ns and percentages of the other studies cited, refer to gainfully employed men only, who were available geographically at the time of the follow-up study.

‡U.S. census (1951) educational and occupational data for men are included for purposes of general comparison.

With regard to the lower end of the IQ range, Table 14 also gives the occupational achievements of two follow-up studies of mentally defective groups. The data reported are in the form of average percentages for the combined groups. Compared to the gifted and control groups, the findings suggest a stronger, less variable relationship between mental deficiency and occupational achievement, as determined mainly by IQ. None of the mental defective groups achieve I and II occupational categories; 23 per cent are in III and IV, and 77 per cent in V and VI. For the control samples, whose mean IQ's are within the average range, the proportion of cases fall in the several categories as shown. Approximately two-thirds of the gifted group attained superior vocational levels (I and II). The presence of 10 and 24 per cent of the gifted in the lower occupational Categories V and VI, and III and IV, respectively, however, suggests again the greater variability and, hence, the potential predictive "error" associated with "good" IQ scores.

Prediction of scholastic achievement by means of the IQ was studied by review of the same investigations. Table 14 also presents the follow-up findings of the same group of men whose IQ's were obtained in childhood. The data are summarized in scatterplot form via averages.

It appears that the IQ has considerable power in predicting scholastic achievement, particularly in the tails of the distribution of IQ's. Compared to the controls and the gifted, however, the lower end of the IQ range (the mental defectives) reveals greater certainty of prediction for the criterion scholastic achievement.

At the upper extreme, the gifted's superiority educationally is self-evident (67 per cent graduated from college). According to Terman and Oden, none of the gifted failed to complete grade school. For the middle and upper range of the predictor, however, the computed percentages, placed in their respective cells, suggest the characteristic variability observed before, and again reveal the twisted pear shape.

What about learning, personality, and the "twisted pear" phenomenon? In his genetic research of dull-bright rats and maze-learning ability, Tryon (1940) found that while the poor maze-learning of the dull rats could be predicted very well, the bright rats varied throughout a wide range of learning scores (errors). Table 15 presents a fourfold table which was obtained by plotting around the median value of the total errors of the seventh generation ($N = 153$), the total errors made by their dull and bright offspring of the 15th to 18th generation. The reason for using the seventh generation as the source for the median value comes from Tryon's observation, "There appears to be a law of diminishing returns, for after the F_7, negligible effects of selective breeding are noted." None of the descendants of the dulls fell in the bright category, whereas 30 per cent of the descendants of the bright ancestors performed in the dull category. The results, in short, suggest that the relation between predictor ancestors and criterion descendants, involving the learning of a complex set of highly integrated acts, is that of the twisted pear.

TABLE 15

PERCENTAGE OF BRIGHT AND DULL STRAINS 15TH–18TH GENERATIONS
WHO FALL ABOVE AND BELOW THE MEDIAN TOTAL ERRORS
OF THE 7TH GENERATION (N = 153)

(From Tryon, 1940)

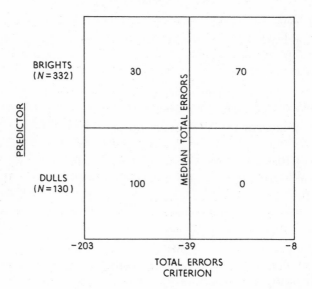

The work of the California-Berkeley group on authoritarianism suggests a similar pattern of differential predictability in personality assessment (Adorno, *et al.*, 1950). While high scorers (authoritarians) and low scorers (nonauthoritarians) "emerge as a result of statistical analysis . . . they consist in accumulations of symptoms frequently found together, but they leave plenty of room for variations of specific features. Furthermore, various distinct subtypes are found within each of the two major portions." Analysis of the prejudiced subjects, however, revealed that they are "on the whole more alike as a group than are the unprejudiced. The latter include a great variety of personalities . . ." (pp. 971–972). It seems, therefore, that a high score on the ethnocentrism scale is more predictive of authoritarianism than are low scores of its absence.

Leaving psychology for a moment, an analogue seems to exist in the actuarial determinations of the life insurance field. For example, having reviewed their experience tables and having ascertained the extent of their errors of prediction, insurance companies confidentially relate obesity to a short span of life and set their premium rates accordingly. As weight approaches nonobesity, however, there appears to be increasing variability in predicting life expectancy. It is, of course, true that no one dies of obesity and the nonobese may die of many other causes; yet as a predictor variable of the probability of life expectancy, insurance companies respect the highly significant relationship found at the "poor"-nonadaptive extreme, i.e., between obesity and short life expectancy.

In their daily practice, my hospital medical colleagues confirm the curvilinear relationship between their tests and their criteria of pathology; at least, they acknowledge implicitly the application of differential predictability. For example, it seems that medical specialists almost always regard a positive test finding ("poor" predictor score) with considerable respect. The reason for this is that their diagnostic techniques are accurate at least 80 per cent of the time when they yield a positive finding, i.e., the false positive rate is low. A negative or even a borderline finding, ("good" to average score) however, is invariably disregarded, if, in the physician's opinion, this finding is at variance with the patient's history, his presenting complaints, his symptoms and other diagnostic data. With a negative ("good" score) finding, therefore, the physician functions with a clinical relativism and a clinical tolerance of variability and errors of prediction.

When we apply our correlation statistics to measure the magnitude of the relationship between a criterion and a predictor, the coefficient thus obtained gives an average, over-all statement of differential predictions of the test. The result, being a statement of the weighted means of the selection ratios of the predictor classes Y_1, Y_2, ... Y_n on the criterion X, is to attenuate the validity coefficient. If the product-moment r is computed without drawing the scatterplot, the plot may or may not be heteroscedastic, and the analyst cannot tell whether there are differential predictions of the various Y classes.

Guilford, among others, has argued for the importance of scatter-gram inspection. With respect to organismic behavior, therefore, the case of linear association and equal variance obtains and applies partially, but not throughout a predictor-criterion relationship. The case of curvilinear association and unequal variance, however, also applies and, therefore, both cases are relevant and deserve our differential appreciation.

It has been said many times before and in many different ways that the behavior of the adaptive, functioning organism is ordinarily highly complex. I think we mean by this a capacity for variable, substitutive, compensatory behaviors. Under the disruptive conditions of pathology or stress, for example, it is as if special homeostatic mechanisms provide a biological and/or psychological smoke screen of adaptiveness. These on-going, restorative processes may be largely responsible for the high rate of "normal" responses or false negatives. It is perhaps no accident that many of our most useful diagnostic methods have been devised to assess pathology in status, i.e., when the camouflage is no longer impenetrable, or when adaptiveness has been or is curtailed beyond a certain point. I am referring here, in particular, to Binet's original mental test—an extraordinarily fine screening device for mental deficiency. It is precisely in the nonadaptive segment, then, that our predictors seem to prove themselves by virtue of their high rate of predictive accuracy. In this connection, it should be pointed out that they are not entirely without predictive power in the adaptive segment either, albeit negative errors lessen their accuracy. It seems, therefore, that when predictor measures are extrapolated beyond that "certain point," i.e., from "poor" to "good," the multivariable complexities of behavior multiply and interfere with our predictive accuracy. Hence, it appears that whatever validity a measure may possess for predicting adaptive behavior, it is likely to be more accurate in predicting nonadaptive behavior.

Perhaps the hidden determinant in all this is the criterion dimension itself extending from the nonadaptive to the adaptive. It, too, appears to have a partial range of certainty and "truth," probably because more is known about the defining criterion points of nonadaptiveness than about those of adaptive behavior. Our test construction procedures provide us with reasonably good techniques and measures of criterion nonadaptive behavior. If, however, the twisted-pear phenomenon possesses the degree of generality suggested by the data reviewed, then there is reason to question the assumptions for extrapolating from the nonadaptive to the adaptive extremes of predictor-criterion relationships.

Is it possible that the observed partial curvilinearity and differential predictive variance are merely artifacts of sampling (of our tests) or of our criterion determinations? Is the twisted pear solely a "clinical" phenomenon, or is it a more general characteristic of the prediction problem? Perhaps these questions are unanswerable at the present time or perhaps we are dealing with a reality of organismic behavior, one of the existentional dilemmas, to borrow a term from Erich Fromm, for the behavioral sciences. It is as if, on the one hand, there is general acceptance of the dynamic nature of organismic adaptation and change, and the variability thereby induced, while, on the other hand, there is the coexisting pursuit of immutable validity coefficients as an attainable goal in the business of understanding and predicting behavior.

Practically all serious discussions of the validity problem point to the great need for obtaining objective criteria. With industrial workers, research workers typically aim here for output data in lieu of foreman ratings. The surface objectivity of such data, because of their quantification, seems almost ideal. Assuming such output data are available (very often not the case, so that experimenters have to make arrangements in advance to collect these), many other measurement problems lurk beneath the surface.

Dr. Rothe, psychologist and Executive Staff Assistant of the Beloit Corporation in Beloit, Wisconsin, has published a series of studies in the Journal of Applied Psychology, *beginning in 1941, on this problem. Mr. Nye is Wisconsin State Director of Apprentice Training. In the following article by these two authors, most of these studies are summarized. This article has been condensed from the original report appearing in that journal (1958, Vol. 42, pp. 182–186).*

Output Rates among Coil Winders

Harold F. Rothe and Charles T. Nye

A series of previous papers has shown that the output rates, or production, of various groups of industrial employees tends to be relatively inconsistent from one period of time to another. It has been hypothesized that this inconsistency might be a function of the motivation, or lack of motivation, in the various situations. It has also been suggested that this inconsistency is not the same thing as low "reliability"; rather, that output is itself a phenomenon deserving study. "The proper subject for the study of industrial output is industrial output itself."

One study revealed different daily work curves from one day to another, rather than a "typical daily work curve." A second study showed a low correlation between the average production for one two-week period compared with the average production for the following two-week period. There was no financial incentive system in operation in that plant. The third study showed a higher correlation between the average production of one week compared with the average production of the next week, covering a period of 16 weeks, in a plant that did have a financial incentive system. Even in this latter situation, however, the week to week consistency was lower than the consistency commonly described in textbooks.

In the present study, data were again taken from the official books of a manufacturing concern and the week to week consistency for a group of employees was determined. The ratio of interindividual differences and the ratio of intra-individual differences were also obtained. These two measures, the consistency and the ratios, were analyzed in the light of the hypotheses previously put forth.

BACKGROUND OF THE STUDY

The data used here were taken from the books of a Midwest manufacturing plant. They cover a group of 27 employees and a period of 38 successive weeks from June 1956 to March 1957. (Actually 39 weeks were covered, but one week in December was omitted because the plant closed for inventory.) The employees were mainly women and all were experienced on their jobs. There were no "learners" in the group. Although there were some slight variations in the jobs, they fall into three basic jobs described in the USES Dictionary of Occupational Titles as coil winder, 6–99.014, rotor-coil winder, 6–99.112, and stator-coil winder, 6–99.131. All employees in the plant, including those involved in this study, were members of a national union under a union-shop contract.

There was no financial incentive system in effect. There had been one, but it had been removed about five years earlier. The employees were performing their regular jobs in their regular workplaces, and each employee governed her own work pace. (No moving belts, no long machine runs, etc.) The data were used for each week in which the employee worked 32 or more hours. Thus, from time to time, the size of the sample dropped below 27 employees. However, in no week were there fewer than 21 employees.

MAIN FINDINGS

The weekly average output for the group ranged from a low of 76.1 per cent for the first week of the study (for week ending June 17) to near the top production index of 91.2 at the close (for week ending March 10). Inspection of the data covering the entire period shows there was an increase in performance early in the period studied and that the group performance later stabilized at a plateau. It is noteworthy that there was a change in departmental foremen at the beginning of this study. A forelady who had previously supervised this department but who had been transferred to another department was transferred back to the coil winding department at the time that happened to be selected for this study. Output climbed immediately upon her return and stabilized again at the high level it had reached previously when this forelady was supervising operations. Although this improved production is undoubtedly a tribute to this forelady, it is also an uncontrolled variable in this study. It is doubtful if the rise in productivity affected the results of this study, but this does indicate the difficulties involved in attempting to do scientific research in an industrial situation.

The correlaton of each employee's performance for one week with his or her performance for the following week was determined by the method of Pearsonian r. The median r is .64; the highest r is .91 and the lowest r is −.03. Thus it is concluded that the week-to-week output was not particularly consistent, and also that there was an extremely large variation in consistency. This latter point is important for psychologists attempting to validate tests (or other activities) against production data. It shows the need for taking production data over a fairly long period of time. If a psychologist happened to select the two weeks correlating .91 he would undoubtedly be most happy, and if he happened to select the two weeks correlating −.03, he would be most unhappy.

The greatest and least amount of productivity for each employee for any one of the 38 weeks was calculated, together with the ratio of best to worst performance of each employee. The median ratio of best to worst performance or the intra-individual ratio is 2.24. (An illustration of the most variable worker, whose intra-individual ratio was 7.20, is the worker with the highest weekly average production of 144 and the lowest weekly average of 20.)

The ratio of best operator to worst operator for each week—the interindividual ratio—was also calculated. Here the median ratio is 2.06. Thus the average ratio of the range of intra-individual performance exceeds the average ratio of the range of interindividual performance. This was also true in the study of butter-wrappers who were also working under nonincentive conditions. But the opposite was true (i.e., the average ratio of the range of *inter*individual performance exceeded the average ratio of the range of *intra*-individual performance) in the study of chocolate-dippers who, perhaps by no coincidence, were on a financial incentive system.

It is also perhaps important to note that the ratios found in this situation were much larger than the ratios found in the study of chocolate-dippers (although smaller than the ratios found in laboratory studies). In that study, the median interindividual ratio was 1.475 and the median intra-individual ratio was 1.18 as contrasted with the 2.06

happened to be selected for this study. Output climbed immediately and 2.24 found here, respectively.

OTHER FINDINGS

Since the correlation of output from one week to the next week was so low ($r = .64$), the data were combined in various ways to determine the effect of using longer periods of time. The most obvious combination was to split the data—to correlate the average production of each of the 27 operators for the first 19 weeks with their average production for the second 19 weeks. The Personian r is .71, which is low for a work sample of this size.

Another r was obtained using the average production of each operator for the four-week periods of greatest plant employment (i.e., when the number of employees in the plant was greatest). The employees whose output data were used in this study formed only a part of one department in a very large plant. Here, as probably almost everywhere, the grapevine carries stories of increasing or decreasing sales and corresponding rises and falls in employment. Thus it was believed that there may be some relationship between output and size of the plant labor force. There were two peaks of employment in the period covered by this study. Production data for the four weeks leading up to and including each of the two peaks were used. The peaks were about six months apart from each other. The obtained r was .25, which suggests a lack of common variables influencing output during those two periods.

Along the same line of reasoning, the average output for each operator during a five-week period of decreasing employment was correlated with the five-week average during a period of increasing employment. The obtained $r = .60$. The writers suspect that the r of .60 found here and the r of .25 in the preceding paragraph are merely chance variations.

The average production for the entire group of 27 operators for each week was correlated with the size of the total plant labor force for that week, and the resulting $r = -.39$. This means that as the employee force decreases, the average production of these coil winders increases, and vice versa. Although this correlation of $-.39$ is statistically significant at between the 1 per cent and 5 per cent levels, it should be realized that it is an indication from one department in one plant. Other data from other situations are needed before much meaning can be attached to these data.

The correlation between total weekly plant employment and weekly output variance of these coil winders is −.02; between number of total plant's employees on layoff and average production of these coil winders, $r = -.03$; between total number on layoff and variance of coil winders production, $r = .02$; between number employed in coil-winding department and average production of these 27 operators, $r = .07$; and between number employed in this department and variance of output of these 27 operators, $r = -.16$. All of these correlations are, of course, insignificant.

DISCUSSION

In an earlier study by the senior author, it was hypothesized that the incentives to work may be considered ineffective when the ratio of the range of intra-individual differences is greater than the ratio of the range of interindividual differences. In the present situation, where there was no financial incentive system, the intra-individual ratio did exceed the interindividual ratio. And in a previous study, with no incentive system in effect, this same relationship between the ratios of inter- and intra-individual differences was found, while in a situation where an incentive system was in effect, the opposite relationship was found. The hypothesis is clearly not proven by this study, but these various studies do seem to point clearly toward a relationship between motivation and inter- and intra-individual differences.

A second hypothesis, which also emerged from previous work, was that if the intercorrelation of output rates for two periods closely related in time is less than .50, the motivation is not highly effective, while intercorrelation higher than .80 indicates very effective motivation. The present facts are generally consistent with this hypothesis, but they vary in amount (or size of coefficient). In the light of the present study, this hypothesis is now changed to say that an intercorrelation of .80 or above indicates effective motivation, and an intercorrelation of .70 or less indicates ineffective motivation. This leaves a twilight zone of between .80 and .70 that needs clarification from further research. (It also tempts one to speculate on the chaos that might exist if a negative or insignificant intercorrelation were to exist!)

The output data were correlated with various other variables such as size of employee force and number of employees on layoff, but the obtained r's were insignificant.

Grouping the weekly output data into 4-, 5-, and 19-week periods and correlating the data for these longer periods did not increase the r significantly over the r for single weeks' outputs correlated.

This study, along with the other output studies, again shows that production data cannot be picked up casually and used to validate tests or other procedures. In this entire series of studies of industrial output, the most striking single result is the lack of consistency from time to time, especially when there is no financial incentive system in operation. A second important result is the wide range of "consistency coefficients" of output data, such that a researcher could be entirely misled by tests of statistical significance if he just happened to select a period of unusually high or low consistency.

Another discouraging result when validity data are secured in everyday performance situations, where again one has production records, is the typically low correlations that result. Rather than abandon further efforts, Dr. Ghiselli in the following article suggests that a second look should be taken at the scattergrams. Here, in an exploratory study involving a group of 193 taxicab drivers, he outlines some suggestions for salvaging some of the data, since the psychometric devices utilized might work only for part of the group. The study is also valuable, since it demonstrates the use of a cross-validation group. The original report appeared in the Journal of Applied Psychology, 1956, *Vol. 40, pp. 374–377. The author is well known in the field of industrial and personnel psychology for his many research reports. He is Professor of Psychology at the University of California at Berkeley.*

Differentiation of Individuals in Terms

of Their Predictability

Edwin E. Ghiselli

When scores on a test are unrelated to criterion scores or are related to them only to a very low degree, the presumption is that the test is of little value. Hence in a prediction or selection situation, tests with low validity are quickly discarded and the entire effort is directed to the development of tests which will yield scores that are substantially related to the criterion.

Even though the validity coefficient of a test is negligible, there is the possibility that, at least with certain individuals, reasonably accurate predictions of criterion performance may be made from scores on the test. As one regards the scatter diagram of the scores on two variables that exhibit a low relationship, it is apparent that some individuals fall on or very close to the line of relations while others depart markedly from it. Thus for some individuals there is quite close correspondence between standard scores on the test and standard scores on the criterion. The remainder of the individuals display to varying degrees differences between standard test and standard criterion scores.

Suppose that it were possible by some other means, perhaps another test, to differentiate those individuals whose test and criterion scores show small discrepancies from those individuals whose test and criterion scores are markedly different. Then it would be possible to screen out a group for which at least reasonably accurate predictions could be made. Thus even though the validity of the test for the entire group is low, for some individuals who can be differentiated beforehand, the test would have some practical utility.

In a somewhat different form, this notion is implicit in dealing with individual cases in clinical and guidance work. Consider the case of a counselor attempting to decide whether a young person should seek education above the secondary school level. If it appears that motivation or interests seem inappropriate, he might not recommend college even though the intelligence test score is high. In effect, what is being said is that when the individual possesses certain other characteristics, there will be little correspondence between test performance and college achievement.

Therefore there is nothing new in the notion that it is possible to differentiate between those individuals for whom a test is a good predictor and those for whom it is a poor one. However, it remains to be seen whether it is possible to make such a differentiation in a systematic and objective fashion. It is the purpose of the present investigation to examine this possibility.

METHODS AND PROCEDURES

Scores from one test and two inventories were obtained on candidates for the job of taxicab driver at the time of hiring. The test consisted of tapping and dotting items, and the inventories consisted of 24 pairs of forced-choice items which sought to get at appropriateness of occupational level and interest in jobs involving personal relationships. The details of these devices have been described elsewhere (Brown & Ghiselli, 1949). Previous investigations have indicated that these devices have some, though modest, validity for various aspects of the job of taxicab drivers.

In the present investigation the criterion of job proficiency consisted of production during the first 12 weeks of employment. Raw production figures were corrected for temporal variation and differences in division in which the driver operated. Records were obtained on 193 men who were randomly divided into two groups, 100 comprising an experimental group, and 93 a cross-validation group.

RESULTS

The validity coefficients of the three predictors together with their intercorrelations for the experimental group are given in Table 16. The validity of the tapping and dotting test at best can be characterized as limited. Neither of the two inventories has any appreciable value as a selective device. It is apparent that any combination of scores on the test and either of the inventories, as through multiple correlation, would have no greater validity than that of the test alone.

TABLE 16
VALIDITY COEFFICIENTS OF AND INTERCORRELATIONS AMONG
PREDICTOR VARIABLES FOR THE EXPERIMENTAL GROUP

Variables	Tapping and Dotting	Occupational Level Inventory	Personal Relation- ships Inventory
Criterion	.259	.055	.125
Difference Score		.318	.126
Tapping and Dotting		.029	.283

For each individual in the experimental group, the difference between his standard score on the tapping and dotting test and his standard criterion score was computed. Differences in sign were ignored; hence an individual with a low difference score was one whose standard test and criterion scores were very similar, and an individual with a large difference score was one whose standard test and criterion scores were very different. The coefficients of correlation between these difference scores and scores on the two inventories are given in Table 16. The coefficient of correlation was found to be of moderate size for the occupational level scale and low for the personal relationships scale. Therefore there was a tendency for those individuals who made a low score on the occupational level inventory to display a correspondence between standard test and criterion scores, and for those individuals who made a high score to show a discrepancy between test and criterion scores. There was little such tendency in the case of the personal relationship inventory.

From the foregoing it would appear that if only those individuals who made low scores on the occupational-level inventory were used, the coefficient of correlation between scores on the tapping and dotting test and the criterion would be greater than the value of .259 obtained for the entire group. However, no such tendency should result from a similar selection on the basis of the personal relationship inventory.

To examine this notion, the validity coefficients for the tapping and dotting test were calculated for the cross-validation group using three degrees of selectivity on the basis of the two inventories. The validity of the test scores were calculated for the one-third and two-thirds earning the lowest scores on the two inventories. The first of these groups should be composed of the one-third of the individuals whose performance is quite predictable, with the least predictable two-thirds discarded. The second group should be composed of the individuals whose performance is fairly well predictable, with the least predictable one-third discarded.

For the one-third of the individuals in the cross-validation whose scores on the occupational-level inventory indicated their job performance should be quite predictable from the tapping and dotting test, the validity coefficient was found to be .664, whereas the validity coefficient for the most predictable two-thirds of the individuals was .323, and that for all cases only .220. On the other hand, for the one-third of the individuals whose scores on the personal relationship inventory indicated their job performance should be most predictable, the validity of the test was .000, for the most predictable two-thirds it was only .130, and for all cases it was .100.

In a practical selection situation, such as the present one with taxicab drivers, a first elimination of applicants can be made by dropping out those individuals for whom prediction of job success by means of the selection test is likely to be poor. Then a second elimination can be made on the basis of the selection test, picking those individuals whose scores are high. Thus in the present case those candidates high on the occupational level inventory could be first eliminated. This process would leave those whose performance is substantially related to scores on the tapping and dotting test. Then those scoring low in this test could be eliminated, resulting in the retention of a group whose average criterion performance is high. If the personal relationship inventory were used, no such benefits should accrue.

The question then is raised as to what proportion of candidates should be dropped out by the first screening and what proportion by the second screening. For example, if it is desired to obtain from a group of individuals 20 per cent whose criterion performance will be significantly better than average, should 40 per cent be dropped in the first screening and 40 per cent in the second screening, or should 20 per cent be dropped in the first screening and 60 per cent in the second screening? No definitive answer to this question can be offered at the present time. Undoubtedly the optimal percentages to be eliminated in the two screenings will be a function of the magnitude of the correlations between the tests, the criterion, and the difference scores.

On purely rational grounds it would appear that the optimal percentages eliminated in the two screenings would be nearly the same. If a very high proportion is eliminated in the first screening, while to be sure the prediction of success of the remainder will be good, there will be so few individuals left to eliminate in the second screening that there will be very little improvement in criterion scores. On the other hand, if very few are eliminated in the initial screening, then the validity of the selection test for the second screening will be so low that even with a high proportion eliminated the gain will be small.

To illustrate the problem, an example using the cross-validation group is presented in Figure 5. The objective of the selection process is taken as the selection of the best 20 per cent of candidates. Then various distributions of elimination between the two screenings can be made of the remaining 80 per cent. At one extreme none can be eliminated in the first screening, and the entire 80 per cent can be eliminated on the basis of the second screening. At the other extreme 80 per cent could be eliminated on the basis of the first screening and none in the second screening. The mean of the standard criterion scores of the "best" 20 per cent of individuals selected by various distributions of percentages of elimination at the two stages were calculated. The mean criterion scores of the individuals remaining after elimination are shown in Figure 5.

Reference to Figure 5 will show that using the occupational level inventory as the basis for the first elimination, when the very large proportion of individuals is eliminated either in the first screening or in the second screening, the final results are poorest. A more equitable division of elimination between first screening and second screening is superior. Best results were obtained when a somewhat larger proportion was eliminated in the first screening, rather than in the second. The personal relationship inventory, which has little or no value in selecting predictable individuals, does nothing to improve the selection of high performers on the criterion.

DISCUSSION

The results of this study point to the possibility of distinguishing applicants whose job performance can be predicted by ordinary selective procedures from those whose performance is poorly predicted. Selective procedures, therefore, can be improved not only by the addition of highly valid predictors to present procedures, but also by the addition of devices to screen out individuals whose levels of aptitude and job proficiency show little correspondence.

The investigation reported here is not sufficiently extensive to furnish many clues concerning the kinds of variables that will be useful in this type of screening. It seems likely that such variables will have a considerable degree of specificity for each particular selection situation.

FIGURE 5

Mean Criterion Scores of Workers Surviving the Selection Process Under Various Conditions of Selection

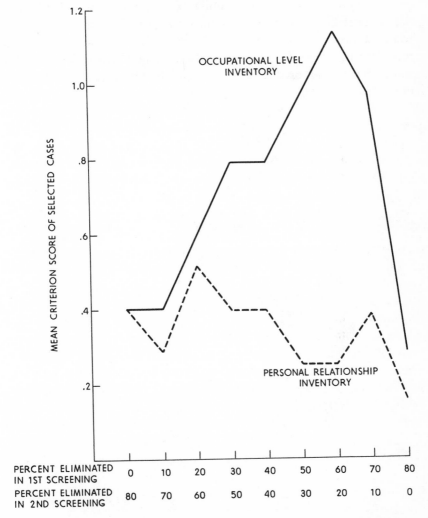

However, the results obtained with the occupational-level inventory do suggest one interesting possibility. Each item in the inventory called for a choice to be made between two jobs in terms of their interest to the testee. The two jobs were similar in nature but one was at a lower and the other at a higher level, e.g., bookkeeping and accounting. Since the job of taxicab driver is only at the semi-skilled level, presumably it would not provide sufficient challenge for a person with higher occupa-

tional ambitions. Therefore low scores on the inventory were taken as the most appropriate.

As was seen, scores on the occupational inventory were unrelated to proficiency, yet they did distinguish those individuals whose aptitude and achievement levels were similar from those whose levels were different. If the inventory does measure occupational goals, then it would appear that inclusion both of individuals whose goals are appropriate and individuals whose goals are inappropriate in a validation study masks the predictive power of the aptitude measure being evaluated.

Especially in office or industrial situations, it is frequently not possible to utilize the standard, "approved" steps in studying the validity of aptitude tests. In many instances, the time element involved is important since, unfortunately for research purposes, many personnel people are not willing to wait several months or years for true validation of test findings. Here is a proposal about "synthetic validity" which ties in job analysis procedures with actual aptitude test content.

Dr. Lawshe is Professor of Industrial Psychology at Purdue University. The article which follows is the first of a series of studies on this subject of synthetic validity which Dr. Lawshe and associates at Purdue's Occupational Research Center have published. Dr. Steinberg is Personnel Director of the Beltone Electronics Corporation in Chicago. The article is a condensed version of the original which appeared in Personnel Psychology, 1955, Vol. 8, pp. 291–301.

A Study in Synthetic Validity:

Exploratory Investigation of Clerical Jobs

C. H. Lawshe and M. D. Steinberg

This research has undertaken the task of attempting to establish test standards when accepted validation procedures are inapplicable. An elemental approach to job analysis has been used, test requirements for the elements have been established, and a procedure for their use is proposed.

The procedure for choosing tests for industrial selection purposes is well agreed upon (job analysis, experimental try-out of tests, checking test scores against a criterion, etc.). However, the extreme variability of job content, the small number of employees reporting to the same supervisor, and many related problems sometimes make the application of these procedures unrealistic or virtually impossible. Especially is this true in many office and clerical situations. Recognition of this fact prompted the senior author to propose the concept of synthetic validity to denote the inferring of validity in a specific situation. The concept is similar to that involved when the time study engineer establishes standard times for new operations, purely on a priori basis through the use of "synthetic times" for the various elements constituting the operation.

Briefly stated, the problem is this: is it possible to discover the ability requirements of small work elements as measured by tests, and in turn to determine the test pattern that should be required for a person who is to perform some combination (possibly unique) of these elements? The research reported here dealt specifically with office or clerical activity.

A job description check list,* consisting of 139 operations or elements constituting clerical activity, was used. Samples from this check list are:

> Makes simple calculations such as addition or subtraction without using a machine.
> Composes routine correspondence or memoranda, following standard operating procedures.
> Compiles numerical or statistical data for tables, charts, rate schedules, or other uses with or without using a machine.
> Approves or rejects applications, requests, claims, or other items, following operational policies or rules of action.

For the aptitude test to measure clerical skills, the Purdue Clerical Adaptability Test was employed. This test consists of the following seven sections: spelling, memory for oral instructions, arithmetic computation, checking, vocabulary, accuracy of copying (handwriting), and arithmetic reasoning. Research has shown these seven sections to be reasonably independent and the scores to be stable.

Fifteen judges, familiar with clerical activity, were asked to estimate the critical test requirement of each operation. For example, with respect to the first operation (see above) involving simple calculations, judges were asked, "How critical is spelling (the first section of the aptitude test) to the performance of this operation?" Similarly, the same question was asked with respect to each of the seven tests for each of the 139 operations in the check list. As a result, certain test areas were designated as being critical for certain operations. To illustrate with the four sample clerical operations cited above, arithmetic computation and arithmetical reasoning were judged as critical for the first operation using simple calculations; spelling (the first section of the test) was judged as critical for the second clerical operation in the list. Some operations were judged to have no critical requirements insofar as these seven tests are concerned, while some operations were judged critical in all seven.

---

*This checklist is available from Southworth's Purdue Book & Supply Stores, 308–10 State Street, West Lafayette, Indiana.

The sample studies consisted of 262 positions in 12 companies. Arrangements were made by mail and standardized instructions were supplied to all cooperating workers. Only five operations in each job were considered. These were the five designated as being most important or constituting the "core" by the supervisor. The use of these five is based on the rationale that it is "highest level" or "most important" elements in a job that differentiate it from other jobs.

The current study rests upon one fundamental assumption, i.e., in general, those incumbents who are currently employed in positions, by and large, possess those qualities which the positions demand of them. The rationale is that if an individual cannot or does not "deliver" on the job, either the employee is replaced, or the job assignment is modified. Actually, we know that this is not universally true; there are no doubt many exceptions, but in general the assumption would seem to be valid.

Specifically, then, this study sought to answer the question, "Are jobs which involve many operations with critical spelling demands presently "manned" by better spellers than are those jobs that involve few operations with critical spelling demands?" Similarly, the same question was asked with respect to each of the other six test areas.

RESULTS

In order to be able to present the data in expectancy table form, the test authors' median (50th percentile) was employed. For example, those positions which had four or five operations judged critical in spelling were found to have incumbents, 84 per cent of whom scored above the median on the spelling test. In expectancy table form, this indicates that the probability of finding a better-than-average speller on a four- or five-critical-operation job is 84 in 100. (See Table 17). Note that the probability of finding higher scorers in spelling diminishes

TABLE 17
EXPECTANCY TABLE SHOWING PROBABILITY OF FINDING A "BETTER-THAN-AVERAGE" SCORER ON THE SPELLING AND VOCABULARY SECTION AMONG EMPLOYEES CURRENTLY EMPLOYED ON POSITIONS HAVING VARIOUS NUMBERS OF CRITICAL OPERATIONS

N Critical Operations Spelling	Probability of Exceeding Median Spelling Score
4 or 5	84
2 or 3	58
0 or 1	45
Vocabulary	
4 or 5	85
1, 2 or 3	46
0	33

as the number of operations with judged critical spelling requirements decreases.

Similarly, with the results for the vocabulary tests in Table 17, it is evident that when a job includes several operations previously designated as having critical test requirements, the probability of finding a higher-than-average test scorer on that job is greater than in the case when the number of operations designated as critical is small.

SUMMARY

Based upon this study, it would then seem that we have made progress toward "synthetically" determining the test requirements for a particular job. The following procedures appear justified:

1. Apply the check list to the position.
2. Have the supervisor identify the five most important operations.
3. Determine how many of these five operations have critical requirements concerning the subsections of the test.
4. Consult expectancy tables presented as above and determine the probabilities of finding a "better-than-average" scorer on each of the subtests.
5. Administer the clerical test to applicants.
6. When the probability is high, look for a high scorer; when it is low, ignore this section of the test.

*A frequent assertion is that aptitude tests, when used in typical
employee-selection situations, save money both from the point of view
of decreased training costs as well as decreased turnover. Data in support of such generally-accepted conclusions are not too frequently
published. Many companies do not have the research staff to work up
such data; other companies prefer to keep such local information from
public scrutiny. The following study, representing research done under
the sponsorship of the Pacific Telephone and Telegraph Company,
provides a clear illustration of the enormous savings in training costs
when even relatively simple clerical aptitude tests are used as part of
the selection process. Dr. Rusmore is Professor of Psychology at San
Jose State College as well as psychological consultant to the company
in question; Mr. Toorenaar is Staff Statistician for the same company.
The article is abstracted from* Personnel Psychology, *1956, Vol. 9,
pp. 39–44.*

Reducing Training Costs by

Employment Testing

J. T. Rusmore and G. J. Toorenaar

The value of applying the cost-accounting concept to criterion construction is generally assumed, yet actual demonstrations of this concept
are rare indeed. The present study shows how certain savings were
demonstrated in a special situation.

Some time after a selection battery for telephone operators had been
introduced into the employment procedure, certain management people
inquired into the test scores of employees who, at the time of termination, had not yet measured up to the accepted performance standards
for telephone operation. A few cases called to the attention of the
research group were found to have such dramatically low test scores
that a systematic study was undertaken.

A feature of special interest in this study is the criterion. It is a
"pass-fail" criterion, a summary evaluation made by the supervisor at
the time of termination. It is suggested that such an evaluation, made

after hope of employee improvement is abandoned, and after the subtle administrative consequences of ratings have lost all meaning, may be truer than evaluations made at any other time. Although no information is available to permit the determination of the reliability of this criterion, it may be held that only a highly reliable criterion would sustain a validity coefficient of the magnitude to be reported in this study.

The predictor variable is an aptitude test battery whose component tests are scored according to the amount of work done in an allotted time and are weighted according to beta coefficients determined in the previous study. The tests are identified as numerical facility, number checking and table reading. Numerical facility is measured by addition and subtraction of one- and two-place numbers, with a time limit of 2 minutes and 40 seconds. Name checking is measured by checking pairs of names to indicate whether the members of the pair are the same or different, with a time limit of 13 minutes. Table reading is measured by reading a telephone-type rate table to determine the cost of long distance calls, with a time limit of five minutes. All tests are speeded.

The tests comprising the present battery were selected by the Wherry-Doolittle method from a group of 11 promising tests which were individually correlated with an 84-item check list criterion ($r_{cc} = .74$). No estimate of test reliability has been made. In an earlier study involving 102 employees, the multiple correlation of the three tests with the check-list criterion was .56.

In the present study, the biserial correlation of the test battery score with the "pass-fail" criterion was .81 ± .06. The 135 telephone operators here involved were hired in the first seven months and terminated in the same year. None was rejected on the basis of test scores. This short-tenure group is the entire population hired and terminated under constant conditions. Sixty employees in this group did not measure up to company standards (failed); 75 employees showed satisfactory performance (passed). The mean score for the "fail" group was 40; for the "pass" group, 58. The significance of the difference between the two means produced a t of 8.1, which well surpasses the one percent level of confidence.

Ghiselli and Brown (1955) have criticized the cost-accounting approach because it is expensive. At least in this instance, usable cost figures for both training and employment were available for the asking. If these cost figures could be reasonably related to a range of cut-off scores, the net gain or loss resulting from the use of any given cut-off score could be estimated. In general, the procedure outlined by Doppelt and Bennett (1953) was followed. Discussions with members of the appropriate operating departments revealed that the cost of rejecting an applicant in a normal labor market was about $40; the cost of training a failure was placed conservatively at $340. For any given cutting score, a net figure could be reached by subtracting the cost of all persons rejected from the savings made by rejecting the training failures.

The net dollar figures were extended from the experimental group to a typical annual employment load for the San Francisco Bay Area. The complete range of test battery scores is plotted against these annual net savings for the Bay Area in Figure 6. The curve has been smoothed to eliminate irregularities.

FIGURE 6
SMOOTHED CURVE, TEST SCORES TO NET SAVINGS IN
TRAINING OPERATORS, BAY AREA, 1951

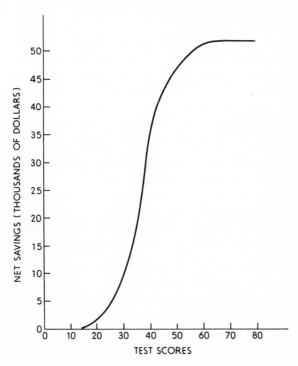

For example, assuming that the current applicant population is not different from the one studied and that management procedures and standards have remained constant, a reasonable cut-off score of 38 on the test score battery would be found to effect savings of $28,000 annually in training cost in the San Francisco Bay Area.

This study deals only with costs in employment and training. It does not touch on the larger issue of differences in productivity, but it does provide an actual demonstration of certain savings made possible by the use of a valid predictor of job success. It is suggested that psychologists in industry may find that such an actual demonstration is useful in facilitating communication between the psychologist and persons directly interested in annual net-dollar savings.

We now come, as a conclusion to this section dealing with validity, to a recent and free-wheeling dissertation on some faulty thinking in this whole area and, again, a plea for the operational approach. The student should read this article as a fairly "radical" approach, since the author demolishes several of the accepted and traditional premises about test validity. While the article rather specifically limits the discussion to "mental testers," the reader would be wise to broaden this concept to include all aptitude and achievement testing programs.

Dr. Ebel is a Vice President at the Educational Testing Service in Princeton, New Jersey. This is one of the most respected test distribution and research centers in the USA, so that any pronouncement by one of its officers carries real weight. The article originally appeared in the American Psychologist, 1961, Vol. 16, pp. 640–647.

Must All Tests Be Valid?

Robert L. Ebel

Validity has long been one of the major deities in the pantheon of the psychometrician. It is universally praised, but the good works done in its name are remarkably few. Test validation, in fact, is widely regarded as the least satisfactory aspect of test development. For this the blame is usually placed on the lack of good criterion measures. To assuage their guilt feelings about inadequate test validation, test constructors from time to time urge their colleagues to go to work on the criterion problem.

It is the purpose of this paper to develop an alternative explanation of the problem, and to propose an alternative solution. The basic difficulty in validating many tests arises, we believe, not from inadequate criteria but from logical and operational limitations of the concept of validity itself. We are persuaded that faster progress will be made toward better educational and psychological tests if validity is given a much more specific and restricted definition than is usually the case, and if it is no longer regarded as the supremely important quality of every mental test.

DIFFICULTIES WITH VALIDITY

There are at least four indications that all is not well with the concept of validity as applied to mental tests. First, test specialists differ in their definitions. Gulliksen remarks that the validity of a test is its correlation with some criterion; Cureton says it is an estimate of the correlation between the raw test scores and the "true" or perfectly reliable criterion measures. Lindquist presents the more traditional notion of validity being the accuracy with which a test measures what it intends to measure. And Edgerton says validity is the extent to which the measuring device is useful for a given purpose. Cronbach has stated that the more fully and confidently a test can be interpreted, the greater is its validity.

No exact scientist would accept such diverse statements as operationally useful definitions of the same quantitative concept. While there is obviously some conceptual similarity, there also are important divergencies. The first specifies correlation with a criterion. The second requires estimation of a corrected correlation coefficient. The third avoids statistical terms, stressing accuracy in relation to the user's intent. The fourth makes validity mean utility. The fifth relates it to interpretability of test scores. What the test developer needs is an operational definition.

Further, the generality of some of these definitions suggests that in the minds of their authors, test validity is almost synonymous with test value. But if validity does mean value, then reliability, convenience in use, adequacy of norms, and even the availability of alternate forms become aspects of validity, and we are left without a term for what Gulliksen and Cureton mean by validity. Using the same term for a variety of concepts leads to serious semantic confusions and to procedural pitfalls as well.

A closely related indication of difficulty with the concept of validity is seen in the diverse forms it must assume to fit different situations. The APA (1954) and the AERA (1955) Technical Recommendations mention four types of validity: content, predictive, concurrent, and construct. Two of these, content and construct, have little in common with the other two, or with each other. Others discuss face and factorial validity in addition to content validity, various types of empirical validity, and intrinsic validity.

Again it may be said truly that these types of validity have some common conceptual elements, but the differences are striking. To encompass all the diverse varieties of validity requires an extremely loose and general definition of the basic idea of validity. Perhaps what we really need is a more concrete and realistic conception of the complex of qualities which make a test good.

A third indication that all is not well with validity is found in this strange paradox. While almost every test specialist agrees that validity is the most important quality of a mental test, almost all of them concur on the general inadequacy of test validation. Nearly 30 years ago, in the early years of objective testing, Ruch (1933) made this comment:

There are in use today at least one thousand different educational and mental tests. Convincing critical and statistical data on the validity, reliability, and norms of these measures are available in probably less than 10 per cent of the cases.

One might reasonably expect that the situation would have improved in the intervening years, but this seems not to have happened. In a spaced sample of reviews of 20 tests in the Fifth Mental Measurements Yearbook (Buros, 1959) only one was found in which the reviewer judged the evidence of validity to be adequate. Ten tests were criticized for lack of evidence of validity. Nine reviewers made no comment about the validation of the tests they reviewed. This in itself is surprising, if validity is indeed the most important quality of any mental test. Our failure to demonstrate consistently that our tests possess the quality we value above all others may mean that we have used the wrong approach in trying to gain evidence of it.

A fourth suggestion that something may be wrong with the mental tester's concept of validity is that corresponding problems of validation seem to be almost nonexistent in the realm of physical measurements. Specialists in this area have written extensively on the measurement of physical properties, but one searches in vain through their writings for a discussion of the validity of physical measurements. They show much concern for operational definitions of quantitative concepts, for limitations on the measurability of certain properties, and for accuracy of measurement. But the question of the validity of a measuring procedure seems to arise only incidentally and indirectly. For some properties, such as the hardness of solids or the viscosity of fluids, different methods of measurement yield inconsistent results. But modern physical scientists seem never to ask which of the methods of measurement is the more valid. One is moved to wonder why this difference between mental and physical measurement. Is it possible that we have fallen into a trap of our own devising when we find it so difficult to validate our mental tests? Have we, in Berkeley's words, "first raised a dust and then complained that we cannot see?"

Refinements in the measurement of distance, for example, are not justified on the basis of superior validity, that is, as closer approximations to the measurement of true distance or true time. They are regarded rather as improvements because they permit reproducible measurement to smaller fractions of existing units of measurement, which is to say that they are justified on the basis of superior reliability.

When a shortcut substitute for some elaborate standard method of measurement is proposed, the question of the validity of the substitute method does arise with logical legitimacy. In such a situation the concept of validity is simple, and the meaning of the term is clear. We will argue for retaining this concept of validity and of restricting the term to this concept. But to ask about the validity of the basic method of measurement, which provides the operational definition of the thing being measured, would seem to most physical scientists as it does to us to be asking a meaningless question.

WHY THE DIFFICULTIES

These observations suggest that the concept of validity itself may be weak scientifically. Most of the definitions of validity can be shown to be derived from the basic notion that validity is the degree to which a test measures what it is supposed to measure. But how does one know what a test is supposed to measure? On a superficial level, perhaps, it may be suggested by the test title—academic aptitude, mathematics achievement, or social studies background, for example—but these suggestions are by no means definitive.

Does the criterion tell us what the test is supposed to measure? It might if criteria were given to us. Usually they are not. They have to be devised, often after the test itself was constructed.

The ease with which test developers can be induced to accept as criterion measures quantitative data having the slightest appearance of relevance to the trait being measured is one of the scandals of psychometry. To borrow a figure of speech from Thorndike, they will use the loudness of the thunder as a criterion for their measurements of the voltage of the lightning. Even in those rare cases where criterion measures have been painstakingly devised, the validity of the test is not determined unless the validity of the criterion has been established. This requires a criterion for the other criterion, and so on ad infinitum. We can pursue such an infinite regress until we are weary without finding a self-sufficient foundation for a claim that the test is valid.

The concept of validity is also weak philosophically. It reflects a belief in the existence of quantifiable human characteristics, such as intelligence or skill in arithmetic, independent of any operations used to measure it. Philosophers call this point of view "realism," but most of them now agree that it is not very realistic. One of Einstein's major contributions was to point out that the concept of time is scientifically meaningless until the clocks used to measure it have been described. This naive faith in the pre-existence of a quantity to be measured is basic to the general conception of validity.

You may recall the story of the three baseball umpires who were discussing their modes of operation and defending their integrity as umpires. "I call 'em as I see 'em," said the first. The second replied, "I call 'em as they are." The third said, "What I call 'em makes 'em what they are." In philosophical terms, the first was an empiricist; the second, a realist; and the third, a positivist. I should like to see test developers be less individualistic in their positivism than baseball umpires are at times, but I think they should be positivists rather than realists. Neither a strike in baseball nor scholastic aptitude in tesing is a useful concept until it has been defined in operational terms.

Many of those concerned with mental measurements however, persist in being philosophical realists. They tend to endow abstractions with a real existence. They think of a real trait which "underlies" a test score, and which is meaningfully there even though their best efforts to measure it will never be more than approximations. They think of intelligence as really existing independent of any operational definition such as those provided by the Binet, the Kuhlman-Anderson, or the Wechsler. They seek to use tests to discover what critical thinking or creativity really are instead of using the tests to define what they mean when they use such terms. They have not yet learned that realistic philosophy is productive mainly of verbal discourse, and that it must be shunned if mental measurement is to advance.

So long as what a test is supposed to measure is conceived to be an ideal quantity, unmeasurable directly and hence undefinable operationally, it is small wonder that we have trouble validating our tests. Only if we are willing to accept some actual test, or other actual method of obtaining criterion measures, as a basic (if somewhat arbitrary) operational definition of the thing we wish to measure, and only if we have some other test or measurement procedure that we wish to check against this standard, do we find the concept of test validity useful. Further, if the test we propose to use provides in itself the best available operational definition, the concept of validity does not apply. A basic definition needs to be clearly meaningful, but it does not need to be, and indeed it cannot be, validated.

One of the by-products of the realistic philosophy is mistrust of appearances and a reverence for the concealed reality. What a test or test item really measures, we warn ourselves, may be quite different from what it appears to measure. But how a person can possibly determine what it really measures without observing something that it appears to measure is never clearly explained. Those who analyze batteries of tests to determine the "underlying" factors trust appearances of what a test is measuring very little, but even they fall back on appearances when they must name the factors discovered or provide verbal descriptions of them.

The source of our concern over the deceitfulness of appearances is probably that what a test appears to measure sometimes seems to be different to different observers or when viewed in a different light. If we resolve not to trust any appearances at all, the problem vanishes, but so does our confidence in the test (and probably our sanity as well). A better course of action is to seek to understand why the appearances were not consistent.

Mistrust of appearances, in turn, leads one to seek completely empirical and deductive procedures of test validation. But completely empirical validation is seldom possible. Strictly speaking it is impossible in principle. We cannot escape judgment regarding the choice of a criterion, nor can we escape appearances (i.e., observations) in getting criterion data. To avoid an infinite regress of criterion validations, one must stop somewhere and accept or proclaim an arbitrary definition of the thing to be measured. Unfortunately this is seldom done. What happens more often is that we accept highly questionable criteria, obtain discouragingly low correlations, and finally give the whole thing up as a bad job.

A third possible explanation for difficulty with validity is that the concept is too broad. If it is made synonymous with value, or utility, or meaning, if it is made to apply to all mental tests including those used to describe persons or control educational processes as well as those used to predict future achievement, it must obviously have many different meanings. Now the trouble with using the same term to mean a variety of different things is that the meanings tend to get tangled up with each other. When the word is used in one particular sense, connotations appropriate to its use in other senses tend to hover about it and suggest irrelevant procedures.

In the case of the term "validity," we tend always to expect evidence in the form of a validity coefficient, even though such coefficients are completely appropriate only to tests used as convenient operational substitutes for more tedious, if somewhat more precise, standard measurement procedures. But when tests are used to describe educational achievement, or to assist in the control of the educational process, validity coefficients usually are quite irrelevant. The fact that they are not naturally relevant in these situations may account for some of the difficulty we encounter in trying to obtain data from which to calculate them. The obvious natural criteria we need simply do not exist in the real world, and must be conjured up from the realm of abstract ideals. Perhaps this is why evidence for the validity of educational tests is so often inadequate and unsatisfactory. Perhaps the notion of correlating test scores with criterion scores to obtain a basic index of test quality has been overgeneralized. Perhaps we have often sought to use it in situations where it does not logically apply.

It may even be that some of us, unconsciously perhaps, are glad to honor with our words a procedure of test validation which has limited applicability in practice. By so doing we exhibit our good intentions. If the procedure will not work in the absence of a good criterion, and if a good criterion is unavailable, we are excused from further effort to demonstrate test quality. We also have, in the well-recognized shortcomings of available criteria, a convenient scapegoat for the lack of good evidence of test quality. It may often be convenient to sweep the problem of test validation under the rug of inadequate or unavailable criteria, especially when we promise ourselves and others to work to get better criteria when we can find the time.

WHAT IS A CRITERION?

At this point it may be appropriate to ask what, after all, is the difference between test scores and criterion measures? Is the difference one of substance or only one of function? In the case of predictive validity the distinction is fairly clear. Test scores come first. Criterion measures are obtained later. In the case of concurrent validity the distinction gets blurred. One distinction suggested by frequent practice is that criterion measures should be ratings based on direct observations of behavior under presumably natural conditions. This would serve to distinguish them from test scores, which are almost always based on assessments of output under carefully controlled and hence somewhat artificial conditions. But ratings based on direct observations of behavior have serious and well-known psychometric shortcomings. This limits their value as criteria.

Indeed the limitation may be more serious than is commonly realized. Though it has often been done, it makes little sense to judge the accuracy with which a test does the job it is supposed to do by checking the scores it yields against those obtained from a less accurate measuring procedure. If a new method of measurement involves a better (and hence different) definition of the trait to be measured, it obviously makes no sense to judge its quality on the basis of degree of agreement with inferior measures. If the new method does not involve a better definition, but only more precise observations, it does make sense to require that the new agree with the old so far as their respective reliabilities will permit, but in this case it is hard to see the old, inferior measure as a standard or criterion for judging the quality of the new. If the criterion is used as a standard for judging the accuracy of the scores from the test, it should always exemplify a measurement procedure clearly superior to (i.e., more relevant and precise than) that embodied in the test.

In theory this could provide a useful distinction between test scores and criterion measures. In practice it seldom does. What usually happens is that the test developer pours all the skill, all the energy, and all the time he has into the process of making an outstanding test. He has none left over to spend on obtaining measurements "clearly superior" to those his test will yield, and under the circumstances would have no stomach for the task anyway. Small wonder that many good tests go unvalidated or poorly validated by conventional psychometric standards.

Predictive validity has long been recognized as one of the standard types, if not the standard type of validity. Many writers have developed the idea that the purpose of all measurement is prediction. There is a special sense in which this is true, though the surveyor or the analytic chemist might be surprised to find himself in the same occupational class as the weather forecaster. Perhaps the statement "All measurement is for prediction" belongs in the same category as the statement "All education is guidance" or even "All flesh is grass." There is a degree of truth in such statements, but if they are taken too literally they can be seriously misleading. If the predictive function of measurement is regarded as the sole function, it leads to the highly questionable conclusion that the best way to judge the quality of a measurement of something is to determine how accurately it predicts something else.

Why should the quality of a Test X as a measure of Trait X be judged by how well it predicts Trait Y when Y is a function not only of X but also of Z, W, and possibly a host of other factors? Is it reasonable to judge the quality of a barometer solely, or even mainly, by the accuracy of the weather forecasts which are made with its help? Or to consider the matter in another way, is it reasonable to suppose that Test X should by itself be a good measure of Trait Y, when Test X consists of verbal analogies, arithmetic problems, etc., while Trait Y is ultimately measured by grades assigned by a variety of teachers in courses from Art to Zoology?

Scores on Test X may indeed be related to measures of Trait Y, and the size of the correlation may indicate, in part, how useful Test X is for a particular task of selection. But loose logic is involved if that correlation is used as a measure of the validity of Test X as a measure of Trait

X. An academic aptitude test does not purport to measure academic success. It should not claim to do more than part of the job of predicting academic success.

Validity, test theorists agree, is specific—specific to a given group of individuals tested, to the treatment given them, and to a given purpose for testing (or to a given criterion). Anyone who uses a published test is almost certain to give it to a different group than the one on which it was validated. For any user's group the test may be more or less valid than it was for the test author's tryout group. Quite possibly the user may even have a somewhat different purpose for testing than the test author had in mind. His criterion may be different. Again this means that the test may be more or less valid than the author reported. Under these conditions, how can a test author possibly publish fully adequate data on validity? The best he can do is to report validity under certain clearly specified and carefully restricted conditions of use. For the majority of possible uses of a test, validation becomes inevitably a responsibility of the test user. There is thus an element of unfairness in the common complaint that test publishers fail to provide adequate data on validity.

ALTERNATIVES

Whether or not you are prepared to agree that validity has serious shortcomings as the primary basis for judging test quality, you may now be interested in what alternatives might be proposed to replace it. What basis for judging test quality would be better than validity? Cronbach's definition may provide a clue. He said: "The more fully and confidently a test can be interpreted, the greater its validity." The interpretability of a test score depends on its meaningfulness. We would suggest that meaningfulness replace validity in the usual lists of major desirable characteristics of a measuring instrument. Before this suggestion is laughed out of hearing, consider what it implies.

One, but only one, of the kinds of information that help to make test scores meaningful is the relation of those scores to other measures of the same persons. When tests are used to predict, or when they are used as convenient substitutes for more exact but more laborious measurement procedures, validity coefficients expressing the relation between test scores and criterion measures may be the most essential basis for meaning. Hence we are not proposing that either the term or the concept of validity be abolished but only that they be restricted to situations in which independent criterion measures are feasible and necessary.

Relationships of test scores to other measures can also add meaning to the test scores even when the other measures do not constitute legitimate criteria. When a test is used in a battery, knowledge of intercorrelations among the scores adds to the meaningfulness of the scores from each test. Such intercorrelations show how much the various tests measure in common, and how much independent information they provide. Construct validation also depends on relations between measures of various kinds, but thus far it has been of more direct interest and value to the psychological theorist than to the psychometrist.

Unless a measure is related to other measures, it is scientifically and operationally sterile. The validity fallacy arises from the assumption that the relation of the measure to one single other measure (the criterion) is all-important. The concept of construct validity has helped to break down this unfortunate stereotype.

What of the other kinds of information that help make test scores meaningful? Most important of all, scientifically, is a description of the operations used to obtain the scores. Operational definitions have always been basic to the meaning of measurements of length, mass, time, and other physical quantities. Such operational definitions should be basic to mental measurements as well. They would be, I am persuaded, had we not been misled by an overgeneralized concept of predictive validity.

Operational definitions of some kinds of test scores, such as speed scores in typewriting, ability scores in spelling, or vocabulary knowledge scores, are not particularly difficult to formulate. For other test scores, the problems seem more formidable. We must acknowledge that the excellence of many current tests has resulted more from the skilled intuitions of the test constructor than from preconceived excellence of design, recorded in truly controlling-test specifications. But there is no apparent reason why an adequate operational definition of the score from any test should be impossible. Such a definition obviously must cover the critical procedures in test construction, in test administration, and in scoring. The development, use, and publication of such operational definitions would, I am persuaded, not only make the test scores more meaningful, but would lead us rapidly to the production of better tests.

Reliability and Norms. There are two other types of information which contribute substantially to the meaningfulness of test scores. These have to do with the reliability of the scores and with the norms of performance for representative groups of examinees. A completely unreliable score is completely meaningless. A perfectly reliable test score is almost certainly meaningful, though it may be particularly significant or useful.

The importance of norms in making test scores meaningful requires no defense here. In the case of most educational tests they are highly useful. In a few special cases they may be unimportant or even irrelevant.

Importance and Convenience. The stress we have placed on meaningfulness of test scores, subordinating validity, reliability, and norms to it, does not mean that it can be regarded as the sole basis for judging the quality of a mental test. There are two other very important elements. One is the importance (usefulness as a basis for effective or satisfying behavior) of the knowledge or abilities required by the test. The other is the convenience of the test in use. The many factors which contribute to the convenience of a test have been well outlined by numerous authors.

A measurement can be completely meaningful and still be completely useless. For example, the number of hairs on a person's head is an operationally definable measurement. It can be related to other measurements of a person such as his age or his IQ. We could estimate its reliability and get norms for it. But it would remain, so far as I know, an almost useless measurement, one of little or no importance. Quite properly I think, critics of current educational tests are as much concerned with the importance of what the test is measuring as they are with the meaningfulness of the scores or with the convenience of the test in use.

CONCLUSIONS

It may be helpful now to summarize in outline form the characteristics which we regard as determining the quality of a mental test or measurement procedure. They are:

1. The importance of the inferences that can be made from the test scores.
2. The meaningfulness of the test scores, based on
   a. An operational definition of the measurement procedure.
   b. A knowledge of the relationships of the scores to other measures, from
      i. Validity coefficients, predictive and concurrent
      ii. Other correlation coefficients or measures of relationship
   c. A good estimate of the reliability of the scores
   d. Appropriate norms of examinee performance
3. The convenience of the test in use.

Must all tests be valid? If the term "valid" is not to be made synonymous with the term "good," if validity is a clearly-defined concept which can be quantified by finding the correlation between test scores and criterion measures, then the answer is clearly "no," on the basis of the considerations discussed in this paper.

These views may be wrong. If so, and if the current conception of validity is philosophically sound and operationally useful, let us in the name of intellectual honesty, support this claim with some good solid evidence. The time is long past for lame apologies and prolix rationalization of failure to demonstrate that good tests have the quality we have said is more important than any other. Perhaps we should recognize the age-old alternatives so far as validity is concerned. Either put up the evidence or withdraw the claim. It is my view that in general, we have not and will not be able to put up satisfactory evidence. On the other hand we should not stop being concerned about test quality. What is proposed here is that we stop beating our heads against a stone wall and step back to look for a way over it or around it. There is one, I think, and this article has attempted to elucidate it.

Having followed the argument thus far, some will say: "You still want valid tests. All you have done is to propose a different term, meaningfulness, to replace validity." This is surely not what I have been trying to do. I hope that your time has not been wasted in reading one side of a purely lexical debate. I hope that these efforts may contribute to the adoption of a more appropriate and productive procedure than validation has been for determining the quality of a test.

*   *   *   *   *

As the reader might well expect, things were not allowed to rest here. Subsequent issues of the American Psychologist *carried some spirited protests and rebuttals to the Ebel article. Jordan and Skager (1962) both sent in contributions. The former felt that Ebel, at the last moment, veered away to a pseudosolution; the latter reminded readers that the ability of a test to predict in the real world is still the essential business and that its absence cannot be compensated by something else. Renner, in another rebuttal (1962), returns to the basic theme that meaningfulness is a necessary part of validity but also that this can never be a substitute for the traditional predictive validity.*

PART EIGHT

INTELLIGENCE

To turn to the USA scene, it should be no surprise that test administrators also meet situations where testees are motivated to "beat the test." This is especially obvious in selection testing where personality inventories are employed and there have been many studies to demonstrate both faking "good" and "bad" in these situations. What may not be so obvious is that motivation can make large differences in performance on a mental ability measure, even with testees that would be presumed to be rather unsophisticated about psychological tests.

Dr. Jennings, the author of this article, is a member of the staff of the Wharton School of Finance and Commerce at the University of Pennsylvania. The test referred to (Wonderlic Personnel Test) is an industrial version of the Otis Higher Mental Examination, both widely used mental ability measures which may be administered in groups and which provide IQ ratings. The article originally appeared in the Journal of Applied Psychology, 1953, Vol. 37, pp. 168–169.

The Motivation Factor in

Testing Supervisors

Eugene E. Jennings

Effectively using psychological testing to aid in selecting supervisory personnel presents an extremely important problem in motivation. The question is whether there are differences in motivation in taking tests for research or for actual promotion purposes. If there are motivational differences between taking tests for research and for keeps, which basis of motivation will elicit test responses that more clearly reflect the individual's actual aptitude?

METHOD

The writer had an opportunity to check this with a sample of 40 supervisors who volunteered initially to participate in a testing program aimed at obtaining for research purposes a measure of the qualities and characteristics identifying the group as a whole. The supervisors were randomly divided into two groups of 20 each. Rough comparability was obtained in age, education, and experience, since differences between these means and sigmas did not exceed the .05 level of significance. The two groups identified as 1 and 2 were given the Wonderlic Personnel Test, Form A.

Three months later the same two groups were given Form B, but supervisors in Control Group 1 were encouraged to cooperate for purely research purposes while supervisors in Experimental Group 2 were asked to cooperate for the purpose of giving management additional information for determining whom among them to promote to higher supervisory levels.

In order to determine which basis of motivation elicited test scores more nearly representative of actual aptitude, a criterion of over-all performance was obtained. Superiors knowing each supervisor in Group 1 ranked them from best to poorest on over-all performance as defined in a training session. The same procedure was followed in evaluating supervisors in Group 2. A reranking of each supervisor in both groups three months later showed the criterion to have an estimated + .89 reliability. Correlations between test scores and criterion for Groups 1 and 2 for both testing situations were obtained by the rank-difference method.

RESULTS

Table 18 shows the mean scores and sigmas for Group 1 and 2 with respect to Forms A and B of the Wonderlic Personnel Test.

Whereas the differences in means and sigmas were not significant between the first and second testing for Control Group 1, Experimental Group 2, believing their performance at the second testing would affect their opportunity for promotion, increased their mean score almost seven points.

However, did supervisors in both Groups 1 and 2 maintain comparable scores in the two testing situations? The correlations by the rank-differences method between first and second testings were +.76 and

TABLE 18
SCORES OF THE WONDERLIC TESTS

	Group 1 (N = 20)	Group 2 (N = 20)	d
Form A			
Means	19.1	19.9	.78
Sigmas	5.5	5.0	.44
Form B — 3 Months later			
Means	20.0	26.6	6.63*
Sigmas	5.7	6.4	.63

*Indicates significant difference beyond .05 level of confidence.

+.39, respectively, for Groups 1 and 2. The former but not the latter is significantly greater than zero, since it exceeds the .05 level of confidence.

Generally, supervisors in Group 1 maintained comparable absolute and relative scores in both testing situations. Supervisors in Group 2 did not maintain absolute and relative scores when advised that promotions would be based on test performance. Inspection revealed that several supervisors changed rank-positions from highest to lowest, and in two cases rank values changed while numerical scores did not.

The correlations between test scores and criterion for Groups 1 and 2 were, respectively, +.41 and +.34 for the first testing and +.37 and +.67 for the second testing. Only the last correlation is significantly greater than zero, since it exceeds the .05 level of confidence.

These data tend to indicate that an insignificant relationship existed between test scores and criterion of over-all performance when the tests were administered for purely research purposes. However, changing the basis of motivation from that of research to that of promotion purposes brought about a highly significant relationship between test scores and criterion.

It might be interesting to mention that two men from Group 2 were actually promoted since the several supervisors up for consideration were just by chance in Group 2. However, their test scores were not helpful in deciding which of the several to promote since all of their scores on the second test were fairly high. But had scores on the first test, given for purely research purposes, been used to aid management in promoting two supervisors, it is doubtful that the two actually selected would have been, since they had two of the lowest scores in their group.

SUMMARY

The problem of whether there are differences in motivation in taking tests for research or for promotion purposes was studied by giving to a group of supervisors two forms of the Wonderlic Personnel Test with a time interval between for research purposes. A second group took the same two forms but the second administration was with reference to possible promotion. The following results were obtained:

1. The promotion motivation produced significant increases in the mean score whereas the control group showed no such increases.

2. The promotion changed the individual's relative standing in the experimental group as shown by the lower correlations between the two tests than occurred in the control group.

3. Scores motivated by promotion purposes had greater validity, as indicated by correlations with a criterion based on ratings of over-all performance.

Although it is very difficult to draw general conclusions, the implications of this study should serve to sound a note of caution to others doing research on aptitude tests in industry to take special pains to control the factor of motivation.

The IQ has come in for a great deal of criticism. An anonymous but facetious critic labelled it "that new tool of infant damnation." This literally becomes very serious business when the IQ score is rigidly used to classify individuals for placement in "slow learner" groups in school or, more significantly, when it is used as a basis for commitment to institutions. It is comforting to think that today test users are more sophsticated in IQ interpretation and, in the main, they are. There are school systems, however, that still insist that a child's IQ must be 74 (and not 75) before he can be admitted into a "retarded" group. Even more serious are "errors" which result in commitment to state institutions.

The following report, based on data obtained from the State Home in Beatrice, Nebraska, is by no means a survey of the whole problem. It is to the credit of the professional staff at Beatrice that this study was completed and also that these re-examinations meant the subsequent discharge of the cases reported here. This report is a condensation of the original which appeared in the American Journal of Mental Deficiency, 1960, *Vol.* 64, *pp.* 907–915. *The authors, Drs. Garfield and Affleck, are both psychologists on the staff of the Nebraska Psychiatric Institute of the University of Nebraska College of Medicine.*

A Study of Individuals Committed to a

State Home for the Retarded Who Were

Later Released as Not Mentally Defective

S. L. Garfield and D. C. Affleck

The diagnosis of mental deficiency with its concomitant problems is not always as simple a matter as it sometimes appears to be on the surface. Not only are there difficulties in differentiating a mentally retarded person from persons with other types of conditions, but an erroneous diagnosis is one which has very serious consequences for the individual concerned and in many cases for the family as well.

Although problems pertaining to the diagnosis and definition of mental retardation have received some attention, comparatively few research studies have been reported on the occurrence of incorrect diagnosis. The concept of "pseudofeeblemindedness," however, has been one evidence of difficulties in this area. More recently, concern has been expressed over problems in the diagnostic differentiation of mental deficiency from childhood autism and childhood schizophrenia. Obviously, the matter of diagnosis is important for proper treatment and disposition.

We became interested in this problem as a result of coming into contact with some cases diagnosed previously as mentally retarded, but who were found on later examination not to be retarded. On a superficial inspection these cases presented a pattern of factors which had led to institutionalization for mental deficiency or to consideration of such action. Usually the individual displayed some behavioral or social difficulty, there was an inadequate home situation, and an intellectual examination had reported an IQ below 75. In several instances, because of behavioral or personality disturbance, such individuals were studied more intensively in our setting and gave indications that they were intellectually above the retarded level. Sometimes the total score on intellectual tests was not too high, but the variability of intellectual performance suggested a state of emotional disturbance which precluded optimal functioning. We were impressed also with the tendency of some psychological examiners to report psychometric data and IQ scores with little sensitivity to other non-cognitive factors which may affect intellectual performance.

THE PRESENT STUDY

As a consequence we were interested in the problem of individuals incorrectly diagnosed as mentally retarded and in the factors that contribute to such problems in diagnosis. In contacts and visits with the staff of the Beatrice State Home, we were informed of 24 individuals who had been re-examined and found not to be mentally retarded. We decided, therefore, to make a study of these 24 cases. We were interested primarily in seeing what types of cases these were, the factors leading to their institutionalization, and the events responsible for their being judged not mentally retarded with subsequent discharge from the institution.

Fourteen of the group were males and ten were females. The group was predominantly white, with only one Negro. The age of institutionalization varied markedly for the subjects in the present investigation. The youngest was four months of age and oldest was 64 years of age at the time of admission. The period of institutionalization ranged widely

—from 1 year 8 months to almost 58 years. Seventeen of the patients had some sort of psychological examination prior to admission and, as might be expected, it was the older cases which had no such examination. While the psychological examinations played a role in the initial admission of most cases, psychological re-examinations at a later time also were instrumental in contributing to the revised judgment concerning the lack of mental retardation.

FACTORS ASSOCIATED WITH COMMITMENT

Although some similarity in patterns was noted among the cases relative to the apparent reasons for admission, there were also unique features which are not too easily categorized. One of the more frequent reasons for being institutionalized appeared to be a combination of social difficulty and lack of an adequate home situation. While this was not always the case, it seemed to be reflected in the comparatively large number who were committed to the State Home from other types of institutions—training schools, orphanages, state hospitals. The largest single group of individuals in this study were those who came to the State Home from another type of institution—11 of the current group of 24 were in this category. Various factors appeared to play a role in the eventual transfer or commitment of these patients to the State Home. These included behavioral difficulties, poor educational progress, and patterns of behavior judged to be unusual or indicative of mental disability. Generally, the individual was seen as having some type of personality or behavioral disturbance, and in most instances a psychological or psychiatric examination was then requested. If the latter indicated a low IQ or clinical judgment of mental deficiency, plans for a transfer to the State Home were instituted. This appeared to be the pattern for this group of individuals, but, of course, one cannot state on the basis of our data how frequently such a pattern occurs.

In the other cases listed, a variety of factors seemed to be responsible, including physical disability, a disturbed home situation, death of parents, and behavior judged unsatisfactory by others in the community. In several of these cases definite pressures were exerted to have the individual removed from the home or community. In one case, for example, the individual and his brother were abandoned by their mother while the father was in the service. After the father remarried there was continued bickering in the home. The boy began to act out his difficulties by stealing, setting fires, and fighting. During this period he received psychiatric treatment with somewhat variable results. The stepmother insisted on his removal from the home and he was eventually institution-

alized in the State Home. In another case, that of a 15-year-old illegiti-
mate girl, institutionalization was requested by a relative with whom
she was living and who was unable to control her. In another instance, a
27-year-old woman living with a man in a common law relationship
was committed because of complaints of abuse filed by a domestic relations worker.

Thus, while the specific situations varied somewhat, in most instances
there were serious difficulties or problems in the current life situation of
the individual. External stresses were particularly notable in the case
histories of the 14 individuals who were committed prior to their 18th
birthday. Very atypical environmental situations are seen in the fact that
eight of these persons were transferred from state or private institutions
and three others came directly from a disrupted or inadequate home situation.

PSYCHOLOGICAL TEST RESULTS

Because the results of the psychological examination played a significant role in the commitment or eventual discharge of a number of these
persons, it is of some importance to make a separate analysis of these
findings. (Table III in the original report should be consulted for
details.) Seven of the subjects had no psychological examination prior
to commitment, and these tended to be those institutionalized some years
ago. In some instances the name of the test was not indicated in the
reports in the case records. In a few cases also, the individual received
an extensive battery of tests including special and less-known instruments, and these results are not included.

The range of scores and the variation in findings are of considerable
interest, even though a competent clinical psychologist today would
not base his diagnostic impression on the IQ alone. Without question,
however, the IQ played an important role in the commitment of the
majority of these cases. Where a low IQ was obtained prior to commitment it was apparently seized upon or utilized as a means of commit-
ting the individual to the State Home. At least from the material available for some cases, one received a feeling that the individual was
viewed as a problem and the opportunity to dispose of the problem was
not to be slighted. For example, in one case when the re-examination at
the State School revealed the individual was not retarded and this was
communicated to the original institution, the latter stated the IQ didn't
matter, since the person was a difficult problem. In this instance and
in a few others there was decided reluctance to take the individual back.

A few comments can be offered with regard to psychological examinations performed prior to commitment. While most of the IQ's obtained were low, little allowance was made in the psychological reports for possible emotional factors which conceivably might have contributed to the lowered level of performance. If a number of these individuals were experiencing difficulties, were away from their home and family, or conceivably were anxious about the test situation, little was said about this and apparently it was not deemed to be of much significance. This was so, even though other data available on the cases, including psychiatric appraisals, made mention of personality difficulties, frequently of severe degree. It is of interest that seven of the 17 cases examined psychologically prior to commitment had been examined psychiatrically or received psychiatric treatment. Nevertheless, little mention was made in the psychological report of the possible influence of such disturbance on test performance. In some instances mention was made of the negativeness or inadequate cooperation of the subject, but this did not seem to influence the interpretation of the test scores. In general, the emphasis was placed on the IQ score and the interpretation of mental deficiency was followed by a prognostic statement to the effect that the individual would never progress beyond a limited level of mental development. Commitment was also recommended in most instances. By and large, these reports were quite positive in terms of the definiteness and conclusiveness of findings. In most instances, they were performed by psychologists who had not received any extensive training in clinical psychology.

In two cases, IQ's in the 80's were reported, but the individual still was committed or retained in the institution. In one of these cases an IQ of 88 by a qualified psychologist was followed by three lower IQ's reported by psychologists with limited clinical training. Even though the report containing the 88 IQ mentioned the possibility of significant emotional disturbance in the child, the later IQ's carried the day and the child was institutionalized by order of the court. In the other such case, institutionalization occurred prior to the psychological examination. This took place 40 years ago and the data are meager. However, the individual remained in the institution approximately 35 years after an IQ of 87 was obtained.

The IQ's secured at a later date in the State Home average considerably higher than those secured earlier. Unfortunately, in not all cases was a psychological examination performed prior to institutionalization, nor was the same test always used in the later examination. This makes the matter of evaluation and interpretation of the data somewhat more complicated. Obviously, different factors might be involved in the various cases, and perhaps no definitive conclusions can be drawn. After reviewing all the available data, however, the present authors believe that the most apparent explanation, at least in a large percentage of those cases tested prior to commitment, concerns the inadequacy of the original examination and the failure to evaluate the importance of emotional factors on intelligence test scores. In over half of these cases, there were data already available pointing to the existence of personality and behavioral disturbance at the time of testing. Secondly, even the brief reports by the examiners made mention of some resistiveness, peculiarity, or other unusual behavior on the part of the subject which was not considered in the evaluation of the test data. To the experienced clinician, this appeared to be definite disregard of personality variables as they affect test scores. Thirdly, in four cases which were examined at our institute, the pattern of test scores and the behavior evident during the testing situation led the clinical psychologist to consider personality disturbance as a significant variable affecting test scores. In these instances, the psychologists felt the patients' intellectual potentials were above that of the mental defective level. Other factors which seemed to play a role in the original test scores were that the individuals were examined at a time when they were experiencing some type of adjustment difficulty, were separated from home and family, were anxious or lacked motivation. It is a time honored colloquialism in mental testing that the examiner must secure rapport and cooperation with the subject in order to secure optimum results. If there seem to be factors interfering with this, the results probably cannot be viewed as valid. This view seemed to be disregarded completely in some of the cases.

While the authors were most impressed with the lack of concern on the part of previous examiners for variables which affect test scores, other explanations are also possible for some of the cases. In two cases (5 and 9), an additional explanation seems obvious. In these two instances, examinations were performed at or before age two, with IQ's in the neighborhood of 50. The IQ's at later ages on the 1937 Stanford-Binet and WISC were in the 80's. This is in line with other studies indicating the relatively poor predictive ability of infant testing. In the third case tested originally at age two, the differences between the early scores and the later ones were not as marked.

Obviously, the findings discussed do not lead automatically to definite interpretations or conclusions. The writers, in going through the case material, were struck with the very inadequate job of psychological examination in a majority of cases, the lack of sensitivity to the importance of personality factors on test scores, and the almost exclusive reliance on the IQ. To us, this was a disturbing finding with very important social consequences. However, other problems also appear to be raised by our data, even though the latter are limited. One concerns the dangers of relying on the results of tests at or before age two. The other, concerning lack of comparability between tests, also has significant practical implications, since most individuals outside of professional psychology tend to react to all IQ's as equivalent, regardless of the test used. When differences occur, which IQ's shall be considered as a basis for practical decisions? While it is certainly true that important decisions should be based on more than the IQ, our data strongly suggest that the IQ carries tremendous weight in such decisions.

FACTORS LEADING TO DISCHARGE

The majority of individuals discharged were identified primarily by two means. One of these was a retesting program instituted relatively recently. The other was the result of someone on the staff noting that an individual functioned better than expected. In these instances the individual was given a psychological examination, and if it appeared to indicate that the individual was not mentally retarded, attempts were made to have the individual discharged. Although various staff members were involved with some of these individuals, it appeared that the staff social workers were those most frequently requesting a re-evaluation because certain individuals impressed them as not being retarded. In one instance, a re-evaluation was requested by an outside agency. The psychologist's findings indicated the individual was not mentally deficient, and a recommendation for discharge was made. In three instances, various patterns of acting out or related problems led to evaluation at our own institution. It can be noted also that generally it was more difficult to get an individual out of the institution than it was to get him in. Not only are there numerous problems to consider in getting a person back into the community at large, but in some instances there was definite opposition from the community organizations which played a role in the original institutionalzation. This is another reason why errors in diagnosis leading to unnecessary or inappropriate institutionalization have unhappy consequences.

DISCUSSION

Our data appear to lend support for the need to evaluate the influence of emotional and environmental factors on tests of intelligence. Such considerations were rarely suggested in pre-commitment reports in this sample. Apparently in the desire to appear "objective," great reliance was placed on test scores alone. This reliance was not only evident in the reports, but in the reaction of social agencies and the courts to the evaluations. Credence is readily granted a reported test score because of its ease of statement and seeming objectivity. When argument did occur initially in some pre-commitment cases, it was largely over discrepant IQ scores. The misuse of IQ scores is very evident in subsequent correspondence about the cases. In some instances, the scores are cited as authoritative estimates of intellectual potential or as positive indications of how much ability the person has, e.g., "This boy has 50 per cent intelligence." "This girl has an IQ of 66 per cent; and since feeblemindedness may be quantitatively defined as any score below 70 per cent, she may be considered definitely feebleminded and classified as a moron."

In the light of these misuses, one may question the advisability of reporting IQ's. Very few persons who use psychological reports appear to understand that an IQ is only a means of ranking a person relative to a standardization group, and that when emotional disturbance is present, such ranking may not be reliable. For such reasons, it seems preferable to have a qualitative evaluation of intellectual functioning where the clinical psychologist translates his test findings into language which is meaningful to laymen and not as subject to misinterpretation.

Somewhat related to these considerations are the problems concerning the limitations of test results secured at very early ages and the matter of comparability of scores on different tests. Undoubtedly more careful research on these problems is needed, particularly in terms of which tests appear to correlate most with other criteria of social adjustment.

The high percentage (46 per cent) of cases in this sample of patients who came from other institutions is also a finding of considerable interest. It would appear that in these cases also, too great attention was given to intellectual factors and test scores when these were in great part symptoms of broader emotional disturbance. The basis for this may rest on the historical availability of institutional care for the mentally retarded and a failure to be adequately sensitive to the total functioning of the person. Where below average (or dull normal) intelligence is combined with anti-social behavior, inadequate home situation or emotional disturbance, institutionalization in a home for the retarded may be viewed as a solution to the problem, particularly if under stress the IQ falls close to the mentally retarded range. It is also possible that unless a child shows grossly psychotic behavior, emotional factors do not receive primary consideration. Related to this may be the fact that institutional facilities for emotionally-disturbed children are relatively scarce and perhaps reserved for those of higher intelligence and grosser disturbance. Outpatient treatment probably is not considered when the home situation is unstable. The net result is that the individual is incorrectly diagnosed and inappropriately institutionalized.

Finally, it should be stated that we have no precise estimate of the extent of the problem reported on here. The current sample is not the result of a statistical survey, and there are undoubtedly variations from setting to setting. Nevertheless, it does emphasize a problem which, though small in number, is important in terms of the welfare of the individual. Periodic reappraisals of the institutionalized individuals in the higher ranges of the mentally retarded would appear justified.

PART NINE

PERSONALITY

Psychological tests are frequently described as either objective or subjective and, typically, this labelling is in terms of the type of item. When most students ask an instructor about a scheduled examination, one inevitable question is whether the test is to be objective or not. By this students mean whether it is to be an essay-type examination or, say, an examination composed of multiple-choice items. A little reflection will show that the form of the item has little to do with whether the test is truly objective. It would be possible—and this is rather frequent with teacher-made achievement tests—to compose a multiple-choice or true-false item that was one hundred per cent subjective.

In the following article, condensed from the original which appeared in the Journal of Counseling Psychology, *1958, Vol. 5, pp. 285–289, Professor Cattell has carefully spelled out the distinctions between objective and subjective and, furthermore, indicated that there are two degrees of the former. Dr. Cattell, who obtained his Ph.D. from the University of London and is now Research Professor of Psychology at the Institute of Personality and Ability Testing at the University of Illinois, is famous for his work in the area of psychometrics, particularly factor analytic or multivariate analyses. He has brilliantly carried on the British psychometric approach here in the USA. He is the author of many books and articles, as well as batteries of psychological tests, in the area of personality and motivation. Dr. Cattell is the author of two large-scale research reports which have resulted in two personality tests: the Objective-Analytic Test Personality Factor Test Battery and the Sixteen Personality Factor Questionnaire.*

What Is "Objective" in
"Objective Personality Tests"?

Raymond B. Cattell

This note to practical psychologists in the mental testing area concerns itself purely with the clarifying of test nomenclature. There is no doubt that much confusion arises in the communications of practical test users, through failure of descriptive precision in the matter here to be discussed.

TWO MEANINGS OF "OBJECTIVE"

The sense in which "objective" has been increasingly used by the present writer and his co-workers is clearly distinct from the older use still appearing in many text books. This older and more trivial sense has mainly been employed by those concerned with teaching teachers the difference between essay examinations and multiple-choice achievement tests, or those preoccupied with biographical inventories and other "itemetric" approaches. It is still given equal weight with other meanings in the texts of well-known educational statisticians.

These meanings, as we shall see, are in a sense two degrees of objectivity. The term "objective," in the first degree, has been used by educational psychologists to indicate a test which requires something different from essay-type appraisal, and involves, instead, an agreed key for selective (multiple-choice) or inventive (open-ended) responses, such that all psychometrists scoring the test will get the same numerical result. However, it happens historically that the pioneers in structured personality research used the term "objective" in a more fundamental sense. In this higher degree of objectivity it was required not only that the test result should be scored similarly by two different psychologists, but that the test stimulus situation, and the whole mode of response, should be such that the subject himself could not fake the response, or distort it to fit his subjective desires for a particular kind of "good or bad" score. That is to say, there could be no "motivational distortion" such as is systematically involved in the questionnaire, i.e., the self-appraisal inventory. Incidentally, these objective tests have been far more varied in type than the pencil and paper inventories, for they have frequently not even broken down into items, but have been measures of global behavior, and have thus not been susceptible to the restricted rules of that branch of psychometrics which we may call "itemetrics." They include miniature situational tests, stylistic tests, misperception tests (projective tests), psychophysiological measures, etc., and are perhaps best illustrated by the 100 or more varieties of scores shown in my own Objective Analytic Personality Factor Test Battery. These tests are, in fact, designed to eliminate the systematic distortion through poor self-knowledge, strong motivation to make a good impression, or dishonesty, which normally reduce both the reliability and the validity of Q′-data. In general, the pioneers in this field have tacitly agreed (and the present writer concurs), in assuming that the first degree of objectivity, i.e., mere scoring objectivity, shall always be present as a prerequisite in such tests, much as one assumes that scores will not have clerical errors, or private manipulations by the examiner. There are, indeed, a considerable number of hard-headed psychometrists who are not even willing to consider that a procedure constitutes a "test" until this initial objectivity of scoring exists.

THREE MEDIA FOR PERSONALITY MEASUREMENT

It is this more radical sense of objectivity which has been consistently employed by the present writer, through 20 years of systematic personality structure investigation. This sense has been implicit in the notion that there are three, and only three, fundamental media through which measured or unmeasured data on personality can be collected, as a basis for research and theory. These three media of observation, which it is important to distinguish, both for theoretical research purposes and for efficiency of practical routine testing work, are:

1. Observations of individual behavior made in the individual's actual life situation, e.g., the behavior embedded in occupation, family relations, social life, etc., unplanned and uneffected by the observations being made. Such data can be obtained by behavior ratings, made by a sufficient number of observers, or by numerical recordings of actual events, e.g., time sampling of specific behaviors, actual records of achievements, automobile accidents, salary, human relations (sociometry). This procedure is more accurately called "life record observation," and has been systematically referred to as "L-data."

2. Observations of personality which come to the psychologist in terms of introspective, verbal, self-record and self-evaluation, typically in inventories, questionnaires, opinionnaires and all the evidence of the consulting room. This gives "mental interiors"—a view of the external behavior constituting L-data, as seen from the unique position of the subject. As just stated, such test data is naturally more subject to faking

and self deception, and does not, in any case, permit the psychometrist to calculate a conspect reliability coefficient, i.e., a correlation between two independent observers (as in L-data) or experimenters as in T-data below, since only one person—the subject—can observe from this particular vantage point. Such observations are symbolized as Q'-data (Q for questionnaire, in the broadest sense). One should distinguish between such Q'-data, in which the subject's statements about himself are accepted as descriptions, and Q-data, in which the questionnaire response itself is merely taken as "behavior," the meaning of which has still to be established by correlation with L-data behavior factors.

3. Observations on personality made by measuring actual behavior in a miniature situation—a test. The person reacts to a standard stimulus situation, and his behavior is measured in ways of which he may not be aware and with interpretations of which he will certainly not be cognizant. This child is called an objective test, or T-data. Some questionnaire response, namely, Q-data but not Q'-data, by virtue of being recorded only as behavior and not as accepted true self-evaluation, can come under the rubric of T-data, but most T-data comes from far more varied miniature situations, as indicated above.

TEST VERSUS CRITERION

It will be noted that both Q- and Q'-data and T-data come from tests, thus contrasting with L-data which comes from everyday life and is, therefore, the realm of criterion data. In calling questionnaire (Q'-data) and objective test (T-data) both test data—in contrast to L-data—we should perhaps stop to define a test as such (self evaluative or objective). In this most general form, therefore a test may be defined as: an artificial, transportable, standardized situation, which the subject recognizes and voluntarily enters, agreeing to respond within specified forms, and the responses to which are measured or classified according to rules agreed upon by psychologists. Although Q'- and T-data contrast with L-data in that both the former are tests, L- and T-data contrast, alternatively, with Q'-data in that the two first are concerned with objectively-measured behavior; while a third grouping would place L- and Q'-data over against T-data in that the two former are concerned with everyday behavior, whereas T-data can be, and commonly is, exotic or artificial.

OTHER DIMENSIONS OF PERSONALITY TESTING

Focusing attention now, within the above trio, only on the test forms of behavior measurement—in order more fully to bring out the properties defined as objective—we should note that tests, like anything else, can in general be defined in terms of either "types" or "dimensions." The division just made between objective and self-evaluative tests is really a dichotomy on a dimension, and permits recognition of other ways of "cutting the cake" to be simultaneously recognized. Indeed, in order not to fall into any confusion about the objective-vs.-self-evaluative dimension, it is desirable to work out two or three other important dimensions, including that of objectivity of scoring, referred to at the beginning. It is necessary at the outset to realize that objectivity of test, as defined here, is quite distinct from reliability and validity. However, objectivity should increase the probability of good validity (by reducing faking), of good reliability (by reducing systematic shifts in the mode of distortion from one test-motivation situation to another) and of certainty of interpretation of the test, e.g., determining the meaning of a factor found in test response.

The most important second dimension, after objective-vs.-evaluative (or self-appraising), is what can most aptly be called rative-vs.-conspective, corresponding to part of that total difference which exists in educational psychology between essay and multiple choice, and in clinical psychology between open-ended projective (or down-right crystal ball, e.g., reading character in handwriting, devices) and tests objectively scored by a key. A more precise terminology than the old "objective-vs.-subjective" is deserved by this dichotomy, and is required to distinguish it from the first and more basic dimension of objectivity just described.

Let us look more closely at what is involved. The essay or rating requires interpretation by the private judgment of the individual psychologist, and the resulting numerical value is a function of the subject's and the psychologist's personalities. (The multiple choice may also rest on no more than one unaided judgment, but it is an explicit, agreed and subsequently common judgment of all the psychologists concerned.) This difference is shown operationally in an index which the present writer, in his survey of reliability coefficients, has called the "conspect reliability coefficient," i.e., the correlation between two examiners or raters to determine how far they "see together" (conspect) in scoring tests. When the conspect reliability coefficient reaches unity, we have what has sometimes been called an objectively-scored test, or what we might now, to avoid confusion, better call a conspective test.

A conspective test might synonymously be named a "key-scored" test, were it not that this is too concrete and awkward a term, since, conceivably, perfectly conspective tests may yet be found that are not key-scored. Besides, conspective brings out the operational relation to the conspect reliability coefficient. The opposite of a conspective test one thinks of by such terms as "equivocal," "examiner-biased," "privately rated," "double-personality-determined," etc., which, though usefully descriptive, are too cumbersome. A correct Latin-derived expression would be "disspective" but since, for psychologists, the meaning of 'personal viewpoints intruding' is now well tied up with the verb "to rate," perhaps "rative" would more briefly and accurately designate the nonconspective scoring of a test.

It should be noted at once that conspective-vs.-rative is not the same dimension in the test world as "selective (fixed choice) vs.-inventive (open-ended)." For an open-ended, inventive-answer, projective test, for example, can have definite scores assigned, for all free responses, by prior agreement among psychologists. This is a third, essentially independent dimension of test design and construction. However, there will be a high prevalence of rative scoring among inventive-answer tests.

THE ESSENTIAL MEANING OF "OBJECTIVE"

Before concluding it is desirable to define more sharply the dichotomy of "objective-vs.-self-appraising" (or "taking self-evaluation at face value") tests, now that it has been sorted out from its confusion with "conspective-vs.-rative." Elsewhere the writer has defined this sense of an objective test as "A test in which the subject's behavior is measured, for inferring personality, without his being aware in what ways his behavior is likely to affect the interpretation." If he is told, as in an inventory, to evaluate himself, and the examiner accepts these descriptions, the test is obviously not meeting these conditions, for the subject knows in what sense to misrepresent in order favorably to affect the score. Only the test defined in this sense as objective escapes the motivated distortion, fakability and situation-sensitivity of the self-appraising test. In an examination of test properties in relation to L-, Q'- and T-data, the nonobjective, self-appraising form does not connote that faking must occur, while absence of self-appraisal design does not guarantee that faking cannot be effective, unless the subject does not know how his behavior is being measured or what inferences are being drawn from it. The Objective-Analytic Test Batteries illustrate the way in which test design can thus leave the subject pretty completely in the dark. He can, of course, still refuse to cooperate, and thus introduce error into his score or give no answers at all; but he cannot fake his behavior successfully to convey some impressions which he falsely (consciously or unconsciously) wishes to make.

To sum up, there are three essentially independent dimensions of test description:

1. Objective-vs.-Self-appraising. This defines the kind of stimulus response situation, and instruction, given to the subject, in terms of the degree of his ignorance of the behavior upon which he will actually be scored.

2. Selective-vs.-Inventive (open-ended), defining the kind of response situation limitations to which the subject agrees to be restricted.

3. Conspective-vs.-Rative, defining the kind of scoring situation in which the examiner is placed, and therefore the magnitude of the conspect reliability among examiners.

These three dichotomous dimensions will yield, (except for incompatibilities) eight (2^3) types of test, for which eight nouns might be used. But it would probably be simpler to depend on use of the present three-fold adjectival description. For example, use of the Rorschach with previously assigned scores for free responses constitutes an objective, inventive, conspective test; (b) certain standardized interview tests give self-appraising, inventive, rative measures; while (c) Scheier's anxiety scale is an objective, selective, conspective test. There may be other dimensions of test description needed for special purposes, but this definition of (1) stimulus situation, (2) response opportunity, and (3) scoring basis, should suffice in general to "place" a test beyond misunderstanding.

A perennial problem with all self-report devices is that of faking —conscious or unconscious. Not only does one have the unexpected situation of the desire on a testee's part to "fake good" but there is also the distinct problem of detection of the "fake bad." The latter is, for obvious reasons, not encountered as frequently as the former, but it does exist—for example, draftees "faking bad" in order to avoid military service. Earlier psychometricians paid little attention to this problem, other than resorting to exhortations for honesty, not requiring testees to sign names, and the like. In recent years, more sophisticated attempts have been made to cope with this problem. These generally are based on giving the testee a real chance to distort answers and then deriving an empirical "fake key" from this. Ruch (1942) was probably the originator of this technique where he first had college students fill out the Benreuter Personality Inventory under normal conditions and, for a second time, as if they were applying for the job of salesman which they sincerely wanted and where they knew the test scores would be used.

With the appearance of the Minnesota Multiphasic Personality Inventory (MMPI), much attention was given to the problem of conscious and unconscious faking. Of all the paper-and-pencil personality inventories, the MMPI has been the subject of the largest amount of research on this issue. Four validity scales were developed by the test authors; other psychologists have continued work towards further refinement. By necessity, most such work has involved college students who are asked to take the MMPI on repeated occasions but under different psychological sets.

In the following report, Drs. Drasgow and Barnette were able to secure a non-student group—candidates in industrial assessments by means of psychological tests for upgrading—where the application of the F — K index (Gough, 1950) brought promising results. The study was done while both authors were serving as counseling psychologists at the University of Buffalo's Vocational Counseling Center (now State University of New York at Buffalo). The report is a condensation of the original article which appeared in the Journal of Consulting Psychology, *1957, Vol. 21, pp. 399–401.*

The F scale of the MMPI is composed of items answered "true" or "false" by very few normals; any testee having several of these was probably careless or inattentive in taking the test. The K scale is the "suppressor scale" of the MMPI. High scores are secured when the testee is desirous of placing himself in a good light; low scores are earned when the testee is either unusually frank or else is adopting a highly defensive attitude. Since K is the longer of the two scales, the arithmetical result of F — K is typically a negative number.

F — K in a Motivated Group

James Drasgow and W. Leslie Barnette, Jr.

A recurring problem in the use of any personality test is the question of dissembling. The Minnesota Multiphasic Personality Inventory (MMPI) contains at least four separate scales (*?, L, K, F*) which directly contribute to evaluating the validity of the scores in the profile. Each one of these four scales assesses validity from a somewhat different approach, but apparently the only promising combination of scales to date is Gough's F minus K.

Several empirical studies have reported on the meaningfuless of the values obtained by subtracting the K raw score from the F raw score. These studies have been especially concerned with establishing optimum cutoff points in the F — K distributions. The distributions that have been studied and reported were obtained from subjects under different conditions, e.g., (a) "normal" subjects who were given no particular instructions designed to affect F — K, (b) normal subjects who were instructed to feign abnormality, (c) normals who were instructed to act more normal, and (d) patients who were given instructions designed to be analogous to those given to the first three "normal" groups. The most rewarding results have been obtained with condition (b). These studies have been well replicated and cutoff scores corroborated. The present study focuses on the unsolved reverse problem of detecting profiles which have been faked to make a "good impression."

In an attempt to discover what precise range of F — K values might be used to discriminate the subjects who were instructed to fake a "good" normal profile, earlier studies have merely concluded that more research was needed.

Why is it that the faked-good profiles have been so difficult to detect? In previous studies with subjects working under fake-good instructions, their motivation is open to question. The choice of motivated subjects by previous researchers appears to have been unfortunate since the probability of finding real differences has been minimized by supplying only instructions to stimulate motivation. The present brief report has therefore focused on this aspect and supplies a group with higher motivation.

SUBJECTS

The University's Vocational Counseling Center provides a job applicant screening service to business and industry. The job applicants from this service formed the group with which we worked. Some of the applicants were applying for jobs with companies without having been previously associated with the company, while others were old-line company employees competing for promotion to a choice spot. All S's were employed males on their "old" jobs at the time of testing. The jobs for which they were being tested included such titles as foreman, salesman, supervisor, superintendent, and vice-president. The jobs can be seen in a framework of advancement and betterment, so that in this society we can reasonably infer an appreciable degree of motivation to get the better job. Many of the men said that they had been working years for the job in question, and that it was not merely a matter of money.

The total number of "industrial cases" with MMPIs available for use in the present study was 92. Within this total pool, 66 profiles had scores within the normal range ($T = 30$ to 70), and 26 profiles had one or more scores outside. The normal sample of 66 cases is utilized here.

The modal person in the sample was a 34-year-old white married male with two children and two years of college. He was currently employed, but trying to get a "better" job.

RESULTS AND DISCUSSION

All scores on all MMPI scales on the profile were within the accepted normal range as stated earlier. The mean raw F was 1.6 and the SD was 1.5; the mean raw K was 17.6 with an SD of 3.2. The difference of —16 for $F — K$ is well beyond the .01 level.

Hunt (1948) reported a mean $F — K$ of —11 for the group of navy prisoners who were asked to make a good impression, but he was dissatisfied with this statistic because too many normals also gave this value. One might then expect an $F — K$ of this size as an indication of a "normal" amount of hypocrisy which may be associated with making a good impression in this society. Gough (1950) gives —7 to —10 as a modal range within which the majority of normals would fall.

A corroborating factor and potential source of explanation for the obtained results appeared in the relationship between a job applicant's $F - K$ and his number of dependents. Because of the restriction in the range of the number of dependents and the non-normal nature of the distribution, a non-parametric correlation technique was used to estimate the association. The correlation was .61 and significant beyond the .01 level. Concomitantly, it is of interest to report that the correlation between $F - K$ and age was zero, while that between $F - K$ and education was —.18 (Pearsonian r's in both instances).

The relatively high relationship indicated by the .61 could probably be interpreted in a variety of ways. The writers would relate it to the American middle class value of upward social mobility. We postulate that the more dependents the client has, the greater will be his felt personal responsibility and that, as a partial consequence, the more motivated he will be to make a good impression so as to secure the proposed upgrading on the job.

SUMMARY

Other MMPI studies involving $F - K$ samples where testees have been requested to fake good are criticized on the ground of inadequate motivation or felt responsibility. Results are presented, utilizing 66 normal MMPI profiles obtained from clients tested for upgrading where evidence was available for high motivation. The mean $F - K$ index for this group was —16. Age and years of education had little or no effect; number of dependents, however, was significantly related to this index. It is proposed that the felt responsibility and upward motivation of these clients are the important factors in producing such elevated $F - K$ indices.

A more slippery criterion problem presents itself in the field of personality measurement, especially where the aim is to screen out the misfits. Here, in the general area referred to as psychiatric screening, the "ability" to be measured is the individual's emotional adjustment. Especially in the military, the assumption is made that not only does such selection result in efficient performance but that it also protects individuals from the consequences of failure (which may often be severe). The article here selected tells of the success with such psychiatric screening in the U.S. Navy during World War II. It originally appeared in the Journal of Consulting Psychology, 1950, Vol. 14, pp. 35–39. *A significant conclusion is that there may be a point reached of diminishing returns. As Dr. Hunt has remarked elsewhere, such psychiatric screening works far better in military rather than in civilian settings since, in the former, the pressures both to "tell the truth" and the penalties for malingering are very great. Dr. Hunt, well known for clinical research, is Professor of Psychology at Northwestern University. Dr. Wittson was the psychiatric consultant. The study was part of a larger research project supported by the Office of Naval Research.*

The specific screening procedures, not described in the accompanying article, have been presented in detail elsewhere (Wittson and Hunt, 1945). Briefly, every entering naval recruit received a brief psychiatric interview averaging between 2–3 minutes per man and conducted by a psychiatrist. From this, plus the regular medical examination, recruits considered fit were immediately passed on to duty. Men judged unfit were admitted to an observation ward for further study; from here they were either separated from the service or returned to duty. Others, in whom some behavioral deviation was suspected but not sufficiently detectable to warrant assignment to this observation ward, were sent on to trial duty and re-examined at a later date.

It should be noted that no specific personality inventories were employed. For various army situations where printed personality inventories were used (actually printed psychiatric interviews) with success, thereby saving the time spent on actual psychiatric interviews, the student should consult Chapters 13–14 of Volume IV of Studies in Social Psychology in World War II *(Princeton University Press, 1950).*

A Validation Study of
Naval Neuropsychiatric Screening

William A. Hunt, Cecil L. Wittson and

Henrietta W. Burton

In an attempt to avoid some of the neuropsychiatric difficulties of World War I, the U.S. Navy in 1941 instituted the neuropsychiatric examination of all incoming recruits as a screening device. Every recruit was given a neuropsychiatric examination upon his arrival at a naval training station. As a result of this examination the recruit was either cleared and sent on to duty, given trial duty with re-examination, or referred to a psychiatric observation ward for further study. If as a result of this further study he was adjudged to be unfit for naval service, his case was presented before an aptitude board and he was discharged as unsuited for active duty. In some cases of severe neuropsychiatric involvement, the recruit might be referred to a hospital and discharged from there through a process of medical survey. By thus getting rid of those men who showed neuropsychiatric symptomatology of an incapacitating nature during training, the Navy hoped to reduce the subsequent rate of neuropsychiatric attrition during service. Owing to the immediate need for a screening program and the tremendous press of military activities, this prophylactic measure was accepted on an apriori basis without experimental validation. While it appears a rational and proper step from the professional point of view, many criticisms were raised concerning its necessity and its efficiency. These criticisms, plus the need for such a screening program in the event of further hostilities, make some experimental investigation of its efficacy mandatory. The present study is an attempt to subject the hypothesis that naval neuropsychiatric screening was efficacious in lowering the subsequent rate of neuropsychiatric attrition during service to more rigorous investigation than has been made previously. The hypothesis that "screening" means less subsequent psychiatric attrition during service may be stated in the following fashion: the more neuropsychiatrically unfit individuals who are removed from a sample of recruits during the recruit training period, the smaller should be the number of medical surveys for neuropsychiatric reasons among that sample during their later military service. Stated in more concise form: if neuropsychiatric screening performed its assumed function, an inverse relation should exist between the recruit screening rate at the naval training station level and the subsequent rate of neuropsychiatric attrition during service.

Three training stations were selected for our study: the USNTS, Newport; USNTS, Sampson; and USNTS, Great Lakes. At all three of these stations the same type of screening procedure was in use. All three neuropsychiatric units were, to the best of our knowledge, at about the same level of professional efficiency. The type of recruit passing through these stations can be considered to be roughly of the same sort. Material from other training stations was available but was not used, owing to the fact that the recruit populations were not comparable to the above three stations, and to the further fact that differences existed in the basic methods of screening. In our three samples, the quality of the recruit populations, the professional competence of the examining staffs, and the examining procedures themselves were all roughly comparable. An experimental check of our hypothesis demands a situation in which there exists large differences between the training station discharge rates in these installations; differences not attributable to these supposedly equated factors of population, staff and procedure. Such a situation existed in April of 1943. This date was selected because at that time there existed one major difference in the screening at these three stations, this difference being the number of men who were being rejected as a result of neuropsychiatric screening. At USNTS, Great Lakes, the psychiatric unit operated with the full support of the local command and was allowed to discharge any recruit who was considered to be unsuited for naval service. While the psychiatric unit operating at USNTS, Newport, received the support and cooperation of the command, the number of special order discharges effected was held to approximately 4 per cent. At the USNTS, Sampson, the commanding officer was not in sympathy with the screening process, and consequently while a number of unfit recruits were being detected by the neuropsychiatric unit, their separation from the service was not approved by the commandant, and few discharges were actually issued. Since there were these wide differences in the number of screening discharges issued during training in our three selected stations, we would assume that if the screening process were effective in cutting down subsequent neuropsychiatric attrition, the later incidence of neuropsychiatric difficulties among the men passing through these stations should be in inverse relation to the rate of discharges during training.

A large sample of recruits (at least 1,000 for each station) was selected from among the men entering these training stations during April of 1943. The recruits were selected at random directly from microfilm copies of the original muster lists of all new recruits arriving at the training station. The screening rate, as well as the subsequent neuropsychiatric attrition, is not derived from any station report or bureau figure, but is taken directly from the service records of the men involved. Each recruit's name and service number was forwarded to the Naval Records Center in Garden City, Long Island, New York, where his individual health record was obtained. The record was then read carefully by one of the investigators and the pertinent information on it was abstracted. As we have said before, as used in this article, screening rate during the training period refers to both the special order discharges by reason of inaptitude and the medical surveys for neuropsychiatric reasons. Subsequent neuropsychiatric attrition is defined as all medical surveys issued for neuropsychiatric reasons during military service subsequent to the training period.

The original samples selected suffered some shrinkage (about 10 per cent) due to the unavailability of records. There are two main reasons for a record being unavailable: the man may be still on active duty, or his record may be lost. Since those men who are still on duty would represent men who have suffered no neuropsychiatric difficulties sufficient for discharge, the attrition rates reported in this article are artificially high, as some "normals" are thus excluded from the population. This is never more than a matter of one or two hundredths of a per cent, however, and since it is distributed equally throughout all samples, it can be overlooked for the purposes of this article. Several repeat studies involving the investigation of the same records on two separate occasions have indicated that lost records do not represent a constant error in any one direction. We may therefore assume that our obtained samples are representative.

Table 19 gives the percentage of screening discharges during training and the percentage of subsequent neuropsychiatric discharges during approximately two-and-a-half years of service through December of 1945. The expected inverse ratio between screening rate and subsequent neuropsychiatric attrition appears and confirms our hypothesis. Apparently, screening was effective in reducing the rate of psychiatric difficulties during service. All these differences are significant at the 2 per cent level or less (less than two chances out of 100 that the differences are due to chance factors), except for the differences in subsequent attrition during service between Newport and Great Lakes samples. While the difference between Newport and Great Lakes in screening rate is significant, the difference in subsequent attrition is not. Thus the added screening discharged at Great Lakes did not produce a significant difference in the later psychiatric discharge rate. This

TABLE 19
RELATION OF TRAINING STATION SCREENING RATE TO
SUBSEQUENT NEURO-PSYCHIATRIC ATTRITION

Training Station	N	% Discharged during training	% Discharged Subsequently	% Discharged Subsequently by Years		
				1943	1944	1945
Great Lakes 1525		4.5	1.5	0.3	0.5	0.7
Newport 1173		2.6	1.8	0.5	0.4	0.9
Sampson 2823		0.7	3.0	0.6	1.0	1.5
Total 5521		2.2	2.4	0.5	0.7	1.1

suggests the possibility of a curve of diminishing returns in neuro-psychiatric screening. It may well be that there is an optimal screening rate above which it is not profitable to go, and that the Commanding Officer at Newport was correct in attempting to set some upper limit to the number of screening discharges.

A further check on this possibility of diminishing returns may be obtained by a study of the subsequent service records of 242 USNTS, Newport, recruits studied by the psychiatric unit in 1943, were sent to duty despite questionable findings. These men represented a borderline group, and included many who would have been discharged had a higher discharge rate been allowed. They are unselected, consecutive cases and the average length of service approximates that of the original group. While the overall subsequent attrition rate was 12.8 per cent, seven times that of the Newport sample reported in Table 19, 87 per cent seem to have made a successful adjustment to service. This bears out the hypothesis of an upper limit for screening. Any final answer to the question of an optimal screening rate, however, must await a great deal more data than is available at present.

Table 19 also gives the psychiatric attrition rate during subsequent service broken down by years. There is increasing attrition rate over the two-and-a-half years covered by this study, showing that neuropsychiatric disability is a function of length of service. In continuing our previously reported study of the recruits who passed through the USNTS, Newport, in September of 1941, we have been able to follow 915 cases during their subsequent service through December of 1945. Here the relation between length of service and psychiatric disability appears clearly, and the increasing rate as time goes on is dramatically illustrated by the sharp rise during 1945, the fourth year of service for the group. The yearly discharge rates for this September, 1941, group are: 1941–42, 0.2 per cent; 1943, 0.5 per cent, 1944, 0.9 per cent; 1945, 2.4 per cent. While the absolute number of discharges for psychoses is too small to be statistically reliable, no clear trend is evident for the psychoses. The increase seems rather to be in the psychoneuroses and personality disorders.

In this connection it is interesting to compare the rates of discharge for neuropsychiatric reasons with those for disciplinary reasons. In the disciplinary category we have included all discharges labeled "bad conduct," "undesirable," or "dishonorable." Table 20 gives the figures

TABLE 20
DISCIPLINARY DISCHARGES AS A FUNCTION OF
LENGTH OF SERVICE

		Per Cent Discharged			
Sample	N	1941–42	1943	1944	1945
Great Lakes '43 1525		....	0.3	0.9	0.7
Newport '43 1173		....	0.3	0.6	1.0
Sampson '43 2823		....	0.3	0.4	0.3
Newport '41 915		1.2	1.2	0.9	0.5

for disciplinary discharges by years for the three samples in this study, plus the September, 1941, sample from USNTS, Newport. An increase with length of service does not appear in the case of those disciplinary discharges.

SUMMARY

A sample of 5521 naval recruits entering three naval training stations during April, 1943, has been followed during two-and-a-half years of subsequent service to determine whether there is any relation between the number of men discharged during training (as the result of neuropsychiatric screening procedures) and subsequent neuropsychiatric attrition during service. An inverse relation appears, indicating that neuropsychiatric screening was successful in reducing subsequent neuropsychiatric attrition. The more recruits discharged for neuropsychiatric reasons during training, the less subsequent neuropsychiatric attrition during service. Subsequent attrition rates are shown to be a function of length of service. This does not appear true for disciplinary discharges.

Personality inventories, especially those of the paper-and-pencil type, have proliferated in recent years ever since the early demonstration in World War I that the Woodworth Personal Data was a useful device for spotting draftees exhibiting emotional instability. Aside from the use of such inventories as psychiatric screening devices, they are sometimes used as source material for the writing of personality descriptions of "normals." To many people—and individuals who would be expected to be sophisticated about psychological tests—it is amazing how "accurate" such descriptions can be. Here are three articles which deal with this topic. Historically, credit should probably go to the late Professor Donald Paterson of the University of Minnesota who first demonstrated what later came to be labelled "the Barnum Effect."

Dr. Marvin Dunnette, who is an industrial psychologist with the Minnesota Mining and Manufacturing Company of St. Paul, Minnesota, called attention to this phenomenon in a letter to the editor which appeared in the American Psychologist, *1957, Vol. 12, pp. 223–25.*

Use of the Sugar Pill by Industrial

Psychologists

Marvin D. Dunnette

I have become increasingly mindful of the importance and lasting significance of one of the classic contributions made by Donald G. Paterson:

CHARACTER READING AT SIGHT OF MR. X
According to the System of Mr. P. T. Barnum

Abilities: Above average in intelligence or mental alertness. Also above average in accuracy—rather painstaking at times. Deserves a reputation for neatness—dislikes turning out sloppy work. Has initiative; that is, ability to make suggestions and to get new ideas, open-mindedness.

Emotions: You have a tendency to worry at times but not to excess. You do get depressed at times but you couldn't be called moody because you are generally cheerful and rather optimistic. You have a good disposition although earlier in life you have had a struggle with yourself to control your impulses and temper.

Interests: You are strongly socially inclined, you like to meet people, especially to mix with those you know well. You appreciate art, painting and music, but you will never be a success as an artist or as a creator or composer of music.

You like sports and athletic events but devote more of your attention to reading about them in the sporting page than in actual participation.

Ambitions: You are ambitious, and deserve credit for wanting to be well thought of by your family, business associates and friends. These ambitions come out most strongly in your tendency to indulge in day-dreams, in building air-castles, but this does not mean that you fail to get into the game of life actively.

Vocational: You ought to continue to be successful so long as you stay in a social vocation. I mean if you keep at work bringing you in contact with people. Just what work you pick out isn't as important as the fact that it must be work bringing you in touch with people. On the negative side you would never have made a success at strictly theoretical work or in pure research work such as physics or neurology.*

Paterson's generalized personality sketch illustrates the "Barnum Effect" in personnel testing and evaluation. Most individuals, confronted with this description of themselves, readily believe that it sizes them up pretty well. They often wonder how the analyst can do such an accurate and insightful job, and they nearly always will accept such "accuracy" as prima-facie evidence of the validity of any of a number of personnel selection and evaluation techniques.

Actually, of course, the sketch cited above does possess a good degree of accuracy; but it is not uniquely accurate for different and specific individuals. Instead, it has a universal appeal; it is accurate for nearly all individuals regardless of their origin, race, or creed. Accuracy is achieved by using relatively trivial generalities. Yet, persons, by and large, are sufficiently naive, psychologically and sufficiently self-centered so that they are amazed by the apparent accuracy of the description. In a word, they have the wool pulled over their eyes. Thus the name "Barnum Effect" has been suggested by Meehl to be used in referring to the spurious sense of accuracy often resulting from this kind of anecdotal validation. Obviously, this sort of verification of psychological evidence has little to recommend it. In terms of the techniques used in "selling" the results, the Barnum method must be placed in a category with such arts as palmistry, graphology, tea leaf reading, and astrology.

Still, it is an unfortunate fact that many otherwise hardheaded businessmen are today behaving in a rather gullible fashion. Not a few industrial psychologists, both within firms and acting as consultants, are making heavy use of anecdotal validation in selling their wares to businessmen. In other words, they are widely prescribing methods which upon examination may be found to be similar to the medic's use of sugar pills. Surprisingly, these techniques are currently enjoying a good

---

*Reproduced as printed on page 47 of *Counseling and Psychology*. New York: Prentice-Hall, 1951.

deal of acceptance. Very likely, however, this acceptance will continue only until such practitioners are asked to produce the evidence.

The analogy, referred to above, between the use of sugar pills and psychological test validation by anecdote deserves further comment. Sugar pills or placebos are, of course, inactive, harmless pills or injections given solely for the psychological effect they may have upon a patient. Placebos are prescribed with full knowledge that they have no effect on the physiological or organic functioning of a person; yet they may have curative values. The psychological effect of receiving medication is potent when it is combined with the patient's respect and awe of the doctor and the belief that the doctor is doing what is best for him. It is widely agreed that from 50 to 70 per cent of the nation's ills may be psychologically determined. Thus, a physician may not be remiss in using the sugar pill to give psychological support to persons suffering from emotionally-induced, physical distress. A physician would be terribly remis, however, were he to prescribe sugar pills to persons suffering from organically-based disorders. The medical fraternity might well frown on such practice; for, in effect, it misrepresents the facts. Such practice holds out to the patient a hope of recovery when, in truth, the sugar-coated pill can have no such effect.

This unfounded medical usage of sugar pills is closely analogous to the practice by many industrial psychologists of capitalizing on the Barnum Effect. Consider a simple illustration: In most industrial firms, one of the most pressing personnel problems has to do with selecting and maintaining an effective, hard-driving sales force. Ineffective selling and excessive turnover among sales personnel can be extremely costly to a firm. Sales managers and other persons charged with the recruitment and selection of salesmen recognize the significance of this problem. It is common, therefore, for them to seek the help of their firm's industrial psychologist or the aid of a personnel consulting firm in discovering and instituting better methods of selection, placement, and promotion of sales personnel. At this point, it is not uncommon for psychologists to administer batteries of psychological tests from which to prepare personality sketches of various candidates. Final decisions to hire, fire, or promote sales candidates often are based on just such psychological test appraisals and the resultant sketches. Proof of the validity of such a procedure in many instances harkens back to testimonies of the uncanny accuracy of such test-based personality sketches. Obviously, the Barnum Effect may play an important role in creating false impressions of the degree to which tests are accurate and valid. The upshot is that psychological test appraisals are being employed by many currently practicing industrial psychologists as sugar-coated pills; they are being used in situations in which there has been failure to demonstrate their true therapeutic value. Further, they are being used often to create a psychological feeling of well-being; yet, in fact, they may have no proven validity for the setting in which they are being employed. In other words, tests (and other sugar pill assessment techniques) are being used with full knowledge that they may not really be useful in increasing the overall effectiveness of a firm's program of selection, placement, and promotion of personnel.

Certainly, the methods of objectively validating tests and other appraisal techniques are sufficiently well defined so that subjective impressions of test validity, based as they are on personality sketches, testimonials, and other anecdotal accounts, should merit nothing but the scorn of business. Admittedly, the problems of criterion definition of jobs, particularly at the management level, have been tough. But mere difficulty of adequate technique for validation must not become the basis for adopting what currently is an "easy out"—the sugar pill assessment technique.

As a matter of fact, it is a common complaint of "sugar pill psychologists" that the problems of test validation are just too tough. They deride the efforts of statistically-oriented psychologists to produce evidence of test validity, and they point mockingly to the "simple-minded folly" of attempting to reduce such a personal and warm thing as the function of business management to the cold and scrutinizing gaze of persons bent on measurement. They continue to rely heavily on the Barnum Effect in gaining acceptance of their wares; the cordial smile and warm handshake are about as important, it seems, as nearly any other single item in the kit of many present day industrial psychologists. Yet, these same psychologists are characterized by complete naiveté when asked to evaluate their program. They can only harken back to the "acceptance" they have gained in the eyes of management; they can offer little or no objective evidence that their inferences and predictions are accurately describing meaningful aspects of on-the-job management behavior. This attitude has been described as an anti-criterion bias.

It is my contention that such a position is not tenable nor even rationalizable. Psychological research in widely separated settings has begun to point the way toward new methods allowing more objective analysis and description of jobs and more rigorous "clinical" analysis and validation of tests and other assessment devices.

It is necessary, for the good of industrial psychology, that the Barnum

Effect be discredited as a method for the validation of psychological tests. Businessmen, as they become aware of its nature and obvious limitations, should demand sophisticated methods of test validation. In order to avoid ills resulting from the "quick cure," businessmen should, at the same time, exercise a degree of patience in their demand for the services of psychologists. It should be up to businessmen to seek objective validity which goes far beyond mere anecdotal accounts. Decisions based on psychological tests should be delayed until good evidence of the tests' validity is presented. At the same time, it is the ethical duty of industrial psychologists to resist the temptation to use tests which have not been properly validated. It is their duty to educate the persons for whom they perform services; further, it is their duty to create and maintain an atmosphere conducive to test research and validation. In many cases, they will need to "unsell" more persons on testing than they will be called upon to sell, and they will need to caution their clients concerning the many qualifications to be attached to test interpretations.

The psychologist who adopts such an approach and who retains a research attitude in his efforts to wisely validate his tests may be excused for an occasional lapse in response to pressure and the demands of expediency. For when the pressure is eased, he will redouble his efforts to validate his tests and to further specify the conditions and limitations of their use. Businessmen obviously need to be aware of methods of appropriate psychological test validation. By demanding a high level of competency from industrial and consulting psychologists, American business will render unprofitable the currently widespread use of questionable and often misguided psychological test appraisals.

University students are by no means immune from the effects of gullibility. To many students, this may come as a surprise. Forer, in an ingenious demonstration in a classroom situation with students in an introductory psychology course, clearly shows how easy it is to secure personal validation of highly specious measures.

Dr. Forer is a practicing clinical psychologist in the Los Angeles area. The original report, of which the following is a condensed version, appeared in the Journal of Abnormal & Social Psychology, 1949, Vol. 44, pp. 118–123.

The Fallacy of Personal Validations:

A Classroom Demonstration of Gullibility

B. R. Forer

This paper is concerned with some of the methodological errors which can affect estimations of the validity of personality interpretations and measuring instruments. Of prime significance is the nature of the interpretations themselves. Personality evaluations can be, and often are, couched in such general terms that they are meaningless in terms of denotability in behavior. Or they may have "universal validity" and apply to everyone.

Possession of two eyes is a characteristic of all vertebrates, hence is of no value as a differentiating factor among vertebrates. The opposing thumb does not distinguish one human being from another. At the psychological level, the acceptance of some cultural taboos appears to be universal among human beings who live within social groups. Virtually every psychological trait can be observed in some degree in everyone. For the purpose of characterizing a particular individual, stipulation of those traits which he demonstrates is a meaningless procedure. It is not in the presence or absence of a trait that individuals differ. The uniqueness of the individual lies in the relative importance of the various personality forces in determining his behavior and in the relative magnitude of these traits in comparison with other persons. Thus the individual is a unique configuration of characteristics, each of which can be found in everyone, but in varying degrees. A universally valid statement, then, is one which applies equally well to the majority or the totality of the population. The universally valid statement is true for the individual, but it lacks the quantitative specification and the proper focus which are necessary for differential diagnosis. In a sense, a universally valid statement is a description of a cultural group rather than a personal psychological datum.

A universally valid personality description is of the type most likely to be accepted by a client as a truth about himself, a truth which he considers unique in him. Many, if not most, individuals are able to recognize the characteristics in themselves—when it is not to their disadvantage—while oblivious to their presence in others. An example is the tendency for students to perceive their own problems in textbooks of abnormal psychology. In such cases the individual lacks the quantitative frame of reference necessary for a critical comparison of the printed description and his own self-evaluation.

At times, confirmation by a client or by some other person familiar with his history is used as a criterion in the validation of diagnostic inferences and procedures. Test results may suggest certain problems and characteristic modes of behavior which therapists or the client, himself, can confirm or deny. Testing the correctness of inferences about a client by requesting his evaluation of them may be called "personal validation." When the inferences are universally valid, as they often are, the confirmation is useless. The positive results obtained by personal validation can easily lull a test analyst or a therapist into a false sense of security which bolsters his conviction in the essential rightness of his philosophy of personality or his diagnostic prowess. Such false validation increases his comfort in using what may have been a dubious instrument.

The crystal-gazer is likely to be aware of some of these points and other pseudo-diagnosticians, though they may be unaware of the fallacies inherent in their procedures, make effective use of "universal validity" and "personal validation" in deceiving their clients. One way in which character analysts secure a reputation for success is through the employment of ambiguous terms that may apply to any mortal person. A naive person who receives superficial diagnostic information, especially when the social situation is prestige-laden, tends to accept such information. He is impressed by the obvious truths and may be oblivious to the discrepancies. But he does more than this. He also validates the instrument and the diagnostician.

EXPERIMENT

The following experiment was performed in the writer's class in introductory psychology to demonstrate the ease with which clients may be misled by a general personality description into unwarranted approval of a diagnostic tool. The writer had discussed his Diagnostic Interest Blank (hereafter referred to as DIB) in connection with the role of personal motivational factors in perceptual selectivity.

The DIB consists of a list of hobbies, reading materials, personal characteristics, job duties, and secret hopes and ambitions of one's ideal person. The test is interpreted qualitatively, and personality dynamics are inferred along lines similar to projective tests. Class members requested that they be given the test and a personality evaluation. The writer acquiesced.

At the next meeting the 39 students were given DIB's to fill out, and were told that they would be given a brief personality vignette as soon as the writer had time to examine their test papers. One week later each student was given a typed personality sketch with his name written on it. The writer encouraged the expressed desire of the class for secrecy regarding the content of the sketches. Fortunately, this was the day on which a quiz was scheduled; hence it was possible to ensure their sitting two seats apart without arousing suspicion. From the experimenter's point of view it was essential that no student see the sketch received by any other student, because all sketches were identical. These statements came largely from a newsstand astrology book. The students were unsuspecting.

The personality sketch contains some material which overlaps with that of Paterson [see pp. 276–277], but consists of 13 statements rather than a narrative description. A further difference lies in the fact that this sketch was designed for more nearly universal validity than Paterson's appears to have been. The sketch consists of the following items:

1. You have a great need for other people to like and admire you.
2. You have a tendency to be critical of yourself.
3. You have a great deal of unused capacity which you have not turned to your advantage.
4. While you have some personality weaknesses, you are generally able to compensate for them.
5. Your sexual adjustment has presented problems for you.
6. Disciplined and self-controlled outside, you tend to be worrisome and insecure inside.

7. At times you have serious doubts as to whether you have made the right decision or done the right thing.
8. You prefer a certain amount of change and variety and become dissatisfied when hemmed in by restrictions and limitations.
9. You pride yourself as an independent thinker and do not accept others' statements without satisfactory proof.
10. You have found it unwise to be too frank in revealing yourself to others.
11. At times you are extroverted, affable, sociable, while at other times you are introverted, wary, reserved.
12. Some of your aspirations tend to be pretty unrealistic.
13. Security is one of your major goals in life.

Before the sketches were passed to the students, instructions were given first to read the sketches and then to turn the papers over and make the following ratings:

a. Rate on a scale of zero (poor) to five (perfect) how effective the DIB is in revealing personality.
b. Rate on a scale of zero to five the degree to which the personality description reveals basic characteristics of your personality.
c. Then turn the paper again and check each statement as true or false about yourself or use a question mark if you cannot tell.

In answer to their requests students were informed that the writer had another copy of their sketch and would give it to them after the data were collected. After the papers had been returned to the writer, students were asked to raise their hands if they felt the test had done a good job. Virtually all hands went up and the students noticed this. Then the first sketch item was read and students were asked to indicate by hands whether they had found anything similar on their sketches. As all hands rose, the class burst into laughter. It was pointed out to them that the experiment had been performed as an object lesson to demonstrate the tendency to be overly impressed by vague statements and to endow the diagnostician with an unwarrantedly high degree of insight. Similarities between the demonstration and the activities of charlatans were pointed out. That the experience had meaning for them was indicated by the fact that at least one-third of the class asked for copies of the sketch so that they might try the trick on their friends.

RESULTS

The data show clearly that the group had been gulled. Ratings of adequacy of the DIB included only one rating below 4. Thus the instrument received a high degree of personal validation. In the evaluation of the sketch as a whole there were five ratings below 4. While a few students were more critical of the sketch than of the DIB, most of them were ready to admit that basic personality traits had been revealed.

The number of specific items accepted as true varied among the group from eight to 13 except for one individual who accepted only five. This same individual rated the test at 4 and the sketch at 2. Mean acceptance was 10.2 items.

No significant relationships were found between any of the ratings and sex, age, occupational background, or grades on the subsequent quiz.

In addition to the high ratings of the DIB which indicate a degree of gullibility or fallacious judgment, further evidence can be seen in the degree to which ratings were made on other than evidential grounds or contrary to the evidence. If the individual accepts all of the items as applying to himself, he is somewhat justified in accepting the instrument; if he rejects all of the items in the sketch, he is justified in rejecting the DIB.

The chi-square test indicates a degree of association, significant at the one-per cent level, between ratings of the sketch (Rating B) and the number of items checked as true. However, the operation of other factors in judgment from part to whole is clearly indicated. For some individuals the presence of eight true statements among the 13 was considered sufficient evidence for acceptance of the sketch as perfect. For others, high, but imperfect, validity was indicated by the acceptance of 12 of the 13 items. It may be said, then, that among this group of students, individuals varied in the degree to which they weighted the truth and falsity of the descriptive items in arriving at an overall evaluation.

Ratings of the DIB as a diagnostic instrument (Rating A) and number of items accepted as true show no significant relationship. On the one hand, estimation of the adequacy of the personality sketch was partially dependent upon the amount of confirmatory evidence. On the other hand, the degree of approval of the test was independent of the degree to which test results agreed with self-evaluations. That is, validation of the test instrument was an all-or-none affair, depending on a certain minimum amount of evidence. The amount of confirmatory evidence set up as a standard varied among the students.

All of the students accepted the DIB as a good or perfect instrument for personality measurement. Most of them can be accused of a logical error in accepting the test on such scanty evidence. Those who accepted the test with a rating of 5 while accepting fewer than all of the 13 statements have demonstrated a disregard for the evidence of their own criticisms. The same can be said for those who rated the test higher than the personality sketch. It is interesting that the student most critical of the personality sketch as indicated in an overall rating of 2 and acceptance of only five items, at the same time rated the DIB at 4.

RECALL OF RATINGS

Since many of the class had indicated their embarrassment at having been "taken in," the writer suspected that the dynamics of the memory process would operate in the direction of healing the results of this assault to self-esteem. The class had been informed of the distributions of ratings. Three weeks later the students were told that the writer had erased the names from their ratings sheets as he had promised. Unfortunately, he would have liked to compare their ratings with their grades on the quiz. Perhaps they would be willing to jot down from memory the ratings they had made of the DIB and the sketch. The rating scales were written on the blackboard. The students were understandably skeptical at first, but ultimately cooperative. Only 32 of the students were present who had taken the DIB and received the sketch.

Results were more or less as expected. In the case of Rating A (of the DIB) no general trends were noted: two students raised their ratings from 4 to 5 and three others lowered their ratings from 5 to 4. On the other hand, Rating B (of the sketch) tended to be lowered. Seven ratings of 5 were lowered to 4 and one rating of 5 was lowered to 3. None was raised. Thus, there is confirmation of a significant lowering in the level of acceptance of the sketch among those who had been most credulous.

CONCLUSIONS

1. Claims of validity for their methods and results by pseudo-diagnosticians can be duplicated or surpassed in the laboratory without the use of a diagnostic instrument. Blindfold personality estimates can be shown to be valid when the method of personal validation (confirmation by the client) is used for descriptive items of approximate universal validity.

2. Validation of a test instrument or of a personality sketch by means of personal validation is a fallacious procedure which presupposes objectivity of self-evaluation and an understanding of other persons on the part of the client.

3. Using the method of personal validation, a fictitious personality sketch can easily deceive persons into approving a diagnostic device, even when there is incomplete acceptance of the sketch itself. A minimum degree of correspondence between the sketch and self-evaluation

appears to engender an attitude of acceptance of the total sketch, and this attitude of acceptance is carried uncritically to the test instrument.

4. The personal validation procedure is likely to yield more fallacious results in the case of overall evaluations of a personality sketch than when specific statements are evaluated individually.

5. When self-esteem is threatened, memory functions operate in such a manner as to avert the threat and enhance self-esteem. Such memory changes are defensive distortions of recall rather than simple forgetting.

6. Clinical psychologists and others who make inferences about personality characteristics may be led into ascribing an excessively high degree of significance to these inferences. There is pressing need for clinicians to submit their own procedures, presuppositions, and, perhaps, projections to experimental scrutiny.

*   *   *   *   *

The interested reader might also enjoy a second report by Stagner (1958) where these same Forer statements were presented as a personality analysis to a group of personnel managers attending a conference at the University of Illinois. Fifty per cent of the group of 68 personnel managers rated the personality description as "amazingly accurate"; 40 per cent as "rather good"; 10 per cent as "about half and half." Stagner also reports similar results were obtained from a group of supervisors as well as from several classes of college students. Stagner concludes that "the present finding need not be limited to personnel managers alone, although they merit special consideration because of their role in deciding upon employee selection devices."

Sundberg (1955) also adapted Forer's statements and presented these fake personality descriptions, along with blind interpretations of MMPI profiles, to a group of college students. The students were unable to pick out their own bona fide personality descriptions except at a chance level; the majority thought that the fake description described them better.

Fake evaluations have typically employed vague, favorable statements about the person which are easily acceptable. Evans (1962) went a step further in supplying fake evaluations to students in an introductory psychology course at Swarthmore which involved extremely negative as well as positive personality ratings. The student reports were made very specific by giving them their results in the form of graphic rating scales with the scale dimensions clearly labelled (examples: integrity, anxiety, stability, aggression). After receiving the fake evaluations, the experimental group responded to a second adjective check list and here this group modified their second self-descriptions significantly in the direction of the fake evaluations previously received. Fur-

thermore, negative evaluations had as much effect as did positive evaluations in accounting for these shifts. Evans suggests that possibly the critical ambiguity here is in the students' understanding of themselves and the resulting uncertainty when asked to compare themselves with others. There is also the readiness of most unsure people to accept an evaluation when it emanates from a supposedly qualified source.

PART TEN

INTERESTS

Of all the many kinds of psychological measurements, research has shown that the most valid, long-term results have been obtained with the Strong Vocational Interest Blank for males. Dr. E. K. Strong, Jr., has pioneered in this research for many years and has become famous for his periodic follow-ups. It would be very difficult to find another psychological test or inventory about which so much long-range data are obtainable. This has, of course, made the SVIB one of the most useful counseling tools with college students.

The most recent publication by Strong (1955) deals with a follow-up of Stanford University students 18 years later. A volume of this size is, of course, too large to condense or abstract for a book of readings of this type. But to give the flavor of the kind of research with which Strong is engaged in, the following article, abstracted from the Journal of Applied Psychology, *1951, Vol. 35, pp. 89–91, is here presented.*

Dr. Strong has been Professor of Psychology at Stanford University since 1923 and is, obviously, one of the senior USA psychologists today. Since about 1950 he has confined all of his efforts at Stanford to vocational interest research.

Permanence of Interest Scores over 22 Years

Edward K. Strong, Jr.

A study of permanence of scores from the Vocational Interest Blank for intervals of time up to ten years was published in 1943. The data were based on test-retests of college seniors, freshmen, and 11th-grade high school students (Strong, 1943).

To the above are now added test-retest correlations for as long a period as 19 years for college freshmen and 22 years for college seniors.

In addition to answering the question: "How permanent are interest scores?" the data throw light upon additional questions. First, is interest similar to memory in that, as time goes on, the agreement between test and retest becomes less? Second, are interests progressively better established as one grows older so that the older one is when tested, the better the agreement between that test and a subsequent one? Third, which affects permanency more in the period from 17 to 44 years of age: (a) interval of time or (b) age at time of taking the test?

The data are based on: (1) seniors at Stanford University first tested in 1927 and retested in 1932, 1937 and 1949, and (2) freshmen first tested in 1930 and retested in 1931, 1939 and 1949. Six different intervals of time can be studied as to their effect upon permanency of interest scores from the data respecting seniors, and similarly, respecting freshmen. Aside from the interval of time factor in the test-retests, there is also the age factor; the seniors varied from 22 to 32 years of age and the freshmen from 19 to 28 years of age at the time of taking the test. The combinations of time interval and age are set forth in Table 21.

TABLE 21
PERMANENCE OF INTEREST SCORES

No. of Subjects (1)	Educational Level (2)	Dates Tested (3)	Age at Time of Test (4)	Interval in Years between Test and Retest (5)	Median Corre- lation (6)	Number of Subjects (7)	Corre- lation (8)
33..........11th grade	....	17	.06	.86		
148..........11th grade	....	17	1.25	.83		
57..........11th grade	....	17	2.33	.81		
50..........College freshmen	1930–31	19	1	.88	100	.83
50..........College freshmen	1930–39	19	9	.67	100	.67
50..........College freshmen	1930–49	19	19	.72	100	.66
50..........College freshmen	1931–39	20	8	.72	100	.72
50..........College freshmen	1931–49	20	18	.72	100	.70
50..........College seniors	1927–32	22	5	.84	100	.78
50..........College seniors	1927–37	22	10	.82	100	.74
50..........College seniors	1927–49	22	22	.75	100	.72
50..........College seniors	1932–37	27	5	.86		
50..........College seniors	1932–49	27	17	.84		
50..........College freshmen	1939–49	28	10	.87	100	.84
50..........College seniors	1937–49	32	12	.88		

METHOD OF ANALYSIS

There are several different ways of measuring permanence of interest scores, but the method used here is that of correlation between the scores constituting the interest profile of the test with the scores of the interest profile of the retest. In other words, the 34 occupational standard scores of a man in the test are correlated with the 34 corresponding scores of that man in the retest. Such correlations indicate how likely it is that the same general deduction from all scores will be valid in the future.

Correlations for men ranging from 17 to 32 years of age and for intervals of time from three weeks to 22 years are given in Table 21. The data for the high school students are from Finch (1935, p. 682) who used the mean to summarize the correlation from many cases. Our summary is in terms of the median of the coefficients. (With our data, medians and means are practically identical, differing on the average by only .005). In most groups the median is based on the first 50 cases in our file. The samples for seniors are not identical, since some men did not take the test in 1932 or 1937; the same is true for the samples of freshmen.

In columns 7 and 8 of Table 21, correlations are given in which the scores of 100 cases have all been plotted in one scatter diagram and one correlation calculated for all the cases. These coefficients average .035 lower than the medians of individual coefficients. It is probable that the data for the few individuals with very low correlations have affected the second set of coefficients to a greater extent than the first set. In any case we believe the median correlation of many individual records is more enlightening than the single correlation based on the intermingling of 100 records.

RESULTS

The correlation coefficients are amazingly high for test-retest cases: .84 for 5 years; .83 for 10 years; and .75 for 22 years with college seniors. A fourth of all the correlations in the six sub-groups of seniors are .90 or higher, up to .994, the highest, and 60 per cent are .80 or higher.

We concluded in 1943 that "approximately the same rank-order is maintained for occupational interest scores for intervals ranging between one and ten years." Now we can add "between one and 22 years." In other words, those who had interests most similar to engineer, lawyer, or minister on the first occasion were the ones who had scores most similar to those same criterion groups on the second occasion, and vice-versa. The data establish the fact that there is greater permanence in interest scores among student than has generally been believed.

We concluded in 1943 that "permanence of interest scores is somewhat less than for intelligence test scores but more permanent over the college period than college grades, and distinctly higher than for atti-

292 PSYCHOLOGICAL TESTS AND MEASUREMENTS

tude test scores." We now wonder whether or not intelligence test scores will prove to be any more permanent than interest scores for periods of 10 to 20 years.

The average reliability of the interest scales upon which the scores are based is about .89. On this basis the correlation between test and retest scores on a single scale should not rise above .89. The correlations considered here are not, however, correlations of scores on a single scale, but correlations between scores on 34 different scales on the test and on the subsequent retest. What the reliability is of 34 scores in a profile has not been calculated. It seemingly must be higher than .89 or we would not have five correlations in Table 21 between .86 and .88 based on cases ranging from 17-year-old boys with an interval of three months to 32-year-old men with an interval of 12 years.

Permanence of interest scores is affected by the two factors of age at the time of taking the test and interval of time between test and retest. From the data in the table it appears that the two factors are of equal importance, for the correlation between permanence and age with time interval partialed out is .818, and between permanence and time interval with age partialed out it is .812.

To the extent that permanence is affected by interval of time we may characterize interests, first, as similar to memories which fade with time, second, as phenomena which progressively change with increasing maturity, and third, as phenomena which shift with experiences peculiar to the individual. We need to know how much all changes in interests are caused by maturation, how much they are caused by individual experiences and how much by forgetting.

According to our calculations, permanence of interests is affected as much by the age at which the test is taken as by interval of time. It has previously been shown that maturation explains many changes in interests—that interests change rapidly from those held at 15 years to those held at about 25 years, and then shift in the reverse direction much more slowly from about 25 years to 55 years of age. Of the change from 15 to 25 years, roughly speaking, one-third of the change in interests is between 15.5 and 16.5 years, one-third between 16.5 and 18.5 years, and one-third between 18.5 and 25 years.

As the changes in interests because of maturation are relatively small from 22 to 32 years of age, we should expect high permanence of interests from men within this age range. This is what is shown in the table, for all the correlations are between .819 and .880 with one exception, and that is for 22-year-old seniors retested 22 years later. On the other hand, the lowest correlations in the table, i.e., .667 to .725, are for younger men, 19 to 20 years old, retested 8 to 19 years later. It is unfortunate that there are no data of still younger men tested over long periods of time, and of older men tested for very short intervals of time.

At least to the extent that permanence increases with age, interests are not to be associated with memory, for memories do not improve as one grows older. If anything, the reverse is the situation. Evidently, interests become better and better established with increasing age; and consequently, the older the man when first tested, the more likelihood that a test and retest will agree. But the data in the table indicate that although permanence is less for young men than older men, it is still remarkably high for young men. The correlation of .81 for 17-year-old boys over an interval of 2.3 years and of .72 for 19-year-old college freshmen over an interval of 19 years are evidence of high permanency of interests among young men.

Interests are not separate entities but are an aspect of activities, which are habits. As we grow older, certain activities are discarded but many more are engaged in continuously. A human being is more than a mere collection of activities, but the sum total of his activities constitutes a vital part of his makeup. It is this part of a man we measure with an interest test. Indirectly, an interest test must measure to some extent man's underlying wants and desires on the one hand, and his abilities on the other hand, for the activities must represent what he wants to do modified by what he is capable of doing.

In any attempt to test a man in order to discover what kind of person he is, it is evident that an interest test should be included in the battery.

*   *   *   *   *

Dr. Strong, in the above article, raised the general issue whether mental ability measures would prove to be any more permanent than interest inventory results. A partial answer to this query is supplied by Berdie (1955) who conducted a ten-year follow-up of University of Minnesota graduates. These results clearly show that the SVIB differentiated better among curricular groups than did other kinds of psychological tests. The prediction of which curriculum a student will graduate from is better made via the SVIB than with either aptitude or achievement tests.

An interesting sidelight on the predictive efficiency of the SVIB has emerged from the follow-up reports from the Study of Adult Development (formerly known as the Grant Study) at Harvard. Here the SVIB has been shown to work more effectively in one "subculture" than in another, and it is because of this new insight that the following article by Dr. McArthur is presented here. What follows is a considerably condensed version of the original report which appeared in the Journal of Applied Psychology, 1954, Vol. 38, pp. 346–353. *Dr. McArthur currently is psychologist at the Harvard University Health Service.*

Long-Term Validity of the Strong Interest Test in Two Subcultures

Charles McArthur

Surprisingly few long-term follow-ups have been made on the Strong Vocational Interest Blank, when one considers that the test has now been in use two decades. Strong (1943) adduces support of four rather indirect propositions:

1. Men continuing in Occupation A obtain a higher interest score in A than in any other occupation.

2. Men continuing in Occupation A obtain a higher interest score in A than other men entering other occupations.

3. Men continuing in Occupation A obtain higher scores in A than men who change from A to another occupation.

4. Men changing from Occupation A to Occupation B score higher in B prior to the change than in any other occupation, including A.

A special 20-year follow-up by Strong (1952) dealt with medical interests only but was reported in a more direct manner. Of 108 Stanford alumni who were physicians 20 years after testing, Strong reports that 70 had A ratings on the physician scale in their undergraduate tests and 14 received a rating of $B+$. In all, then, 78 per cent of these men who made careers as doctors had had a "high" physician score when tested in college.

PROCEDURE

The Sample.   A series of 61 participants in the Study of Adult Development were given the Strong Vocational Interest Blank in the academic year 1939–1940. These young men were part of a longer series selected for inter-disciplinary long-term study on the basis of their apparent "normality." All were sophomores at the time in Harvard College. We can now test the predictive power of the Strong over a fourteen year interval from 1939 to 1953.

SVIB as a Predictor. How well did the Strong taken in college predict the occupations of these men 14 years later? In Table 22 an assessmen of the correctness of prediction is made in terms of "Good Hits," "Poor Hits," and "Clean Misses." The definitions of these terms are implicit in the claims made by Strong; he feels that a good hit may

TABLE 22
FOURTEEN-YEAR VALIDATION: STRONG VOCATIONAL INTEREST BLANK

Validity	Direct	Indirect	Total
Good Hit	.22	5	27
Poor Hit	7	5	12
Clean Miss	14	7	21
Total	43	17	60

be counted when a man enters an occupation for which he scored A or which had the 1st, 2nd, or 3rd highest ranking score on his test. Less credence is given to a B+ score when it is outranked by many others, yet such scores are usually regarded as "worth some consideration" in counseling. They are here called "Poor Hits." Anything below these criteria is taken to be a "Clean Miss."

The table also specifies whether or not a scale offered a "Direct" or "Indirect" measure of interest. The indirect measures are often no fair test at all, yet a counselor might in practice be forced to make just this sort of inference (as using the Author-Journalist scale to assess the advisability of teaching drama) for lack of other evidence.

Sixty cases could be used for validation, one man being in an occupation for which no scoring scale seemed even indirectly pertinent. It becomes apparent by inspection of Table 22 that some accuracy is lost through the necessity of using indirect measures. The fairest evaluation of the Strong's predictive power may be had from the 43 men whose occupations can be directly tested. Of these, only one-third are Clean Misses. Just half were hit well.

These figures are slightly lower than those given by Strong in his follow-up of medical interests. There, about one out of four tests turned out to be complete misses. Yet one must remain pleased with an instrumen that under "blind conditions" (these tests were all unscored until 1952) predicts future behavior even half the time.

STRONG'S FIRST PROPOSITION

Had a counselor used these tests in 1939 to suggest to the boys their likeliest future vocation, he would have been downright misleading only once in every three attempts. Yet even the "good" tests would have presented him with a grave difficulty: the tests containing accurate predictions also contain too many "extraneous solutions." Like a mathematician solving a cubic equation, the counselor must enter the problem with the expectation that not all the answers offered will be real and pertinent.

Whatever its letter rating, the scale most pertinent to future choice of occupation ranked anywhere from 1st to 33rd highest out of the 44 scales for which each test was scored. The median rank of the most pertinent scale was 5th. That means that the counselor using these tests could have expected, on the average, four "extraneous solutions" with higher-ranking scores than the true solution. It is, of course, true that the "extraneous" quality of certain high scores is obvious: few would counsel a tone-deaf boy to be a musician.

Strong (1943) states that "a college student who continues ten years in the same occupation enters an occupation in which he ranks second or third best." Like our group as a whole, our men who continued in the same occupation (not considering interruption by the war) entered occupations in which, on the median, they had ranked fifth best. Once again, our figures are slightly less impressive than Strong's. It is certainly not true among our cases, men "continuing in Occupation A obtain a higher interest score in A than in any other occupation."

STRONG'S SECOND PROPOSITION

The proposition that men engaged in an occupation score higher on that occupational scale than all other men is well supported by our data. That is, doctors outscore controls on the physician scale, lawyers outscore controls on the law scale, etc. (Controls are simply all the rest of the 61 cases.) This is true for every directly scaled occupation that occurs more than once.

Strong's second proposition seems to be valid.

STRONG'S LAST TWO PROPOSITIONS

Seventeen of our 60 men have made changes in occupation other than shifts enforced by entering the armed services. Often, these men abandoned two or more vocations before settling on the job they are engaged in today. Strong's follow-up data showed that men who abandoned an occupation were likely to possess lower scores on that occupational scale than the scores made by men who continued on the job. Strong found that rule to hold "except for the records of two individuals," while we, except for one instance of tie, find it to be entirely so.

Another generalization Strong offers about men who change vocational fields is that they will proceed from a field in which they have a low score into a field in which they score high. That was true of nine of our changeable men, seven men going contrary to their tests and entering new jobs for which their test scores were lower. (One man changed between jobs with identical scores.) These figures run faintly in the right direction, probably looking even less convincing than the data from which Strong felt that Proposition 4 was "almost but not quite sustained."

CONTENTMENT IN OCCUPATION

As Strong has pointed out (1952), "the validity of an interest test should be measured in terms of satisfaction" but for this "there is no satisfactory measure." The Study of Adult Development has accumulated much data on expressed satisfaction and dissatisfaction with occupational choice, through the use of annual questionnaires.

The 1953 questionnaires were still coming in when this was written. Of the 60 men in whom we are interested, 37 had returned their questionnaires. There was, as a matter of fact, some tendency for the men engaged in occupations for which they possessed a favorable Strong score to return their questionnaires early! (Three-quarters of them had done so, as against half the men with lower scores.) For this, Fisher's p comes out .09. This is not so trivial an indication as it may appear; the study staff has long been aware that among people who are hardest to hear from are those who have a sense of not having succeeded.

Several 1953 questions were pertinent to an inferrable sentiment of job satisfaction. There were 13 men, in all, who showed some evidence of discontent, in answer to one or another of the questions. These 13, who are "less than completely happy about their jobs, only three scored A on the Strong.

OTHER EVIDENCE

These findings, though not so favorable to the test as Strong's results, nonetheless suggest that the test has its usefulness. Furthermore, someone familiar with the study participants cannot help feel that, however inaccurate its predictions of behavior, the test is measuring interests.

There is the evidence, for example, of the correlated pair of scores: lawyer and public administrator. Some men enter the law because they have politics in mind. Cases 20, 25, and 27 are examples. In Case 27, the public administrator score matches that for lawyer. In Case 25, the lawyer score is low; the choice of lawyer would seem to have been contraindicated. That would have been correct. Case 25 escapes being one of our dramatically unhappy group only because the practice of law is rationalized as a means to a political end. The Strong has measured the relative interest in law and politics quite accurately. Some indication of the injustice of "occupations entered" as a criterion of interest may be had from Case 20. This man is reported as a lawyer, and his low score on that scale makes him count in the validation as a "poor hit." Yet he, too, intends to use law as a stepping-stone into politics, a fact that was not shown in the table, since circumstances have prevented his carrying out his plans. His score on public administrator is an A. That is also the scale on which he ranks first.

One is impressed by the logic underlying the relative efficiency of the test in predicting well or poorly certain occupational choices. Engineers, ministers, and teachers seem to be highly predictable; all three are likely to choose their vocation in response to an inner "call." By contrast, men who are in their own business the Strong simply does not predict. Another way of saying these facts would be to assume that the Strong tested interest and that the difference in prediction represented differences in the importance of interest as a factor in various sorts of career choice. The very patterning of the failures of the test therefore confirms its validity as a measure of interest.

PRIVATE AND PUBLIC SCHOOL RESULTS

Suppose we explore the consequences of postulating that the Strong does measure interests. We infer that the test will predict future job choices only for those men who (consciously or unconsciously) give weight to their own interests when they choose a career. For men who do not follow their interest, the test will not predict. We therefore expect the Strong's "validity" to vary between groups known to take their own interests more or less seriously. A major instance of such a prediction is provided by our tests from men who prepared for Harvard at public and private secondary schools.

The public school boy has usually been raised in the "American success culture," described by many anthropologists. His parents' efforts focused on preparing the boy for future vocational achievement. Job choice has been for him a vital matter; his future self-esteem will hinge on his job-title and on how well he does within his occupational field. As one study participant explained it, "I have satisfied myself as to my ability to compete successfully with most of my contemporaries."

The private school boy will often have been reared in a variant orientation, ably described by Kluckhohn (1950), where child-rearing was intended to perpetuate in him a "preferred personality." Occupational role will have been subordinated to family social patterns. In our 1953 questionnaires, eleven private school boys, but only three public school boys, put family interest or personal breadth ahead of achievement values when discussing their "personal future." As Kluckhohn so nicely phrased it, the contrast is between two subcultures, one emphasizing a "doing" and the other a "being" orientation.

One consequence of this subcultural contrast is a difference in the importance assigned to interests when men make their vocational choice. In the "success culture" a son is expected to surpass (therefore often bypass) his father's occupation. Choosing a job is for him a vital matter, the more so because the choice is so greatly "up to him." So much hinges on his making a "right" choice, calculated to yield maximal success, that he will often consult his own interest pattern, either introspectively or with formal aid from a vocational counselor. By contrast, the purest case of the upper class variant is a man whose permitted choices are limited to three: trustee, lawyer, or doctor. (The study has witnessed dramatic conflicts within upper-class men when personal "calls" gave way before the pressure of tradition.) While the average private school boy is not subjected to so focal a pressure, he will nevertheless possess values reinforcing the tangible demand that he join his father or uncle in "the business," and the intangible expectation that he will first of all be the "right sort." As one participant wrote, "As near as I can tell, I have those (personal) qualities in some small measure, so I think it foolish to spend time thinking about my future."

If all this is true, we arrive at the prediction that interests will matter less, and therefore the Strong will be less valid when applied to the behavior of private school boys. Table 23 shows this to be the case. Chi-square suggests p less than .05; if we combine cells (avoiding the low cell and isolating the relation between public school attendance and "Good Hits"), we can apply Fisher's formula and arrive at p below .01. Our proposition seems well validated.

If we translate Table 23 into percentage, we discover that three-quarters of the public school tests gave some sort of "hit" on the occupation engaged in fourteen years after testing. That is exactly the figure reported by Strong (1952) for his 20-year follow-up. If, on the

TABLE 23
VALIDITY OF STRONG TEST APPLIED TO PUBLIC AND PRIVATE
SCHOOL BOYS

Validity	Public	Private	Total
Good Hit	19	8	27
Poor Hit	4	8	12
Clean Miss	8	13	21
Total	31	29	60

other hand, we try to apply the test to private school boys, our predictions will be useless almost half the time.

Splitting out the public school cases, we can try revalidating Strong's four propositions. Proposition 1 fares better: men engaged in Occupation A still do not have "a higher interest score in A than in any other occupation" but the median rank of the pertinent scale is third, where formerly it was fifth. That is more consistent with Strong's claim, quoted earlier, that the occupation continued in will have ranked first, second, or third. Proposition 2 is no better for the public school group alone; that is because some occupations (engineer, chemist) attract high scores from public school, while others (lawyer, minister) attract higher scores from private school. At any rate, Proposition 2 was already verified sufficiently. Proposition 3 was already verified in every comparison, and so cannot be improved. There is one scale (public administrator) on which Proposition 3 is false for the private school group but true for the public school group. Proposition 4 is about equally valid in both groups.

DISCUSSION

This finding will raise various questions, some of which can be answered from our data. To forestall one, the "private school effect" cannot be explained in terms of income. It is true that the Strong is less accurate when applied to families receiving over $16,000 per year, but this figure marks only the upper quartile of our income statistics, while the "private school effect" is visible at all income levels. For example, in the second income quartile, with income held reasonably constant between four and six thousand dollars, public school tests score good hits 75 per cent of the time, private school tests only 40 per cent. In all income quartiles that are adequately represented by public school cases, the proportion of misleading tests remains about one in four; in all income quartiles that are adequately represented by private school cases, the proportion of misleading tests remains about one in two.

These figures suggest that it is the fact of having attended private school (or of being reared in a subculture from which one is sent to a private school), rather than income, and somewhat independently of social class, that depressed the validity of the test. Several explanations suggest themselves. The most obvious would be that the Strong was validated against public school graduates. Next most obvious might be that attending private school is one of those "experiences affecting interests" that Super warns us have been too little studied.

SUMMARY AND CONCLUSIONS

A 14-year follow-up was made of Strong Vocational Interest Blanks administered in 1949 to participants in the Study of Adult Development. The validity of the test as a predictor of occupational choice at first appeared to be slightly lower than that reported by Strong. Of Strong's four validation propositions, two were confirmed, one (that lawyers outscore non-lawyers on the law scale, etc.) strikingly, the other (that lawyers obtain one of their best scores on the law scale, etc.) less so. The median test offered four "extraneous" predictions.

It was possible to demonstrate a relation between conformity to choices commended by the test and future vocational happiness. Choosing a job for which one had (some years before) scored "A" also seemed to reduce the likelihood of developing fatigue, irritability or other symptoms of strain.

The proposition was offered that SVIB validly measured interests, but that failure to predict what job a man would choose could be explained in terms of his making the choice on some basis other than interest. Certain case histories supported this idea as did the apparent pattern in occupations which the test predicted accurately and which it did not.

As a corollary of this preposition it was predicted that the Strong would be applicable to boys who attended a public secondary school but less useful for boys who had prepared in a private preparatory institution. That was the case. The predictive validity of the test among the public school group was almost exactly that originally reported by Strong. Among private school boys, the test was inapplicable half of the time. Further, Strong's first validation proposition was improved in the public school group, the median test record offering only two extraneous predictions.

The import of this finding may be read in one of two ways. If we assume the anthropological theories about the American middle and upper classes to be true, then this is a demonstration that "invalidity" in the Strong arises because interests do not determine choice rather than from failure of the test to measure interests. On the other hand, the implication that there may be a distinct psychology of the upper class is also pointed out.

From all this may be drawn the following conclusions:

1. The Strong has at least the validity claimed for it as a measure of interests.

2. Its most rigorous validation criterion will be the prediction of actual behavior, but even that criterion is met at least 1 time in 2.

3. We may regard as critical for understanding the use of the test Strong's proposed "future calculations as to how much other factors, such as economic conditions, family pressures, etc., affect a man's occupational career." In this respect, attention should be called to upper class variants of the American personality.

Further study of: (a) the effects of environmental pressure in conflict with interests measured by the Strong, and (b) the differences between public and private school personalities, will be made from Study of Adult Development data.

The other big name in the field of interest measurement is that of Professor G. Frederic Kuder whose Kuder Preference Record—of which there are a variety of forms—is very widely known. In contrast to the SVIB, which is sometimes described as an empirical type of interest inventory, the Kuder has been labeled a descriptive interest inventory. In recent years, however, Professor Kuder has begun research on empirically-derived keys for the new Form D (Occupational) of his Preference Record. Currently some 40 special occupational scoring keys are available.

At the 1953 meetings of the American Psychological Association, Professor Kuder delivered a paper on future developments in self-report inventories. Because of his long association with interest measurement, he was particularly fitted to assume the role of prognosticator. His paper was subsequently published in Educational & Psychological Measurement, *1954, Vol. 14, pp. 265–271, and what follows is a slighty altered version. Dr. Kuder has been Professor of Psychology at Duke University since 1948.*

Expected Developments in Interest

and Personality Inventories

G. Frederic Kuder

I approach this subject with considerable hesitation. I have an uneasy feeling there are some who believe that the best possible progress, so far as self-inventories are concerned, would be simply to eliminate them. Perhaps, indeed, that will be their ultimate fate, and perhaps I should now take my seat. However, these questionnaires seem to be rather robust at the moment. Perhaps, therefore, you will not take it amiss if I spend a few moments on what may happen to them in the fairly near future.

SPECIFICATIONS FOR COLLECTIONS OF ITEMS

In the next few years I expect considerable progress in formulating specifications for collections of items designed to be scored for a number of criteria. We cannot expect the set of items assembled on the first or second attempt to be particularly well balanced or to be the most efficient possible for the time required. A series of analyses and revisions is almost inevitable. But a few guiding principles should shorten the process of developing a good instrument. We are now in a position, I believe, where we can, on the basis of theory and experience, set down various specifications for such a collection of items. One of the requirements might well be that the items should be fairly evenly distributed throughout factor space in the general domain appropriate to the criteria. A similar requirement might be that the collection should be assembled in such a way that it will be possible to develop, without distortion, a fairly reliable measure in any direction within the factor space represented.

In setting up specifications for our hypothetical collection of items, we would also do well to remember that it is often more important to get representation of a fairly large number of different and pertinent areas than it is to obtain large samples of a very few areas. Here is an instance in which cultural lag is particularly noticeable in the measurement field. We have known for years, for example, that given two tests of equal validity but with only half enough time available for administering both tests, it is almost always better, from the standpoint of validity, to cut both tests in half than to use only one of the tests. This principle, when generalized, means that it is better to put the emphasis on trying out, systematically, items in as many promising and relatively independent areas as possible. This approach can be carried to the absurd extreme, but I do not think our errors have generally been in that direction.

The approach mentioned almost necessarily involves some sacrifice in reliability of measurement in each specific area, but in many cases any resulting loss in validity will be more than compensated for by the more complete coverage of factors related to a selected criterion. If we can have both high reliability and good coverage, so much the better, but practical considerations are likely to force some compromise between the two. There is, no doubt, a happy medium which is best for the limitations imposed by each specific situation, and I expect to see considerable theoretical and empirical work done on this problem.

THE DETECTION AND PREVENTION OF FAKING

The detection of faking is a subject which is of particular importance in this field of interest and personality. It would seem to be self-evident that there is no way of compelling any one to answer questions carefully and sincerely. Evidence from many studies leaves little room for doubt that interest and personality inventories can be faked. Whether a subject chooses to prevaricate is another matter which apparently depends pretty much upon the situation and the disposition of the subject. It appears that sincere answers often are actually obtained even when it would seem to be to the advantage of the subject to dissimulate.

Whether a person has chosen to fake may be an academic question in many cases. But there are many situations in which there is strong motivation for distorting answers, and methods for determining whether faking has occurred become important. The MMPI is the outstanding example today of a test for which evidence on this point is available. I expect to see rather intensive research on this problem, and suspect some interesting devices will be built into new tests.

Methods for discouraging and preventing faking are also likely to be worked out. In this connection, I look for a trend in occupational inventories away from items with obvious vocational significance. One of the first interest inventories developed consisted entirely of titles of occupations. Such items are, of course, the most obvious kind possible. We know, by now, that some questions can be found which are related to job satisfaction and which are not obvious to the subject. In the course of time, we may be able to build inventories composed entirely of such items. This trend will probably be a slow one, for we discover the less obvious items only by the tedious process of trial and error.

THE USE OF INVENTORIES AS PROJECTIVE DEVICES

Another promising trend is the one involving having items answered under hypothetical conditions. If these conditions are made vague enough, this procedure amounts to using inventories as projective devices. If we ask a subject to answer a blank so as to make the best impression on anyone who might see the answers, the subject can interpret "anyone" in any way he sees fit, and, we hope in a way characteristic of his own general attitudes. Items administered in this form can, of course, be analyzed with respect to various criteria, and the pattern they make with the same items administered under standard conditions can also be analyzed with respect to the criteria. One nice advantage of the hypothetical approach is that the items are probably much more difficult to fake. It is possible that the conventional form of administration may sometimes be dispensed with altogether, as in the case of certain empathy tests.

It has been my experience that quite often the scores from tests given under the hypothetical conditions have little or no relation to scores obtained under standard conditions. For example, I find that a scale concerned with a preference for being active in groups correlates almost exactly zero with itself when taken first in the standard way and then so as to make the best possible impression. This is true also of a scale concerned with a preference for familiar and stable situations. And yet these scales are actually somewhat more reliable when given according to the best impression directions than when taken in the standard fashion. Differences between the scores are, therefore, highly reliable, and give promise for study as predictor variables.

PATTERN INTERPRETATION

The importance of the reliability of the differences between scores is a point which has often been overlooked. Whenever profiles are used, there is implicit in the situation an evaluation of differences between scores. I expect more and more emphasis to be given to the importance of the reliability of these differences. We know that the differences between scores on two highly correlated tests are themselves quite unreliable. Yet how often are differences between such tests treated as though they were highly significant! On the other hand, if tests are uncorrelated, the differences in scores are just as reliable as scores on the original tests. If profiles are to mean anything, the differences between the variables in them must be reliable. This requires inevitably that the measures used must be selected and developed so as to overlap relatively little. For profile analysis we need reliable and independent measures, and I expect more emphasis on this objective in the future. It is a happy coincidence that such sets of measures simplify greatly the job of developing prediction equations.

There will, of course, be continued attention and progress in the interpretation of sets of test scores. These techniques will vary from the extremely simple ones which require little work and time to those that are costly in terms of time and money, but which are designed to squeeze a maximum of information out of the available data. It will be recognized, of course, that the technique appropriate for any situation will depend upon a number of considerations. I hope that some principles as to which technique is likely to be most fruitful within the limitations of a specific situation will be developed for the guidance of test technicians and counselors.

Now that the use of larger and larger numbers of cases apparently is becoming feasible, I expect to see more projects using the method of studying people with identical patterns, following certain Weather Bureau techniques used for weather predictions. This approach, of course, has the notable advantage that it does not assume linear relations among the variables involved. There will also no doubt be more and more attention given to patterns of responses to individual items and to patterns of responses to small groups of items.

ITEM ANALYSIS

Quite a bit of attention has been given in recent years to the development of techniques of item analysis which take account of item overlapping when combining selected items for the prediction of a criterion, without actually computing the item intercorrelations—a job which is usually not feasible. There is room for much more progress along this line, however. I think there will be considerable application of an approach which I shall call the "criterion vector" method of test construction. This method involves building up a test by selecting items. so that the composite will have as nearly as possible the same order of correlations with the tests in the experimental battery as the criterion has with them. If all true variance in the items is accounted for by the tests in the battery, this approach is as effective as considering item intercorrelations, but it involves getting only the correlations of each item with all the tests rather than with all other items and is, therefore, a practical procedure even when the number of items is large.

Of course all this work to allow for item overlapping becomes unnecessary if a composite of items is well designed. If the items are evenly distributed in factor space, as suggested earlier, the centroid of the items with significant validities should come close to coinciding with the criterion vector. In this case, all that is necessary in the construction of a scale is to obtain the correlations of the items with the criterion. The overlapping of items is automatically allowed for. However, the development of such composites will be a time-consuming task. We can expect that the objective of a perfectly uniform distribution of items in factor space will be only approximately achieved. In the meantime, there will continue to be a need for other techniques which allow for item overlapping.

In the face of the trend toward short-cut methods of allowing for item overlapping, we may note that machines have been developed which make it easier to obtain large tables of item intercorrelations, and I expect to see larger and larger tables of this sort. One investigator has recently obtained the 44,850 intercorrelations of 300 items. I hesitate to guess how large a job some courageous soul will tackle within the next ten years. I note with some incredulity that one writer has mentioned at least the possibility of getting the 499,500 intercorrelations from a thousand items.

FACTOR ANALYSIS

There will, no doubt, be more factor analyses. In the future, however, I expect more success in building tests which come close to matching the factors identified by the analyses. The identification of factors does not automatically endow an investigator with good measures of those factors, but this fact has not always been recognized. One does not have to look far in the personality field to find batteries of measures which overlap markedly, although designed to measure factors which are found in the original analysis to be theoretically independent. I think that by now we have more insight into the problem and principles involved, and recognize that the job is not quite as simple as it may have at first appeared. We know that it is not enough merely to attempt to build a measure of a factor by the method of internal consistency. As items are selected for a factor, the correlations of the growing composite with the other factors must be carefully controlled. The criterion vector method of test construction, mentioned previously, is appropriate to this situation when the factor for which the scale is being constructed is taken as the criterion. In the future, we should be more successful in building tests to fit the factors.

I also expect to see more use of suppressor variables in the future. We are likely to see more attempts to develop alternatives for preference items which have equal appeal or apparent equal social approval, although I am inclined to regard this objective as a will-o'-the-wisp. I think the empirical search for promising theoretical variables will continue to be fruitful in this field. There will no doubt be growing interest in tests of empathy. I expect to see increased attention given to the satisfaction a person gets from a course or a job as a criterion. All in all, we can look forward to quite a number of interesting developments.

PART ELEVEN

CRITIQUES

OF

TESTING

To conclude this set of readings, and to avoid any contention of professional bias, two "lay" critiques of psychological testing are here presented, plus a third from a "professional." The first of these is by William H. Whyte, Jr., one of the editors of Fortune Magazine, *where this article originally appeared in the September, 1954, issue. Mr. Whyte is probably best konwn for his stimulating and controversial book,* The Organization Man *(1956). An expanded version of this article appeared in the appendix to this book under the title, "How To Cheat on Personality Tests." What is reproduced here is a considerably abbreviated version of the original* Fortune *piece.*

Mr. Whyte is one of the most apt of the critics of personality testing, especially when utilized for industrial assessments. He rightly gives credit to the psychologists themselves, who have not stood aside and unprotestingly allowed these practices to go undetected. A more recent and more angry protest, but in the exposé journalist tradition, is the book by Gross (1962) with the "loaded" title of The Brain Watchers. *The fire here is mostly directed at the use of projective tests for industrial evaluations, but the typical paper-and-pencil type of personality inventory also comes in for heavy criticism. Unlike Mr. Whyte, Mr. Gross only occasionally refers to the efforts of the psychologists themselves to right some of these wrongs. Curious readers may also want to consult the appendix to the Gross volume, where the author presents his "Corporate Adjustment Inventory" which, he states, is based on current "question-and-answer personality test theories" (sic) and which*

309

he has developed solely as illustrative material for the testee. Self-scoring directions are provided and some interpretative suggestions given for the guidance of a hypothetical personnel man who has the decision of whether to hire or not.

The Fallacies of "Personality" Testing

William H. Whyte, Jr.

Business is being tantalized by a fascinating possibility. After a long experimentation period with school children, college students, and inmates of institutions, applied psychologists are becoming more and more confident that with "personality" tests they can come close to answering the hitherto elusive question of who will succeed and who won't.

At first there were only rough measures—such as how introverted and neurotic a man is—but there are now in regular business use tests that tell a man's superiors his degree of radicalism versus conservatism, his practical judgment, social judgment, degree of perseverance, stability, contentment, hostility to society, and latent homosexuality. Some psychologists are tinkering with a test of sense of humor. To probe even deeper, testers are also applying the "projective" techniques like the Rorschach Ink Blot Test, which lead the subject into x-raying himself for latent feelings and psychoses.

America's secondary-school educators were the first to seize upon these tests, but business is catching up very quickly indeed. Two years ago only about a third of U.S. corporations used personality testing; since then the proportion has been climbing—of the 63 corporations checked by *Fortune,* 60 per cent are using personality tests, and these include such bellwether firms as Sears, General Electric, and Westinghouse. While there are still some executives vigorously opposed to personality testing, all the signs point to a further increase.

But the really significant development is in personality testing. In perhaps 25 per cent of the country's corporations, the tests are used not merely to help screen out those who shouldn't get into the organization, but to check up on people who are already in it. And the people being checked on, furthermore, are not workers so much as management itself. Some of these companies don't bother to give personality tests to workers at all; aside from the fact that testing can be very expensive, they feel that the limited number of psychologists available should concentrate on the more crucial questions.

HOW NEUROTIC ARE EXECUTIVES?

Should Jones be promoted or put on the shelf? Just about the time an executive reaches 45 or 50 and begins to get butterflies in his stomach wondering what it has all added up to and whether the long-sought prize is to be his after all, the company is probably wondering, too. Where once the man's superiors would have threshed this out among themselves, in some companies they now check first with the psychologists to find out what the tests say. At Sears, for example, for the last ten years no one has been promoted in the upper brackets until the board chairman has consulted the tests. At Sears, as elsewhere, the formal decision is, of course, based on other factors also, but the weight now being given test reports makes it clear that for many a potential executive, the most critical day he spends in his life will be the one he spends taking tests.

One result has been the rise of a considerable industry. In the last five years the number of test blanks sold has risen 300 per cent. The growth of psychological consulting firms has paralleled the rise; in addition to such established firms as the Psychological Corporation, literally hundreds of consultants are setting up shop. Science Research Associates of Chicago, a leading test supplier, reports that within the last twelve months, 700 new consultants have asked to be put on its approved list of customers. Colleges are also getting into the business; through research centers like Rensselaer Polytechnic's Personnel Testing Laboratory, they have become directly competitive with leading commercial firms.

The types of service offered vary greatly. Some firms will do the entire operation by mail; for example, the Klein Institute for Aptitude Testing, Inc., of New York, within 48 hours of getting the completed test back will have an analysis on its way to the company. Usually, however, the job is done on the premises. Sometimes the consultant group, like the Activity Vector Analysts, will process the entire management group at one crack. More usually the analysts, very often a group of professors in mufti, will come in and study the organization in order to find the personality "profiles" best suited for particular jobs. They will then tailor a battery of tests and master profiles. Though the analysts may help out with the machinery of testing, the company's personnel deparment generally handles the rest of the job.

A dynamic would appear to be at work. The more people that are tested, the more test results there are to correlate, and the more correlations, the surer are many testers of predicting success or failure, and thus the more reason there is for more organizations to test more and more people. At Westinghouse Electric, for example, 10,000 management men have already been coded onto IBM cards thát contain, in addition to vital statistics and work records, the men's personality-test ratings. What with the schools already doing much the same thing, with electronics making mass testing increasingly easy, there seems no barrier to the building of such inventories for every organization— except common sense. For a large question remains: leaving aside for the moment the matter of invasion of privacy, have the tests themselves been really tested?

WHO FLUNKED?

In an effort to find out, *Fortune* did some extensive testing of its own. What was under investigation, let it be made plain, was not the use of tests as guides in clinical work, or their use in counseling when the individual himself seeks the counseling. Neither was it the problem of ethics raised by the work of some practitioners in the field, interesting as this bypath is. What we have addressed ourselves to is the validity of "personality" tests as a standardized way of rating and slotting people. Question: do the tests really discriminate the man of promise from the run of the mill—or do they discriminate against him?

What would happen if the presidents of our largest corporations took the same tests that future executives are being judged by? What would happen if the tests were applied to a group of scientists, not just average scientists, but a group of the most productive ones in the world? Would they be rated as good risks? Would their scores jibe with their achievements? By actually giving tests to 60 exceptional persons, we found out. Conclusion: if the tests were rigorously applied across the board today, half of the most dynamic men in business would be out walking the streets for a job.

The effects of the day-to-day use of tests are less spectacular, but they are nonetheless far reaching. For the tests, *Fortune* submits, do not do what they are supposed to do. They do not do what they are supposed to do because, for one thing, they are not scientific. Neither in the questions nor in the evaluation are they neutral; they are, instead, loaded with debatable assumptions and questions of values. The result, deliberate or not, is a set of yardsticks that reward the conformist, the pedestrian, the unimaginative—at the expense of the exceptional individual whom management most needs to attract.

WHAT IS "PERSONALITY"?

To a large degree the growing acceptance of personality tests rests on prestige by association, for these tests at first glance seem no more than an extension of the established methods of aptitude testing. The difference, however, is crucial. What is being measured in aptitude and intelligence testing are responses that can be rated objectively—such as the correctness of the answer to 2 + 2 or the number of triangles in a bisected rectangle. The conclusions drawn from these aptitude and intelligence scores are, furthermore, limited to the relatively modest prediction of a man's minimum ability to do the same sort of thing he is asked to do on the tests. If the tests indicate that a man has only 5,000 words in his vocabulary, it is a reasonable assumption that he won't do particularly well in a job requiring 50,000 words. If he is all thumbs when he puts wiggly blocks together, he won't be very good at a job requiring enough manual dexterity to put things like wiggly blocks together.

To jump from aptitude testing to personality testing, however, is to jump from the measurable to the immeasurable. The mathematics is impeccable—and thus entrapping. Because "percentiles" and "coefficients" and "standard deviations" are of themselves neutral (and impressive sounding), the sheer methodology of using them can convince people that they are translating uncertainty, the subjective into the objective, and eliminating utterly the bugbear of value judgments. But the mathematics does not eliminate values, it only obscures them. No matter how objective testers try to be, even in the phrasing of their questions they are inevitably influenced by the customs and values of their particular world.

Questions designed to find your degree of sociability are an example. In some groups the reading of a book is an unsocial act, and the person who confesses he has at times preferred books to companions might have to be quite introverted to do such a thing. But the question is relative; applied to someone in a climate where reading is normal— indeed, the source of much social talk—the hidden "value judgment" built into the test can give a totally unobjective result. People are not always social in the same terms; a person who would earn himself an unsocial score by saying he would prefer bridge to bowling with the gang is not necessarily unsocial, and he might even be a strong extrovert. It could be that he just doesn't like bowling.

If the layman gags at the phrasing of a question, testers reply, sometimes with a chuckle, this is merely a matter of "face validity." They concede that it is better if the questions seem to make sense, but they claim that the question itself is not so important as the way large numbers of people have answered it over a period of time. To put it in another way, if 100 contented supervisors overwhelmingly answer a particular question in a certain way, this means something, and thus no matter whether the question is nonsensical or not, it has produced a meaningful correlation coefficient.

LOGROLLING WITH STATISTICS

Meaning what? This is not the place to go into a lengthy dissertation on statistics, but two points should be made about the impressive test charts and tables that so often paralyze executives' common sense. A large proportion of the mathematics is purely internal; that is, different parts of the tests are compared with each other rather than with external evidence. Second, the external evidence used in many "validation" studies will be found on closer examination to consist of the scores persons made on similar personality tests rather than such untidy matters as how they actually performed on the job. That there should be a correlation between test scores is hardly surprising; test authors are forever borrowing questions from each other (some questions have been reincarnated in as many as ten or twelve different tests) and what the correlations largely prove is how incestuous tests can be.

But how much have scores been related to individual behavior? Among themselves psychologists raise the same question, and for muted savagery there is nothing to match the critiques they make of each other's tests. The Bernreuter Personality Inventory is a particular case in point. This is by far the most widely used test in business (1953 sales by Stanford University Press, one of several distributors: one million copies). Yet a reading of the professional journals shows a long succession of negative results; when psychologists independently checked Bernreuter scores against other, more objective evidence of what the people tested were like, they found no significant relationships, and sometimes reverse correlations.

As top psychologists point out, a really rigorous validation would demand that a firm hire all comers for a period of time, test them, seal away the tests so that the scores would not prejudice superiors, and then, several years later, unseal the scores and match them against the actual performance of the individuals involved. This has rarely been even attempted. To be sure, a good bit of work on the performance of groups has been done; for example, a group considered more productive has an average score on a test higher than another group. The average of a group, however, tells us very little about the individuals involved, for some of the "best" people will have lower test scores than some of the "poor" ones.

Testers evade this abyss by relying on a whole battery of tests rather than on just one or two. But no matter how many variables you add you cannot make a constant of them. If a man has a high "contentment index" and at the same time a very high "irritability index," does the one good cancel the other bad? Frequently the tester finds himself right back where he started from. If he is a perceptive man he may make a very accurate prognosis, but when, several years later, the prognosis turns out to be true, this is adduced as evidence of the amazing accuracy of test scores.

And there is the matter of the "profile." Testers collate in chart form personality scores for groups of people in different occupations to show how they compare with other adults on several personality traits. This is generally expressed as a "percentile" rating; if 30 salesclerks' sociability scores average somewhere around the 80th percentile, for example, this indicates that the average salesclerk is more sociable than 79 out of 100 adults. Thus a man being considered for a particular kind of job can be matched against the master profile of the ground. If the shoe fits, he is Cinderella.

Profiles are also worked up for jobs in individual companies. At Sears, Roebuck, there are charts that diagram the optimum balance of qualities required. Here is the one on executive values:

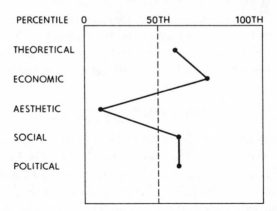

A man does not have to match this profile exactly, but it won't help him at all if his line zigs where the chart zags. Take a man who scores considerably higher than the 10th percentile on aesthetic values, for example; such people, Sears notes, "accept artistic beauty and taste as a fundamental standard of life. This is not a factor which makes for executive success. . . . Generally, cultural considerations are not important to Sears executives, and there is evidence that such interests are detrimental to success."

THE ECHO

Sears has every right to de-emphasize certain qualities and emphasize others; and in hewing to this type, it should be noted, Sears has built up one of the most alert management groups in the country. But the profile is not to be confused with science. When they are used as selection devices, tests are not a neutral tool; they become a large factor in the very equation they purport to solve. For one thing, the tests tend to screen out—or repel—those who would upset the correlation. If a man can't get into the company in the first place because he isn't the company type, he can't very well get to be an executive in it and be tested in a study to find out what kind of profile subsequent executives should match. Long before personality tests were invented, of course, plenty of companies had proved that if you hire only people of a certain type, then all your successful men will be people of that type. But no one confused this with the immutable laws of science.

Bias, in short, is no longer personalized; now it's institutionalized. For the profile is self-confirming. When it doesn't screen out those who fail to match it, it will mask the amount of deviance in the people who do pass. Few test takers can believe the flagrantly silly statement in the preamble to many tests that there are "no right or wrong answers." There wouldn't be much point in the company's giving the test if some answers weren't regarded as better than others. "Do you daydream frequently?" In many companies a man either so honest or so stupid as to answer "yes" would be well advised to look elsewhere for employment.

THE COMPANY "TYPE"

Even when the man who should have looked elsewhere slips through, the profile will be self-confirming. For the profile molds as well as chooses; it is, as Sears puts it, a statement of "the kind of behavior we have found to be desirable." Several years of give and take, and the organization will smooth the man out. Thus when the psychologists do their "validating," or re-checking, later, he will score near enough to the median to show them how right they were all along.

Up to a point the company "type" has some virtue; any first-rate organization must have an *esprit de corps,* and this implies a certain degree of homogeneity. But the pitfalls are many, for while a self-confirming profile makes for a comfortable organization, it eventually can make for a static one. Even the largest corporations must respond to changes in the environment; a settled company may have its very existence threatened by technological advances unless it makes a bold shift to a new type of market. What, then, of the pruning and molding that adapted it so beautifully to its original environment? The dinosaur was a formidable animal.

THE FIGHT AGAINST TALENT

Are the people who don't score well necessarily the misfits? Almost by definition the dynamic person is an exception—and where aptitude tests reward, personality tests often punish him. Look at the profiles and test scoring keys, and you will find that you will come closer to a high score if you observe two rules:

(1) When asked for word associations or comments about the world, give the most conventional, run-of-the-mill, pedestrian answer possible.

(2) When in doubt about the most beneficial answer to any question, repeat to yourself:

> I loved my father and my mother, but my father a little bit more.
> I was a happy, normal American boy and everybody liked me.
> I like things pretty much the way they are.
> I never worry about anything.
> I love my wife and children.
> I don't let them get in the way of company work.
> I don't care for books or music much.

CHOOSE (A), (B), (C), (D).

The sheer mechanics of the tests also punish the exceptional man. A test with prefabricated answers is precisely the kind of test that people with superior intelligence find hardest to answer. How big was that fire in the basement of the theatre? This is not a quibble; it is the kind of question that occurs to the intelligent mind, and the ability to see shadings, to posit alternatives, is virtually indispensable to judgment, practical or otherwise.

We now come to *Fortune's* experiment. With the stipulation by *Fortune* that their individual scores should not be identified, 14 corporation presidents and board chairmen agreed to take a battery of tests including Personal Audit, Thurstone Temperament, and the Test of Practical Judgment. Next, 12 of the country's most brilliant scientists (previously studied in connection with "The Young Scientists," *Fortune,*

June, 1954) agreed to do the same. As a further check, 29 rising middle-management men who had been picked to attend an advanced-management school took the Thurstone and Practical Judgment tests.

Here are the highlights of the test results.

1. Not one corporation president had a profile that fell completely within the usual "acceptable" range, and two failed to meet the minimum profile for foremen. On the How Supervise? questions, presidents on the average got only half the answers right, thus putting them well down in the lower percentiles. They did particularly badly on the questions concerning company-employee-relations policies. Only three presidents answered more than half of these questions correctly.

2. The scientists' Personal Audit profile were more even than the presidents'—if anything, they scored as too contented, firm, and consistent. They did, however, show up as extremely misanthropic, over half falling under the 20th percentile for sociability.

3. The middle-management executives scored well on stability and sociability, but on practical judgment only three were at or over the mean indicated for executive work.

4. The range of scores was so great as to make a median figure relatively meaningless. On the Thurstone "S" score for sociability, for example, only eight of the 43 management men fell between the 40th and the 60th percentiles, the remainder being grouped at either extreme.

5. Internally, the scores were highly contradictory. Many of the same people who got high "steadiness" scores on the Personal Audit scored very badly for "stability" on the Thurstone test. Similarly, many who scored high on "contentment" had very low "tranquillity" scores.

THE ABNORMAL NORMS

One explanation for this great variance between results and the standard norms would be that the men in the sample were answering frankly and thus their scores could not be properly compared with the standard norms given. But if this is true, then we must conclude that the norms themselves embody slanted answers. Another explanation of their showing would be that they scored low because they were in fact neurotic or maladjusted, as the tests said. But this leaves us with a further anomaly. If people with an outstanding record of achievement show up as less well "adjusted" than the run-of-the-mill, then how important a yardstick is adjustment? Fortune's sample, of course, is small. So is the supply of outstanding talented people.

The study of a man's past performance, the gauging of him in the personal interview, are uncertain guides; executives are right to use them with humility. But they are still the key, and the need is not to displace them, but to become more skilled with them. The question of who will be best in a critical situation cannot be determined scientifically before the event. No matter how much information we may amass, we must rely on judgment, on intuition, on the particulars of the situation—and the more crucial the situation, the less certain can we be of prediction. It is an immensely difficult task, perhaps the most difficult one that any management faces. But the question cannot be fed into a computer, nor can it be turned over by proxy for someone else to decide. Any management that so evades its most vital function needs some analysis of its own.

THE RIGHT TO PRIVACY

And doesn't the individual have some rights in this matter, too? Our society has taught him to submit to many things; thousands of civilians who went into the military meekly stood naked in long lines waiting for their numbered turn in the mass physical examinations. Many civilians who have been asked to work on government projects have submitted to being fingerprinted and to the certainty that government agents would soon be puzzling their friends and neighbors with questions about their backgrounds. In these cases a man can console himself that there is a reason; that if he is to enjoy the benefits of collective efforts he must also pay some price.

But there is a line. How much must a man testify against himself? The bill of rights should not stop at the corporation's edge. In return for the salary the organization gives the individual, it can ask for superlative work from him, but it should not ask for his psyche as well. Here and there, we are happy to report, some declarations of independence have been made. Last year the executives of a large and well-known New England corporation were subjected by the management to psychological examination by an outside consultant. Whether it was because of the consultant's manner or because of the New England character, the executives at length revolted. Let them be judged, they said, for their work. As for their inner feelings—that, as one man said who was almost fired for saying so, that was no one's damn business but their own.

*　　　*　　　*　　　*　　　*

As a postscript to Whyte's article, the reader may be interested in learning that his suggested "rules" have been put to experimental test by Shaw (1962).

Ninety-four upperclassmen, majors in Business Administration at the University of Florida, took the Bernreuter Personality Inventory. They were told to imagine themselves as applicants for a supervisory position in a manufacturing plant, to assume they really wanted the job and that, as a part of the application procedure, they were requested to take this test. One half of the group knew Whyte's rules and were requested to fill out the inventory on this basis; the other half were asked to complete the blank honestly. The resulting profiles were then submitted to seven personnel supervisors, representing four industrial organizations which currently employed the Bernreuter as part of their selection procedures. Each supervisor was requested to indicate which "person" he would prefer (and each supervisor was free to accept or reject both.). As expected, the "honest" scores differed significantly from the "dishonest" ones, yet the latter were chosen significantly more often by the personnel people. Furthermore, 52 per cent of the profile pairs were checked "would hire neither." Shaw concluded that following Whyte's rules offers no great advantage in a situation of this type.

Taking a more molecular approach, Dr. Hoffman, who is Professor of Mathematics at Queens College, has made an independent study of tests, particularly those attempting to locate young people of exceptional talent or tests, such as "College Boards," which play so large a role in the admission policies of many colleges. He became involved in problems of testing when he published a criticism of the selection methods used by the Westinghouse Science Talent Search in 1943. As a result he was asked to undertake a yearly commentary on the Westinghouse tests. Several years ago the Ford Foundation put Dr. Hoffman in touch with officials of the Educational Testing Service, probably the most prestige-full test developer in the country. Here, also, he was asked to become a consultant—something he declined because, he said, "I wanted to have a free hand."

What follows is a condensation of Dr. Hoffman's hard-hitting article which originally appeared in Harper's Magazine *for March, 1961, (Vol. 222, pp. 37–44) and which has since been expanded into book form with the title,* The Tyranny of Testing *(1962). Here Dr. Hoffman details his extensive charges against the multiple-choice format of test items and their defense, generally along statistical lines where, in essence, the items can be shown to be vague or ambiguous. Especially where science questions are concerned, precision is crucial, and much of Dr. Hoffman's attack is aimed in this direction, as the following quotations and excerpts, both from the* Harper's Magazine *article and from his book will show.*

The Tyranny of Multiple-Choice Tests

Banesh Hoffmann

There is no escaping the testers with their electrical scoring machines. They measure out IQ's at regular intervals and assess our scholastic achievement throughout our school days. They stand guard at the gateway to National Merit Scholarships, and they tell admissions officers how many points' worth of college aptitude we possess. They pass on our qualifications for graduate study and entry to professional schools. They classify us en masse in the Army. They screen us when we apply for jobs—whether in industry or government. They are even undertaking to certify our worth when we come up for promotion to positions far outranking their own.

The nation, in short, is placing enormous reliance on machine-graded multiple-choice tests as a measure of ability. But, unhappily, it can be shown that they have grave defects. Our confidence in them can have dangerous consequences, not only for education but for the strength and vitality of the nation. The whole question of multiple-choice testing needs thorough re-examination—and it is not getting it.

Few of the people who take these tests give much thought to where they come from. For the most part, they are not made up by the schools and other organizations that administer them. They are bought or rented. Test-making has developed into a large, lucrative, and increasingly competitive business—some of the test publishers employ traveling salesmen to promote their wares. If you have a valid reason for giving a test, you can probably find an appropriate one already in stock. Or you can commission a test-making organization to construct one to suit your special needs—although the cost may run to many thousands of dollars.

The most recent edition of the *Mental Measurements Yearbook,* a compendium of information used throughout the testing industry, reviews 957 different tests (most of them the multiple-choice type) produced by some 173 organizations, of which 28 issue catalogues of the tests they have for sale or hire. It is difficult to estimate how many millions of machine-graded multiple-choice tests are administered each year; the National Merit Scholarship Tests alone now account for half a million.

The bulk of the tests used in this country are produced by five organizations. Their work is not simple. The very concept of multiple-choice tests is the result of years of research by test psychologists seeking ever more precise ways of measuring human abilities. A test emerges from an intricate collaboration. First an expert on test-making, usually one trained in psychology, maps out the test with experts in the subject to be tested and then calls on these, or other, subject experts to submit questions which can be graded by scoring machines. Test experts and subject experts reject many of the questions and reword others. The surviving questions are then "pretested" on people comparable to those for whom the test is intended, and a statistical dossier is compiled for each question. If a question is answered correctly mainly by the "better" examinees it is a good question. If it is answered correctly mainly by the "poorer" ones it is a bad question. If a fair number of the "better" examinees favor one answer and a comparable number another answer, the question is probably ambiguous. If everyone gets it right, it is useless. And so on.

In the light of the pretest statistics, still further questions are rejected or rewritten, and ultimately a rigorously screened version of the test emerges. It is now ready to be given to the people for whom it was constructed, but the process is by no means over. The test is given a preliminary tryout and the results receive elaborate statistical analysis. This yields a variety of important technical information—for example, a numerical measure of the test's success in fulfilling the purpose for which it was constructed.

The test-makers put this information into a "manual" which accompanies the test. And even then the process is not necessarily at an end, for the manual may be revised in the light of statistics accumulated during actual use of the test; and sometimes the test itself is revised.

MELANCHOLY FLAWS

The services of the test-makers understandably have been in heavy demand. They aim to meet urgent and large-scale needs; to sort out millions of servicemen; to give reliable information to college admissions officers about the abilities of candidates for entrance; to deal with increasingly large groups of job candidates in private business. Busy executives—especially those who secretly lack confidence in their own judgment—are only too happy to hand over to professional testers the job of deciding who is worthy and who is not.

For such clients, the multiple-choice test has strong and obvious appeal. It combines efficiency and economy with the splendid advantage of being labeled "objective": it can be graded quickly by machine or with a scoring stencil that even a child can use. No subjective element enters the process of grading. (Of course, highly subjective judgments may enter the test-makers' decisions as to which answers are to be counted as right and which wrong.)

The great question that the public must ask of the multiple-choice testing industry is not how quick and economical its products are but, simply, how good the tests are themselves. Significant flaws in the tests we use so widely should certainly be of vital concern. The test-makers, by their impressive scientific ritual of psychological expertise, pretesting, and statistical analysis, have created a widespread impression that their products must surely be free of such flaws, an impression especially prevalent among people with unshakable confidence in scientific routines, no matter how or by whom applied. Yet there is melancholy evidence to the contrary.

How would you feel, for example, if, on applying for a responsible position, you were given a test with questions like this:

You are an editor forced to turn down a scholarly book which you think is a good piece of work but which will not sell. Which one of the following statements would best inform the author of your decision without discouraging him?

(A) You'll probably think me grossly mercenary when I tell you that, good though I think it is, I must turn down your book because it would have very little commercial success.

(B) You are obviously unfamiliar with the requirements of the publishing business—through no fault of your own. The point is that your book would have a very limited sale, and therefore we cannot accept it.

(C) Having read your book with great care, I must admit that it is a creditable effort. However, we doubt that it would have a great enough sale to justify our publishing it.

(D) We feel that your book is an important contribution in its field. But, since so few readers are interested in that field, we find that we cannot fit the book into our publishing program.

You cannot, of course, ask your examiner what he meant by "would best inform the author of your decision without discouraging him." You are not allowed to ask questions; nor even to explain your answer. You must simply pick a letter—A, B, C, or D; you will be judged right if you pick the one the tester wants, wrong if you do not. If you fail to pick the wanted answer, and thereby jeopardize your chances of getting the job, it will be small consolation to you to know that neither one of the two editors on whom I tried this question picked the right answer.

This question is a product of the Educational Testing Service. It is taken verbatim from a booklet, *Sample Questions from the Foreign Service Officer Examination,* put out by the U.S. State Department. It is intended to test "the candidate's ability to recognize the appropriateness of certain forms of expression to specific situations."

I tried it on several of my colleagues. Here are their choices (I omit their various cogent reasons): a professor of classics—D; a public relations man—C; a personnel director—C; a professor of music widely known for his writing ability—A; a professor of English—A; a professor of anthropology—C; two professors of anthropology acting in concert (after long wavering between A and D)—A; a professor of English—D; a dean—C. And not one of them had a kind word to say for the question. (The test-makers happen to consider answer D the best.)

Do questions of this sort really test what is claimed? Do they not rather test ability to fathom what is in the mind of the examiner?

When a question is merely ambiguous, like the one above, you have at least a sporting chance. But there are some questions that load the dice against you if your ability is far above the average. These occur far too frequently.

DUBIOUS NATIONAL MERIT

Those who produce and administer tests have strong interests in defending their effectiveness, and they often cite statistics to show that the high scores of those who did well on the tests were confirmed by their later performance. Consider, for example, the National Merit Scholarship Corporation, which each year awards many millions of dollars' worth of college scholarships all over the nation and gives valuable testimonials in the form of certificates of merit to many thousands of runners-up. In its latest annual report, it speaks with pride of the accomplishments of the National Merit Scholars in college. Among other things, it says "about 82 per cent (of the scholars) rank in the top quarter of their classes, even though many have selected colleges of very high academic standing."

This is a curious boast. In 1959, out of 478,991 candidates for the Merit Scholarships, all but 10,334 were eliminated from further consideration because of their scores on a qualifying test, and ultimately a mere 920 received Merit Scholarships. In four years, out of 959,683 candidates, only 3,465 were awarded scholarships. The scholars are certainly a select group. Yet we gather from the corporation's statement that not all of this presumed elite went to colleges of very high academic standing and that, nevertheless, almost 20 per cent of them failed to rank even in the first quarter of their classes. Do these facts encourage faith in the screening process?

Again, the corporation says in its report that "the national examinations have been praised as among the best available for determining aptitude and readiness to profit from a college education," and nowhere does it make any adverse remarks about these tests (except inadvertently, as in the above boast).

The corporation cannot always have been satisfied with its qualifying test, for in 1958 it not only made an abrupt change in the nature of the test but took the contract away from the Educational Testing Service and gave it to Science Research Associates.

What of the new National Merit tests? These are two reviews of the April 1958 test in the *Fifth Mental Measurements Yearbook*. One of them is, on the whole, favorable, though it does not give the glowing impression that the corporation's words might convey to the unwary reader. The reviewer characterizes the quality of the individual questions as "acceptable," and he is by no means convinced that the new type of test is an improvement over the old. Of course, it is natural for the corporation to put its case in as favorable a light as possible. Foundations and industrial corporations have entrusted it with the distribution of enormous sums of money for scholarships and it has become, willingly or not, a by no means negligible force in the affairs of the nation. So it is understandable that the corporation did not take public notice of the other critic, who complains that data supplied along with the test by Science Research Associates "exhibited characteristics suggestive of too much emphasis on salesmanship," and cites "as a wholesome contrast" the literature prepared by Educational Testing Service for their earlier form of the test.

The critic goes on to point out, among other things, that the test "was not suited to its task of identifying potential scholarship recipients" because it was not difficult enough for the superior candidates, and that "considerable psychometric naiveté is exhibited in several sections of the Technical Manual," a charge he documents by pointing out significant flaws in the interpretation of statistics. He remarks briefly that some of the questions are poorly written. He says that the parts of the test that deal with social studies and natural science measure almost entirely reading ability and general verbal aptitude, and in this connection he points out that the statistics cited by Science Research Associates show scores on the social studies part to be about as good a measure of ability in natural science as they are of ability in social studies, and vice versa. He ends with the following words:

"In conclusion, the (qualifying test) and the literature distributed about it did not seem to be a step forward. The reviewer is concerned that assessment psychology has been retarded and may have lost ground through the production and use of this test. He is amazed and disturbed that such inferior work can be conducted and tolerated on such a large scale. It is hoped that it will not be repeated."* The people who take the tests, of course, know nothing of such criticisms and the tests go merrily on.

STATISTICS SHOW

Can anything be done about the multiple-choice tests? Must we simply accept them passively? It is not difficult to find prominent educators and other commentators who have launched wide-ranging protests against them. For example:

The tests deny the creative person a significant opportunity to demonstrate his creativity, and favor the shrewd and facile candidate over the one who has something of his own to say.

---

*Editor's note: The reviewer in question is Dr. Benno Fricke, Chief of Evaluation and Examinations Division, University of Michigan.

They penalize the candidate who perceives subtle points unnoticed by less able people, including the test-makers.

They are apt to be superficial and intellectually dishonest, with questions made artificially difficult by means of ambiguity because genuinely searching questions do not readily fit into the multiple-choice format.

They too often degenerate into subjective guessing games in which the candidate does not pick what he considers the best answer out of a bad lot, but rather the one he believes the unknown examiner would consider the best.

They neglect skill in disciplined expression.

They have, in sum, a pernicious effect on education and the recognition of merit.

But such criticisms do not seem to disturb the test-makers, who, well entrenched and growing more powerful every day, have developed a strikingly effective routine for dealing with their critics.

When confronted with general criticisms, they make a show of patient reasonableness. Of course they welcome concerned criticism, they say. But the critic is just an amateur offering mere opinion, not scientific fact. After all, they are experts, and they know. Having said this, they go on to extol the virtues of their product. They speak proudly of the professional competence of the people who make their tests—recently the president of the Educational Testing Service boasted of "hundreds of outstanding teachers from schools and colleges" who work with his organization. They point to the elaborate scientific ritual they follow in constructing and evaluating their tests. Insisting that "statistics show . . ." they surround themselves with such an aura of scientific infallibility that few people realize that the test-makers have avoided answering the criticism aimed at them.

There is, I suggest, a way to penetrate this defense. Instead of making general criticisms, one should exhibit specific test questions, such as presented above; declare that they are defective; and challenge the test-makers to defend these questions specifically.

The test-makers intensely dislike this sort of challenge because it puts them in a quandary. They have to be wary of conceding that the questions are bad and claiming that they are rare exceptions, for they do not know how many more examples the challenger has in reserve. On the other hand, if they defend a bad question by their "statistics show . . ." maneuver, they risk the implication that their use of statistics is improper or that their statistics are untrustworthy. If they defend the question by referring to the scientific ritual used in constructing their tests, they undermine faith in the efficacy of that ritual. If they defend it by pointing to the high caliber of their staff experts and consultants, they may well start people wondering whether the caliber is high enough. Therefore, a sharply focused challenge of specific questions seems the one effective means by which the quality of multiple-choice tests can be called into question.

It is important to point out, however, that no matter how many defective sample questions one could find, no more than a prima facie case could be made against the testers, because most of the important tests used for competitive selection purposes are kept secret. Even if the sample questions are found to be defective, we still have no way of knowing whether they fairly reflect the tests themselves. In short, there is at present no way for a comprehensive and independent judgment of the tests to be made in the public interest.

One solution to this dilemma could be the formation of a completely independent board of eminent educators and scholars which could have access to the whole range of questions produced by the testing organizations. Committee members could examine the actual tests and the statistical evidence concerning them, consult with experts and their critics, and form an opinion as to the real worth of current tests. The scope of their critique should extend far beyond the technical reviews of tests now published in the *Mental Measurements Yearbooks*. The committee could open up the question whether the multiple-choice format is really suited to measuring the various kinds of ability tested today. If they found the tests wanting, they might recommend alternative approaches to testing to supplement or supplant the multiple-choice method. And they could consider the merits of the rather hesitant steps already being taken within the testing industry to augment the role of essay questions in certain testing programs.

If, however, they found that present tests are doing a generally effective job, we would have the assurance that this was a conclusion arrived at not merely by the test-makers and their clients, but by a distinguished independent board acting in the public interest.

AN "AVERAGE" QUESTION

How will the testing organizations respond to this proposal? Judging from their past reactions to outside criticism, we may be sure they will not readily accept such an intrusion into what they mistakenly regard as their domain. However, if there were an explicit and convincing public demonstration that their present methods are producing dangerously defective questions, it is hard to see how they could honorably and responsibly ignore it or hamper an independent committee of inquiry.

With this in mind, I have compiled a challenge to the testers based on the sample questions in two booklets put out by the College Entrance Examination Board. Their tests are, of course, among the best known and most important used in America today, and they are made by the Educational Testing Service, which is generally recognized as the leading test-making organization. Of the 234 questions in these two booklets, I have picked 12, arbitrarily limiting myself to 5 per cent of the supply. All the questions in the booklets had originally appeared in College Entrance examinations. Thus they have been subjected not only to the rigorous screening, pretesting, and statistical analysis which all examination questions undergo, but also to a further screening which qualified them to serve as illustrations of the kind of questions to be expected on these tests.

I have already challenged the merits of two of these questions publicly, one in an appendix appearing in Jacques Barzun's book, *The House of Intellect,* the other in an article in the Spring 1959 issue of *The American Scholar.* The president of the Educational Testing Service replied officially to the latter in the Autumn 1959 issue of The American Scholar, but instead of defending or discussing the question itself he gave an almost classical example of the test-makers' response to criticism. (It was here, for instance, that he spoke of the "hundreds of outstanding teachers" who have helped to construct the tests.) He made no defense at all of the defective question itself. One could wish for a more responsive reply.

I have space here to present [one more question] of the 12 constituting the challenge. Since the two that have already appeared were from the booklet describing the Scholastic Aptitude Tests, I shall here give [one question] from the booklet *Science,* published in 1954, which describes the Science Achievement Tests. It gives an indication of the extraordinary manner in which the College Entrance Examination Board measures scientific caliber. The question is quoted with permission of the College Board. I am, of course, prepared to exhibit the other questions selected from the College Entrance booklets; but space does not permit me to include them here.

Do not be deterred by the presence of unfamiliar technical terms. The defects in the questions are so striking that they tower above the technical background, and no scientific knowledge is needed in order to understand their nature. If, therefore, some of the terms are obscure, simply ignore them.

Here is question 54 in *Science.* It is listed as belonging to "Chemistry" and its degree of difficulty is said to be "average."

54. The burning of gasoline in an automobile cylinder involves all of the following except

    (A) reduction
    (B) decomposition
    (C) an exothermic reaction
    (D) oxidation
    (E) conversion of matter to energy.

The average chemistry student quickly picks the wanted answer, E, doubtless arguing that conversion of matter into energy refers to nuclear reactions and is inappropriate here.

But the student who is unfortunate enough to understand, even if only in an elementary way, what $E = mc^2$ is really about finds himself at a distinct disadvantage. He knows that in certain nuclear reactions energy is released through the breaking of nuclear bonds. He knows, too, that in the burning of gasoline the energy released comes from the dissociation of chemical bonds, that these chemical bonds contribute, however minutely, to the rest mass of the substances involved in the reaction, and that the released energy—all of it—comes from the diminution of this rest mass. Thus here, just as in nuclear reactions, there is "conversion of matter into energy." So the superior student correctly concludes that none of the given answers is correct.

One might try to defend the question by saying that since matter is a form of energy, answer E is tautological. But, quite apart from the fact that the wording is customary, any tautology would make E a fortiori valid, and thus unacceptable as an answer.

TOO CRUCIAL FOR TRUST

Admittedly there is no easy solution to the problem of testing. That is why the committee I advocated earlier should include creative people of commanding intellectual stature who could bring fresh vision to the testing situation, especially as it affects those gifted young people whose talents do not conform to the statistically-based norms of the multiple-choice testers. Only a minority of such a committee should consist of test psychologists or professional test-makers. Perhaps one way to bring such a group into being would be through appointment—with or without foundation help—by scholarly organizations of the highest repute—for instance, the American Council of Learned Societies, the National Academy of Sciences, and the Modern Language Association.

It would be premature to anticipate the conclusions of such a committee. Certainly there is a case for the usefulness of multiple-choice tests, properly constructed, in a limited range of testing. It is possible that their quality can be much improved. But if it is decided that their very format makes them inappropriate for broader testing purposes, their tight grip on our educational system should be broken. Testing in this country is too crucial an activity to be accepted on trust.

*   *   *   *   *

As one might suspect, a great deal of heat was generated by this attack. The burden of the rebuttal largely fell on the shoulders of the Educational Testing Service. Mr. Henry Chauncy, ETS President, protested to Harper's (in the May, 1961, issue). To quote Mr. Chauncy:

As is evident in his article, . . . Mr. Hoffmann dismisses evidence with amazing ease—when the subject lies outside his own field. His method is to ferret out questions which he thinks would appear ambiguous to the exceptional student, and then assume that all potential geniuses will see them his way, score poorly, and be lost to society. He has never presented evidence to support his thesis. All our evidence is to the contrary. Quite the reverse, tests have frequently identified the brilliant student not otherwise recognized.

Dr. Hoffmann selected a test item from the Foreign Service Officer Examination Handbook for criticism—the item about the editor who was forced to turn down a scholarly manuscript because he felt it would not sell. For the record, here is the official ETS explanation of the item. (ETS prepared an official handout for all interested readers of the Hoffmann article and the following is taken from that source.)

The item is designed to test sensitivity to the reactions of others to written communication. Presumably, this would be an important quality in Foreign Service Officers. Obviously, this is a difficult quality to measure by any means. And it certainly can't be measured by giving a person a question in which logic or accuracy of grammatical knowledge will produce the correct answer. A certain amount of ambiguity is part and parcel of this kind of test. The distinctions must be rather small and subtle in order to have any kind of measure at all. On any one item, even a very sensitive and perceptive person might, by a particular line of reasoning, give the wrong response. However, if 50 or more such questions are asked, the sensitive, perceptive person will agree, more often than the person lacking in sensitivity, with the answers selected by panels who have prepared the questions following a carefully developed plan.

For example, the thinking of the panel which prepared the item quoted above was somewhat like this:

Obviously, Option B is the least diplomatic response. A reader might very logically interpret the statement as meaning, "You are obviously an ignoramus, but, of course, I know that your ignorance is not your own fault."

Option A is somewhat better than Option B, but it doesn't avoid discouraging the author; it simply permits him to project his feeling of hopelessness in a mercenary world on the editor. It is small comfort to know that a grossly mercenary editor *thinks* the book is good (but isn't really sure).

Option C comes closer to the mark, but in comparison with Option D, it is clearly second best. The dollar signs are somewhat disguised ("we doubt that it would have great enough sale") and the editorial "we" is used to soften the refusal, but the response abounds in clichés which wound—without intent. The basis of judgment is put in the singular. The only person who has read the book is the writer of the letter. And having read it with great *care* (not especially suggestive of perception, and certainly not of sympathy) the *one* man *must admit* that the *effort is creditable*. If I say I am forced to admit, I suggest that my approach has been negative, and I really don't want to make the judgment forced upon me. As for *effort;* this suggests, "Well, anyway, you tried—but so what!" The ultimate wound is the word *creditable;* this word is reserved for the efforts of amateurs.

In contrast, Option D provides the ultimate compliment to a scholar—"an important contribution in its field"—and focuses on the limited number of people competent to appreciate the work rather than on the number of dollars they might generate for the publisher. *We* is used throughout; it may be the editorial *we*, but it does not hit the reader with the condescending tone of Option C. The author is encouraged, in a sense, to try to reach his limited audience in some other way—perhaps by microfilming the manuscript.

*   *   *   *   *

The above would make Answer D seem best. It does so, Dr. Hoffmann points out (1962, pp. 168–171), by using a double standard—"switching its sensitivity on and off, reacting with unnecessary sharpness to the 'I think' in Answer A but not saying a word about the 'We feel' in the answer it wishes to defend . . ." Dr. Hoffmann goes on to remark that this Answer D is both impersonal and unimaginative and that it has about it the "chill air" of a form letter—and an insincere one at that. Answer A, on the other hand, could have easily come from a gentleman and it has a kind of warm and personal touch. It is this answer that Dr. Hoffmann supports. But in the end, he remarks, there is probably no "best" answer to the question since it is truly an ambiguous item, a point which ETS admitted.

*   *   *   *   *

The other test item to which Dr. Hoffmann calls attention is the one about the burning of gasoline in an automobile cylinder. The thinking behind the framing of the alternatives to this question is discussed and explained by Fornoff (1962). What follows is an abstract of Dr. Fornoff's comments about this particular test item. The original article appeared in Physics Today, *(1962, Vol. 15, pp. 36ff). Dr. Fornoff is a member of the Test Development Division of ETS.*

I am one of those people whose identity is hidden by the letters ETS which Dr. Banesh Hoffmann has attacked with such determination. My responsibility, shared directly with two colleagues and indirectly with many more, is the preparation of science tests. I have a doctorate in chemistry from the Ohio State University, and I spent a postdoctoral year at the University of California. I have been on the faculties of three good universities, Lehigh, Kansas State, and Rutgers, but I must admit that there are many things that I do not know. Contrary to Dr. Hoffmann's suspicion, I believe that my colleagues and I do know a few things.

We are aware, for instance, of Einstein's relation, $E = mc^2$. I did not write the question on the burning of gasoline in an automobile cylinder that Dr. Hoffmann has been working to make famous, and I do not know who did write it. Despite Dr. Hoffmann's comments, I believe there is a reasonable context associated with the question and that this context is normally discerned by chemistry students who understand change.

This question was never used in a test given for evaluating student performance. It has been tried out twice in what we call pretests, tests given to learn about the questions, not about the students. The second of these pretestings took place last spring when some 400 college-freshman chemistry students from eight colleges took the pretest. A random sample of 300 of the answer sheets was studied in detail. Performances of the top quintile of the students were worth noting.

Two of these top 60 students omitted the question. This is what Dr. Hoffmann seems to assume that superior students would do. Twenty-seven of them said that the burning of gasoline did not involve decomposition, and 11 of them said that reduction was not involved. Still, three times as many students from this group as from the bottom quintile chose the keyed response, conversion of matter to energy, as not being involved in this process.

This question was written for the booklet from which Dr. Hoffmann quotes. In a communication directly to ETS back in 1955 or 1956, Dr. Hoffmann pointed out what he considered to be the weakness of the question, and the ETS staff at that time recognized that some people might miss the context in which the question was written. The question for the booklet was therefore revised, and since the 1957 edition has had for its fifth option, "conversion of energy to matter." The facts do not substantiate the assertion that ETS does not know about $E = mc^2$, and I believe that the question as originally worded tested an important understanding of chemical change.

I shall continue to be concerned that the committees charged with the preparation of ETS science tests be composed of the best people who will accept the appointments and will spend the necessary time at their tasks. I shall regrettably expect that a few of the questions included in the tests will be subject to interpretations which the committees will miss. But I shall continue to believe that, despite the limitations by these "defective" questions, superior students will get superior scores on multiple-choice tests, that the complicated admission practices will guarantee college admission to the superior students who apply for admission, and that both the colleges who do the selection and the students who are considered by these colleges benefit from careful selection based, in part, on multiple-choice tests.

*   *   *   *   *

Dr. Hoffmann answered Dr. Fornoff in Physics Today *(1962, Vol. 15, pp. 80ff.). ETS has earlier defended this question by saying that the good student would be aware that the* classical *concepts of matter and chemical change are the frame of reference here (rather than, say, the model of modern physics as represented by the Einstein equation). This same student would also recognize that the first four processes listed as alternatives (reduction, decomposition, exothermic reaction, oxidation) are obviously involved in burning gasoline and so he easily selects response E as the answer (conversion of matter to energy). Dr. Hoffmann (1962, pp. 186–188) rejects such an explanation: Einstein's famous equation is over 50 years old and the question, as stated, is clearly easier for the student who does not understand this equation than for the one who does.*

The original Hoffmann article in Harper's *also included a discussion of a "difficult" question belonging to chemistry. Limitations of space preclude presentation here; the whole matter is set down in detail in Hoffmann's recent book (1962, pp. 189–195) where he states that the ETS defence was invalid, since blunders were made in it, and the supposedly clinching argument boomeranged. Dr. Hoffmann feels that the way out of these difficulties is to set up a distinguished committee of inquiry to study, among other things, the quality of these tests and testmakers. Such a committee should have on it creative people of outstanding intellectual stature, and it should not be composed primarily of professional test-makers. Dr. Hoffmann feels that wise testers know the limitations of current tests and that, after all, all methods of evaluating people have their defects, so that we should not allow one particular method to dominate the field.*

Dr. Hoffmann reports a huumorous anecdote (1962, p. 158) which can serve as a concluding note to this particular critique. Harper's Magazine *publishes a special edition for student use which contains a section discussing the issue's contents and suggesting topics for classroom use. Questions are also provided. When the editors got around to discussing "The Tyranny of Multiple-Choice Tests," six of the questions appeared in multiple-choice format!* Dr. Hoffmann *reports he was not always sure himself as to the "best" answer.*

Dr. Hoffmann *is not alone. One almost gets the impression there has been instituted an "open season" to hunt down testers, so much so that, at the Spring, 1963 meetings of the New York State Psychological Association, an overflow crowd attended a symposium entitled "Test and Protest" where the panelists discussed these recent critics. A new critical voice is that of Koerner (1963) who, in writing about the very sad state of schools of education in the USA,* briefly discusses the National Teacher Examinations sponsored by ETS. In a sort of left-handed way, he excuses ETS since it is restricted to testing only what educationists tell ETS they are trying to do in their teacher-training programs. The "absurd questions" to be found in some of these examinations probably screen out not only the flagrantly incompetent but also the "exceptionally able but unorthodox persons." Too often the testee is forced to choose among "pre-packaged ambiguities, none of which may represent* his *answer but which he must reason his way through to what he supposes the testers may have had in mind in asking the question" (footnote, p. 256).*

The publication flow continues unabatedly. As this volume goes to press, still another "lay" volume, clearly negative and in the exposé journalism tradition, has come off the press purporting to highlight the abuses of educational tests from the kindergarten IQ's through the college entrance tests (Black, 1963). The volume is advertised as a* must *for all parents "of a child who wants to go to a good college."*

---

*To give the flavor, Koerner speaks of Ed.D. programs as generally showing more often than not "a weak candidate put through a weak program by a weak faculty to earn a weak degree" (1963, p. 184).

The critics of psychological testing are by no means solely the lay people, and the impression should not *be gained that the psychologists and measurement specialists have been silent on these same issues— as well as others. Even casual inspection of the various volumes of the* Mental Measurements Yearbooks, *wherein critical reviews written by the professionals appear, will offer ample testimony of the tough-minded attitudes of these people.*

In a recent book discussing the whole area of measurement in guidance (Rothney, Danielson & Heimann, 1959), the authors, clearly professional people in education and psychology and who are actually involved in either counselor training or in the administration of guidance centers, come up with the discouraging suggestion that the best possible way to improve tests would be to declare a moratorium on their production for several years. During that time the poor and obsolete tests would wither away and some real gains might be made. Does it not seem strange, these authors ask, that in a country where butcher and grocer scales are inspected regularly—even policed—that a test distributor may sell such products without any supervision? "After reading many test manuals one is often left with the feeling that 'there ought to be a law.' ...The greatest hope for the immediate future (is) seen in increased consumer sophistication as antidotes to high pressure sales promotion campaigns of test publishers. This sophistication (is) seen as necessary if counselors are to find tests useful in the important tasks that they undertake (pp. 323, 350).

Dr. John Schlien, who is Assistant Professor of Psychology at the University of Chicago and who is also a member of the staff of the University's Counseling Center, has also raised what might be termed a "Rogerian voice" on this whole issue of psychological testing and social control. The following article, a condensation of Dr. Shlien's original article, "Mental Testing and Modern Society," appearing in The Humanist* *(1958, Vol. 18, pp. 356–364), presents a challenging and certainly disenchanted view of the entire matter.*

---

*Published by the American Humanist Association, Yellow Springs, Ohio.

Mental Testing and Modern Society

John M. Shlien

In our aspirations for a rational secular society, we who think of ourselves as humanists sometimes reach out toward newly-developed instruments which are not as rational as they seem to be, and much less humane. We hope that these instruments will provide technical means for achieving what are primarily moral ends. Sometimes they do. A new parliamentary procedure, life insurance, a new source of cheap energy, a divorce law—perhaps these are examples of means which have the desired influence in relieving some of the elemental strife in the human condition and in distributing power more equitably; or at least, as the cynic puts it, in "spreading the injustice around." We seize upon or have foisted upon us such means, thinking that they will lead to a better-planned society. Thus we have bought and been sold the whole field of "mental testing"—a somewhat old-fashioned term covering measures of attitudes, aptitudes, skills, knowledge, preferences, various aspects of intelligence, and more recently in particular, personality characteristics.

No reader can have escaped first-hand experience with at least some of these. If young enough, he may have been handed some cubes while being supported in his crib, in order to see if he, like most of his contemporaries, will hold one, carry it to his mouth, and in general, be "normal." No unkindness is intended, and he is too young to know the pangs of failure in an evaluation—yet. Mommy will do the suffering for him, if need be, or enjoy the satisfaction of his averageness. Or, if the reader is old enough, he may have been tested in order to judge his readiness for retirement, or to diagnose his possible senility. During the in-between years, he will have his share of the 40 to 60 million tests given yearly in this country. They are likely to play a part in his assignments throughout school, and to affect, increasingly, his possibilities for entering college. He may meet them many times in applying for jobs. He may be required to act as a subject for new ones being developed while he is in college (thus having the relatively happy status of a "control" or "normal") and may be examined prior to marriage for his readiness in general and his compatibility with his proposed partner. (Bills have been introduced in some state legislatures to make this as compulsory as blood tests.) If he is married by a newly-ordained minister he may often have the satisfaction of knowing that the minister has an adequate personal adjustment for his task, since he was probably evaluated by the Rorschach test before assignment to a parish. In the Army, in the Navy, in sickness, in health—no use belaboring the point; you have only to consult your neighbor, and your own experience. To put it simply, many decisions in the lives of many people will be based on the results of "mental tests." If these decisions importantly affect our private and communal lives, it is important for the public to know a good deal about the tests. The public does not. In many instances, the public is not supposed to.

It is generally said that the aim of science is prediction and control, though understanding is aim enough for some of the best scientists. These tests are intended, above all, to be scientific—that is their main justification—and since they share the aims of science, many questions need to be publicly considered. Some are technical, some are ethical. The first kind of question asks, essentially, *"Can* modern tests really *predict* human behavior?"* The answer is not clear, but is relatively easy to come by. The second question is, *"Should* modern tests *control* human behavior?"* This is more difficult. In brief, my own answer would be that if tests really could predict behavior, then they should also control it, because it is better to use the truth than to avoid it. If man is really predictable, he may as well be controllable. (It also works the other way—when he is most controlled, he is most predictable. Limit his freedom and you can better predict where he will be and what he will do. Frustrate him and you reduce his reactions to a few; but when he is truly free, he may invent beyond the scope of your measures.) As it turns out, he is not very predictable—only partly so—therefore, the ethical question bears heavily upon us. We are soon pretending to control when in fact we cannot predict.

The technical questions hinge on problems of validity, reliability, criteria, and certain assumptions about human nature. Validity is usually reported in terms of a correlation coefficient. Though the figure does not intend to lie, it has an inflated quality about it which permits us to think of it as being higher than it really is. In our ordinary mathematical conceptions, the number 70 in a scale of zero to 100 is a respectable number. But 70 is about as high as a correlation coefficient of validity *ever* goes, and it means less than you might think. Of the many ways in which a correlation could be interpreted, a fair one is the per cent of forecasting efficiency. Efficiency is the extent to which a test reduces the error in one's prediction, and the prediction is, of course, based upon the correlation. Small forecasting efficiencies correspond to most correlation coefficients, especially those below 50 (or 13 per cent better than chance). One would have to get correlations of around .95 (which represent a 69 per cent improvement over chance)—which in reality are never obtained—to achieve the kind of forecasting which would minimize error to an extent that would not do violence to many individuals. But at least half of the tests reported and used today have validity coefficients of .50 or less. The great majority are below .60, with very few as high as .70. *On the whole,* this means that tests are not very useful for selection. They can be made to be useful if one is willing to expend some people to whom the tests are unfair. For instance, if a scholastic aptitude test has a range of scores from 0 to 100, and a validity coefficient of .50, a decision to admit only students with a "critical" score of 90 or above would practically eliminate academic failures. But there would be a great many with scores below 90 who would also have been successful students, had they the chance.

Another technical problem is the matter of finding reliable criteria against which to validate tests. A test stems, in the first place, from experience and judgment. Someone makes observations about people, and then, more or less wisely, decides to objectify, perhaps to disguise, his observations and judgments. He devises a situation shorter in time than the performance he wants to predict, and this is his test. But he must now validate it; and two things hinder him. One is the lack of reliable criteria. If six clinicians cannot agree upon the psychiatric classification of a patient (and often they cannot), then a test which aims to diagnose has no stable mark at which to shoot. Or if a foreman cannot rate a worker or group of workers in a consistent way on two or more occasions (and often he cannot), a test of aptitude for that job, no matter how cleverly constructed, cannot prove itself. And if a worker does not himself present a consistent performance to be rated (and often he does not), this too makes his original test score subject to error in prediction. Finally, if either the test or the person taking it (or both) was unreliable in the first place, and might thus beget a significantly different score on two or more occasions (and this happens), again error is introduced and validity is lowered.

Can tests predict behavior? Not very well. Tests suffer from a lack of basic validity (wisdom, insight, understanding) in the first place. What inherent validity does exist suffers further from the instability of the test, of the judgments against which the test is appraised, and of the person who takes the test. In other words, people cannot be predicted very well because they are fairly unpredictable. They change.

INCLUSION AND EXCLUSION—AN ETHICAL DILEMMA

Some of the ethical problems have already reared their heads. A primary one is the violence done to the individual by tests which have so little validity that they can only be made useful by application to large numbers of people, many of whom will be unfairly treated, as in the example of the cut-off score for college entrance. Is the elimination of academic failures worth the price of excluding a good man who could well succeed, given the chance? The economics involved is not technical, but ethical. It is worth noting that the great impetus for psychological testing started in this country with the Army Alpha during World War I, and developed on a really massive scale in World War II. Tests were no more valid than they are now, but since in war the individual as such matters not at all, while planes costing millions matter a great deal, validity coefficients from .10 to .35 were usefully applied to large masses of men. But, for all the organization intended and logistics involved, war is the very negation of human planning. It is a mistake, and we have made it, to transfer the economics of war to a peacetime society. We have deceived ourselves into thinking that a fairly dull tool, which cut some costs in the vast waste of war, is much sharper than it really is. It is for that reason—not because the tests are monsters—that our mis-uses of tests are monstrous. A few years ago, the Director of the Federal Security Commission announced that we would need "a government agency to sift the (high school) graduates, determine how many, who will be assigned to military service, to college training and to industry." For those who prize individual freedom, it would be discouraging enough if such selection could in fact be well done. The outrage lies in the fact that it can't be well done, but is suggested as if it could, anyway. It continues. Another Defense Department official suggested that we all wear dogtags around our necks, bearing with our names and blood types, our IQ's, and that only those with higher IQ's be admitted to the limited space in atomic bomb shelters! It is true that there are individual differences in IQ. On the whole, they do not correlate very highly with anything, but there are these differences, and many more besides. What do we want to do about them?

When we use them to *in*clude, they seem in general beneficial. That critical score of 90 on the scholastic aptitude test may help a "poor but worthy" student to obtain a scholarship. Good, though still others are being excluded, "unfairly." Is exclusion by test any more unfair or damaging than exclusion by other misfortunes, such as lack of money? Hard to say, but it seems that the test speaks with more finality. One can earn money, but the test tends to assign a fixed status, hard to change, seemingly beyond redress for most. People change, and therein lies the hope of the world. Growth and education depend upon it. But an underlying assumption vaguely held by all of us about the test is that it assigns a status which is static. IQ is supposed to be relatively stable, personality to be fixed in the first few years. Once we have been told that someone has a certain personality trait, mental status, aptitude, we and perhaps he, too, tend to resist the possibility of change. The tester himself resists the idea of change. It makes people unpredictable. He would like to think of their variability as "error" in measurement, to be eliminated. To him, every score is a prediction. When he classes a boy as "pre-delinquent" he has an investment in that prediction, not because he is more vindictive than the social worker, teacher, therapist, or parent, but because he cannot handle change so well. For this reason, and insofar as we join him in it, exclusion by test is particularly damaging.

Exclusion by test helps to maintain human semi-slavery and to prevent social inventiveness. We use tests to exclude those in the lowest grades from any but the lowest grade jobs. This is our way of dealing with the age-old problem—who shall do the most onerous work? Garbage collection is an unpleasant task. It falls to those "civil servants" who are judged least fitted for better jobs. We leave it at that, just as we would leave cotton picking to the illiterate southern worker if the economics of inflation did not introduce the automatic cotton-picking machine. In Sweden, garbage removal has been designed so that it is handled with one standard type of can, the lid of which screws on tightly. These are picked up by the collectors, driven to the disposal plant, and by machine are unscrewed, emptied, and steam washed. The drivers merely return the cans. They have special concessions in working hours and similar rewards. A source of human degradation is removed. We would have to do this if we were to forego the method of exclusion by test. One makes the best use of one's intelligence when one invents with it, rather than relying on someone else's lower status to solve the problem. Thus we do not really meet the problem if we follow the current suggestion of a British scientist "to breed high-IQ apes to take over low-IQ human jobs."

SPREADING THE INJUSTICE AROUND

Plato had a better—at least more equitable—idea when in his *Republic,* the onerous tasks were assigned on an age-grading basis, so that everyone passing through adolescence served the tables, for instance. Yet he, too, had the same narrow idea of individual differences to which modern testers cling. In Book II, Socrates puts it: . . . "that, in the first place, no two persons are born exactly alike, but each differs in natural endowments, one being suited for one occupation and another for another." And further, "But we cautioned the shoemaker, you know, against attempting to be an agriculturalist, or a weaver or a builder besides, with a view to our shoemaking work being well done; and to every artisan we assigned in like manner *one occupation; namely, that for which he was best fitted* . . . " Again, it is true there are individual differences, but this does not mean that any single task is the "one best fit" for any man. One thing we can learn from the experience of war and modern industry with its labor shifts is that most men can do a variety of different jobs, and do them equally well. The image given by Plato, and held in hope by the unreconstructed test technician, is almost that of the "idiot savant"—a man who can do one thing and that alone well. That would indeed make prediction and assignment much more feasible. It is just not true. Individual differences fluctuate, and do so across a broad scale covering many different capacities with a single person.* He may work best who changes work occasionally. We may caution "shoemaker, stick to your last" and miss the old craftsman who deserted us for the real estate business; but it's our misfortune, and none of his own.

It is not just the lower grades of workers and warriors and their problems we have to consider. In the world vision of the tester, ministers and kings must be selected and assigned, too. It has been seriously proposed (in a Presidential address to the Division of Evaluation and Measurement of the American Psychological Association)—as well as half-seriously by many—that the "ideal social structure" would utilize tests to qualify candidates for the highest political offices, in combination with or substituting for elections. This is, in a way, simply extending civil service to higher levels. There are many faults in our political government, but civil service has not cured them. It cannot really eliminate incompetence or corruption. For one thing, the placement tests are not that good. Further, the test results are usually merged with experience or service ratings, somewhat unreliable and easily controlled by the party in power. Given a bad situation to start with, civil service can only limit it, and may serve to anchor corruption firmly in office, so that a reform government has no chance to change the administration.

---

*And I would assert that these differences are the keystone of democracy, rather than its inherent undoing, as Plato and others would have it.

Further, if the testing system is extended to the higher realms, who is to test the testers? In the final anlysis, who could, except themselves? But that is not so serious a question, except as it reflects the always-dangerous power problem when decisions about many are handed to a few. The testing psychologist, like other people, is eager to rise, somewhat on the make for power, and sometimes motivated by what a famous psychoanalyst called "the narcissistic need to know what is wrong with somebody else." Certainly his position as the man who devises and administers tests of others gives him status and security of a sort not often equalled psychologically. But is he the "baby brother" who will grow into the menacing Big Brother of 1984, as *Life* magazine suggested? When he is not sufficiently self-critical, he has plenty of professional colleagues who more than make up for that.

EFFICIENCY IS NOT ENOUGH

The most important point of weakness is our own gullibility. We do not know what tests can and cannot do, nor do we know what we want from life. Tests are sold to us on the basis of their "efficiency." Aside from the validity of this claim, the idea of efficiency itself needs to be re-examined. It is often a short-term concept, and a short-sighted one. Suddenly speaking, the most efficient way to get exactly the proteins you need is to take a bite of the nearest person. To get to the ground floor, jump out of the window. But these very immediate goals are not our complete or real ones. Until we have thought about these, we cannot use efficiency, even if it can be delivered. Long-term efficiency may rest much more upon people going where and doing what they want than on placing them where tests say they fit best.

Meanwhile, tests are here to stay, partly because they are entrenched in our social and industrial order, partly because they have some validity. As far as validity is concerned, they may already be as good as they can get. Their real usefulness can increase only when a sophisticated, unintimidated public can face them for just what they are worth.

BIBLIOGRAPHY

ADORNO, T. W., *et al. The Authoritarian Personality.* New York: Harper & Brothers. 1950.

AMERICAN EDUCATIONAL RESEARCH ASSOCIATION, COMMITTEE ON TEST STANDARDS. *Technical Recommendations for Achievement Tests.* Washington, D.C.: AERA, 1955.

AMERICAN PSYCHOLOGICAL ASSOCIATION. *Technical Recommendations for Psychological and Diagnostic Techniques.* Washington, D.C., APA, 1954.

BALLER, W. R. "A Study of the Present Social Status of a Group of Adults Who, When They Were in Elementary Schools, Were Classified as Mentally Deficient." *Genetic Psychological Monograph,* 1936, Vol. 18, pp. 165–244.

BARNES, E. H. "The Relationship of Biased Test Responses to Psychopathology." *Journal of Abnormal & Social Psychology,* 1955, Vol. 51, pp. 286–290.

BARNES, E. H. "Response Bias and the MMPI." *Journal of Consulting Psychology,* 1956, Vol. 20, pp. 371–374.

BENNETT, G. K. and DOPPELT, J. E. "Item Difficulty and Speed of Response." *Educational & Psychological Measurement,* 1956, Vol. 16, pp. 494–496.

BERDIE, R. F. "Aptitude, Achievement, Interest, and Personality Tests: A Longitudinal Comparison." *Journal of Applied Psychology,* 1955, Vol. 39, pp. 103–114.

BLACK, H. *They Shall Not Pass.* New York: William Morrow & Co., Inc., 1963.

BOYLE, D. J. and HAGIN, W. V. "The Light Plane as a Pre-Primary Selection and Training Device: I. Analysis of Operational Data." *USAF Human Resources Research Center Technical Report,* 1953, No. 53–33.

BROWN, C. W. and GHISELLI, E. E. "Age of Semi-Skilled Workers in Relation to Abilities and Interests." *Personnel Psychology,* 1949, Vol. 2, pp. 497–511.

CLARK, W. W. and TIEGS, E. W. *Technical Report on the California Achievement Tests, 1957 Edition.* Los Angeles: California Test Bureau, 1958.

COMREY, A. L. "An Operational Approach to Some Problems in Psychological Measurement." *Psychological Review,* 1950, Vol. 57, pp. 217–228.

COUCH, A. and KENISTON, K. "Yeasayers and Naysayers, Agreeing Response Set as a Personality Variable." *Journal of Abnormal & Social Psychology,* 1960, Vol. 60, pp. 151–174.

CRONBACH, L. J. "Response Sets and Test Validity." *Educational & Psychological Measurement,* 1946, Vol. 6, pp. 475–494.

CRONBACH, L. J. "Further Evidence on Response Sets and Test Design." *Educational & Psychological Measurement,* 1950, Vol. 10, pp. 3–31.

CRONBACH, L. J. *Essentials of Psychological Testing.* New York: Harper & Brothers, 1949. (2nd edition, 1960.)

DOPPELT, J. E. and BENNETT, G. K. "Reducing the Costs of Training Satisfactory Workers by Using Tests." *Personnel Psychology*, 1953, Vol. 6, pp. 1–8.

DUBOIS, P. H. *Multivariate Correlational Analysis.* New York: Harper & Brothers, 1957.

DUBOIS, P. H. and BUNCH, M. E. "A New Technique for Studying Group Learning." *American Journal of Psychology*, 1949, Vol. 62, 272–278.

DVORAK, B. J. "Differential Occupational Ability Patterns." *Bulletin of the Employment Stabilization Research Institute,* 1935, Vol. 3, No. 8. Minneapolis: University of Minnesota Press.

DVORAK, B. J. "The General Aptitude Test Battery." *Personnel & Guidance Journal,* 1956, Vol. 35, pp. 145–152.

EVANS, C. C. "Influence of 'Fake' Personality Evaluations on Self-Description." *Journal of Psychology,* 1962, Vol. 53, pp. 457–463.

FAIRBANK, R. E. "The Subnormal Child—17 Years After." *Mental Hygiene,* 1933, Vol. 17, pp. 177–208.

FINCH, F. H. "The Permanence of Vocational Interest." *Psychological Bulletin,* 1935, Vol. 32, p. 682 (abstract).

GERSHON, A., GUILFORD, J. P. and MERRIFIELD, P. R. *Figural and Symbolic Divergent-Production Abilities in Adolescent and Adult Populations.* Report No. 29, Psychological Laboratory, University of Southern California, Los Angeles, April, 1963.

GHISELLI, E. E. and BROWN, C. W. *Personnel and Industrial Psychology.* New York: McGraw-Hill, 1955.

GOUGH, H. G. "The F minus K Dissimulation Index for the Minnesota Multiphasic Personality Inventory." *Journal of Consulting Psychology,* 1950, Vol. 14, pp. 408–413.

GRIGG, A. E. and THORPE, J. S. "Deviant Responses in College Adjustment Clients: a Test of Berg's Deviation Hypothesis." *Journal of Consulting Psychology,* 1960, Vol. 24, pp. 92–94.

GRIMSLEY, G. "A Comparative Study of the Wherry-Doolittle and a Multiple Cutting-Score Method." *Psychological Monograph,* 1949, Vol. 63, No. 297.

GROSS, M. L. *The Brain Watchers.* New York: Random House, 1962.

GUILFORD, J. P. "The Structure of Intellect." *Psychological Bulletin,* 1956, Vol. 53, pp. 267–293.

GUILFORD, J. P. and MERRIFIELD, P. R. *The Structure of Intellect Model: Its Uses and Implications.* Report No. 24, Psychological Laboratory, University of Southern California, Los Angeles, April, 1960.

HELLER, K., MYERS, R. A. and KLINE, L. V. "Interviewer Behavior as a Function of Standardized Client Roles." *Journal of Consulting Psychology,* 1963, Vol. 27, pp. 117–122.

HOFFMAN, B. *The Tyranny of Testing.* New York: Crowell-Collier, 1962.

HOLTZMAN, W. H. and BITTERMAN, M. E. "A Factorial Study of Adjustment to Stress." *Journal of Abnormal & Social Psychology,* 1956, Vol. 52, pp. 179–185.

HUNT, H. F. "The Effect of Deliberate Deception on the Minnesota Multiphasic Personality Inventory." *Journal of Consulting Psychology,* 1948, Vol. 12, pp. 396–402.

JORDON, N. and SKAGER, R. W.   "Validity and Meaning." *American Psychologist,* 1962, Vol. 17, pp. 205–207.

JURGENSEN, C. E.   "Report on the Classification Inventory." *Journal of Applied Psychology,* 1944, Vol. 28, pp. 445–460.

KATZELL, R. A.   "Cross-Validation of Item Analysis." *Educational & Psychological Measurement,* 1951, Vol. 11, pp. 16–22.

KLUCKHOLM, F. R.   "Dominant and Substitutive Profiles of Cultural Orientations: Their Significance for the Analysis of Social Stratification." *Social Forces,* 1950, Vol. 28, pp. 376–393.

KNAUFT, E. B.   "A Selection Battery for Bake Shop Managers." *Journal of Applied Psychology,* 1949, Vol. 33, pp. 304–315.

KOERNER, J. D.   *The Miseducation of American Teachers.* Boston: Houghton Mifflin Company, 1963.

KURTZ, A. B.   "The Simultaneous Prediction of Any Number of Criteria by the Use of a Unique Set of Weights." *Psychometrika,* 1937, Vol. 2, pp. 95–101.

MACMEEKAN, A. M.   *The Intelligence of a Representative Group of Scottish Children.* London: University of London Press, 1940.

McGEE, R. K.   "Response Style as a Personality Variable; By What Criterion?" *Psychological Bulletin,* 1962, Vol. 59, pp. 284–295.

McNEMAR, Q.   "More on the Wilson Test." *Psychological Bulletin,* 1958, Vol. 55, pp. 334–335.

MASLING, J.   "The Effects of Warm and Cold Interaction on the Interpretation of a Projective Protocol." *Journal of Protective Techniques,* 1957, Vol. 21, pp. 377–383.

MAYO, G. D. and DuBOIS, P. H.   "Measurement of Gain in Leadership Training!" *Educational & Psychological Measurement,* 1963, Vol. 23, pp. 23–31.

MUSSEN, P. E. (ed.).   *Handbook of Research Methods in Child Development.* New York: John Wiley, 1960.

NORMAN, W. T.   "Relative Importance of Test Item Content." *Journal of Consulting Psychology,* 1963, Vol. 27, pp. 166–174.

RENNER, K. E.   "Must All Tests Be Valid?" *American Psychologist,* 1962, Vol. 17, pp. 507–508.

RICHARDSON, N. W.   "The Relation Between the Difficulty and the Differential Validity of a Test." *Psychometrika,* 1936, Vol. 1, pp. 33–49.

ROE, A.   *The Psychology of Occupations.* New York: John Wiley, 1956.

ROTHNEY, J .W. N., DANIELSON, P. J. and HEINMANN, R. A.   *Measurement for Guidance.* New York: Harper & Brothers, 1959.

RUCH, F. L.   "A Technique for Detecting Attempts to Fake Performance on the Self-Inventory Type of Personality Test." In McNemar, Q. and Merrill, M. A. (eds.), *Studies in Personality.* New York: McGraw-Hill, 1942, pp. 229–234.

RUCH, G. M.   "Recent Developments in Statistical Procedures." *Review of Educational Research,* 1933, Vol. 3, pp. 39–40.

SECHREST, L. and JACKSON, D. N.   "Deviant Response Tendencies: Their Measurement and Interpretation." *Educational & Psychological Measurement,* 1963, Vol. 23, pp. 33–53.

SHAW, M. E.   "The Effectiveness of Whyte's Rules: 'How to Cheat on Personality Tests.' " *Journal of Applied Psychology,* 1962, Vol. 46, pp. 21–25.

STAGNER, R.   "The Gullibility of Personnel Managers." *Educational & Psychological Measurement*, 1958, Vol. 11, pp. 347–352.

STRONG, E. K., JR.   *Vocational Interests of Men and Women*. Stanford, Calif.: Stanford University Press, 1943.

STRONG, E. K., JR.   "Twenty-Year Follow-up of Medical Interests." In Thurstone, L. L. (ed.), *Applications of Psychology*. New York: Harper & Bros. 1952, pp. 111–130.

STRONG, E. K., JR.   *Vocational Interests 18 Years After College*. Minneapolis, University of Minnesota Press, 1955.

SUNDBERG, N. D.   "The Acceptability of 'Fake' versus 'Bona Fide' Personality Test Interpretations." *Journal of Abnormal & Social Psychology*, 1955, Vol. 50, pp. 145–147.

TERMAN, L. M. and MERRILL, M. A.   *Measuring Intelligence*. New York: Houghton Mifflin, 1937.

TERMAN, L. M. and ODEN, M. H.   "The Gifted Child Grows Up." *Genetic Studies of Genius*, Vol. 4. Stanford: Stanford University Press, 1947.

THORNDIKE, R. L.   *Personnel Selection: Test and Measurement Techniques*. New York: John Wiley, 1949.

TRYON, R. C.   "Genetic Differences in Maze-Learning Ability in Rats." *Yearbook of the National Society for the Study of Education*, 1940, Vol. 39, Part I, pp. 111–119.

U.S. DEPT. OF LABOR, BUREAU OF EMPLOYMENT SECURITY.   *GATB Norms for Ninth and Tenth Graders*. Washington, D. C., 1959.

U.S. DEPT. OF LABOR, BUREAU OF EMPLOYMENT SECURITY.   *Guide to the Use of the General Aptitude Test Battery*. Washington 25, D. C.: Govt. Printing Office, 1958.

VERNON, P. E. and PARRY, J. B.   *Personnel Selection in the British Forces*. London: University of London Press, 1949.

WESMAN, A. G.   "Effect of Speed on Item-Test Correlation Coefficients." *Educational & Psychological Measurement*, 1949, Vol. 9, pp. 51–57.

WHYTE, W. H., JR.   *The Organization Man*. New York: Simon & Schuster, 1956.

WILSON, K. V.   "A Distribution-Free Test of Analysis of Variance Hypotheses." *Psychological Bulletin*, 1956, Vol. 53, pp. 96–101.

WITTSON, C. L. and HUNT, W. A.   "Three Years of Naval Selection." *War Medicine*, 1945, Vol. 7, pp. 218–221.

Subject Index

A

Achievement tests
  overlap with intelligence tests, 22
  school uses, 22–23
  and time limits, 99
American Institute for Research, 178
Army Air Force tests, 163–77

B

Barnum Effect, 277–80
"Being" orientation, 299
Bernreuter Personality Inventory, 314, 319
Bias and test profiles, 316

C

California Achievement Tests, 58
California Test of Mental Maturity, 22
Chicago Non-Verbal Examination, 97–98
Clerical Speed and Accuracy Test, 97–99
Closure factor, 119
College Entrance Examination Board, 329
Conspect reliability, 263
Consulting firms and testing, 311
Correlation
  and forecasting efficiency, 339
  Irish, 78
Cost reduction of training via tests, 229–32
Creative thinking, 125, 127
Criterion/criteria
  contamination, 176
  definition difficulties, 238
  dimensionality, 197–202
  objective and subjective, 132–34, 136
  occupational norms, 132-44
  reliability of, 156–59, 339
  short vs. long range, 189–94
  "space," 197
  unreliability of, 104
  using output data, 212–17
  validity of, 135
  vector method, 307
Cross-validation, 145–47, 150–54, 220–22

D

Derived scores, 22, 59
Deviation hypothesis, 76–86, 88
Deviation IQ, 22

Differential Aptitude Tests, 97
Digit-symbol tests, 98
Dimensionality of ciriteria, 197–202
"Doing" orientation, 299
Double cross-validation, 153
DuBois-Bunch Learning Test, 185

E

Educational Testing Service, 107, 233, 321, 326–36
Ethics, 26–31, 340–43
Executive testing, 311–12, 315–19

F

Facade, "warm" and "cold" of testee, 45–50
Factor analysis, 107–29, 308
Faking
  with MMPI, 304–05
  personality tests, 266
First-order factors, 119

G

"g," 115, 119
General Aptitude Test Battery, 131–44, 195
Grade placement score, 22–23, 59, 63
Grading
  in AAF, 176
  and residual gain, 183
Gullibility
  and Barnum Effect, 277–80
  of university students, 281–88

H

Heteroscedasticity, 204, 209
How Supervize? 318

I

Intellect, structure of, 124–29
Intelligence tests, intercorrelations, 115
Interaction
  examiner subject, 45–50
  with preschool children, 51–56
  therapist-client, 50
Interest measurement, 289–308
Iowa Tests of Educational Development, 22
IQ tests
  and commitment, 252–53
  misuse, 256

IQ tests—*Cont.*
  Scottish Survey, 57
Irish correlations, 78
Item content
  importance of, 86
  unimportance of, 81–82

JK

Jurgensen Classification Inventory, 148–54
Kuder Preference Record, 303

L

L-data, 261
Longitudinal samples, 138–41, 144

M

Maturation and factor analysis results, 120
Measurement
  definition, 12
  fundamental, 2–10, 16
Mechanical aptitude, 122
Memory factor, 118
Mental defectives
  and achievement, 206
  and incorrect diagnosis, 249–57
Mental Measurement Yearbook, 322, 325, 328
Minnesota Multiphasic Personality Inventory,
  82-83, 266–69, 287, 304–05
Misuse
  IQ tests, 256
  personality tests, 310–19
Multiple cutting-score, 7, 131, 141, 188,
  190–92, 195–96

N

National Defense Education Act, 17
National Merit Scholarship Corporation,
  325–26
Non-verbal classification test in Samoa, 43–
  44
Norms
  age-grade relation, 63
  comparability of, 30, 60
  curriculum differences, 62–63
  not standards, 19, 57–44
  occupational and GATB, 131–44
  samples in test development, 138–44
  total population, 69
  unnecessary sex norms, 65–72
Number factor, 117

O

Objective tests
  personality, 260–65
  tyranny of, 321–30
Occupational choice and factor scores, 121
Operationism, 16
Output as criterion, 212–17
Overlap, item, 307

P

Participant observation, 54
Perceptual defense, and reliability, 102–5
Perceptual factor, 118–19
Perceptual Reaction Test, 78–84, 88
Personality tests
  fallacies, 310–19
  and gullibility, 281–88
  objective, 260–65
Personnel managers
  and Barnum Effect, 278–80
  gullibility of, 287
Politics and law interest, 298
Power vs. speed, 100
Primary Mental Abilities, 111, 113–26
Privacy and personality tests, 319
Private vs. public schools, and interest meas-
  urement, 289–302
Profile analysis, 306, 315
Promotion, motivation for, 245–48
Psychiatric screening, 270–75
Purdue Clerical Adaptability Test, 226

R

Radio Code Aptitude Test in Samoa, 42–44
Range of talent, 162, 169, 175, 196
Rapport
  with preschool children, 51–56
  vs. testee facade, 45–50
Recognition threshold score, 104
Reliability
  conspect, 263
  and perceptual defense, 102–5
  score variability, 19, 50
  and time limits, 95–101
Residual gain
  vs. final grade, 183
  and leadership, 186–87
Response set, 73–101
  and obsessives, 89–92
  for promotion on job, 245–48

S

Samoa, testing in, 39–44
Sampling
  longitudinal, 139–41, 144
  random, 57
  stratified, 58, 59–62
Scales, ordinal, 6, 8
Science Research Associates, 326
Scotland IQ survey, 57
Score variability, 19
  with "warm" vs. "cold" facade, 50
Score weights, determination of, 151
Scoring key, absence of, 148
Screening in Navy, 270–75
Second-order factors, 119
Space factor, 116
  and mechanical aptitude, 122
Speed of Decision Test, 88–93

Speeded tests
  vs. power, 100
  and reliability, 95–101
Standardized testing
  procedures in, 60–62
  in Samoa, 39–44
  values, 18
  in Viet Nam, 34–38
Stanford-Binet Test, 22–114
  in Scottish survey, 57
Stanine, 162
  and AAF success, 166–70, 172–77
  and commercial pilots, 179–81
Statistics
  fallacies with tests, 314–15, 326–27
  and forecasting efficiency, 338–39
  and test pre-testing, 322, 332–33
Strong Vocational Interest Blank
  and income, 300
  permanence of scores, 289–98
  with subcultures, 298–302
Suppressor variables, 308
Synthetic validity, 225

T

T-data, 262
Test interpretation
  cautions, 26–31
  errors, 18–25
Test items
  and factor space, 304

Test items—*Cont.*
  overlap, 307
Test publishers, 311, 326
Thurstone Temperament Schedule, 318
Training costs, reduction by tests, 229–32

U

United States Employment Service, 131
  test development studies, 138–44

V

Validity
  difficulties with, 233–34
  ignoring by Germans, 155
  and item analysis, 152, 314
  item validity index, 146
  with proficiency gains, 183–86
  synthetic, 225
Variability of scores, 19, 50
Verbal comprehension factor, 117–18
Viet Nam, testing in, 34–38
Vocational counseling
  and factor scores, 121
  and tests, 21

W

Wherry-Doolittle technique, 140, 142, 188,
  190–93, 196, 230
Wonderlic Personnel Test, 245–48
Word fluency factor, 117
Work sample test and speed, 95

Author Index

A

Adorno, T. W., 208
Afflect, D. C., 249
Asch, M. J., 87

B

Barnes, E. H., 82
Barnette, W. L., 266
Barzun, J., 329
Bauernfeind, R. H., 65
Bennett, G. K., 96, 230
Berdie, R. F., 293
Berg, I. A., 76, 89
Bitterman, M. E., 103
Black, H., 335
Boyle, D. J., 172
Brown, C. W., 219, 230
Buros, O., 235
Burton, H. W., 271
Byrne, D., 102

C

Cattell, R. B., 260
Chauncey, H., 331
Christal, R. E., 171
Clark, W. W., 70
Comrey, A. L., 1
Couch, A., 87
Cronbach, L. J., 73, 77, 99, 188
Cureton, E. E., 145

D

Danielson, P. J., 336
Darley, J. G., 78
Dingle, H., 11
Dion, R., 58
Doppelt, J. E., 96, 230
Drasgow, J., 266
Dubois, P. H., 183, 184, 186
Dunnette, M. D., 276
Dvorak, B. J., 131, 195

E

Ebel, R. L., 233
Evans, C. C., 287

F

Finch, F. H., 291

Fisher, J., 203
Flanagan, J. C., 162, 178
Forer, B. R., 281
Fornaff, F. J., 332
French, J. W., 107
Fricke, B. G., 326

G

Galton, F., 114, 116
Garfield, S. C., 249
Gershon, A., 129
Ghiselli, E. E., 197, 218, 219, 230
Goodman, C. H., 111
Gough, H. G., 266, 268
Grigg, A. E., 85
Grimsley, G., 188
Gross, M. L., 309
Guilford, J. P., 124, 129

H

Hagin, W. V., 172
Heiman, R. A., 336
Heller, K., 50
Hoffmann, B., 86, 321, 331, 334
Holcomb, J., 102
Holtzman, W. H., 103
Hunt, W. A., 268, 271

J

Jackson, D. N., 85, 86
Jenkins, J. G., 155
Jennings, E. E., 245
Jordon, N., 244

K

Katzell, R. A., 153
Keniston, K., 87
Kirkpatrick, J. J., 148
Kluckhohm, F. R., 299
Knauft, E. B., 150
Koerner, J. D., 335
Krumboltz, J. D., 171
Kuder, G. E., 303
Kurtz, A. B., 199

L

Landreth, C., 51
Lawshe, C. H., 225

Levine, A. S., 39

M

McArthur, C., 294
McCarthy, D., 26
Macmeeken, A. M., 57
McGee, R. K., 85
McNemar, Q., 174
Manning, W. H., 183
Masling, J., 45
Mayo, G. D., 186
Merrifield, P. R., 129
Merrill, M. A., 57
Metfessel, N. S., 74
Mussen, P. E., 51

N

Norman, W. T., 86
Nye, C. T., 212

O

Oden, M. H., 205

P

Parry, J. B., 188
Paterson, D. G., 276, 283
Plato, 342

R

Renner, K. E., 244
Richardson, H. W., 9
Ricks, J. R., 26
Rothe, H. F., 212
Rothney, J. W. N., 336
Ruch, F. L., 266
Ruch, G. M., 235

Rusmore, J. T., 229

S

Sax, G., 74
Schlien, J. M., 336
Sechrest, L., 85, 86
Shaw, M. E., 320
Skager, R. W., 244
Socrates, 342
Spearman, C., 115
Stagner, R., 287
Steinberg, M. D., 225
Strong, E. K., Jr., 289, 294–97, 380
Sundberg, N. D., 287

T

Terman, L. L., 57, 205
Thorndike, R. L., 188
Thorpe, J. S., 85
Thurstone, L. L., 113
Tiegs, E. W., 70
Toorenaar, G. J., 229
Tryon, R. C., 207

V

Vernon, P. E., 188
Viteles, M. S., 189

W

Wesman, A. G., 95, 100
Whyte, W. H., Jr., 309
Wickert, F. R., 33
Wilson, K. V., 173
Wittson, C. L., 270, 271
Womer, F. B., 17
Worbois, G. M., 189

This book has been set on the Linotype in 12 and 10 point Garamond Light, leaded 1 point. Part numbers are in 24 point Girder Light; part titles are in 24 point Garamond Light. Article titles and bylines are in 18 and 14 Garamond Bold. The size of the type page is 27 by 46½ picas.